# AVENGERS

# THE CONTEST

MARK GRUENWALD, BILL MANTLO, STEVEN
GRANT, STEVE ENGLEHART & TOM DEFALCO

## PENCILERS
JOHN ROMITA JR., AL MILGROM, BOB HALL,
KEITH POLLARD, MARSHALL ROGERS,
JACKSON GUICE & RON FRENZ

## INKERS
PABLO MARCOS, AL MILGROM, TOM PALMER,
BILL SIENKIEWICZ, AL WILLIAMSON, BOB
LAYTON, KEVIN NOWLAN & BOB WIACEK

## COLORISTS
ANDY YANCHUS, PATRICIA DEFALCO,
MICHELE WOLFMAN, CHRISTIE SCHEELE,
DON WARFIELD, CARL GAFFORD
& GREGORY WRIGHT

## LETTERERS
JOE ROSEN, TOM ORZECHOWSKI
& KEN LOPEZ

## EDITORS
MARK GRUENWALD & TOM DEFALCO

## FRONT COVER ARTISTS
JOHN ROMITA JR, BOB LAYTON
& CHRIS SOTOMAYOR

## BACK COVER ARTISTS
ED HANNIGAN, AL MILGROM & TOM SMITH

**AVENGERS: THE CONTEST.** Contains material originally published in magazine form as CONTEST OF CHAMPIONS #1-3, WEST COAST AVENGERS ANNUAL #2 and AVENGERS ANNUAL #16.
First printing 2012. ISBN# 978-0-7851-6199-8. Published by MARVEL WORLDWIDE, INC., a subsidiary of MARVEL ENTERTAINMENT, LLC. OFFICE OF PUBLICATION: 135 West 50th Street,
New York, NY 10020. Copyright © 1982, 1987 and 2012 Marvel Characters, Inc. All rights reserved. $16.99 per copy in the U.S. and $18.99 in Canada (GST #R127032852); Canadian
Agreement #40668537. All characters featured in this issue and the distinctive names and likenesses thereof, and all related indicia are trademarks of Marvel Characters, Inc. No similarity
between any of the names, characters, persons, and/or institutions in this magazine with those of any living or dead person or institution is intended, and any such similarity which may exist
is purely coincidental. **Printed in the U.S.A.** ALAN FINE, EVP - Office of the President, Marvel Worldwide, Inc. and EVP & CMO Marvel Characters B.V.; DAN BUCKLEY, Publisher & President
- Print, Animation & Digital Divisions; JOE QUESADA, Chief Creative Officer; TOM BREVOORT, SVP of Publishing; DAVID BOGART, SVP of Operations & Procurement, Publishing; RUWAN
JAYATILLEKE, SVP & Associate Publisher, Publishing; C.B. CEBULSKI, SVP of Creator & Content Development; DAVID GABRIEL, SVP of Publishing Sales & Circulation; MICHAEL PASCIULLO,
SVP of Brand Planning & Communications; JIM O'KEEFE, VP of Operations & Logistics; DAN CARR, Executive Director of Publishing Technology; SUSAN CRESPI, Editorial Operations Manager;
ALEX MORALES, Publishing Operations Manager; STAN LEE, Chairman Emeritus. For information regarding advertising in Marvel Comics or on Marvel.com, please contact John Dokes,
SVP Integrated Sales and Marketing, at jdokes@marvel.com. For Marvel subscription inquiries, please call 800-217-9158. **Manufactured between 4/11/2012 and 4/30/2012 by R.R.
DONNELLEY, INC., SALEM, VA, USA.**

10 9 8 7 6 5 4 3 2 1

COLLECTION EDITOR
**MARK D. BEAZLEY**

ASSISTANT EDITORS
**NELSON RIBEIRO & ALEX STARBUCK**

EDITOR, SPECIAL PROJECTS
**JENNIFER GRÜNWALD**

SENIOR EDITOR, SPECIAL PROJECTS
**JEFF YOUNGQUIST**

RESEARCH
**JEPH YORK**

PRODUCTION
**COLORTEK**

BOOK DESIGNER
**MICHAEL CHATHAM**

SENIOR VICE PRESIDENT OF SALES
**DAVID GABRIEL**

SVP OF BRAND PLANNING &
COMMUNICATIONS
**MICHAEL PASCIULLO**


EDITOR IN CHIEF
**AXEL ALONSO**

CHIEF CREATIVE OFFICER
**JOE QUESADA**

PUBLISHER
**DAN BUCKLEY**

EXECUTIVE PRODUCER
**ALAN FINE**


SPECIAL THANKS TO MIKE O'SULLIVAN

THE CONTEST

You ever have one those days? You know the kind I mean. You wake up late because you forgot to set the clock radio. The person before you uses all the hot water, leaving you to shiver in the shower. Your shoelace breaks as you rush to get dressed. Coffee splashes over your new outfit. Your bus is late, and your boss earlier.

Yeah, one of those days!

*Contest of Champions* was one of those assignments.

This limited series holds a very special place in comic book history. It marks the very first time that all the super heroes of one comic book company ever gathered to fight a common foe. Sure, most companies regularly teamed up their most popular heroes. Teams like DC's *Justice Society of America* and Marvel's *All-Winners Squad* first appeared in the 1940s, and their *Justice League* and *Avengers* counterparts are still being published today.

*Contest* was something new. It was the most ambitious project of its day. *Secret Wars*, *Crisis on Infinite Earths*, and countless other company-wide crossovers all followed the template established by *Contest*.

Cool, huh?

Except *Contest* was never supposed to be a limited comic book series.

I wasn't actually there for the first part of the story, but here's the way I heard it. *Contest* was originally conceived as a tie-in for the 1980 Olympics, and was designed to be published as a single *Marvel Treasury Edition*. (One of those 10-by-13-inch giant comic books that the major companies used to publish. Look around your favorite back issue store, and you might find one. It'll be worth your effort. They're a real treat!)

Sometime during 1979, writers Mark Gruenwald, Bill Mantlo, and Steven Grant brainstormed the basic plot for the story you're about to read. Young John Romita Jr., who was just starting his artistic career, was assigned to pencil the job, and Pablo Marcos was handling the inking chores. (I'm afraid I don't know who was the book's original editor.)

Production immediately began on the book, and the pages started flowing. Everything was going just fine.

Until the United States pulled out of the 1980 Olympics.

Since the country was boycotting the Olympics, the powers-that-be decided it didn't make a lot of sense to publish a tie-in. Contest was cancelled.

Sort of.

Nobody told Pablo.

Living somewhere in South America at the time, Pablo had the forty or so penciled pages that JR Jr. had already completed. Since no one was hassling him for the pages, he worked on them in his spare time. He'd occasionally ask about them, be told there was no hurry, and put them aside to work on a more pressing assignment.

Two years passed.

It was now 1981. By this time I had become

an editor at Marvel and Mark Gruenwald had been assigned as my assistant.

We were in our office one day when Pablo showed up with his forty odd pages, and asked when he'd receive the end of the job.

I had no idea what he was talking about. Mark not only did, but he immediately realized how we could exploit those pages.

Racing to Jim Shooter, who was Marvel's editor in chief at the time, Mark proposed that we break the story into three parts and publish it as a limited series. Jim quickly agreed.

Mark called Bill, who immediately made the necessary adjustments to the plot, and then we somehow conned JR into finishing it.

Sounds simple, no?

Unfortunately, *Contest* was one of those assignments.

As we started to prepare the first issue of the limited series, we realized that a lot of changes had occurred in the Marvel Universe between 1979 and 1981. Costumes had been redesigned, new characters had been added, and teams had different members.

And so we started the long task of making the necessary corrections. The very long task!

Heck, that series had so many art adjustments that we felt compelled to give Babyface Bob Layton, the guy who made most of them, a special credit.

I told you it was one of those assignments.

The first issue eventually went off to the printer.

We were midway through the second issue when I was struck by a very terrible and personal tragedy.

Jim Shooter decided to make Mark a full editor.

Don't get me wrong! I thought Mark's promotion was long overdue. I was convinced he'd become one of the greatest comic book editors of all time. (And I was right!)

But I certainly didn't want to get stuck with *Contest*. It was one of those assignments.

Lucky for me, Mark had grown very attached to Contest and asked if I'd let him edit the final issue.

Sure!

No problem!

Be my guest!

I couldn't ditch it fast enough.

Mark supervised the last issue, made all the final corrections, gave me a copy to proofread, got my okay, and sent the comic to the printer.

End of story, right?

Not quite.

(SPOILER WARNING: If you haven't already read *Contest*, you'd better do so before reading further because I'm about to reveal some major story points.)

For reasons that befuddled me, the final issue of *Contest* seemed to generate an exceptional amount of mail. It didn't make any sense. The series was over. We had no place to publish such letters. Why were people writing?

The answer came one day when Jim Shooter invited Mark and me into his office.

Jim was holding all three issues of *Contest*, and he wasn't smiling.

Seems we screwed up.

The Grandmaster had won the first round of the contest.

The Unknown had taken the second.

The third went to the Grandmaster.

And the fourth ended when Shamrock touched the golden globe. The copy on the final page read, "Final score: Grandmaster – 3, Unknown – 1."

It appeared that the Grandmaster had won.

But Shamrock was on the Unknown's team.

The game was actually a tie and neither Mark nor had realized it.

Jim was not pleased. He asked us what we were going to do about it. I, of course, had no idea. Mark not only did, but he immediately informed Jim that the mistake was put in deliberately to set up a sequel. (I don't think Jim ever fell for that line, but Contest had certainly sold well enough to deserve a sequel so he approved it on the spot.)

Mark volunteered to call Bill and John, and I sighed with relief. I was finally through with Contest.

Not quite.

For various reasons, Bill and John could never find time in their busy schedules to do the promised sequel.


Years passed.

I had forgotten all about it until one afternoon when Mark dropped by the office. He informed me that he was finally going to wrap up Contest in the two Avengers Annuals that were scheduled to be published in 1987. Steve Englehart was the regular writer of West Coast Avengers and would write the first half, but Mark needed someone for part two.

Since I shared equal blame for the initial screwup, that happy task was dropped on me.

Fine!

Be that way!

Okay!

To my surprise, this particular writing assignment, which included six art teams (a sure recipe for disaster if I ever heard one), went without a hitch.

I had a truly great time working with Englehart and all the art teams, and the book was published without a single problem.


Contest had suddenly become a real pleasure.

At least until I received a flood of mail protesting my characterization of Hawkeye at the end of the tale. (People also objected to Captain America's final line about his bow-toting buddy.)

What can I say? I thought Hawk's final solution his personality. I still do. You, however, are free to disagree.

Anyway, at long last, it seemed like Contest was finally out of my life.

At least until Polly Watson asked me to write this introduction.

What more can I say.

I told you it was one of those assignments.

Tom Defalco
1999

BY TOM DEFALCO

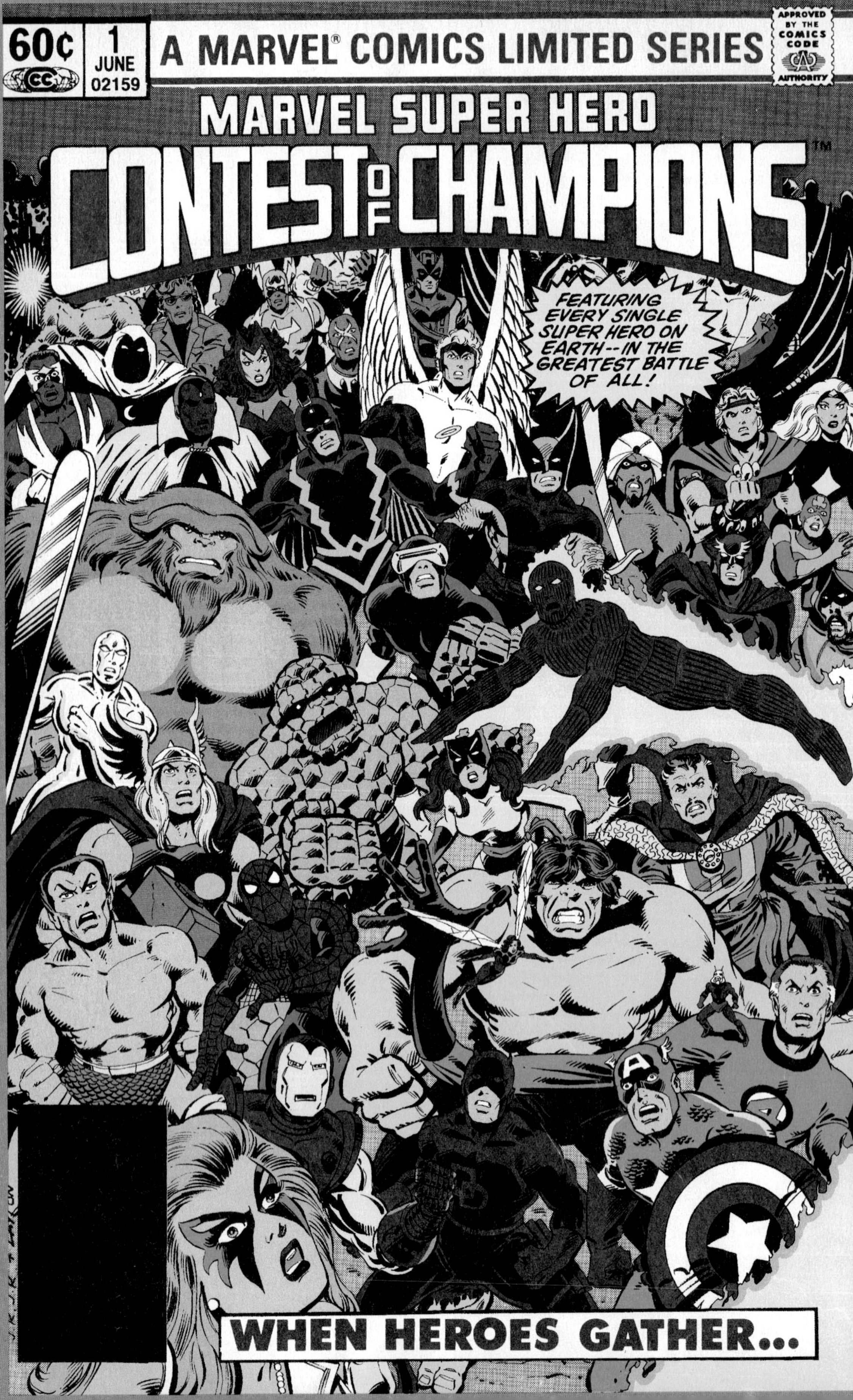
60¢
CC
1
JUNE
02159
A MARVEL® COMICS LIMITED SERIES
APPROVED BY THE COMICS CODE CA AUTHORITY
MARVEL SUPER HERO
CONTEST OF CHAMPIONS™
FEATURING EVERY SINGLE SUPER HERO ON EARTH--IN THE GREATEST BATTLE OF ALL!
WHEN HEROES GATHER...

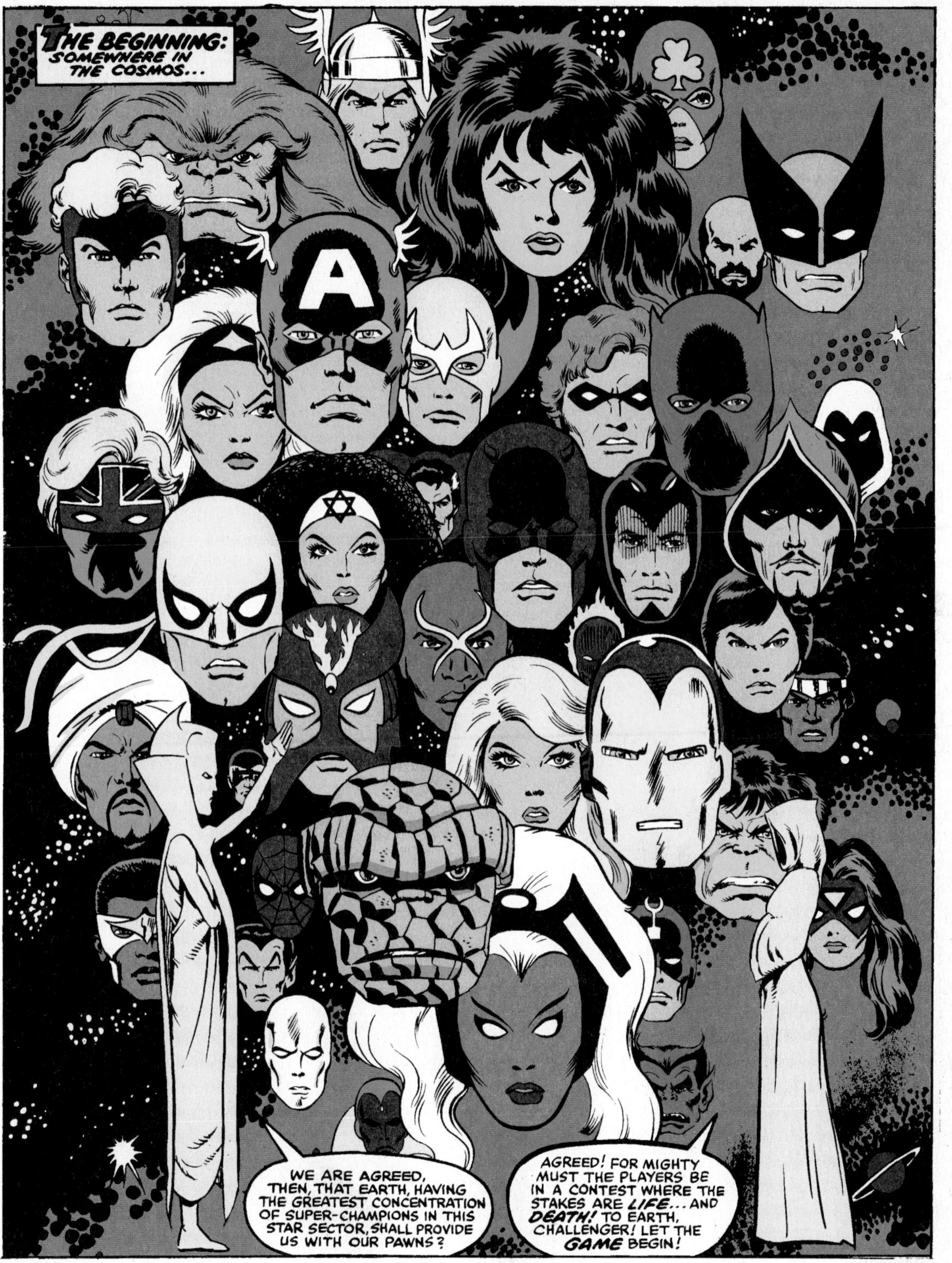
THE BEGINNING: SOMEWHERE IN THE COSMOS...
WE ARE AGREED, THEN, THAT EARTH, HAVING THE GREATEST CONCENTRATION OF SUPER-CHAMPIONS IN THIS STAR SECTOR, SHALL PROVIDE US WITH OUR PAWNS?
AGREED! FOR MIGHTY MUST THE PLAYERS BE IN A CONTEST WHERE THE STAKES ARE LIFE... AND DEATH! TO EARTH, CHALLENGER! LET THE GAME BEGIN!

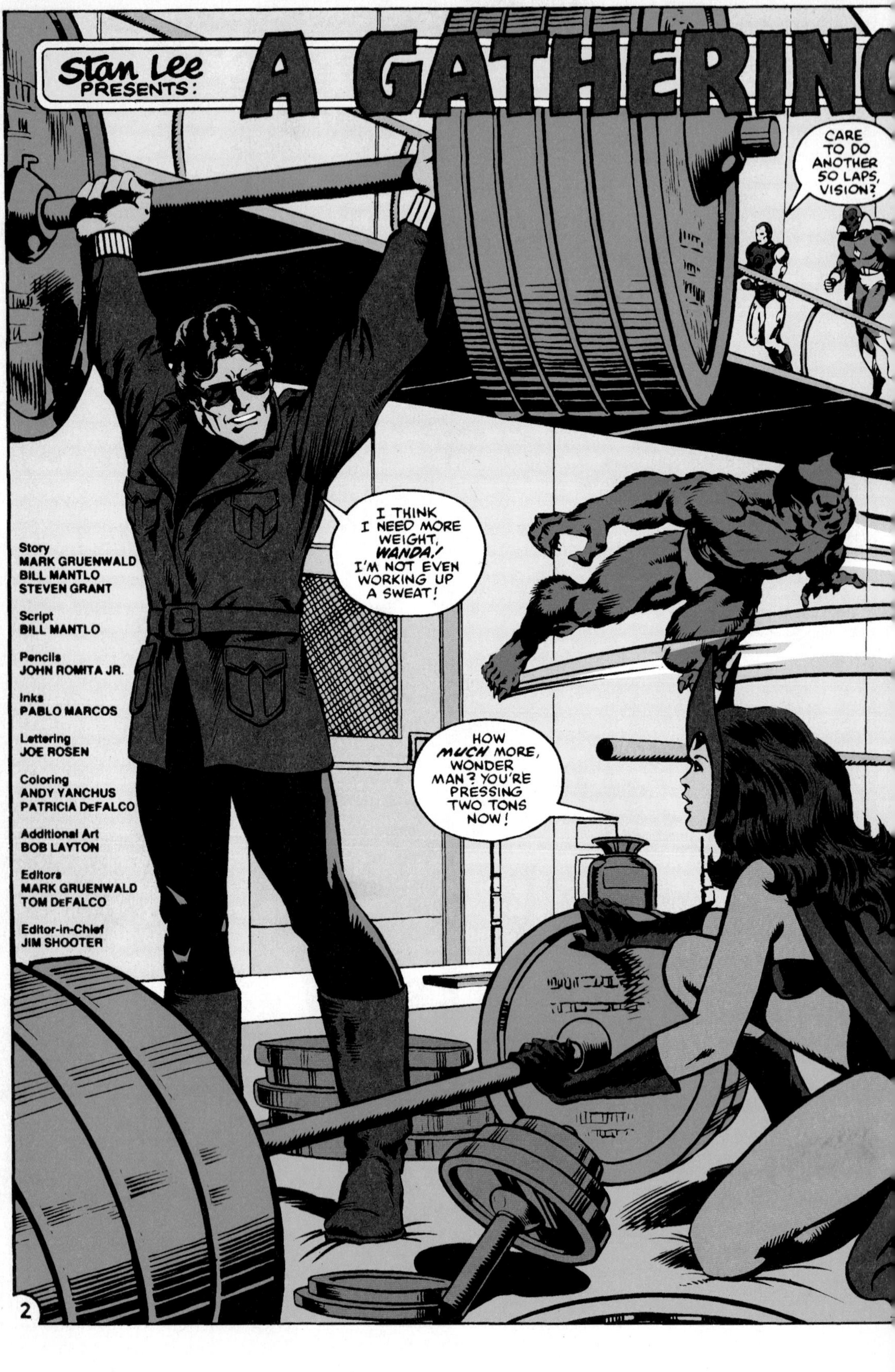
Stan Lee PRESENTS:
A GATHERING
CARE TO DO ANOTHER 50 LAPS, VISION?
I THINK I NEED MORE WEIGHT, WANDA! I'M NOT EVEN WORKING UP A SWEAT!
Story
MARK GRUENWALD
BILL MANTLO
STEVEN GRANT
Script
BILL MANTLO
Pencils
JOHN ROMITA JR.
Inks
PABLO MARCOS
Lettering
JOE ROSEN
Coloring
ANDY YANCHUS
PATRICIA DeFALCO
Additional Art
BOB LAYTON
Editors
MARK GRUENWALD
TOM DeFALCO
Editor-in-Chief
JIM SHOOTER
HOW MUCH MORE, WONDER MAN? YOU'RE PRESSING TWO TONS NOW!
2

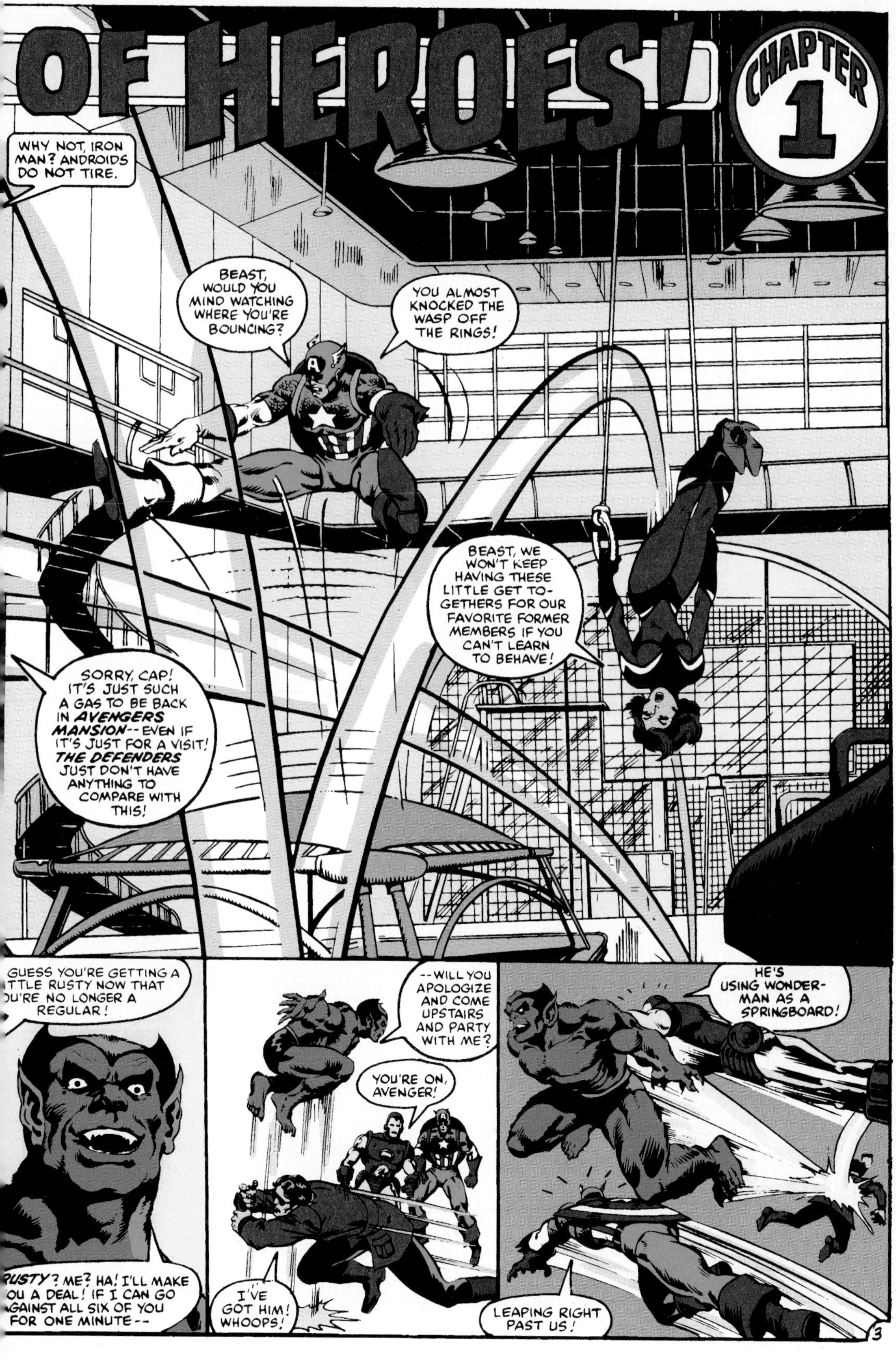
OF HEROES!
CHAPTER 1
WHY NOT, IRON MAN? ANDROIDS DO NOT TIRE.
BEAST, WOULD YOU MIND WATCHING WHERE YOU'RE BOUNCING?
YOU ALMOST KNOCKED THE WASP OFF THE RINGS!
BEAST, WE WON'T KEEP HAVING THESE LITTLE GET TO-GETHERS FOR OUR FAVORITE FORMER MEMBERS IF YOU CAN'T LEARN TO BEHAVE!
SORRY, CAP! IT'S JUST SUCH A GAS TO BE BACK IN AVENGERS MANSION-- EVEN IF IT'S JUST FOR A VISIT! THE DEFENDERS JUST DON'T HAVE ANYTHING TO COMPARE WITH THIS!
GUESS YOU'RE GETTING A TTLE RUSTY NOW THAT OU'RE NO LONGER A REGULAR!
RUSTY? ME? HA! I'LL MAKE OU A DEAL! IF I CAN GO GAINST ALL SIX OF YOU FOR ONE MINUTE--
--WILL YOU APOLOGIZE AND COME UPSTAIRS AND PARTY WITH ME?
YOU'RE ON, AVENGER!
I'VE GOT HIM! WHOOPS!
HE'S USING WONDER-MAN AS A SPRINGBOARD!
LEAPING RIGHT PAST US!
3

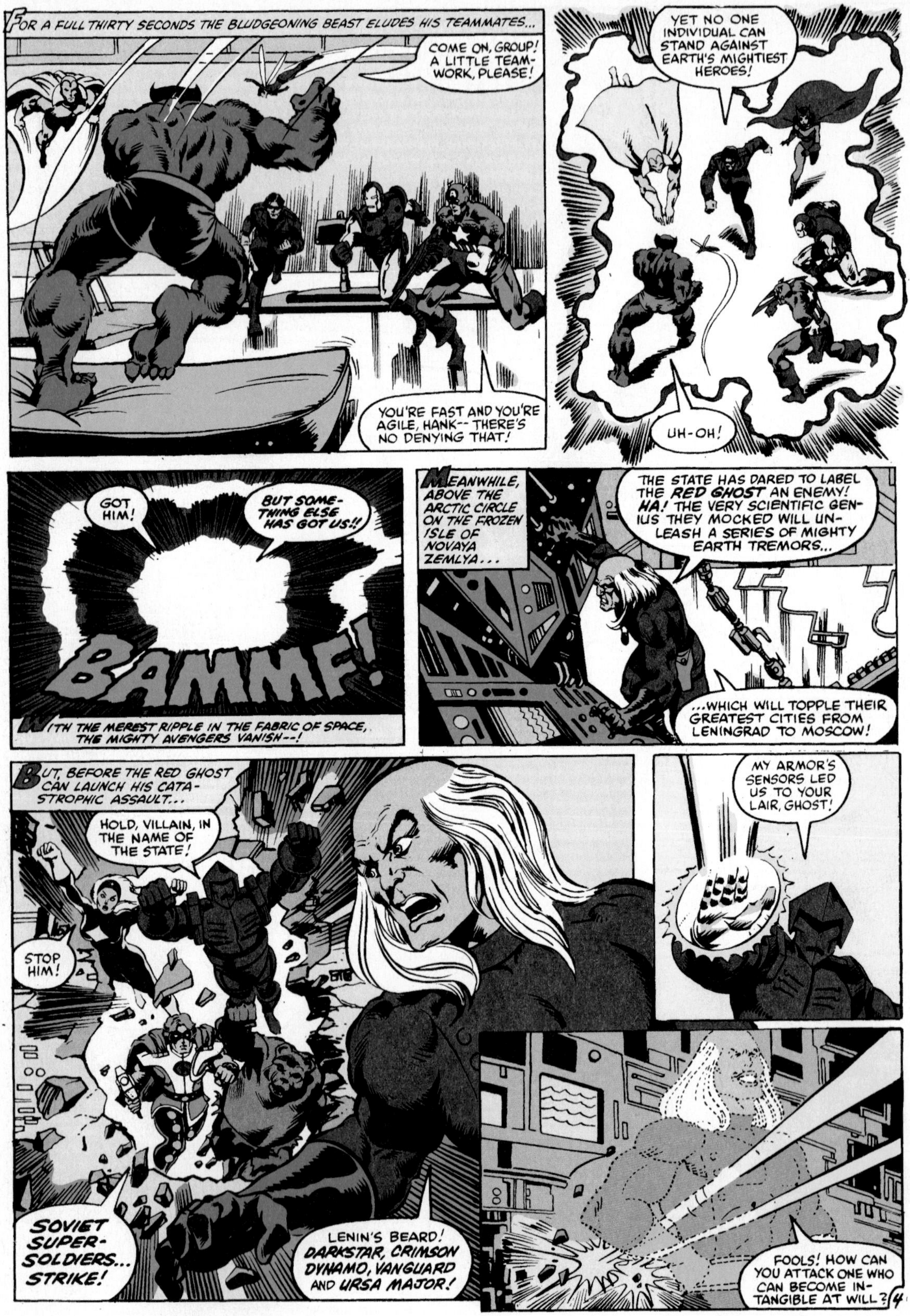

FOR A FULL THIRTY SECONDS THE BLUDGEONING BEAST ELUDES HIS TEAMMATES...
COME ON, GROUP! A LITTLE TEAM-WORK, PLEASE!
YOU'RE FAST AND YOU'RE AGILE, HANK-- THERE'S NO DENYING THAT!
YET NO ONE INDIVIDUAL CAN STAND AGAINST EARTH'S MIGHTIEST HEROES!
UH-OH!
GOT HIM!
BUT SOME-THING ELSE HAS GOT US!!
BAMMF!
WITH THE MEREST RIPPLE IN THE FABRIC OF SPACE, THE MIGHTY AVENGERS VANISH--!
MEANWHILE, ABOVE THE ARCTIC CIRCLE ON THE FROZEN ISLE OF NOVAYA ZEMLYA...
THE STATE HAS DARED TO LABEL THE RED GHOST AN ENEMY! HA! THE VERY SCIENTIFIC GEN-IUS THEY MOCKED WILL UN-LEASH A SERIES OF MIGHTY EARTH TREMORS...
...WHICH WILL TOPPLE THEIR GREATEST CITIES FROM LENINGRAD TO MOSCOW!
BUT, BEFORE THE RED GHOST CAN LAUNCH HIS CATA-STROPHIC ASSAULT...
HOLD, VILLAIN, IN THE NAME OF THE STATE!
STOP HIM!
SOVIET SUPER-SOLDIERS... STRIKE!
LENIN'S BEARD! DARKSTAR, CRIMSON DYNAMO, VANGUARD AND URSA MAJOR!
MY ARMOR'S SENSORS LED US TO YOUR LAIR, GHOST!
FOOLS! HOW CAN YOU ATTACK ONE WHO CAN BECOME IN-TANGIBLE AT WILL?
4

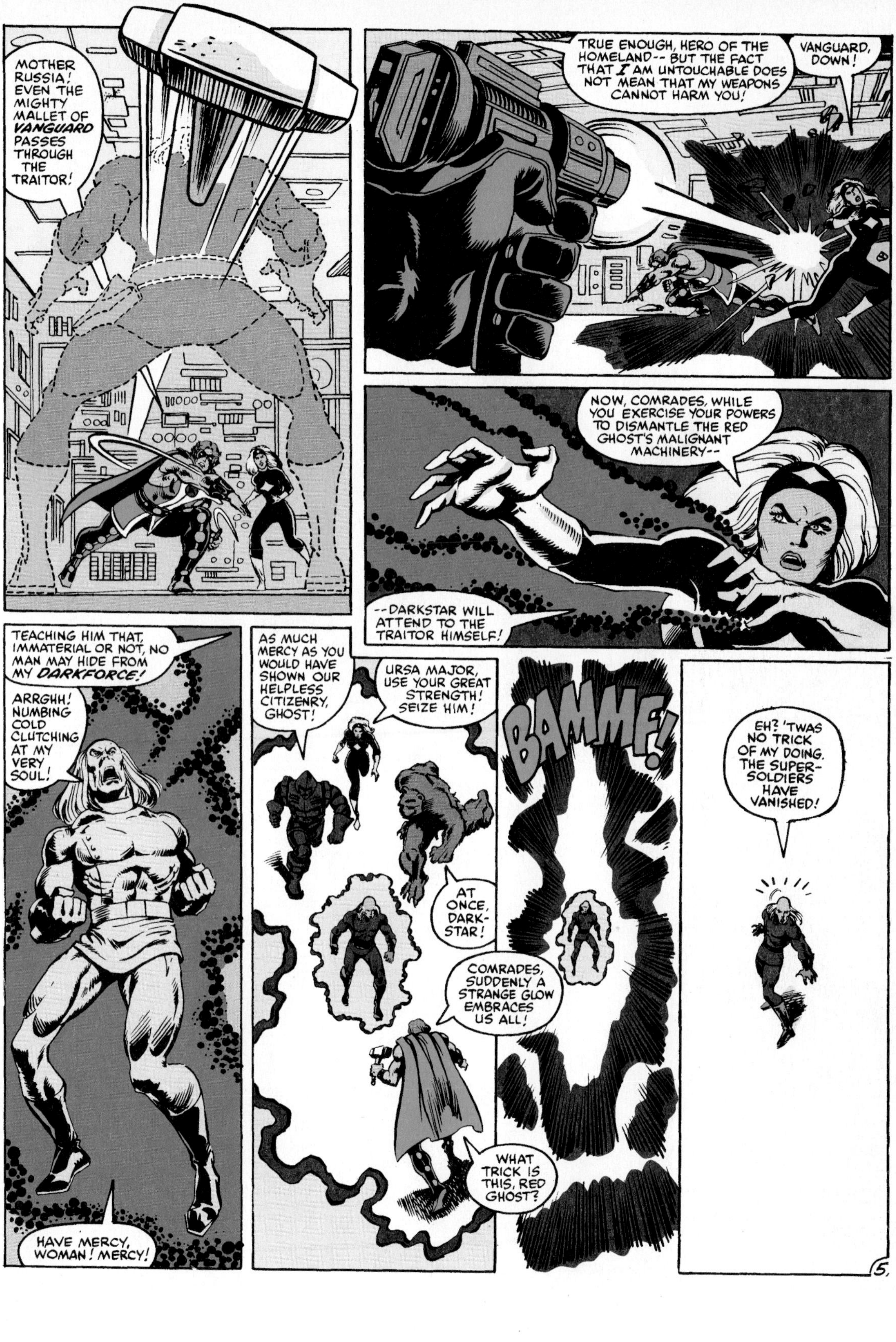
MOTHER RUSSIA! EVEN THE MIGHTY MALLET OF VANGUARD PASSES THROUGH THE TRAITOR!
TRUE ENOUGH, HERO OF THE HOMELAND-- BUT THE FACT THAT I AM UNTOUCHABLE DOES NOT MEAN THAT MY WEAPONS CANNOT HARM YOU!
VANGUARD, DOWN!
NOW, COMRADES, WHILE YOU EXERCISE YOUR POWERS TO DISMANTLE THE RED GHOST'S MALIGNANT MACHINERY--
--DARKSTAR WILL ATTEND TO THE TRAITOR HIMSELF!
TEACHING HIM THAT, IMMATERIAL OR NOT, NO MAN MAY HIDE FROM MY DARKFORCE!
ARRGHH! NUMBING COLD CLUTCHING AT MY VERY SOUL!
HAVE MERCY, WOMAN! MERCY!
AS MUCH MERCY AS YOU WOULD HAVE SHOWN OUR HELPLESS CITIZENRY, GHOST!
URSA MAJOR, USE YOUR GREAT STRENGTH! SEIZE HIM!
AT ONCE, DARK-STAR!
COMRADES, SUDDENLY A STRANGE GLOW EMBRACES US ALL!
WHAT TRICK IS THIS, RED GHOST?
BAMMF!
EH? 'TWAS NO TRICK OF MY DOING. THE SUPER-SOLDIERS HAVE VANISHED!
5

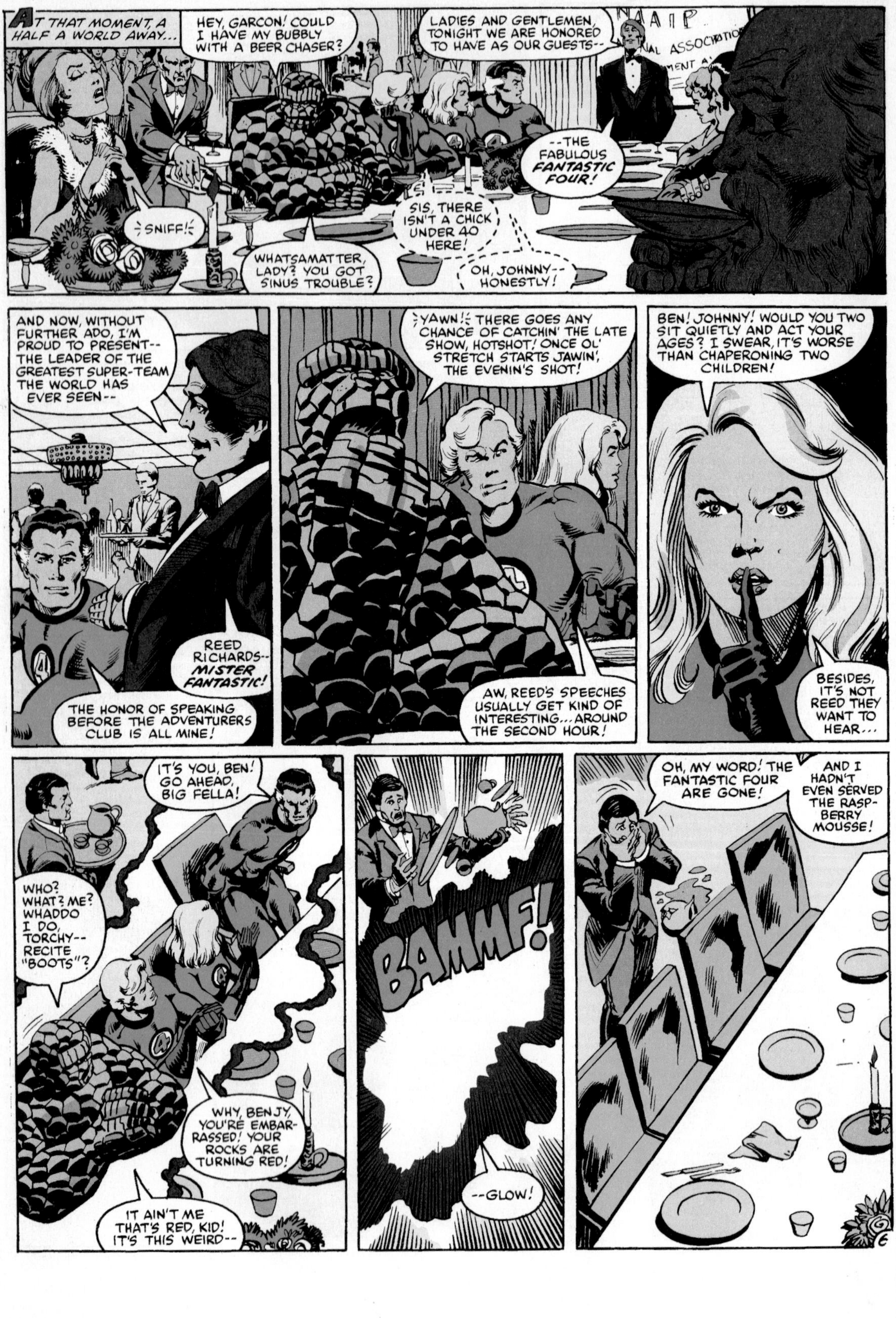
AT THAT MOMENT, A HALF A WORLD AWAY...
HEY, GARCON! COULD I HAVE MY BUBBLY WITH A BEER CHASER?
LADIES AND GENTLEMEN, TONIGHT WE ARE HONORED TO HAVE AS OUR GUESTS--
--THE FABULOUS FANTASTIC FOUR!
SIS, THERE ISN'T A CHICK UNDER 40 HERE!
OH, JOHNNY-- HONESTLY!
SNIFF!
WHATSAMATTER, LADY? YOU GOT SINUS TROUBLE?
AND NOW, WITHOUT FURTHER ADO, I'M PROUD TO PRESENT-- THE LEADER OF THE GREATEST SUPER-TEAM THE WORLD HAS EVER SEEN--
REED RICHARDS-- MISTER FANTASTIC!
THE HONOR OF SPEAKING BEFORE THE ADVENTURERS CLUB IS ALL MINE!
YAWN! THERE GOES ANY CHANCE OF CATCHIN' THE LATE SHOW, HOTSHOT! ONCE OL' STRETCH STARTS JAWIN', THE EVENIN'S SHOT!
AW, REED'S SPEECHES USUALLY GET KIND OF INTERESTING... AROUND THE SECOND HOUR!
BEN! JOHNNY! WOULD YOU TWO SIT QUIETLY AND ACT YOUR AGES? I SWEAR, IT'S WORSE THAN CHAPERONING TWO CHILDREN!
BESIDES, IT'S NOT REED THEY WANT TO HEAR...
IT'S YOU, BEN! GO AHEAD, BIG FELLA!
WHO? WHAT? ME? WHADDO I DO, TORCHY-- RECITE "BOOTS"?
WHY, BENJY, YOU'RE EMBARRASSED! YOUR ROCKS ARE TURNING RED!
IT AIN'T ME THAT'S RED, KID! IT'S THIS WEIRD--
BAMMF!
--GLOW!
OH, MY WORD! THE FANTASTIC FOUR ARE GONE!
AND I HADN'T EVEN SERVED THE RASPBERRY MOUSSE!
6

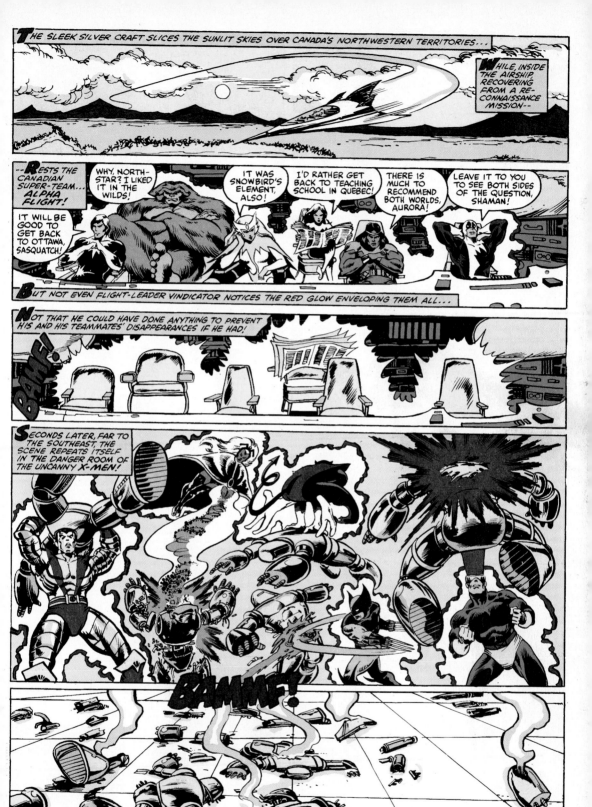

THE SLEEK SILVER CRAFT SLICES THE SUNLIT SKIES OVER CANADA'S NORTHWESTERN TERRITORIES...

WHILE, INSIDE THE AIRSHIP, RECOVERING FROM A RECONNAISSANCE MISSION--

--RESTS THE CANADIAN SUPER-TEAM... ALPHA FLIGHT!

IT WILL BE GOOD TO GET BACK TO OTTAWA, SASQUATCH!

WHY, NORTH-STAR? I LIKED IT IN THE WILDS!

IT WAS SNOWBIRD'S ELEMENT, ALSO!

I'D RATHER GET BACK TO TEACHING SCHOOL IN QUEBEC!

THERE IS MUCH TO RECOMMEND BOTH WORLDS, AURORA!

LEAVE IT TO YOU TO SEE BOTH SIDES OF THE QUESTION, SHAMAN!

BUT NOT EVEN FLIGHT-LEADER VINDICATOR NOTICES THE RED GLOW ENVELOPING THEM ALL...

NOT THAT HE COULD HAVE DONE ANYTHING TO PREVENT HIS AND HIS TEAMMATES' DISAPPEARANCES IF HE HAD!

BAMF!

SECONDS LATER, FAR TO THE SOUTHEAST, THE SCENE REPEATS ITSELF IN THE DANGER ROOM OF THE UNCANNY X-MEN!

BAMMF!

7

13

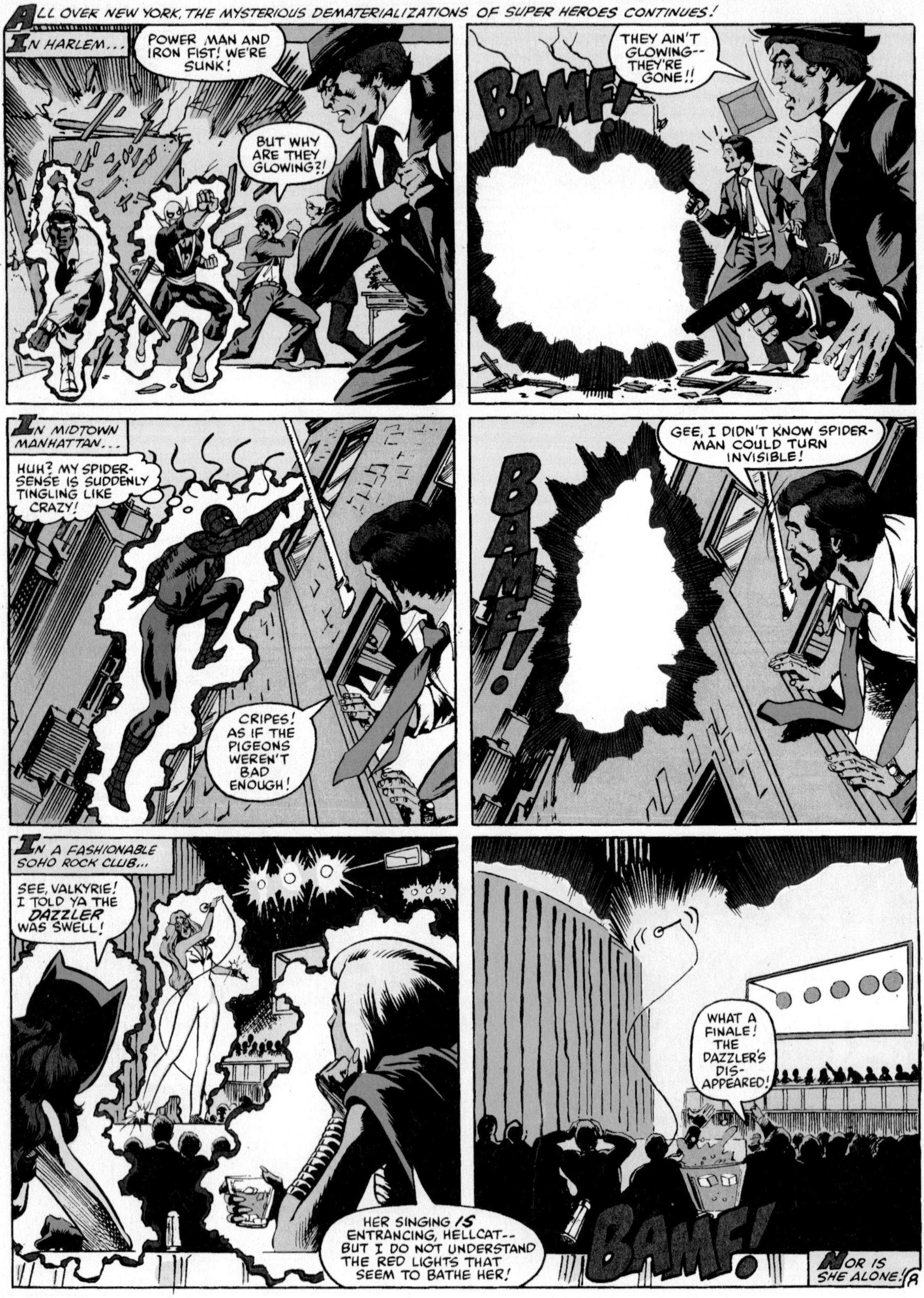
ALL OVER NEW YORK, THE MYSTERIOUS DEMATERIALIZATIONS OF SUPER HEROES CONTINUES!
IN HARLEM...
POWER MAN AND IRON FIST! WE'RE SUNK!
BUT WHY ARE THEY GLOWING?!
BAMF!
THEY AIN'T GLOWING-- THEY'RE GONE!!
IN MIDTOWN MANHATTAN...
HUH? MY SPIDER-SENSE IS SUDDENLY TINGLING LIKE CRAZY!
CRIPES! AS IF THE PIGEONS WEREN'T BAD ENOUGH!
BAMF!
GEE, I DIDN'T KNOW SPIDER-MAN COULD TURN INVISIBLE!
IN A FASHIONABLE SOHO ROCK CLUB...
SEE, VALKYRIE! I TOLD YA THE DAZZLER WAS SWELL!
HER SINGING IS ENTRANCING, HELLCAT-- BUT I DO NOT UNDERSTAND THE RED LIGHTS THAT SEEM TO BATHE HER!
WHAT A FINALE! THE DAZZLER'S DIS-APPEARED!
BAMF!
NOR IS SHE ALONE!

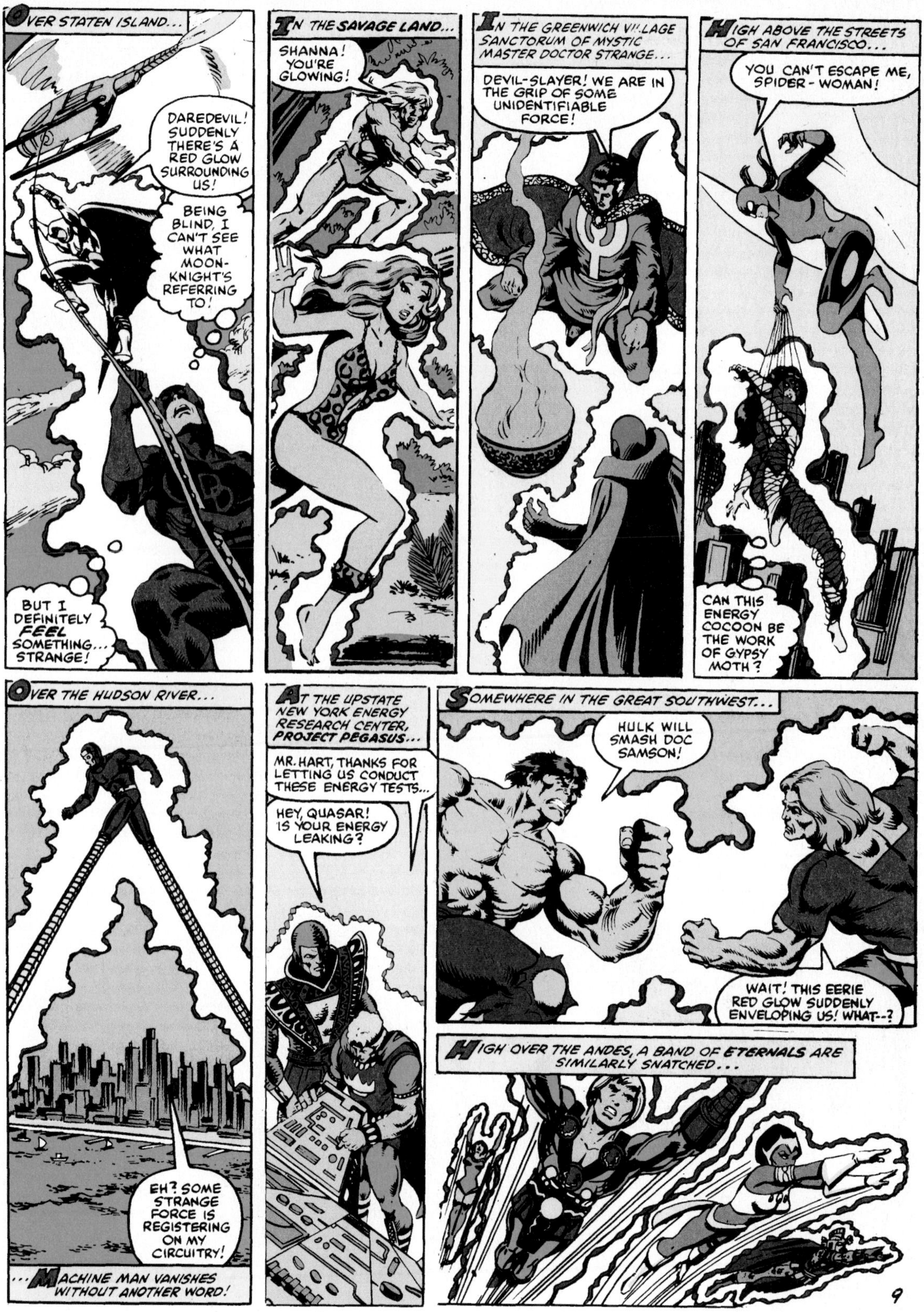
OVER STATEN ISLAND...
DAREDEVIL! SUDDENLY THERE'S A RED GLOW SURROUNDING US!
BEING BLIND, I CAN'T SEE WHAT MOON-KNIGHT'S REFERRING TO!
BUT I DEFINITELY FEEL SOMETHING... STRANGE!
IN THE SAVAGE LAND...
SHANNA! YOU'RE GLOWING!
IN THE GREENWICH VILLAGE SANCTORUM OF MYSTIC MASTER DOCTOR STRANGE...
DEVIL-SLAYER! WE ARE IN THE GRIP OF SOME UNIDENTIFIABLE FORCE!
HIGH ABOVE THE STREETS OF SAN FRANCISCO...
YOU CAN'T ESCAPE ME, SPIDER-WOMAN!
CAN THIS ENERGY COCOON BE THE WORK OF GYPSY MOTH?
OVER THE HUDSON RIVER...
EH? SOME STRANGE FORCE IS REGISTERING ON MY CIRCUITRY!
...MACHINE MAN VANISHES WITHOUT ANOTHER WORD!
AT THE UPSTATE NEW YORK ENERGY RESEARCH CENTER, PROJECT PEGASUS...
MR. HART, THANKS FOR LETTING US CONDUCT THESE ENERGY TESTS...
HEY, QUASAR! IS YOUR ENERGY LEAKING?
SOMEWHERE IN THE GREAT SOUTHWEST...
HULK WILL SMASH DOC SAMSON!
WAIT! THIS EERIE RED GLOW SUDDENLY ENVELOPING US! WHAT--?
HIGH OVER THE ANDES, A BAND OF ETERNALS ARE SIMILARLY SNATCHED...
9

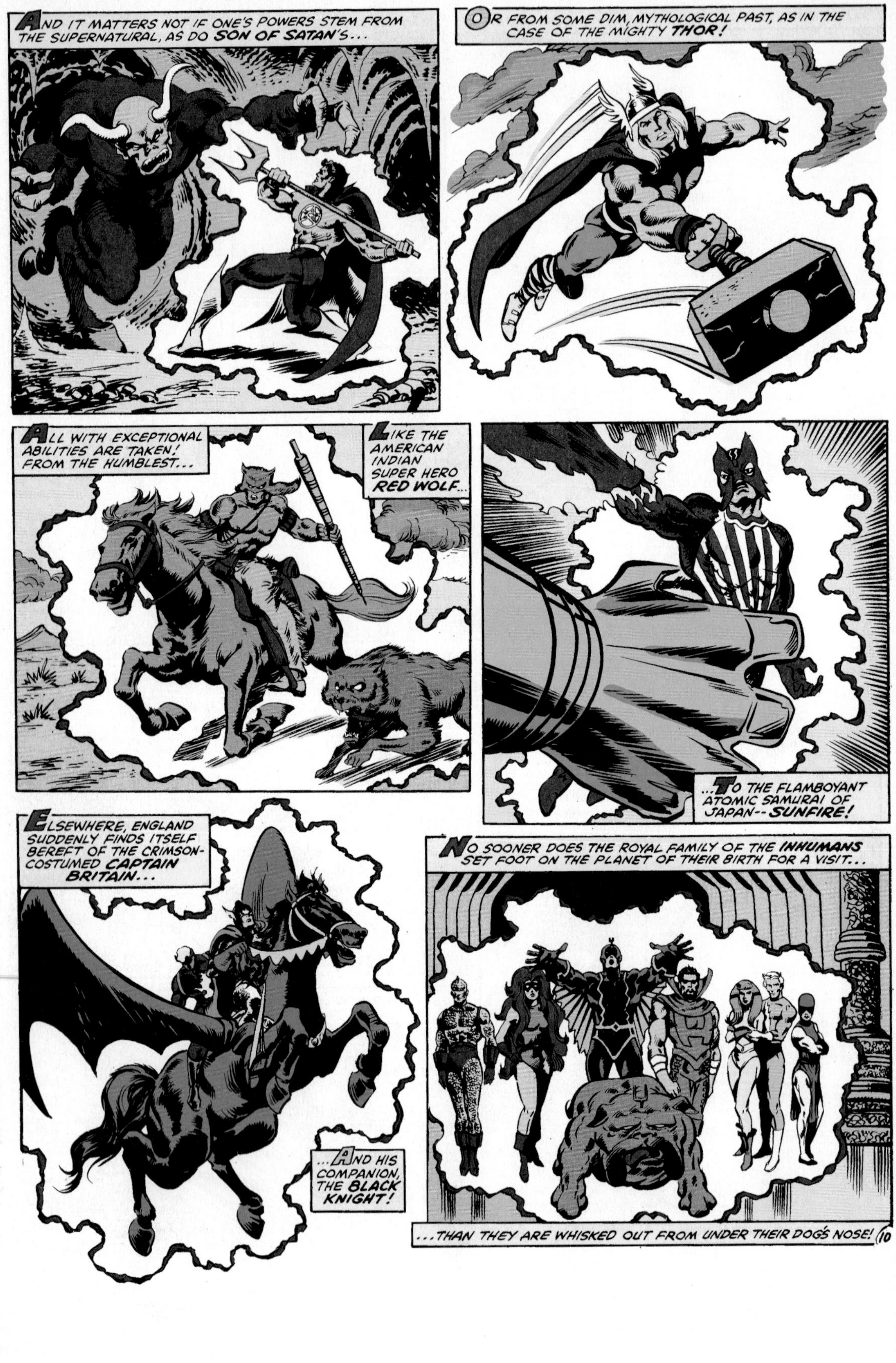
AND IT MATTERS NOT IF ONE'S POWERS STEM FROM THE SUPERNATURAL, AS DO SON OF SATAN'S...
OR FROM SOME DIM, MYTHOLOGICAL PAST, AS IN THE CASE OF THE MIGHTY THOR!
ALL WITH EXCEPTIONAL ABILITIES ARE TAKEN! FROM THE HUMBLEST...
LIKE THE AMERICAN INDIAN SUPER HERO RED WOLF...
...TO THE FLAMBOYANT ATOMIC SAMURAI OF JAPAN--SUNFIRE!
ELSEWHERE, ENGLAND SUDDENLY FINDS ITSELF BEREFT OF THE CRIMSON-COSTUMED CAPTAIN BRITAIN...
...AND HIS COMPANION, THE BLACK KNIGHT!
NO SOONER DOES THE ROYAL FAMILY OF THE INHUMANS SET FOOT ON THE PLANET OF THEIR BIRTH FOR A VISIT...
...THAN THEY ARE WHISKED OUT FROM UNDER THEIR DOG'S NOSE!
10

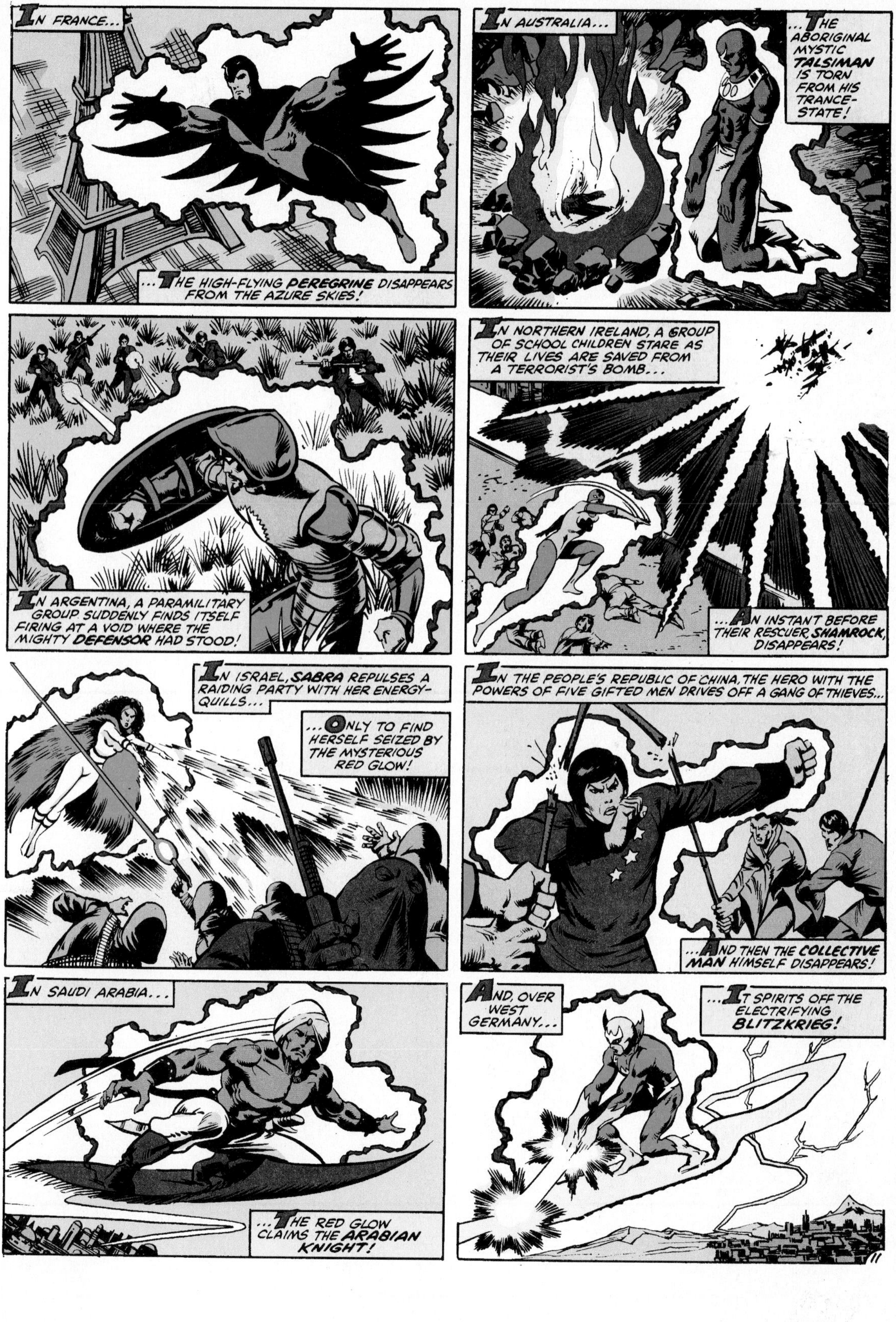
IN FRANCE...
...THE HIGH-FLYING PEREGRINE DISAPPEARS FROM THE AZURE SKIES!
IN AUSTRALIA...
...THE ABORIGINAL MYSTIC TALSIMAN IS TORN FROM HIS TRANCE-STATE!
IN ARGENTINA, A PARAMILITARY GROUP SUDDENLY FINDS ITSELF FIRING AT A VOID WHERE THE MIGHTY DEFENSOR HAD STOOD!
IN NORTHERN IRELAND, A GROUP OF SCHOOL CHILDREN STARE AS THEIR LIVES ARE SAVED FROM A TERRORIST'S BOMB...
...AN INSTANT BEFORE THEIR RESCUER, SHAMROCK, DISAPPEARS!
IN ISRAEL, SABRA REPULSES A RAIDING PARTY WITH HER ENERGY-QUILLS...
...ONLY TO FIND HERSELF SEIZED BY THE MYSTERIOUS RED GLOW!
IN THE PEOPLE'S REPUBLIC OF CHINA, THE HERO WITH THE POWERS OF FIVE GIFTED MEN DRIVES OFF A GANG OF THIEVES...
...AND THEN THE COLLECTIVE MAN HIMSELF DISAPPEARS!
IN SAUDI ARABIA...
...THE RED GLOW CLAIMS THE ARABIAN KNIGHT!
AND, OVER WEST GERMANY...
...IT SPIRITS OFF THE ELECTRIFYING BLITZKRIEG!
11

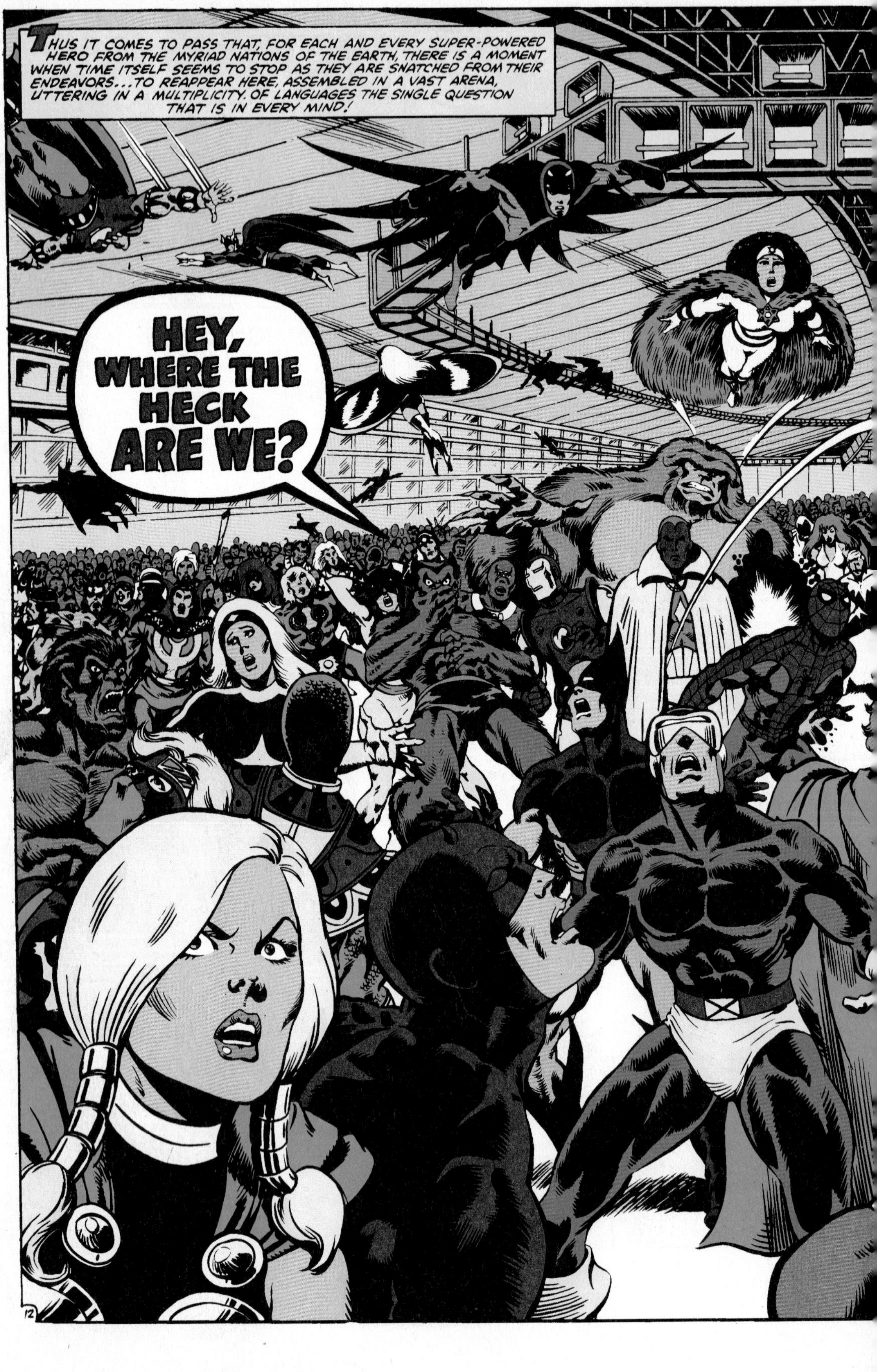
THUS IT COMES TO PASS THAT, FOR EACH AND EVERY SUPER-POWERED HERO FROM THE MYRIAD NATIONS OF THE EARTH, THERE IS A MOMENT WHEN TIME ITSELF SEEMS TO STOP AS THEY ARE SNATCHED FROM THEIR ENDEAVORS...TO REAPPEAR HERE, ASSEMBLED IN A VAST ARENA, UTTERING IN A MULTIPLICITY OF LANGUAGES THE SINGLE QUESTION THAT IS IN EVERY MIND!
HEY, WHERE THE HECK ARE WE?
12

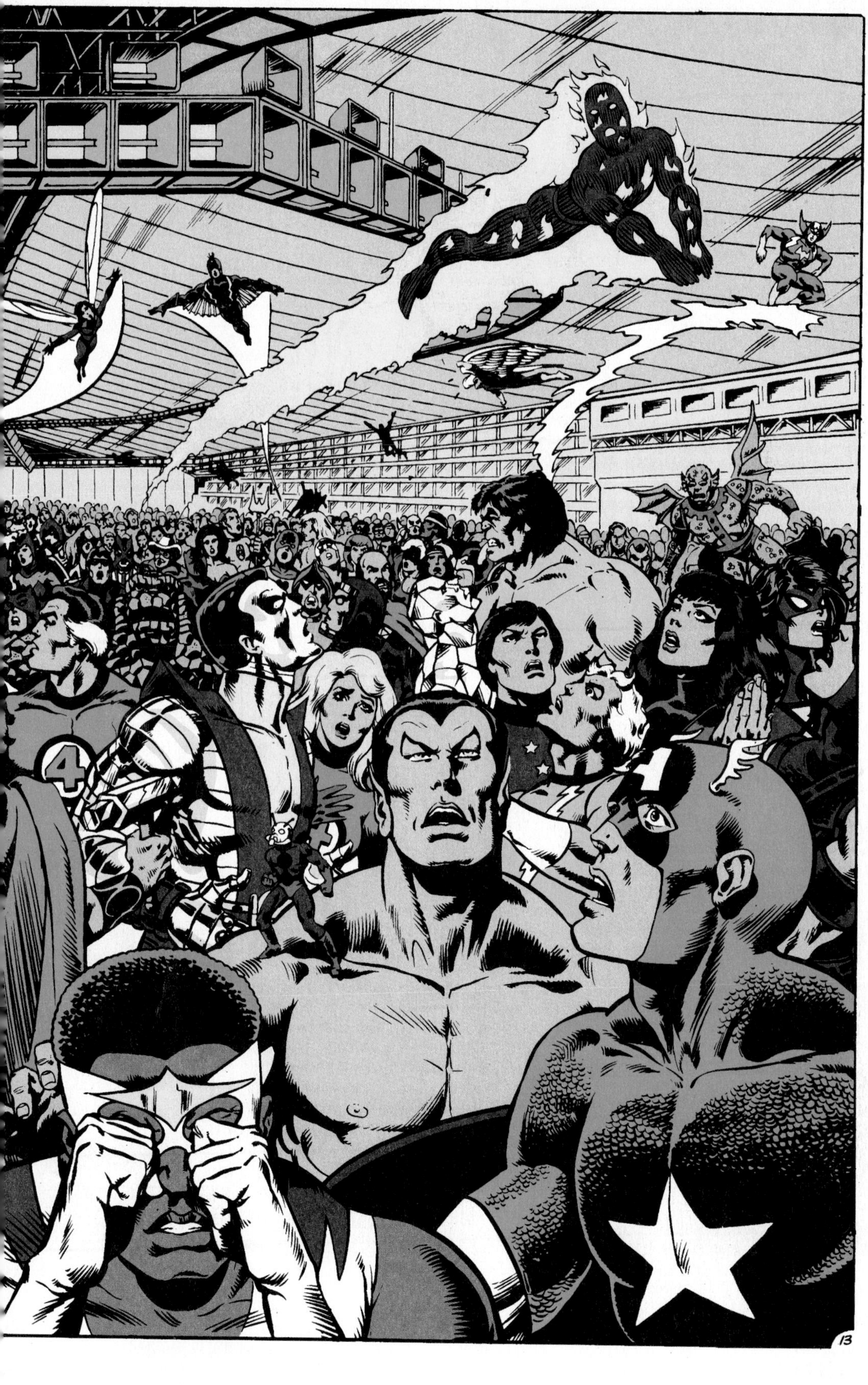

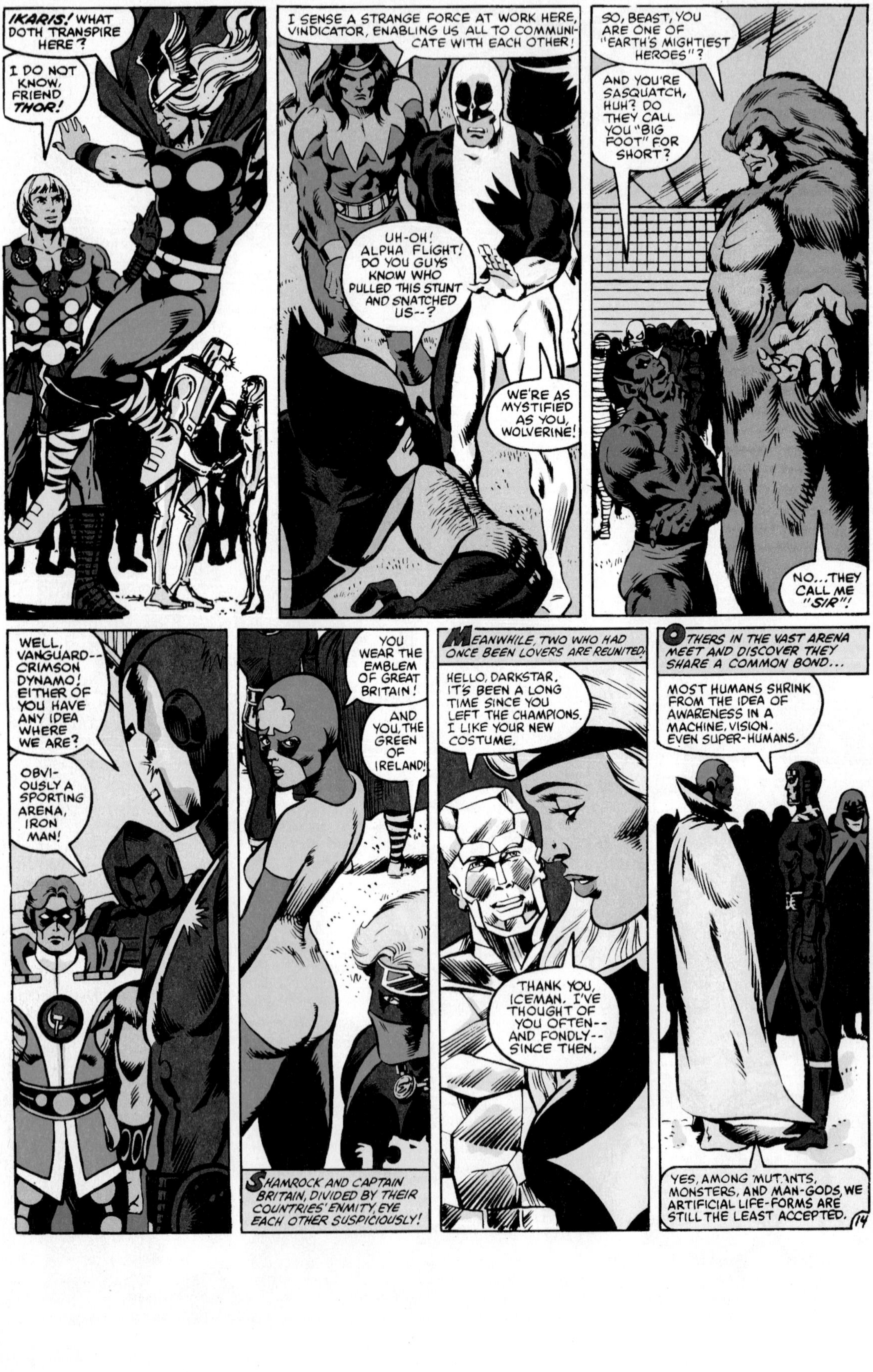
IKARIS! WHAT DOTH TRANSPIRE HERE?
I DO NOT KNOW, FRIEND THOR!
I SENSE A STRANGE FORCE AT WORK HERE, VINDICATOR, ENABLING US ALL TO COMMUNICATE WITH EACH OTHER!
UH-OH! ALPHA FLIGHT! DO YOU GUYS KNOW WHO PULLED THIS STUNT AND SNATCHED US--?
WE'RE AS MYSTIFIED AS YOU, WOLVERINE!
SO, BEAST, YOU ARE ONE OF "EARTH'S MIGHTIEST HEROES"?
AND YOU'RE SASQUATCH, HUH? DO THEY CALL YOU "BIG FOOT" FOR SHORT?
NO...THEY CALL ME "SIR"!
WELL, VANGUARD--CRIMSON DYNAMO! EITHER OF YOU HAVE ANY IDEA WHERE WE ARE?
OBVIOUSLY A SPORTING ARENA, IRON MAN!
YOU WEAR THE EMBLEM OF GREAT BRITAIN!
AND YOU, THE GREEN OF IRELAND!
SHAMROCK AND CAPTAIN BRITAIN, DIVIDED BY THEIR COUNTRIES' ENMITY, EYE EACH OTHER SUSPICIOUSLY!
MEANWHILE, TWO WHO HAD ONCE BEEN LOVERS ARE REUNITED!
HELLO, DARKSTAR, IT'S BEEN A LONG TIME SINCE YOU LEFT THE CHAMPIONS. I LIKE YOUR NEW COSTUME.
THANK YOU, ICEMAN. I'VE THOUGHT OF YOU OFTEN--AND FONDLY--SINCE THEN.
OTHERS IN THE VAST ARENA MEET AND DISCOVER THEY SHARE A COMMON BOND...
MOST HUMANS SHRINK FROM THE IDEA OF AWARENESS IN A MACHINE, VISION. EVEN SUPER-HUMANS.
YES, AMONG MUTANTS, MONSTERS, AND MAN-GODS, WE ARTIFICIAL LIFE-FORMS ARE STILL THE LEAST ACCEPTED.
14

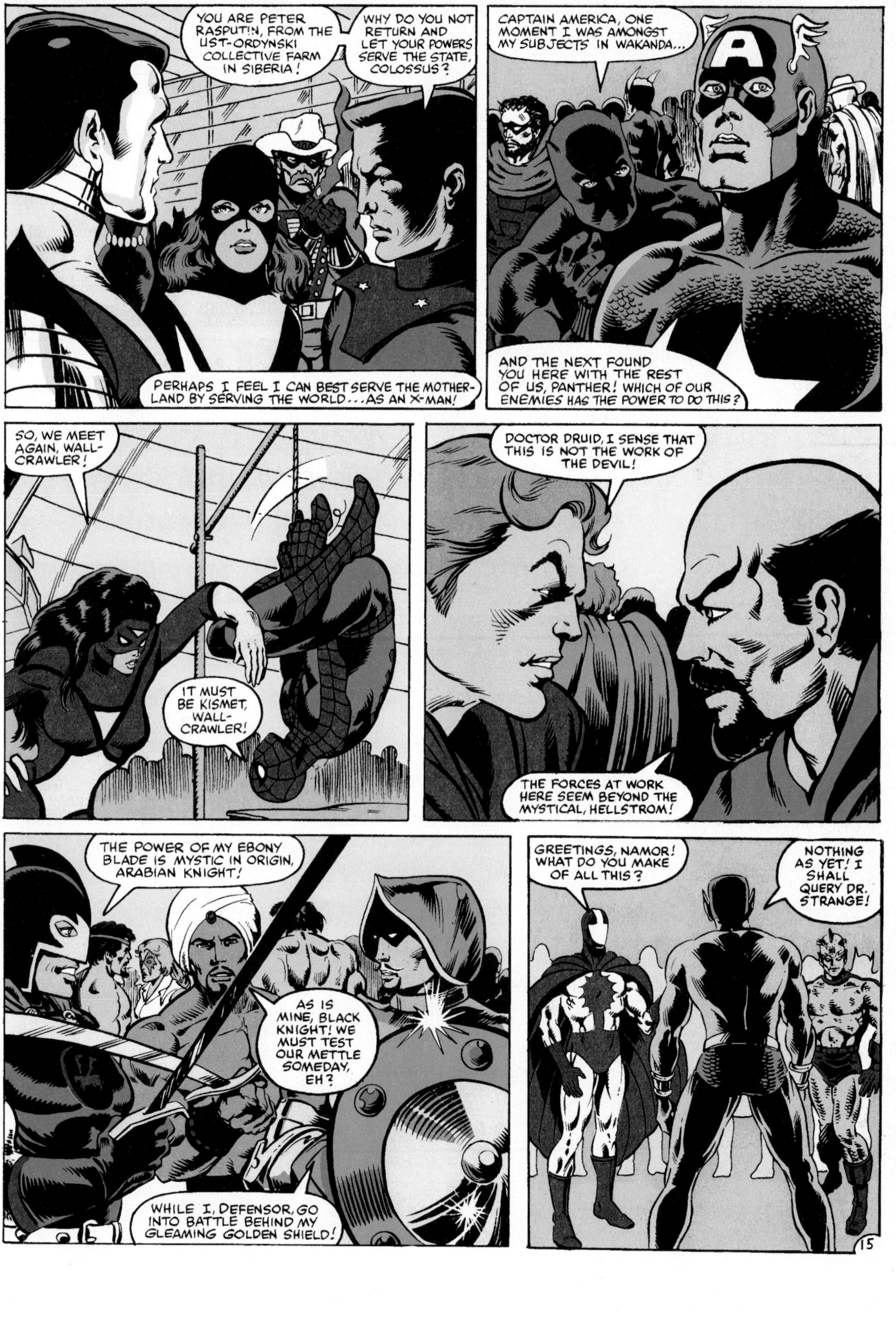
YOU ARE PETER RASPUTIN, FROM THE UST-ORDYNSKI COLLECTIVE FARM IN SIBERIA!
WHY DO YOU NOT RETURN AND LET YOUR POWERS SERVE THE STATE, COLOSSUS?
PERHAPS I FEEL I CAN BEST SERVE THE MOTHER-LAND BY SERVING THE WORLD... AS AN X-MAN!
CAPTAIN AMERICA, ONE MOMENT I WAS AMONGST MY SUBJECTS IN WAKANDA...
AND THE NEXT FOUND YOU HERE WITH THE REST OF US, PANTHER! WHICH OF OUR ENEMIES HAS THE POWER TO DO THIS?
SO, WE MEET AGAIN, WALL-CRAWLER!
IT MUST BE KISMET, WALL-CRAWLER!
DOCTOR DRUID, I SENSE THAT THIS IS NOT THE WORK OF THE DEVIL!
THE FORCES AT WORK HERE SEEM BEYOND THE MYSTICAL, HELLSTROM!
THE POWER OF MY EBONY BLADE IS MYSTIC IN ORIGIN, ARABIAN KNIGHT!
AS IS MINE, BLACK KNIGHT! WE MUST TEST OUR METTLE SOMEDAY, EH?
WHILE I, DEFENSOR, GO INTO BATTLE BEHIND MY GLEAMING GOLDEN SHIELD!
GREETINGS, NAMOR! WHAT DO YOU MAKE OF ALL THIS?
NOTHING AS YET! I SHALL QUERY DR. STRANGE!
15

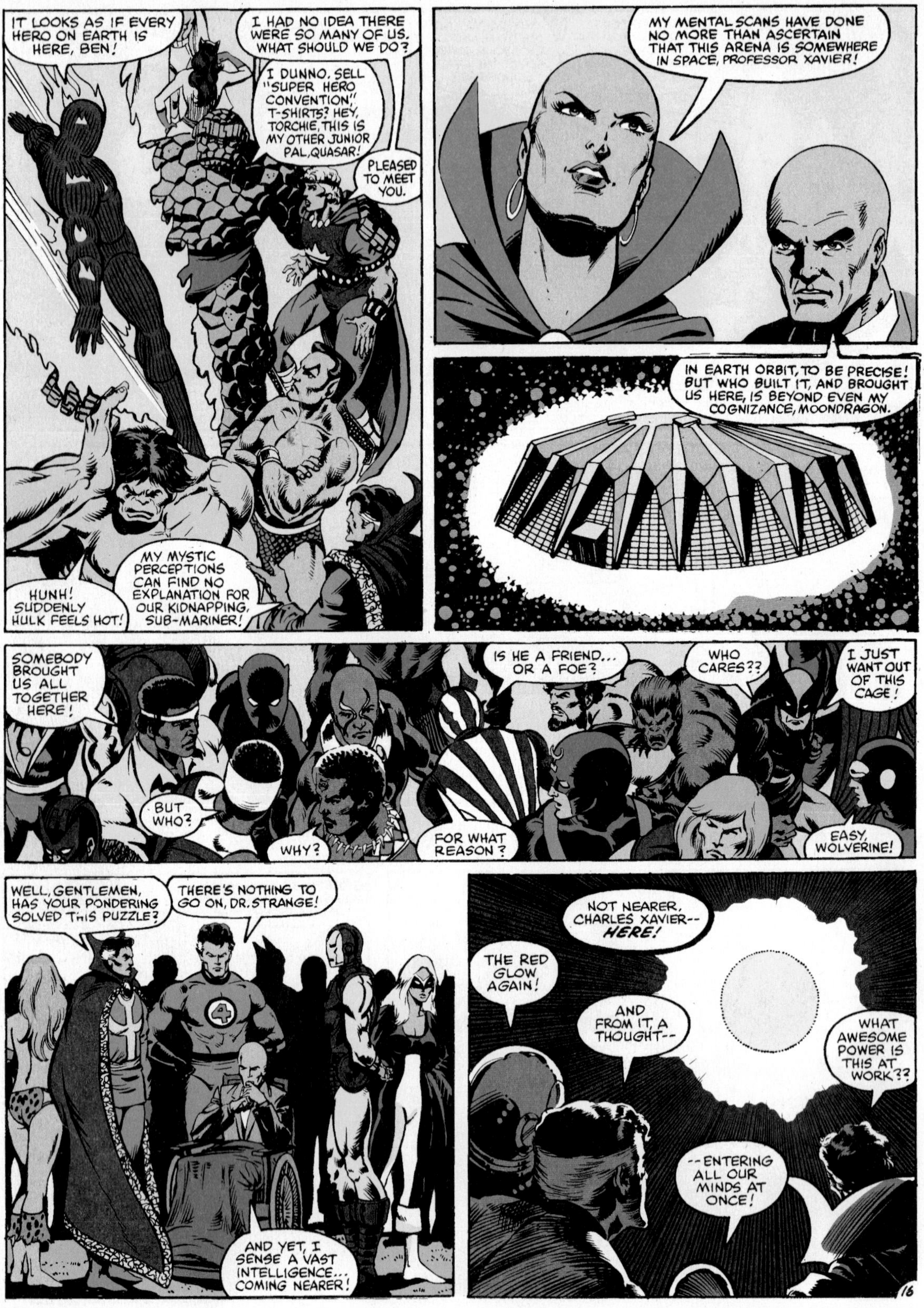
IT LOOKS AS IF EVERY HERO ON EARTH IS HERE, BEN!
I HAD NO IDEA THERE WERE SO MANY OF US. WHAT SHOULD WE DO?
I DUNNO. SELL "SUPER HERO CONVENTION" T-SHIRTS? HEY, TORCHIE, THIS IS MY OTHER JUNIOR PAL, QUASAR!
PLEASED TO MEET YOU.
HUNH! SUDDENLY HULK FEELS HOT!
MY MYSTIC PERCEPTIONS CAN FIND NO EXPLANATION FOR OUR KIDNAPPING, SUB-MARINER!
MY MENTAL SCANS HAVE DONE NO MORE THAN ASCERTAIN THAT THIS ARENA IS SOMEWHERE IN SPACE, PROFESSOR XAVIER!
IN EARTH ORBIT, TO BE PRECISE! BUT WHO BUILT IT, AND BROUGHT US HERE, IS BEYOND EVEN MY COGNIZANCE, MOONDRAGON.
SOMEBODY BROUGHT US ALL TOGETHER HERE!
BUT WHO?
WHY?
IS HE A FRIEND... OR A FOE?
FOR WHAT REASON?
WHO CARES??
I JUST WANT OUT OF THIS CAGE!
EASY, WOLVERINE!
WELL, GENTLEMEN, HAS YOUR PONDERING SOLVED THIS PUZZLE?
THERE'S NOTHING TO GO ON, DR. STRANGE!
AND YET, I SENSE A VAST INTELLIGENCE... COMING NEARER!
NOT NEARER, CHARLES XAVIER-- HERE!
THE RED GLOW AGAIN!
AND FROM IT, A THOUGHT--
WHAT AWESOME POWER IS THIS AT WORK??
--ENTERING ALL OUR MINDS AT ONCE!
16

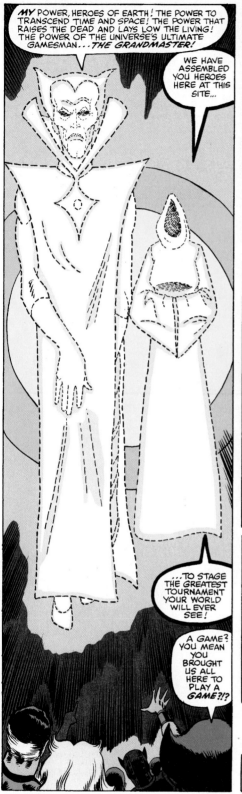

MY POWER, HEROES OF EARTH! THE POWER TO TRANSCEND TIME AND SPACE! THE POWER THAT RAISES THE DEAD AND LAYS LOW THE LIVING! THE POWER OF THE UNIVERSE'S ULTIMATE GAMESMAN...*THE GRANDMASTER!*

WE HAVE ASSEMBLED YOU HEROES HERE AT THIS SITE...

...TO STAGE THE GREATEST TOURNAMENT YOUR WORLD WILL EVER SEE!

A GAME? YOU MEAN YOU BROUGHT US ALL HERE TO PLAY A *GAME?!?*

EXACTLY! AND, AS THE *INERTIA-GLOW* HOLDS YOU PARALYZED BEFORE US...

...SO TOO DOES IT HOLD YOUR WORLD IN THRALL!

BY DRAWING UPON ALL THE POWER OF THE *ELDERS OF THE UNIVERSE* WE HAVE PLACED EVERY LIVING BEING ON YOUR PLANET IN A STATE OF SUSPENDED ANIMATION! IF YOU REFUSE TO PLAY OUR GAME, WE SHALL NOT RELEASE YOUR PLANET! IF YOU DO PLAY, EARTH WILL BE FREED AT GAME'S END!

THE RULES OF THE GAME ARE THESE: FOUR OBJECTS-- QUARTERS OF THE GLEAMING GOLDEN GLOBE OF LIFE-- WILL BE HIDDEN AT THE FOUR CORNERS OF THE EARTH!

MY FACELESS OPPONENT AND I WILL EACH CHOOSE TWELVE CHAMPIONS TO SEEK OUT THE OBJECTS!

WHICHEVER OF US AMASSES THE MOST PIECES, WINS!

AND IF *I* WIN, I WILL BE GRANTED THE POWER TO RESTORE LIFE TO MY BROTHER, THE *COLLECTOR!*

23

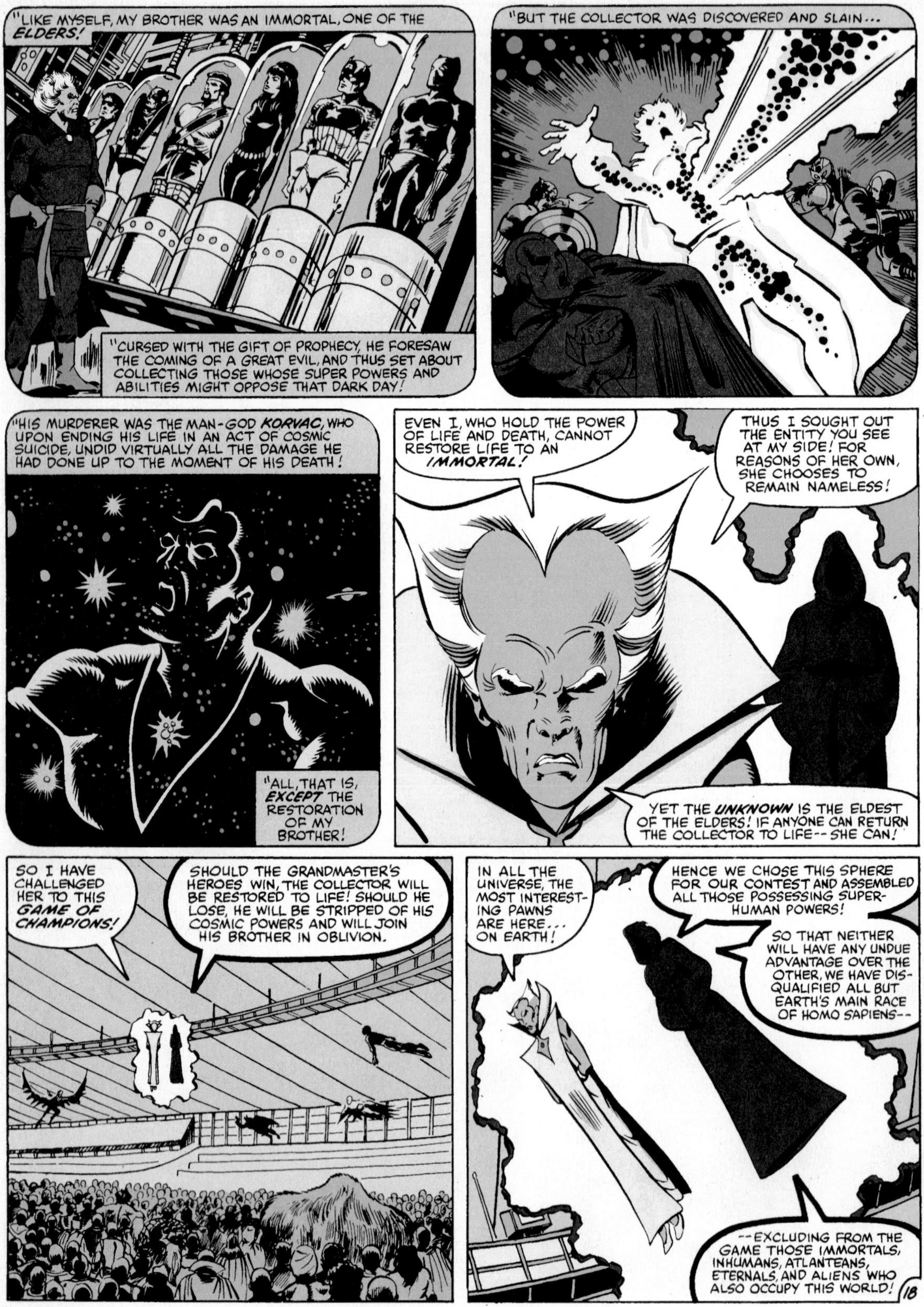
"LIKE MYSELF, MY BROTHER WAS AN IMMORTAL, ONE OF THE ELDERS!
"CURSED WITH THE GIFT OF PROPHECY, HE FORESAW THE COMING OF A GREAT EVIL, AND THUS SET ABOUT COLLECTING THOSE WHOSE SUPER POWERS AND ABILITIES MIGHT OPPOSE THAT DARK DAY!
"BUT THE COLLECTOR WAS DISCOVERED AND SLAIN...
"HIS MURDERER WAS THE MAN-GOD KORVAC, WHO UPON ENDING HIS LIFE IN AN ACT OF COSMIC SUICIDE, UNDID VIRTUALLY ALL THE DAMAGE HE HAD DONE UP TO THE MOMENT OF HIS DEATH!
"ALL, THAT IS, EXCEPT THE RESTORATION OF MY BROTHER!
EVEN I, WHO HOLD THE POWER OF LIFE AND DEATH, CANNOT RESTORE LIFE TO AN IMMORTAL!
THUS I SOUGHT OUT THE ENTITY YOU SEE AT MY SIDE! FOR REASONS OF HER OWN, SHE CHOOSES TO REMAIN NAMELESS!
YET THE UNKNOWN IS THE ELDEST OF THE ELDERS! IF ANYONE CAN RETURN THE COLLECTOR TO LIFE-- SHE CAN!
SO I HAVE CHALLENGED HER TO THIS GAME OF CHAMPIONS!
SHOULD THE GRANDMASTER'S HEROES WIN, THE COLLECTOR WILL BE RESTORED TO LIFE! SHOULD HE LOSE, HE WILL BE STRIPPED OF HIS COSMIC POWERS AND WILL JOIN HIS BROTHER IN OBLIVION.
IN ALL THE UNIVERSE, THE MOST INTERESTING PAWNS ARE HERE... ON EARTH!
HENCE WE CHOSE THIS SPHERE FOR OUR CONTEST AND ASSEMBLED ALL THOSE POSSESSING SUPER-HUMAN POWERS!
SO THAT NEITHER WILL HAVE ANY UNDUE ADVANTAGE OVER THE OTHER, WE HAVE DISQUALIFIED ALL BUT EARTH'S MAIN RACE OF HOMO SAPIENS--
--EXCLUDING FROM THE GAME THOSE IMMORTALS, INHUMANS, ATLANTEANS, ETERNALS, AND ALIENS WHO ALSO OCCUPY THIS WORLD!
18

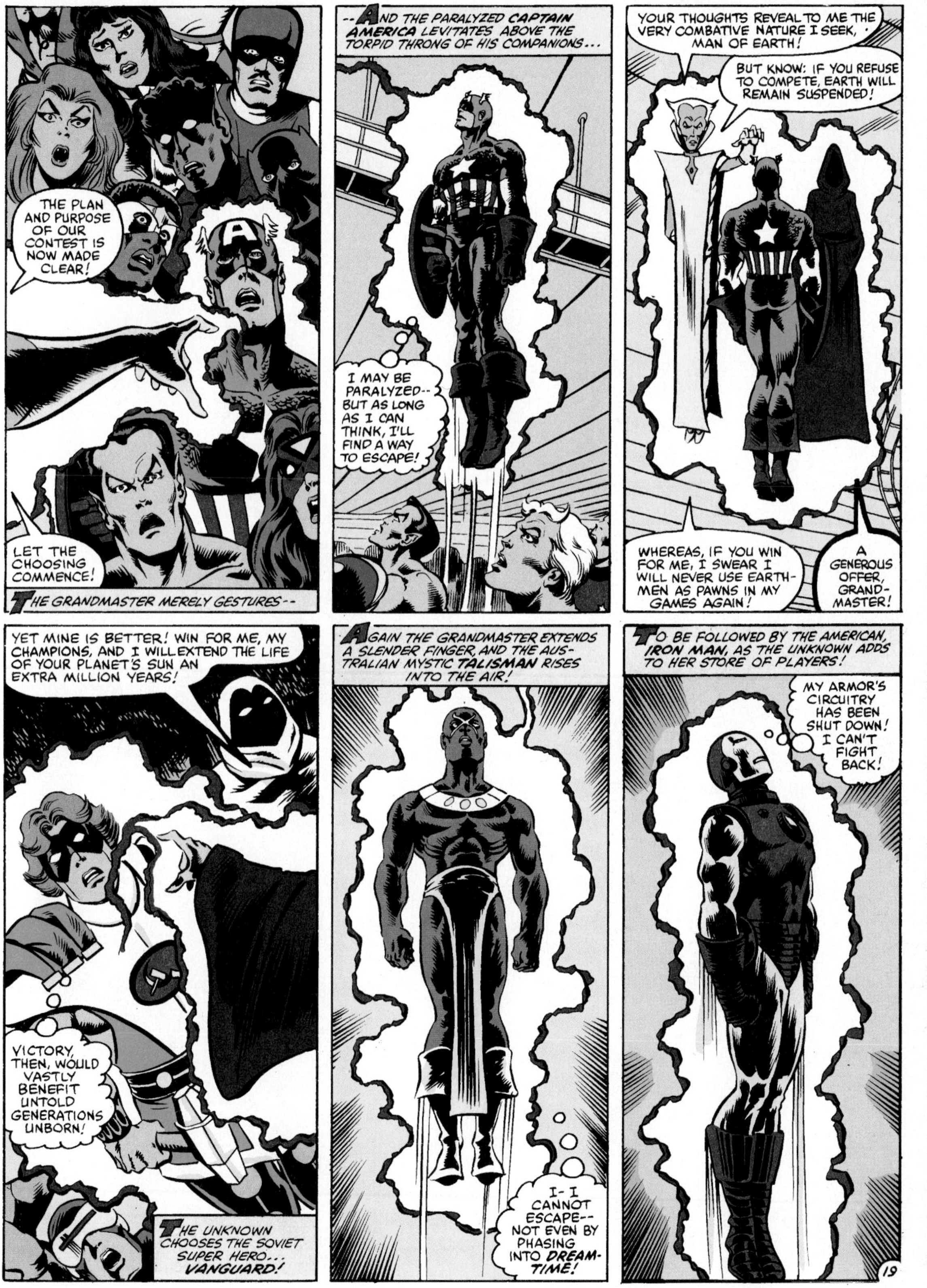
THE PLAN AND PURPOSE OF OUR CONTEST IS NOW MADE CLEAR!
LET THE CHOOSING COMMENCE!
THE GRANDMASTER MERELY GESTURES--
--AND THE PARALYZED CAPTAIN AMERICA LEVITATES ABOVE THE TORPID THRONG OF HIS COMPANIONS...
I MAY BE PARALYZED-- BUT AS LONG AS I CAN THINK, I'LL FIND A WAY TO ESCAPE!
YOUR THOUGHTS REVEAL TO ME THE VERY COMBATIVE NATURE I SEEK, MAN OF EARTH!
BUT KNOW: IF YOU REFUSE TO COMPETE, EARTH WILL REMAIN SUSPENDED!
WHEREAS, IF YOU WIN FOR ME, I SWEAR I WILL NEVER USE EARTHMEN AS PAWNS IN MY GAMES AGAIN!
A GENEROUS OFFER, GRANDMASTER!
YET MINE IS BETTER! WIN FOR ME, MY CHAMPIONS, AND I WILL EXTEND THE LIFE OF YOUR PLANET'S SUN AN EXTRA MILLION YEARS!
VICTORY, THEN, WOULD VASTLY BENEFIT UNTOLD GENERATIONS UNBORN!
THE UNKNOWN CHOOSES THE SOVIET SUPER HERO... VANGUARD!
AGAIN THE GRANDMASTER EXTENDS A SLENDER FINGER, AND THE AUSTRALIAN MYSTIC TALISMAN RISES INTO THE AIR!
I-I CANNOT ESCAPE-- NOT EVEN BY PHASING INTO DREAM-TIME!
TO BE FOLLOWED BY THE AMERICAN, IRON MAN, AS THE UNKNOWN ADDS TO HER STORE OF PLAYERS!
MY ARMOR'S CIRCUITRY HAS BEEN SHUT DOWN! I CAN'T FIGHT BACK!
19

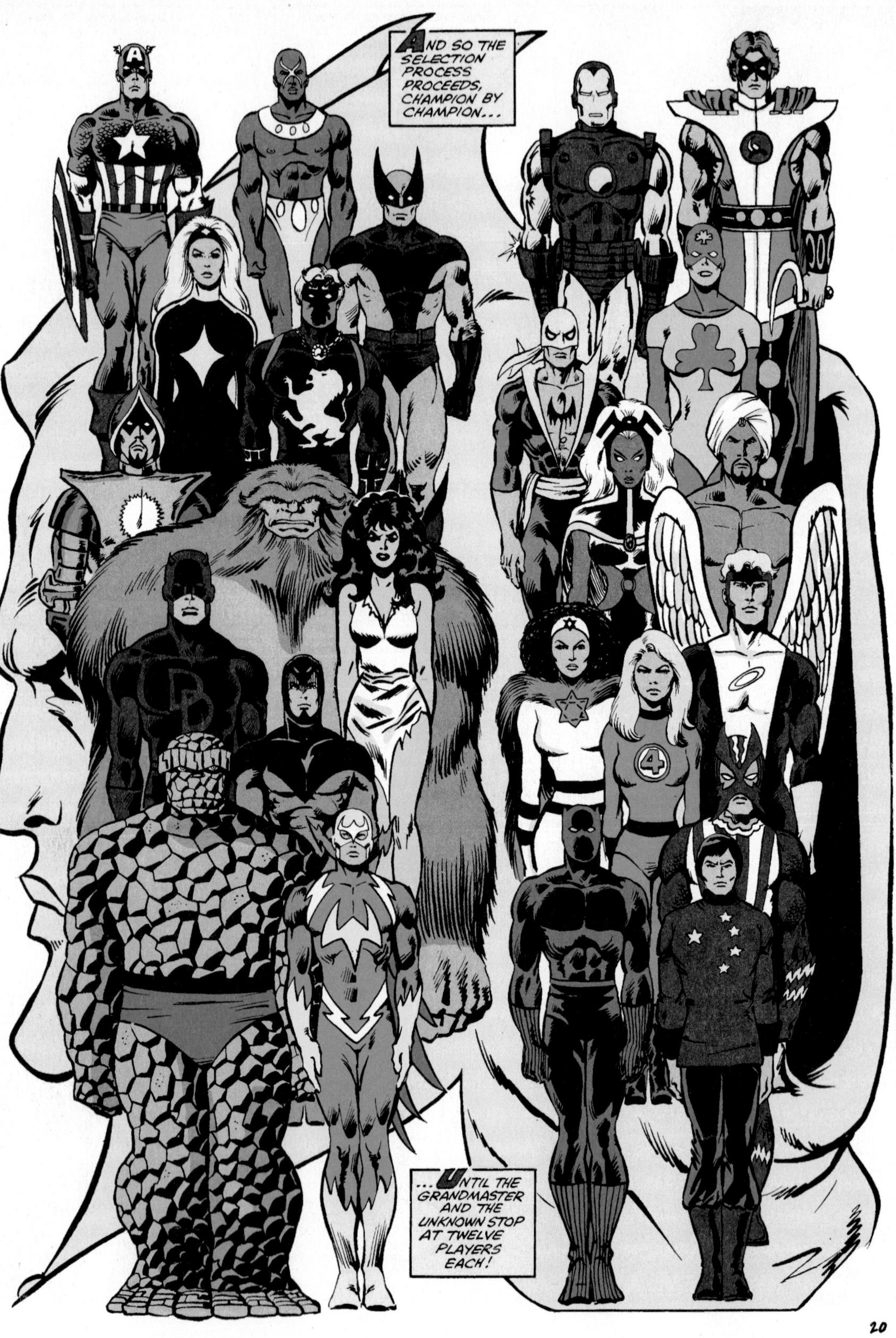
AND SO THE SELECTION PROCESS PROCEEDS, CHAMPION BY CHAMPION...
...UNTIL THE GRANDMASTER AND THE UNKNOWN STOP AT TWELVE PLAYERS EACH!
20

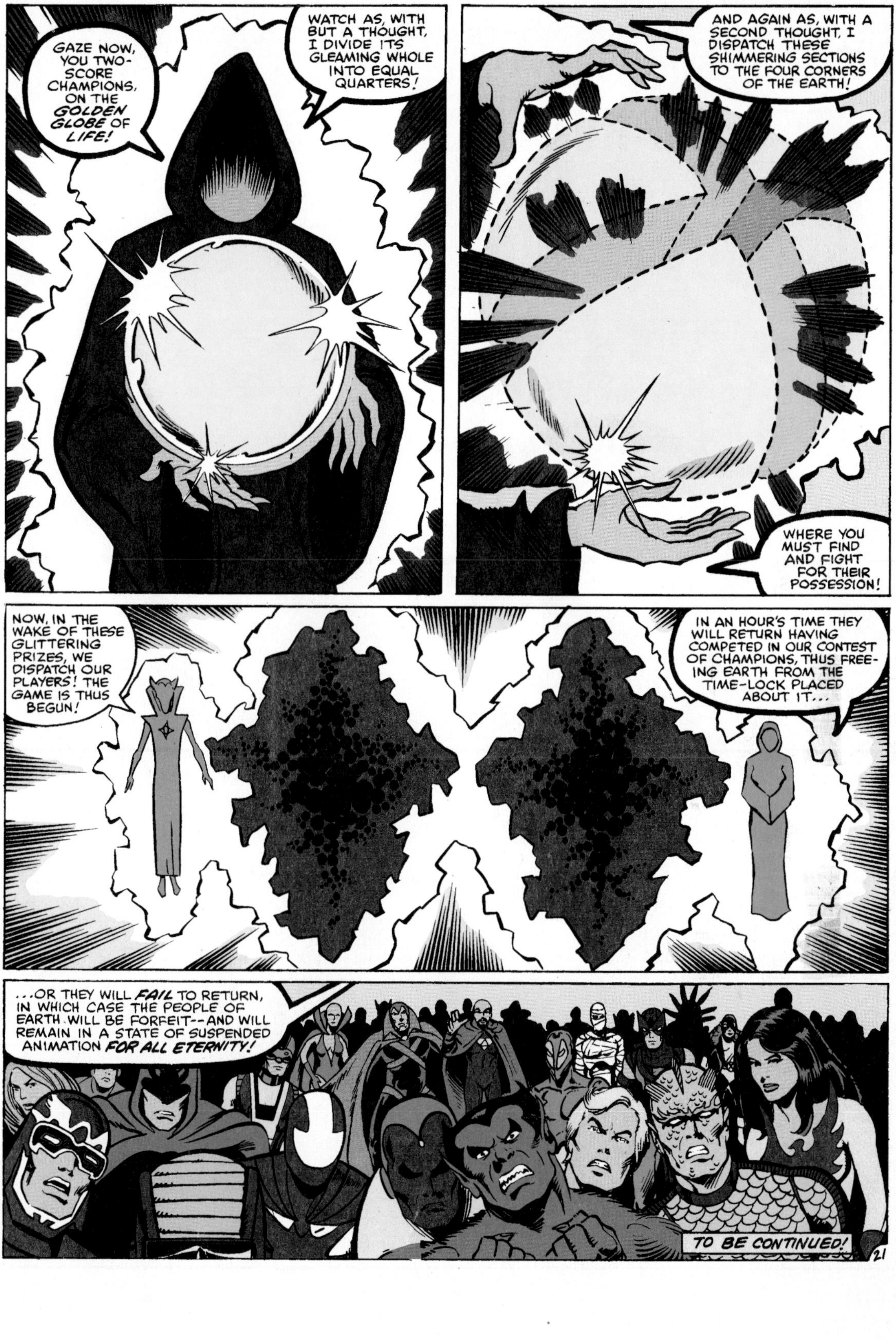
GAZE NOW, YOU TWO-SCORE CHAMPIONS, ON THE GOLDEN GLOBE OF LIFE!
WATCH AS, WITH BUT A THOUGHT, I DIVIDE ITS GLEAMING WHOLE INTO EQUAL QUARTERS!
AND AGAIN AS, WITH A SECOND THOUGHT, I DISPATCH THESE SHIMMERING SECTIONS TO THE FOUR CORNERS OF THE EARTH!
WHERE YOU MUST FIND AND FIGHT FOR THEIR POSSESSION!
NOW, IN THE WAKE OF THESE GLITTERING PRIZES, WE DISPATCH OUR PLAYERS! THE GAME IS THUS BEGUN!
IN AN HOUR'S TIME THEY WILL RETURN HAVING COMPETED IN OUR CONTEST OF CHAMPIONS, THUS FREEING EARTH FROM THE TIME-LOCK PLACED ABOUT IT...
...OR THEY WILL FAIL TO RETURN, IN WHICH CASE THE PEOPLE OF EARTH WILL BE FORFEIT--AND WILL REMAIN IN A STATE OF SUSPENDED ANIMATION FOR ALL ETERNITY!
TO BE CONTINUED!
21

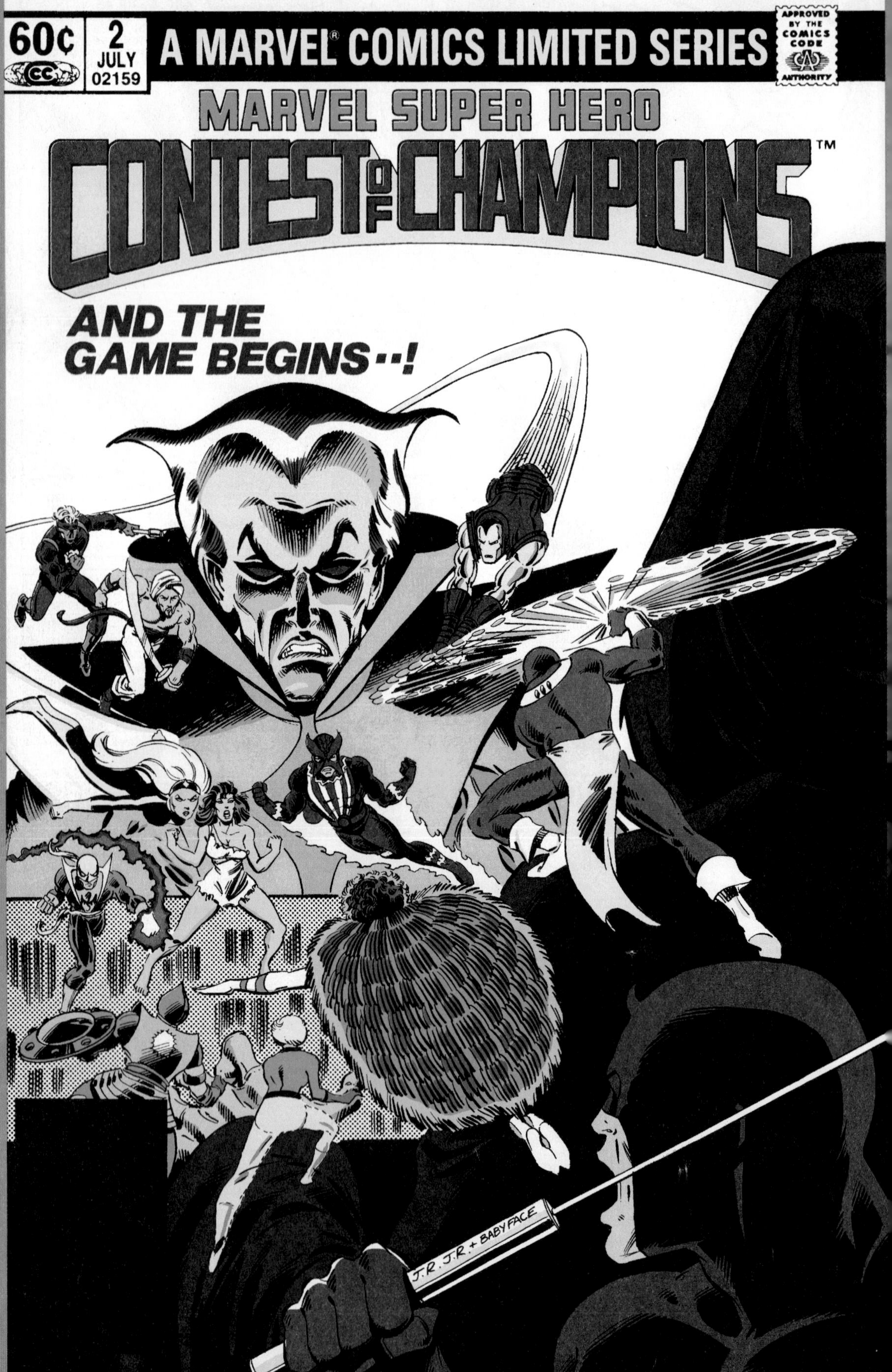
60¢
2
JULY
02159
CC
A MARVEL® COMICS LIMITED SERIES
APPROVED BY THE COMICS CODE CA AUTHORITY
MARVEL SUPER HERO
CONTEST OF CHAMPIONS™
AND THE GAME BEGINS--!
J.R.J.R. + BABYFACE

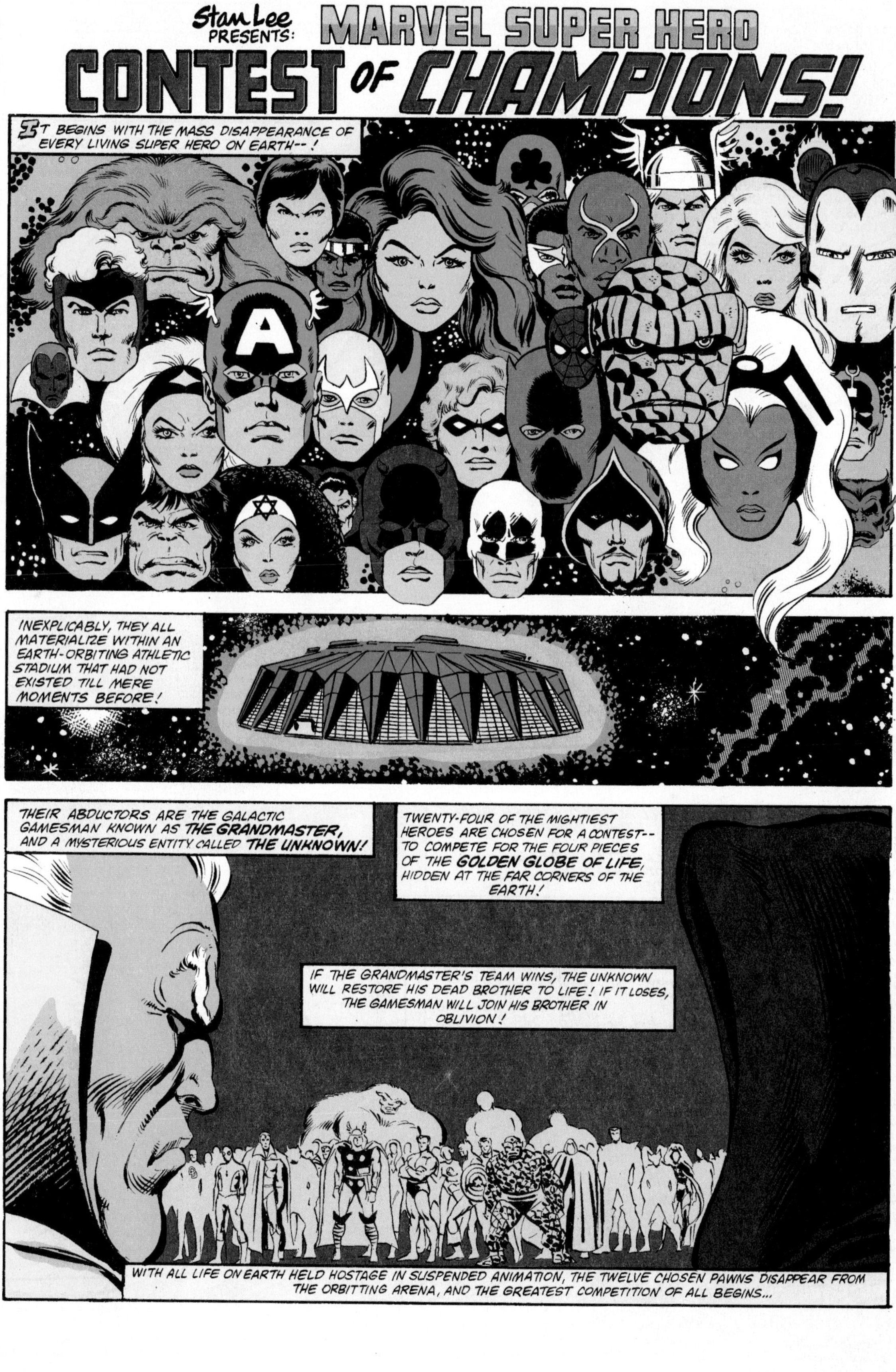
Stan Lee PRESENTS:
MARVEL SUPER HERO CONTEST OF CHAMPIONS!
IT BEGINS WITH THE MASS DISAPPEARANCE OF EVERY LIVING SUPER HERO ON EARTH-- !
INEXPLICABLY, THEY ALL MATERIALIZE WITHIN AN EARTH-ORBITING ATHLETIC STADIUM THAT HAD NOT EXISTED TILL MERE MOMENTS BEFORE!
THEIR ABDUCTORS ARE THE GALACTIC GAMESMAN KNOWN AS THE GRANDMASTER, AND A MYSTERIOUS ENTITY CALLED THE UNKNOWN!
TWENTY-FOUR OF THE MIGHTIEST HEROES ARE CHOSEN FOR A CONTEST-- TO COMPETE FOR THE FOUR PIECES OF THE GOLDEN GLOBE OF LIFE, HIDDEN AT THE FAR CORNERS OF THE EARTH!
IF THE GRANDMASTER'S TEAM WINS, THE UNKNOWN WILL RESTORE HIS DEAD BROTHER TO LIFE! IF IT LOSES, THE GAMESMAN WILL JOIN HIS BROTHER IN OBLIVION!
WITH ALL LIFE ON EARTH HELD HOSTAGE IN SUSPENDED ANIMATION, THE TWELVE CHOSEN PAWNS DISAPPEAR FROM THE ORBITTING ARENA, AND THE GREATEST COMPETITION OF ALL BEGINS...

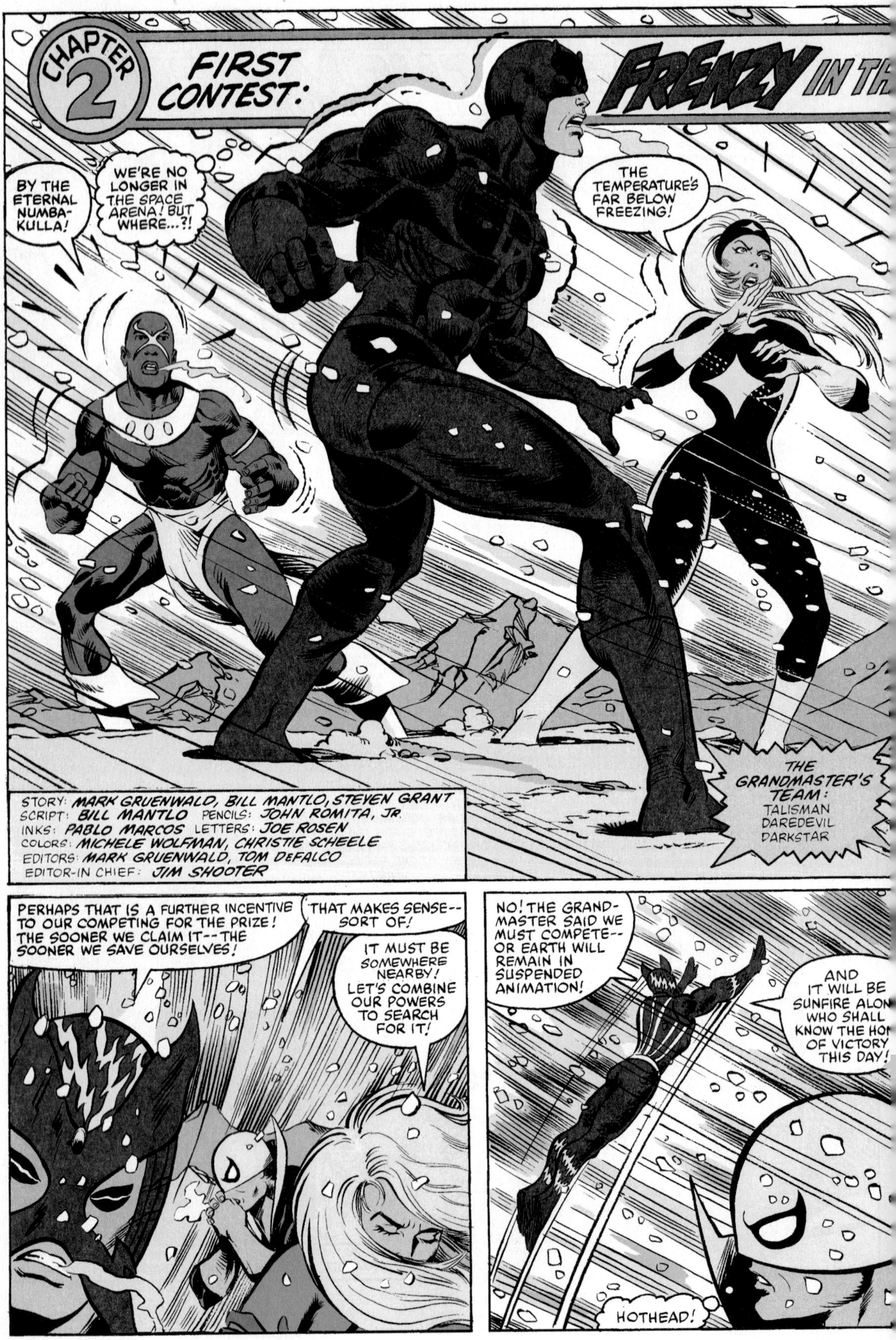

CHAPTER 2
FIRST CONTEST:
FRENZY IN TH
BY THE ETERNAL NUMBA-KULLA!
WE'RE NO LONGER IN THE SPACE ARENA! BUT WHERE...?!
THE TEMPERATURE'S FAR BELOW FREEZING!
THE GRANDMASTER'S TEAM: TALISMAN DAREDEVIL DARKSTAR
STORY: MARK GRUENWALD, BILL MANTLO, STEVEN GRANT
SCRIPT: BILL MANTLO PENCILS: JOHN ROMITA, JR.
INKS: PABLO MARCOS LETTERS: JOE ROSEN
COLORS: MICHELE WOLFMAN, CHRISTIE SCHEELE
EDITORS: MARK GRUENWALD, TOM DeFALCO
EDITOR-IN CHIEF: JIM SHOOTER
PERHAPS THAT IS A FURTHER INCENTIVE TO OUR COMPETING FOR THE PRIZE! THE SOONER WE CLAIM IT--THE SOONER WE SAVE OURSELVES!
THAT MAKES SENSE--SORT OF!
IT MUST BE SOMEWHERE NEARBY! LET'S COMBINE OUR POWERS TO SEARCH FOR IT!
NO! THE GRAND-MASTER SAID WE MUST COMPETE--OR EARTH WILL REMAIN IN SUSPENDED ANIMATION!
AND IT WILL BE SUNFIRE ALON WHO SHALL KNOW THE HON OF VICTORY THIS DAY!
HOTHEAD!

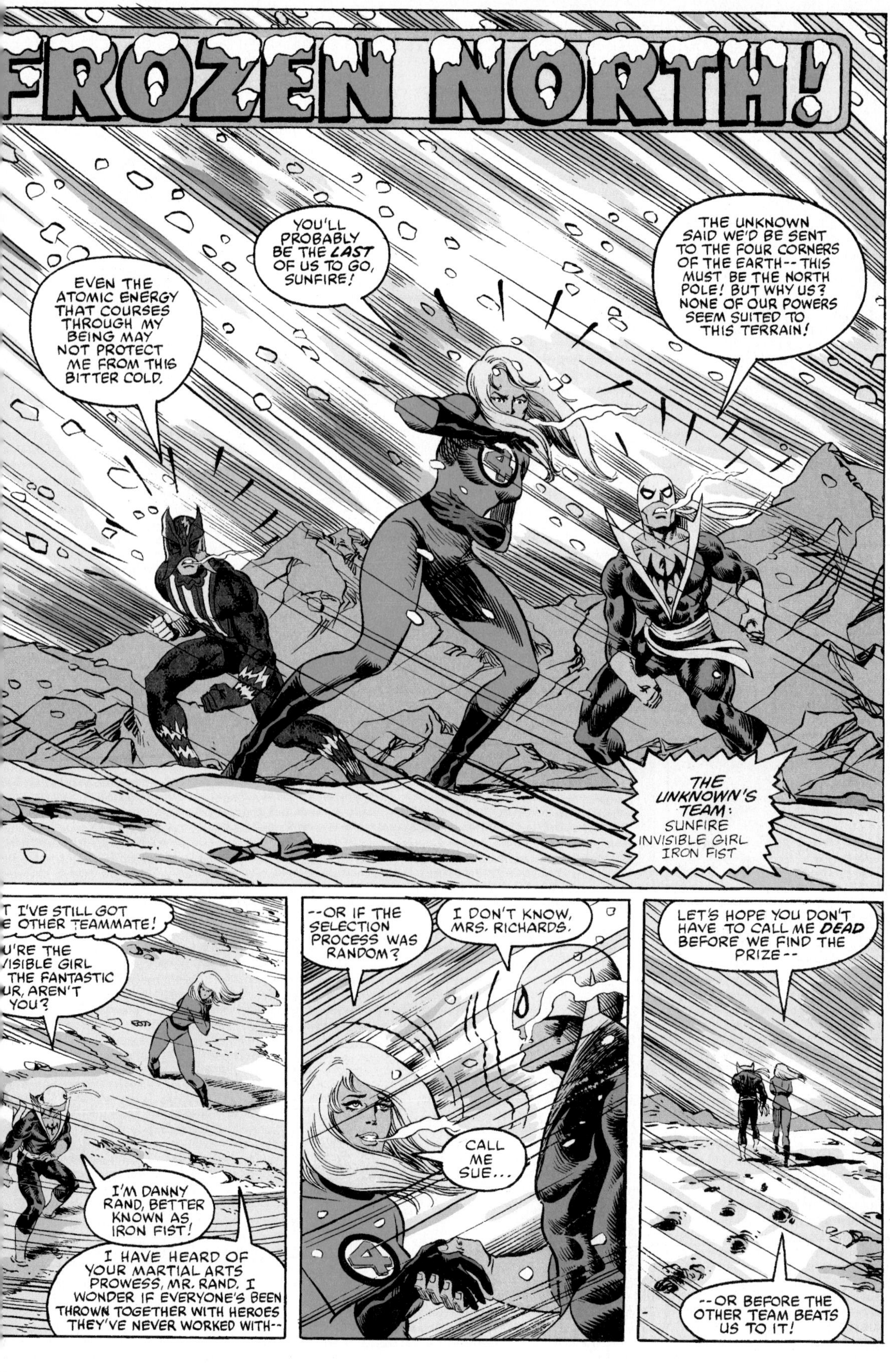
FROZEN NORTH!
EVEN THE ATOMIC ENERGY THAT COURSES THROUGH MY BEING MAY NOT PROTECT ME FROM THIS BITTER COLD.
YOU'LL PROBABLY BE THE LAST OF US TO GO, SUNFIRE!
THE UNKNOWN SAID WE'D BE SENT TO THE FOUR CORNERS OF THE EARTH-- THIS MUST BE THE NORTH POLE! BUT WHY US? NONE OF OUR POWERS SEEM SUITED TO THIS TERRAIN!
THE UNKNOWN'S TEAM: SUNFIRE INVISIBLE GIRL IRON FIST
I'M DANNY RAND, BETTER KNOWN AS IRON FIST!
I HAVE HEARD OF YOUR MARTIAL ARTS PROWESS, MR. RAND. I WONDER IF EVERYONE'S BEEN THROWN TOGETHER WITH HEROES THEY'VE NEVER WORKED WITH--
--OR IF THE SELECTION PROCESS WAS RANDOM?
I DON'T KNOW, MRS. RICHARDS.
CALL ME SUE...
LET'S HOPE YOU DON'T HAVE TO CALL ME DEAD BEFORE WE FIND THE PRIZE--
--OR BEFORE THE OTHER TEAM BEATS US TO IT!

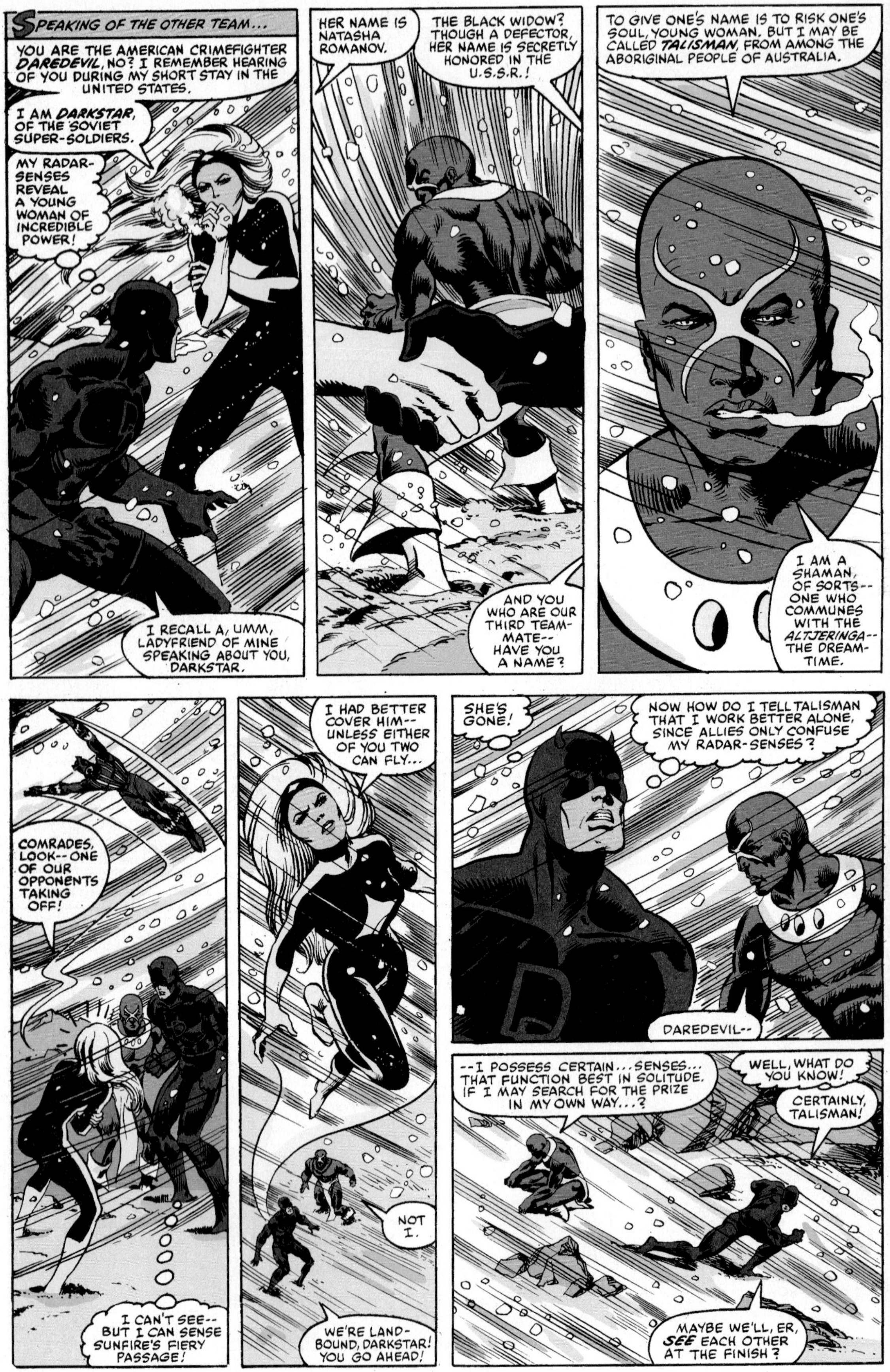

SPEAKING OF THE OTHER TEAM...
YOU ARE THE AMERICAN CRIMEFIGHTER DAREDEVIL, NO? I REMEMBER HEARING OF YOU DURING MY SHORT STAY IN THE UNITED STATES.
I AM DARKSTAR, OF THE SOVIET SUPER-SOLDIERS.
MY RADAR-SENSES REVEAL A YOUNG WOMAN OF INCREDIBLE POWER!
I RECALL A, UMM, LADYFRIEND OF MINE SPEAKING ABOUT YOU, DARKSTAR.
HER NAME IS NATASHA ROMANOV.
THE BLACK WIDOW? THOUGH A DEFECTOR, HER NAME IS SECRETLY HONORED IN THE U.S.S.R.!
AND YOU WHO ARE OUR THIRD TEAM-MATE-- HAVE YOU A NAME?
TO GIVE ONE'S NAME IS TO RISK ONE'S SOUL, YOUNG WOMAN. BUT I MAY BE CALLED TALISMAN, FROM AMONG THE ABORIGINAL PEOPLE OF AUSTRALIA.
I AM A SHAMAN, OF SORTS-- ONE WHO COMMUNES WITH THE ALTJERINGA-- THE DREAM-TIME.
COMRADES, LOOK-- ONE OF OUR OPPONENTS TAKING OFF!
I CAN'T SEE-- BUT I CAN SENSE SUNFIRE'S FIERY PASSAGE!
I HAD BETTER COVER HIM-- UNLESS EITHER OF YOU TWO CAN FLY...
NOT I.
WE'RE LAND-BOUND, DARKSTAR! YOU GO AHEAD!
SHE'S GONE!
NOW HOW DO I TELL TALISMAN THAT I WORK BETTER ALONE, SINCE ALLIES ONLY CONFUSE MY RADAR-SENSES?
DAREDEVIL--
--I POSSESS CERTAIN...SENSES... THAT FUNCTION BEST IN SOLITUDE. IF I MAY SEARCH FOR THE PRIZE IN MY OWN WAY...?
WELL, WHAT DO YOU KNOW!
CERTAINLY, TALISMAN!
MAYBE WE'LL, ER, SEE EACH OTHER AT THE FINISH?

THUS, A SHORT TIME LATER...

A SILVER-TRESSED SUPER HEROINE FLYING TOWARDS ME?

IF SHE AND HER TEAMMATES CAN BE OVERPOWERED FIRST--

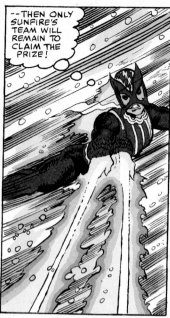

--THEN ONLY SUNFIRE'S TEAM WILL REMAIN TO CLAIM THE PRIZE!

LENIN'S GHOST! TWIN SPEARS OF FLAME ARCING PAST ME!

MY ORIENTAL OPPONENT OUGHT NOT TO PROVOKE--

--ONE WHO CAN RETALIATE BY SUMMONING...THE DARKFORCE!

BY THE SACRED SUN OF JAPAN!

A GIANT HAND OF EBONY ENERGY REACHING TO ENGULF ME!!

MEANWHILE, FAR BELOW...

IRON FIST, LOOK! THAT'S DAREDEVIL!

MAYBE WE OUGHT TO KEEP HIM COVERED-- IN CASE HE FINDS THE PRIZE.

NO! THE FIRST BLOW'S ALREADY BEEN STRUCK OVERHEAD!

IF WE'RE GOING TO BEAT THE GRAND-MASTER'S PLAYERS--

--WE'D BETTER JOIN THE FRAY... FAST!

THIS IS SO UNLIKE WORKING WITH THE FANTASTIC FOUR!

33

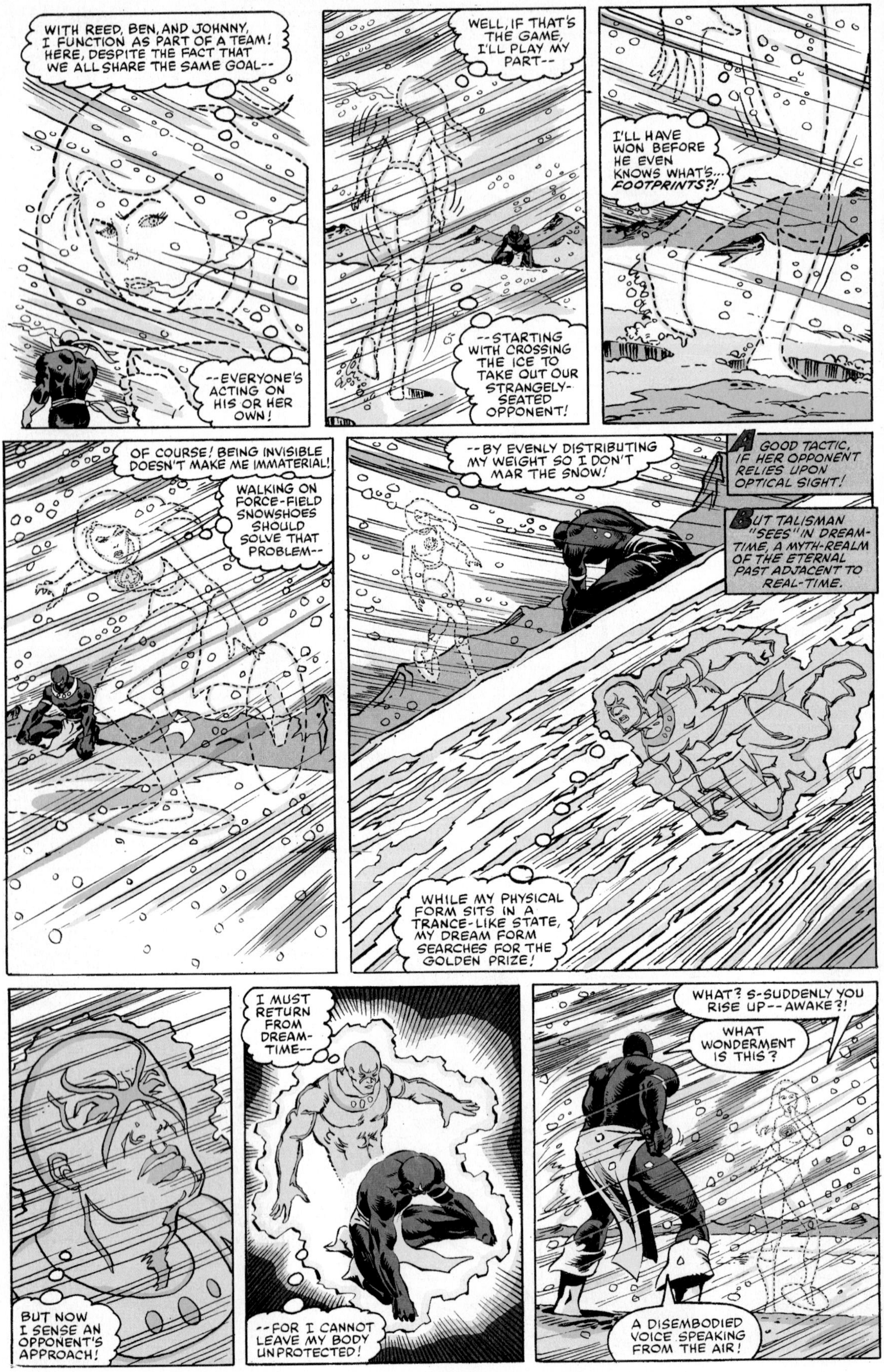
WITH REED, BEN, AND JOHNNY, I FUNCTION AS PART OF A TEAM! HERE, DESPITE THE FACT THAT WE ALL SHARE THE SAME GOAL--
--EVERYONE'S ACTING ON HIS OR HER OWN!
WELL, IF THAT'S THE GAME, I'LL PLAY MY PART--
--STARTING WITH CROSSING THE ICE TO TAKE OUT OUR STRANGELY-SEATED OPPONENT!
I'LL HAVE WON BEFORE HE EVEN KNOWS WHAT'S... FOOTPRINTS?!
OF COURSE! BEING INVISIBLE DOESN'T MAKE ME IMMATERIAL!
WALKING ON FORCE-FIELD SNOWSHOES SHOULD SOLVE THAT PROBLEM--
--BY EVENLY DISTRIBUTING MY WEIGHT SO I DON'T MAR THE SNOW!
A GOOD TACTIC, IF HER OPPONENT RELIES UPON OPTICAL SIGHT!
BUT TALISMAN "SEES" IN DREAM-TIME, A MYTH-REALM OF THE ETERNAL PAST ADJACENT TO REAL-TIME.
WHILE MY PHYSICAL FORM SITS IN A TRANCE-LIKE STATE, MY DREAM FORM SEARCHES FOR THE GOLDEN PRIZE!
BUT NOW I SENSE AN OPPONENT'S APPROACH!
I MUST RETURN FROM DREAM-TIME--
--FOR I CANNOT LEAVE MY BODY UNPROTECTED!
WHAT? S-SUDDENLY YOU RISE UP--AWAKE?!
WHAT WONDERMENT IS THIS?
A DISEMBODIED VOICE SPEAKING FROM THE AIR!

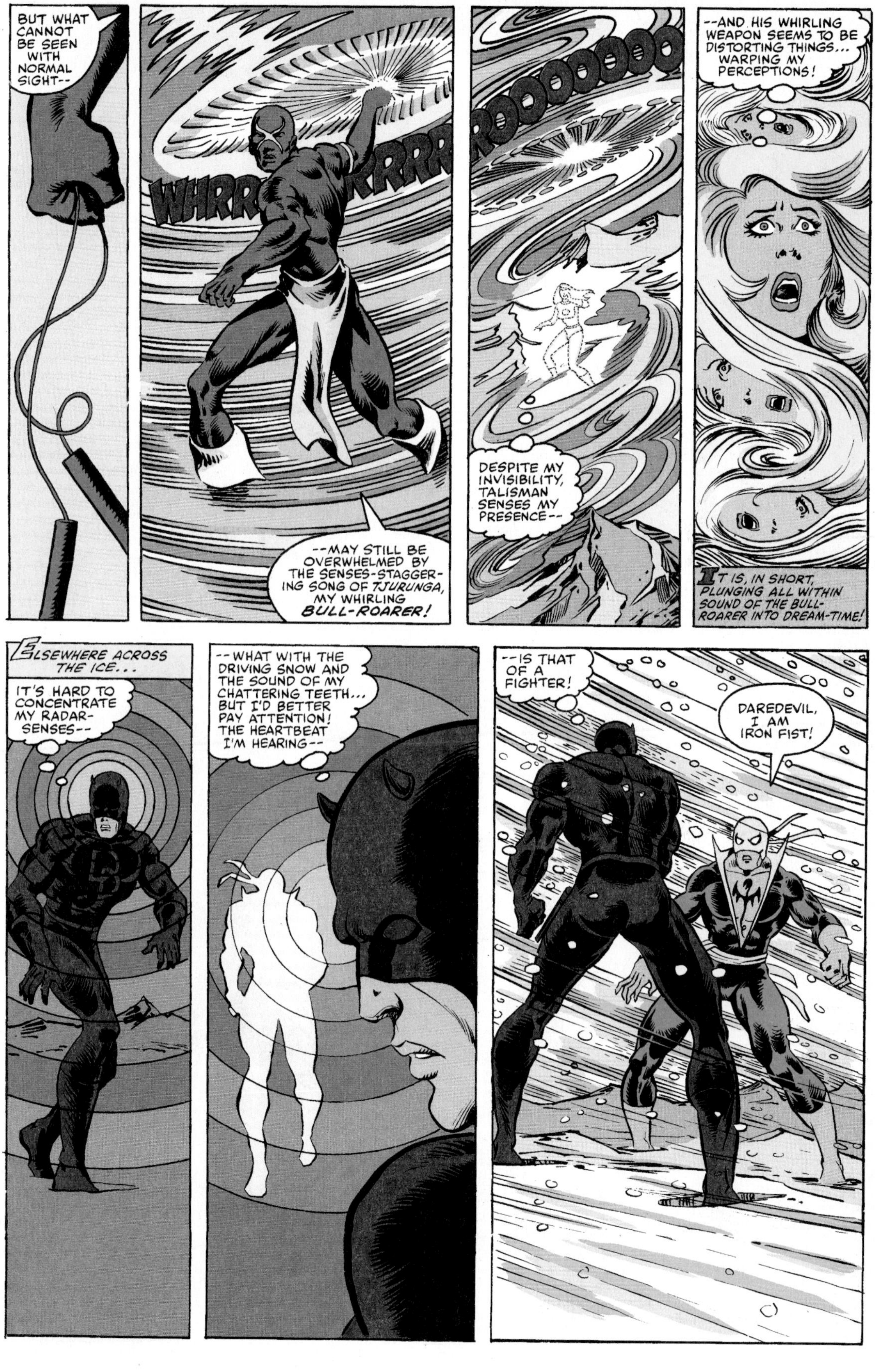
BUT WHAT CANNOT BE SEEN WITH NORMAL SIGHT--
WHRRRKRRRRROOOOOOOOO
--MAY STILL BE OVERWHELMED BY THE SENSES-STAGGERING SONG OF TJURUNGA, MY WHIRLING BULL-ROARER!
DESPITE MY INVISIBILITY, TALISMAN SENSES MY PRESENCE--
--AND HIS WHIRLING WEAPON SEEMS TO BE DISTORTING THINGS... WARPING MY PERCEPTIONS!
IT IS, IN SHORT, PLUNGING ALL WITHIN SOUND OF THE BULL-ROARER INTO DREAM-TIME!
ELSEWHERE ACROSS THE ICE...
IT'S HARD TO CONCENTRATE MY RADAR-SENSES--
--WHAT WITH THE DRIVING SNOW AND THE SOUND OF MY CHATTERING TEETH... BUT I'D BETTER PAY ATTENTION! THE HEARTBEAT I'M HEARING--
--IS THAT OF A FIGHTER!
DAREDEVIL, I AM IRON FIST!

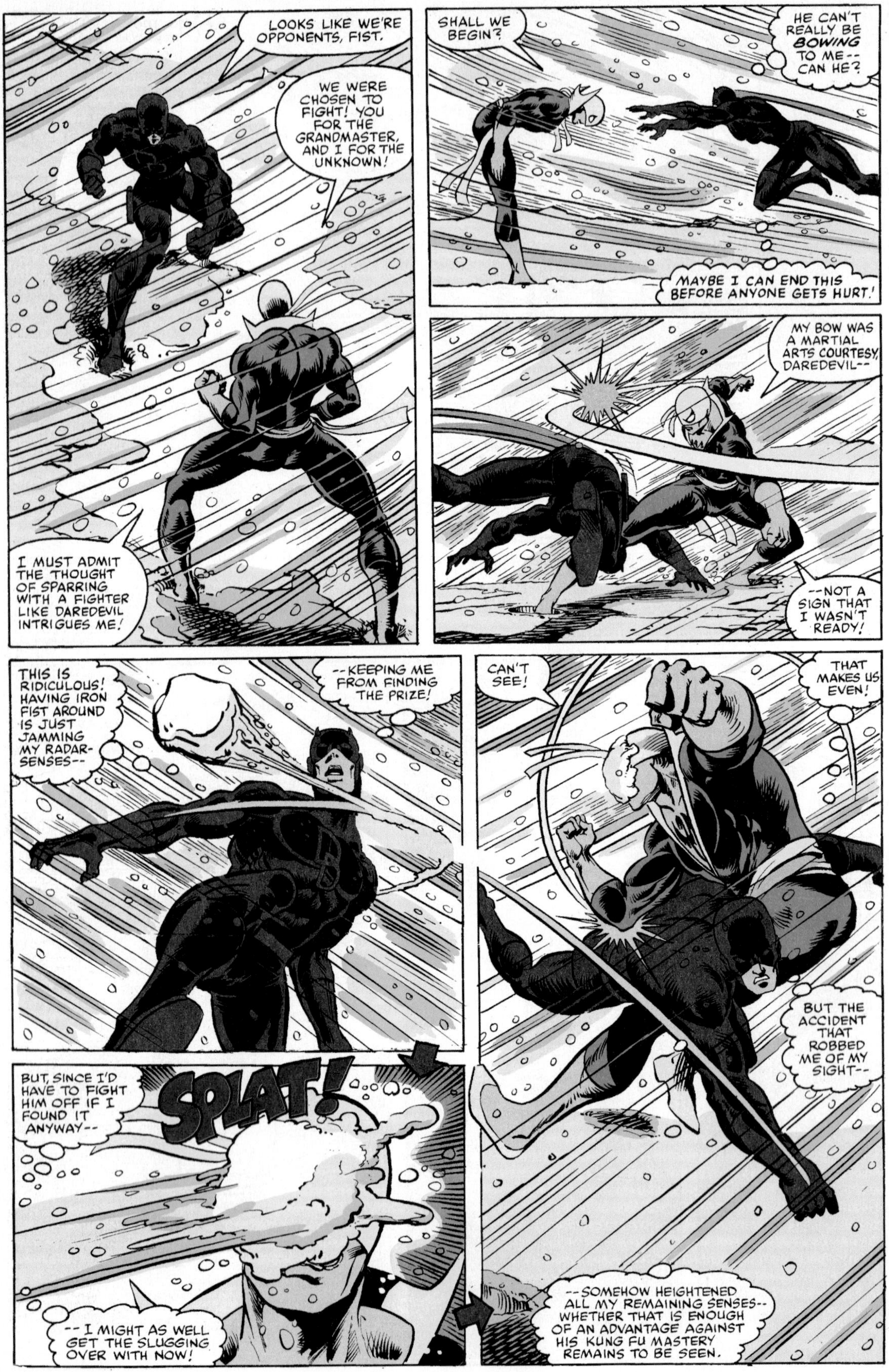
LOOKS LIKE WE'RE OPPONENTS, FIST.
WE WERE CHOSEN TO FIGHT! YOU FOR THE GRANDMASTER, AND I FOR THE UNKNOWN!
I MUST ADMIT THE THOUGHT OF SPARRING WITH A FIGHTER LIKE DAREDEVIL INTRIGUES ME!
SHALL WE BEGIN?
HE CAN'T REALLY BE BOWING TO ME-- CAN HE?
MAYBE I CAN END THIS BEFORE ANYONE GETS HURT!
MY BOW WAS A MARTIAL ARTS COURTESY, DAREDEVIL--
--NOT A SIGN THAT I WASN'T READY!
THIS IS RIDICULOUS! HAVING IRON FIST AROUND IS JUST JAMMING MY RADAR-SENSES--
--KEEPING ME FROM FINDING THE PRIZE!
BUT, SINCE I'D HAVE TO FIGHT HIM OFF IF I FOUND IT ANYWAY--
SPLAT!
--I MIGHT AS WELL GET THE SLUGGING OVER WITH NOW!
CAN'T SEE!
THAT MAKES US EVEN!
BUT THE ACCIDENT THAT ROBBED ME OF MY SIGHT--
--SOMEHOW HEIGHTENED ALL MY REMAINING SENSES--WHETHER THAT IS ENOUGH OF AN ADVANTAGE AGAINST HIS KUNG FU MASTERY REMAINS TO BE SEEN.

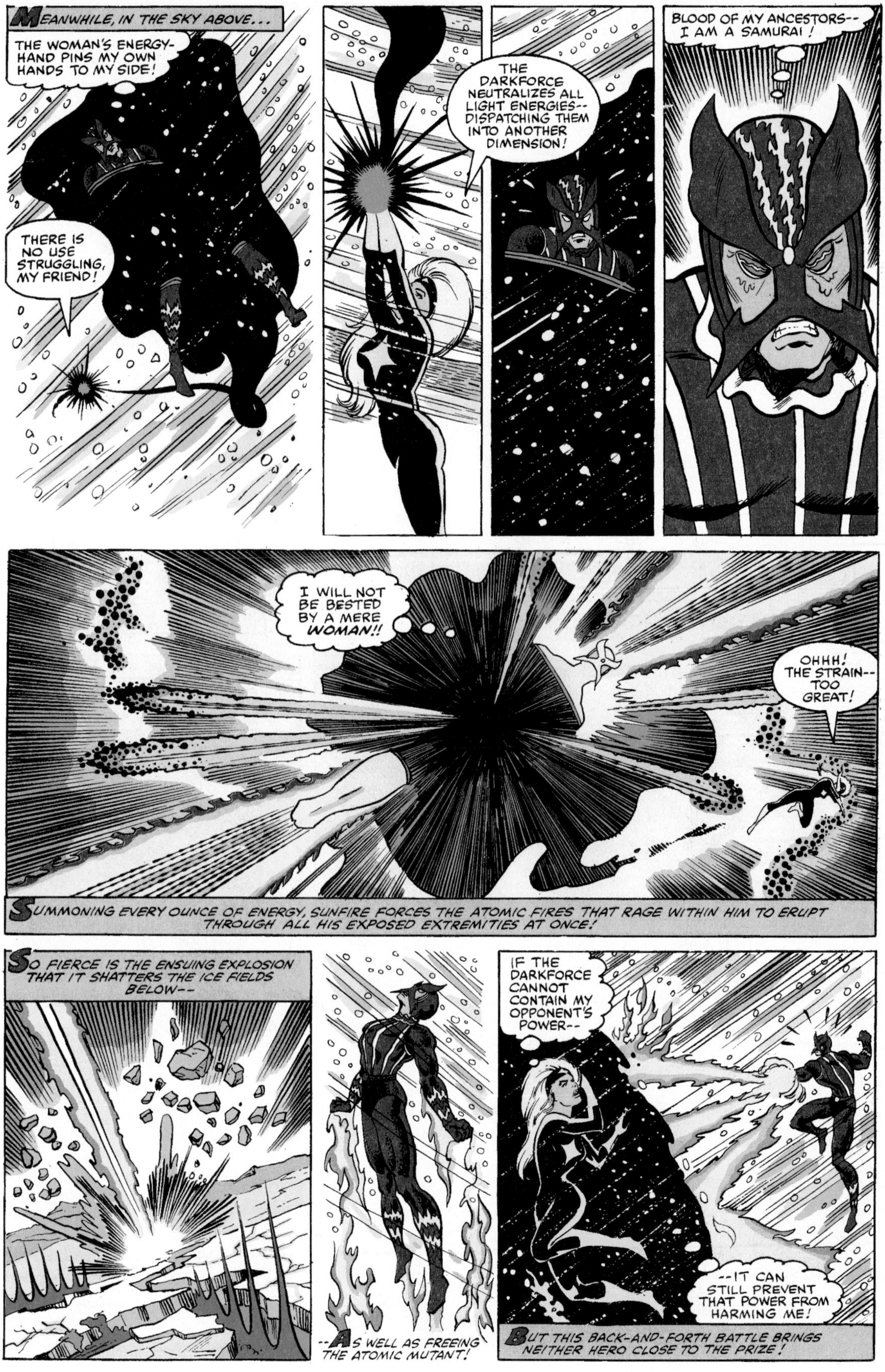
MEANWHILE, IN THE SKY ABOVE...
THE WOMAN'S ENERGY-HAND PINS MY OWN HANDS TO MY SIDE!
THERE IS NO USE STRUGGLING, MY FRIEND!
THE DARKFORCE NEUTRALIZES ALL LIGHT ENERGIES--DISPATCHING THEM INTO ANOTHER DIMENSION!
BLOOD OF MY ANCESTORS--I AM A SAMURAI!
I WILL NOT BE BESTED BY A MERE WOMAN!!
OHHH! THE STRAIN--TOO GREAT!
SUMMONING EVERY OUNCE OF ENERGY, SUNFIRE FORCES THE ATOMIC FIRES THAT RAGE WITHIN HIM TO ERUPT THROUGH ALL HIS EXPOSED EXTREMITIES AT ONCE!
SO FIERCE IS THE ENSUING EXPLOSION THAT IT SHATTERS THE ICE FIELDS BELOW--
--AS WELL AS FREEING THE ATOMIC MUTANT!
IF THE DARKFORCE CANNOT CONTAIN MY OPPONENT'S POWER--
--IT CAN STILL PREVENT THAT POWER FROM HARMING ME!
BUT THIS BACK-AND-FORTH BATTLE BRINGS NEITHER HERO CLOSE TO THE PRIZE!

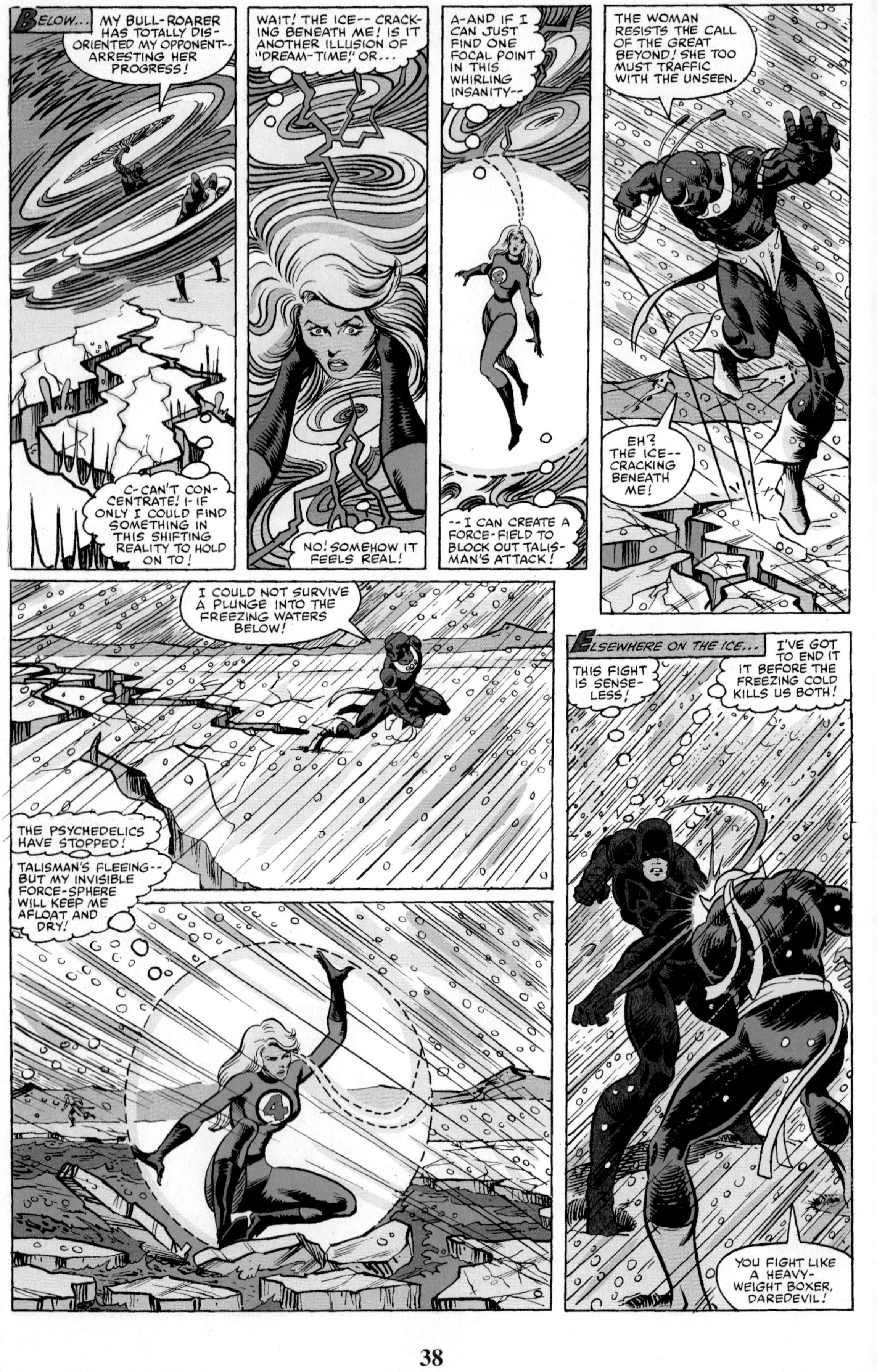
BELOW...
MY BULL-ROARER HAS TOTALLY DISORIENTED MY OPPONENT--ARRESTING HER PROGRESS!
C-CAN'T CONCENTRATE! I-IF ONLY I COULD FIND SOMETHING IN THIS SHIFTING REALITY TO HOLD ON TO!
WAIT! THE ICE-- CRACKING BENEATH ME! IS IT ANOTHER ILLUSION OF "DREAM-TIME," OR...
NO! SOMEHOW IT FEELS REAL!
A-AND IF I CAN JUST FIND ONE FOCAL POINT IN THIS WHIRLING INSANITY--
--I CAN CREATE A FORCE-FIELD TO BLOCK OUT TALISMAN'S ATTACK!
THE WOMAN RESISTS THE CALL OF THE GREAT BEYOND! SHE TOO MUST TRAFFIC WITH THE UNSEEN.
EH? THE ICE--CRACKING BENEATH ME!
I COULD NOT SURVIVE A PLUNGE INTO THE FREEZING WATERS BELOW!
THE PSYCHEDELICS HAVE STOPPED!
TALISMAN'S FLEEING--BUT MY INVISIBLE FORCE-SPHERE WILL KEEP ME AFLOAT AND DRY!
ELSEWHERE ON THE ICE...
THIS FIGHT IS SENSELESS!
I'VE GOT TO END IT IT BEFORE THE FREEZING COLD KILLS US BOTH!
YOU FIGHT LIKE A HEAVY-WEIGHT BOXER, DAREDEVIL!

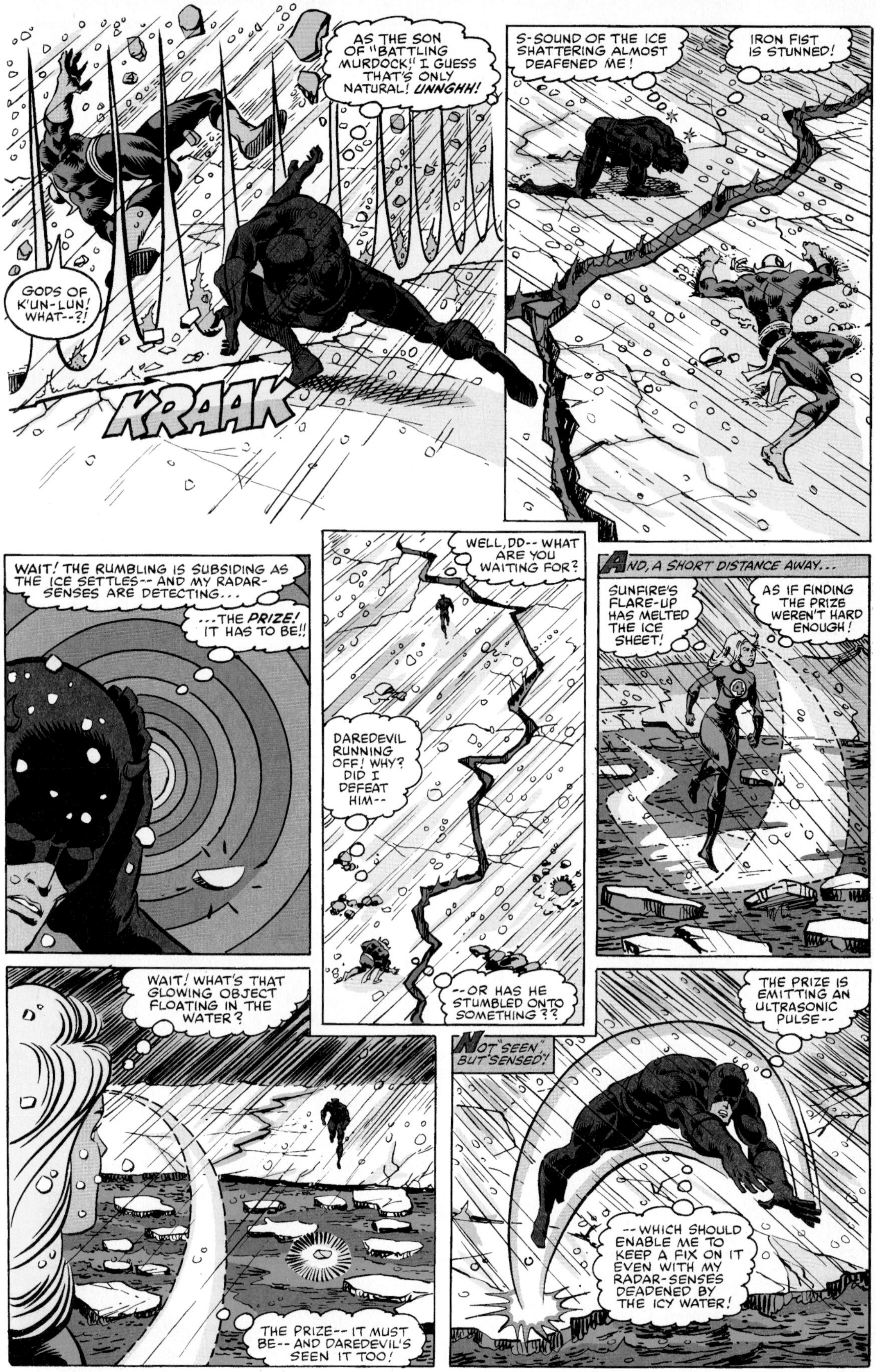
AS THE SON OF "BATTLING MURDOCK," I GUESS THAT'S ONLY NATURAL! UNNGHH!
GODS OF K'UN-LUN! WHAT--?!
KRAAK
S-SOUND OF THE ICE SHATTERING ALMOST DEAFENED ME!
IRON FIST IS STUNNED!
WAIT! THE RUMBLING IS SUBSIDING AS THE ICE SETTLES-- AND MY RADAR-SENSES ARE DETECTING...
...THE PRIZE! IT HAS TO BE!!
WELL, DD-- WHAT ARE YOU WAITING FOR?
DAREDEVIL RUNNING OFF! WHY? DID I DEFEAT HIM--
--OR HAS HE STUMBLED ONTO SOMETHING??
AND, A SHORT DISTANCE AWAY...
SUNFIRE'S FLARE-UP HAS MELTED THE ICE SHEET!
AS IF FINDING THE PRIZE WEREN'T HARD ENOUGH!
WAIT! WHAT'S THAT GLOWING OBJECT FLOATING IN THE WATER?
THE PRIZE-- IT MUST BE-- AND DAREDEVIL'S SEEN IT TOO!
NOT "SEEN," BUT "SENSED"!
THE PRIZE IS EMITTING AN ULTRASONIC PULSE--
--WHICH SHOULD ENABLE ME TO KEEP A FIX ON IT EVEN WITH MY RADAR-SENSES DEADENED BY THE ICY WATER!

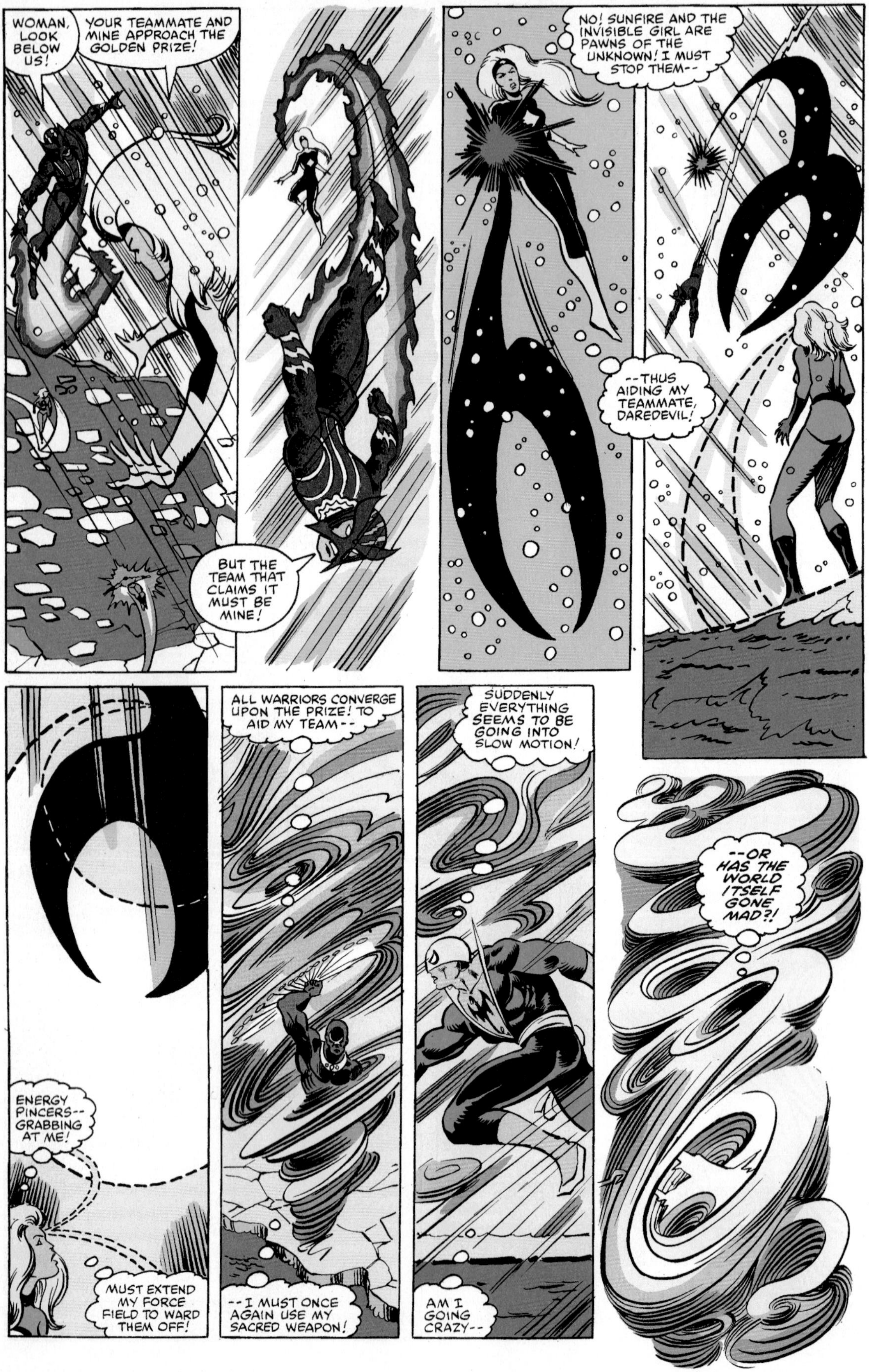
WOMAN, LOOK BELOW US!
YOUR TEAMMATE AND MINE APPROACH THE GOLDEN PRIZE!
BUT THE TEAM THAT CLAIMS IT MUST BE MINE!
NO! SUNFIRE AND THE INVISIBLE GIRL ARE PAWNS OF THE UNKNOWN! I MUST STOP THEM--
--THUS AIDING MY TEAMMATE, DAREDEVIL!
ENERGY PINCERS-- GRABBING AT ME!
MUST EXTEND MY FORCE FIELD TO WARD THEM OFF!
ALL WARRIORS CONVERGE UPON THE PRIZE! TO AID MY TEAM--
--I MUST ONCE AGAIN USE MY SACRED WEAPON!
SUDDENLY EVERYTHING SEEMS TO BE GOING INTO SLOW MOTION!
AM I GOING CRAZY--
--OR HAS THE WORLD ITSELF GONE MAD?!

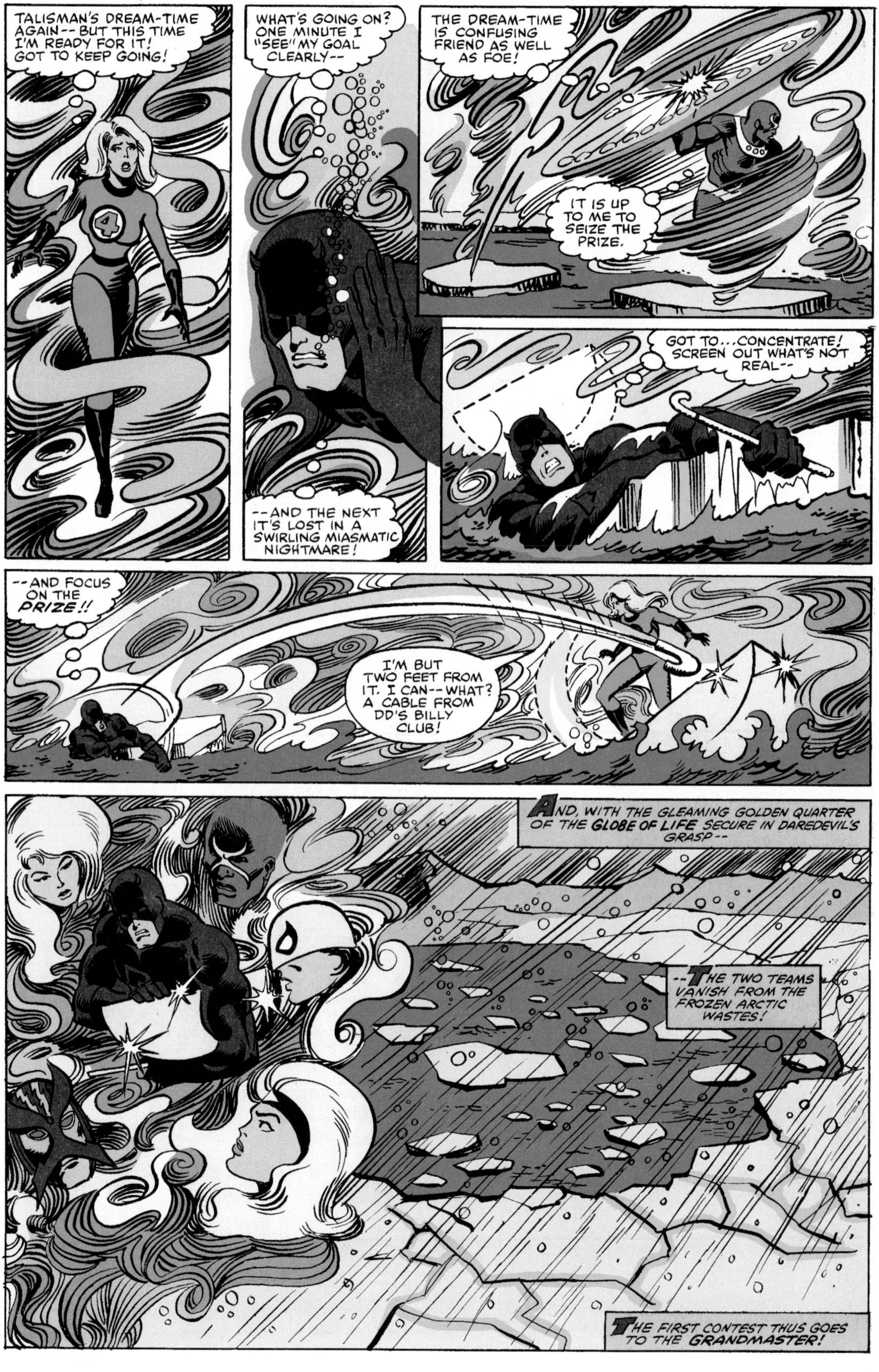

TALISMAN'S DREAM-TIME AGAIN--BUT THIS TIME I'M READY FOR IT! GOT TO KEEP GOING!
WHAT'S GOING ON? ONE MINUTE I "SEE" MY GOAL CLEARLY--
--AND THE NEXT IT'S LOST IN A SWIRLING MIASMATIC NIGHTMARE!
THE DREAM-TIME IS CONFUSING FRIEND AS WELL AS FOE!
IT IS UP TO ME TO SEIZE THE PRIZE.
GOT TO...CONCENTRATE! SCREEN OUT WHAT'S NOT REAL--
--AND FOCUS ON THE PRIZE!!
I'M BUT TWO FEET FROM IT. I CAN--WHAT? A CABLE FROM DD'S BILLY CLUB!
AND, WITH THE GLEAMING GOLDEN QUARTER OF THE GLOBE OF LIFE SECURE IN DAREDEVIL'S GRASP--
--THE TWO TEAMS VANISH FROM THE FROZEN ARCTIC WASTES!
THE FIRST CONTEST THUS GOES TO THE GRANDMASTER!

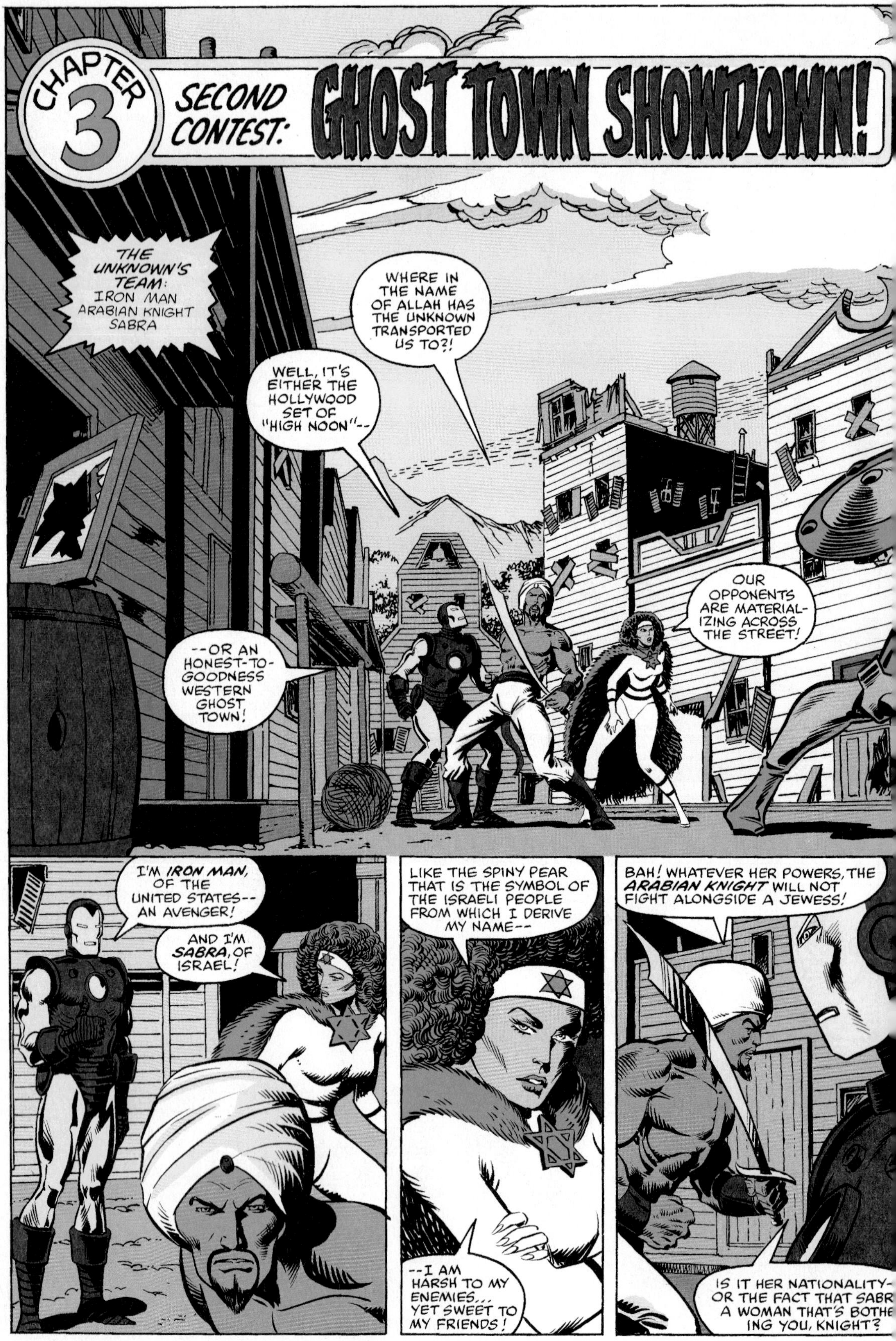
CHAPTER 3
SECOND CONTEST: GHOST TOWN SHOWDOWN!
THE UNKNOWN'S TEAM: IRON MAN ARABIAN KNIGHT SABRA
WHERE IN THE NAME OF ALLAH HAS THE UNKNOWN TRANSPORTED US TO?!
WELL, IT'S EITHER THE HOLLYWOOD SET OF "HIGH NOON"--
--OR AN HONEST-TO-GOODNESS WESTERN GHOST TOWN!
OUR OPPONENTS ARE MATERIALIZING ACROSS THE STREET!
I'M IRON MAN, OF THE UNITED STATES--AN AVENGER!
AND I'M SABRA, OF ISRAEL!
LIKE THE SPINY PEAR THAT IS THE SYMBOL OF THE ISRAELI PEOPLE FROM WHICH I DERIVE MY NAME--
--I AM HARSH TO MY ENEMIES... YET SWEET TO MY FRIENDS!
BAH! WHATEVER HER POWERS, THE ARABIAN KNIGHT WILL NOT FIGHT ALONGSIDE A JEWESS!
IS IT HER NATIONALITY-OR THE FACT THAT SABR A WOMAN THAT'S BOTHE ING YOU, KNIGHT?

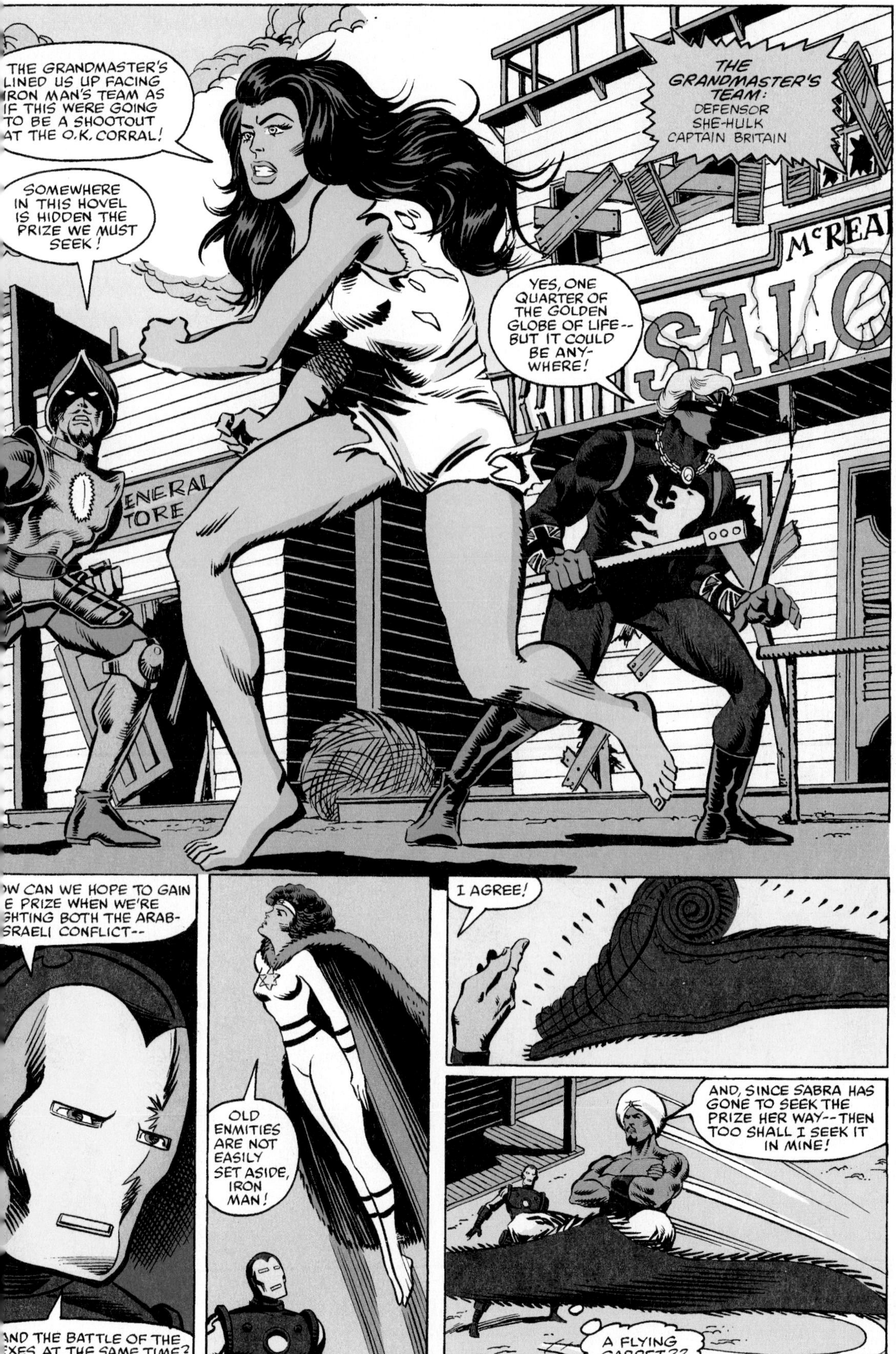
THE GRANDMASTER'S LINED US UP FACING IRON MAN'S TEAM AS IF THIS WERE GOING TO BE A SHOOTOUT AT THE O.K. CORRAL!
THE GRANDMASTER'S TEAM: DEFENSOR SHE-HULK CAPTAIN BRITAIN
SOMEWHERE IN THIS HOVEL IS HIDDEN THE PRIZE WE MUST SEEK!
YES, ONE QUARTER OF THE GOLDEN GLOBE OF LIFE-- BUT IT COULD BE ANY-WHERE!
McREA
SALO
ENERAL TORE
W CAN WE HOPE TO GAIN E PRIZE WHEN WE'RE GHTING BOTH THE ARAB-SRAELI CONFLICT--
AND THE BATTLE OF THE EXES AT THE SAME TIME?
OLD ENMITIES ARE NOT EASILY SET ASIDE, IRON MAN!
I AGREE!
AND, SINCE SABRA HAS GONE TO SEEK THE PRIZE HER WAY--THEN TOO SHALL I SEEK IT IN MINE!
A FLYING CARPET??

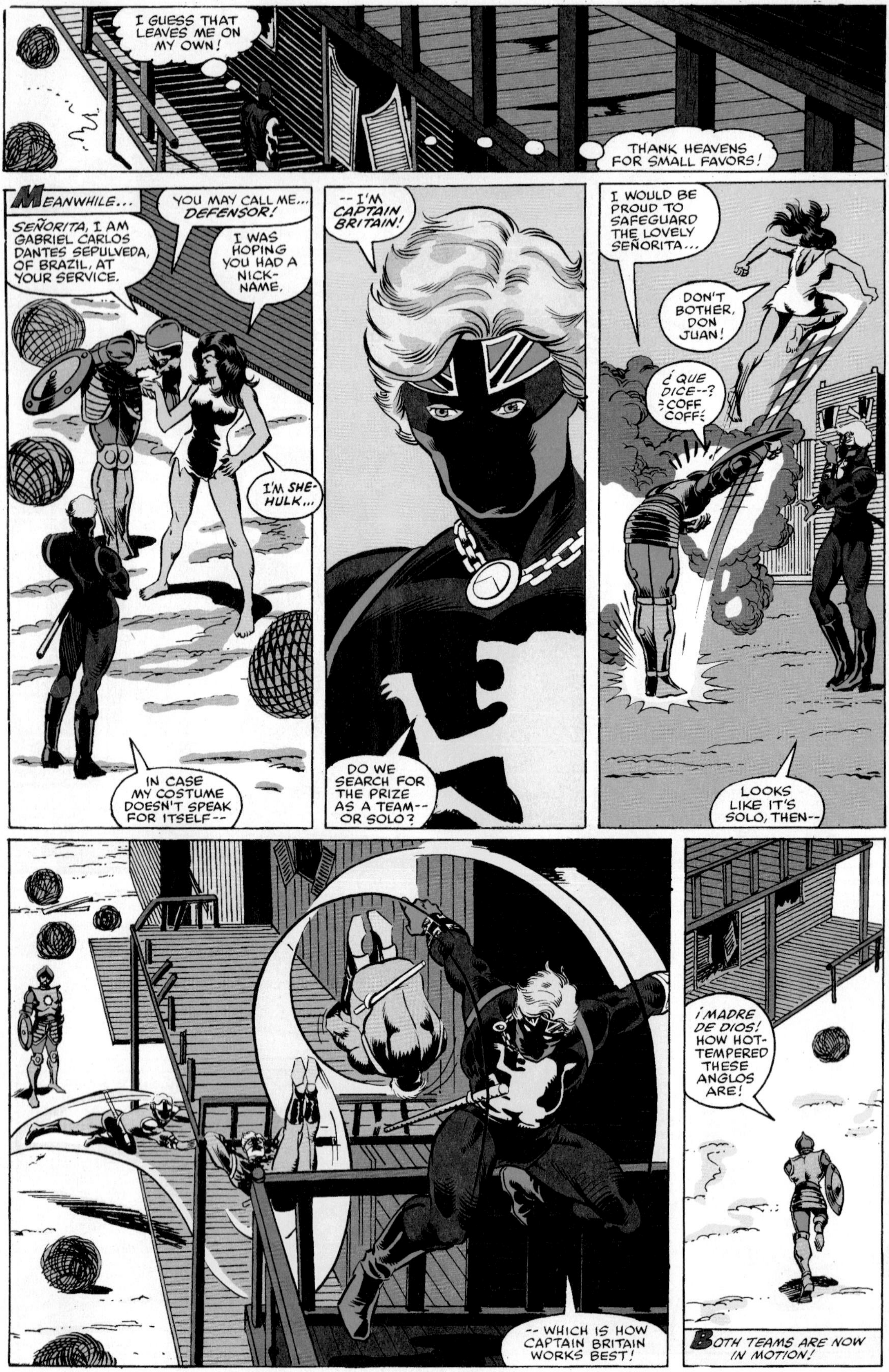
I GUESS THAT LEAVES ME ON MY OWN!
THANK HEAVENS FOR SMALL FAVORS!
MEANWHILE...
SEÑORITA, I AM GABRIEL CARLOS DANTES SEPULVEDA, OF BRAZIL, AT YOUR SERVICE.
YOU MAY CALL ME... DEFENSOR!
I WAS HOPING YOU HAD A NICK-NAME.
I'M SHE-HULK...
IN CASE MY COSTUME DOESN'T SPEAK FOR ITSELF--
-- I'M CAPTAIN BRITAIN!
DO WE SEARCH FOR THE PRIZE AS A TEAM--OR SOLO?
I WOULD BE PROUD TO SAFEGUARD THE LOVELY SEÑORITA...
DON'T BOTHER, DON JUAN!
¿QUE DICE--? COFF COFF!
LOOKS LIKE IT'S SOLO, THEN--
-- WHICH IS HOW CAPTAIN BRITAIN WORKS BEST!
¡MADRE DE DIOS! HOW HOT-TEMPERED THESE ANGLOS ARE!
BOTH TEAMS ARE NOW IN MOTION!

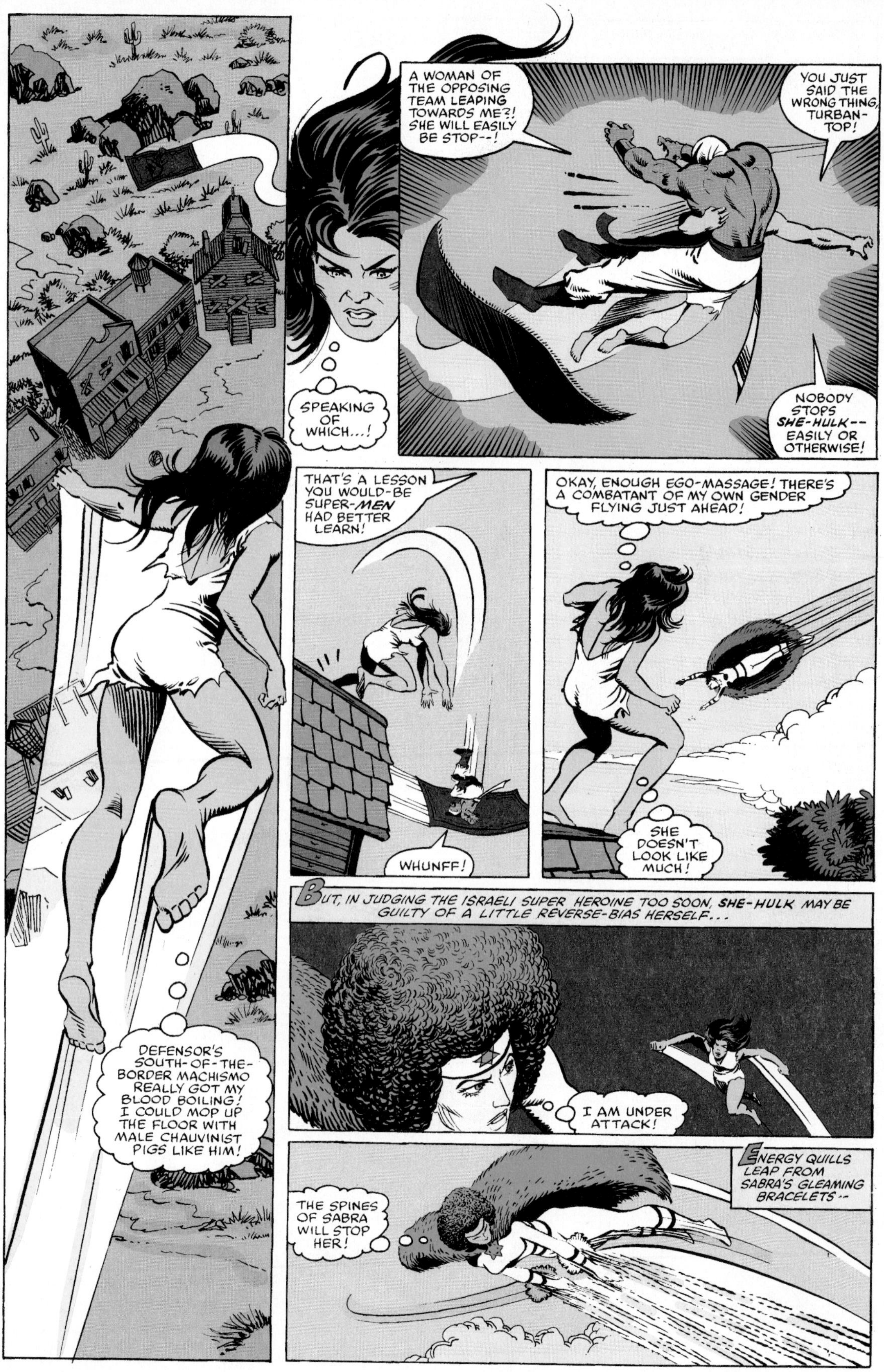
A WOMAN OF THE OPPOSING TEAM LEAPING TOWARDS ME?! SHE WILL EASILY BE STOP--!
YOU JUST SAID THE WRONG THING, TURBAN-TOP!
SPEAKING OF WHICH...!
NOBODY STOPS SHE-HULK-- EASILY OR OTHERWISE!
DEFENSOR'S SOUTH-OF-THE-BORDER MACHISMO REALLY GOT MY BLOOD BOILING! I COULD MOP UP THE FLOOR WITH MALE CHAUVINIST PIGS LIKE HIM!
THAT'S A LESSON YOU WOULD-BE SUPER-MEN HAD BETTER LEARN!
WHUNFF!
OKAY, ENOUGH EGO-MASSAGE! THERE'S A COMBATANT OF MY OWN GENDER FLYING JUST AHEAD!
SHE DOESN'T LOOK LIKE MUCH!
BUT, IN JUDGING THE ISRAELI SUPER HEROINE TOO SOON, SHE-HULK MAY BE GUILTY OF A LITTLE REVERSE-BIAS HERSELF...
I AM UNDER ATTACK!
ENERGY QUILLS LEAP FROM SABRA'S GLEAMING BRACELETS--
THE SPINES OF SABRA WILL STOP HER!

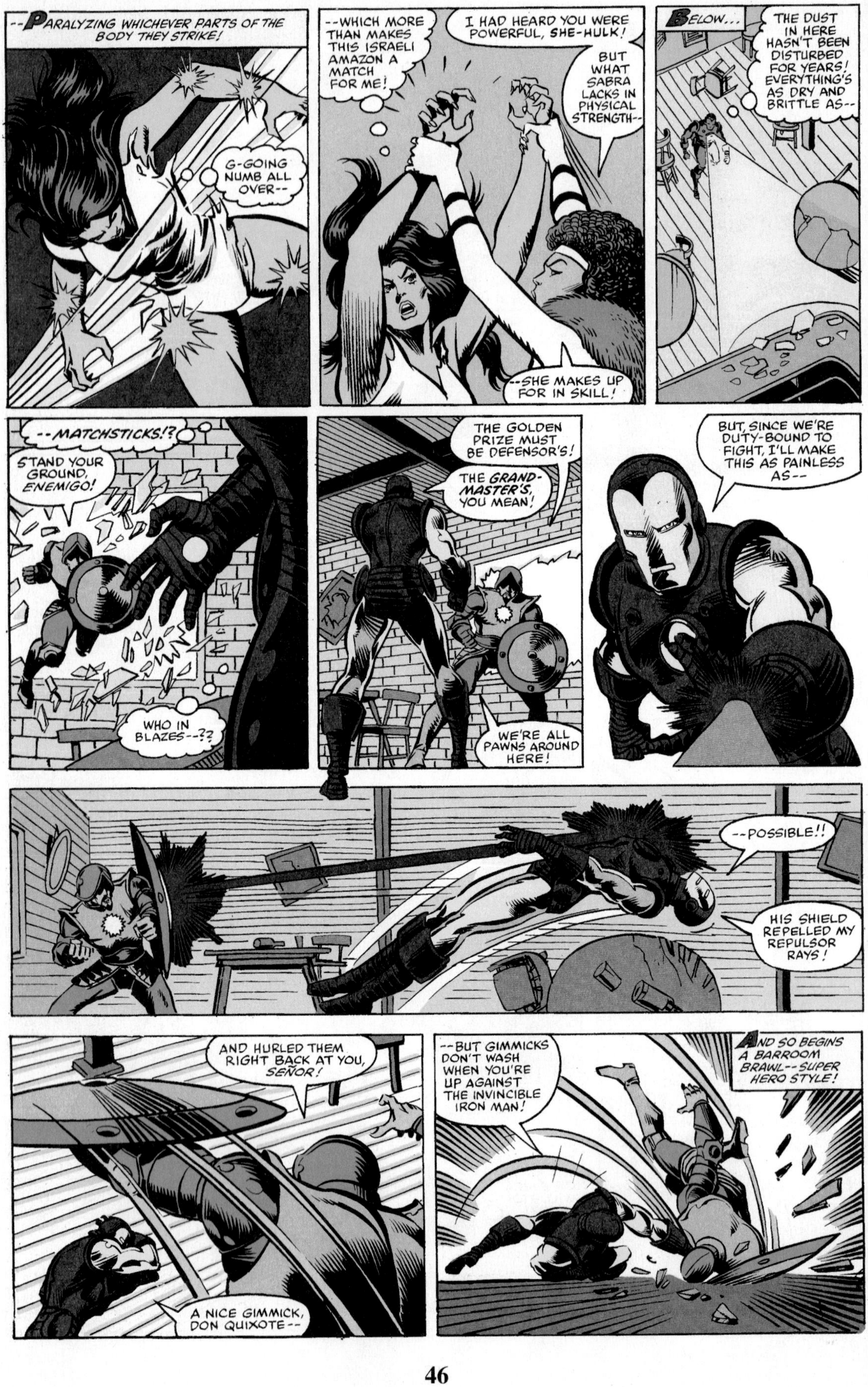
--PARALYZING WHICHEVER PARTS OF THE BODY THEY STRIKE!
G-GOING NUMB ALL OVER--
--WHICH MORE THAN MAKES THIS ISRAELI AMAZON A MATCH FOR ME!
I HAD HEARD YOU WERE POWERFUL, SHE-HULK!
BUT WHAT SABRA LACKS IN PHYSICAL STRENGTH--
--SHE MAKES UP FOR IN SKILL!
BELOW...
THE DUST IN HERE HASN'T BEEN DISTURBED FOR YEARS! EVERYTHING'S AS DRY AND BRITTLE AS--
--MATCHSTICKS!?
STAND YOUR GROUND, ENEMIGO!
WHO IN BLAZES--??
THE GOLDEN PRIZE MUST BE DEFENSOR'S!
THE GRAND-MASTER'S, YOU MEAN!
WE'RE ALL PAWNS AROUND HERE!
BUT, SINCE WE'RE DUTY-BOUND TO FIGHT, I'LL MAKE THIS AS PAINLESS AS--
--POSSIBLE!!
HIS SHIELD REPELLED MY REPULSOR RAYS!
AND HURLED THEM RIGHT BACK AT YOU, SEÑOR!
A NICE GIMMICK, DON QUIXOTE--
--BUT GIMMICKS DON'T WASH WHEN YOU'RE UP AGAINST THE INVINCIBLE IRON MAN!
AND SO BEGINS A BARROOM BRAWL--SUPER HERO STYLE!

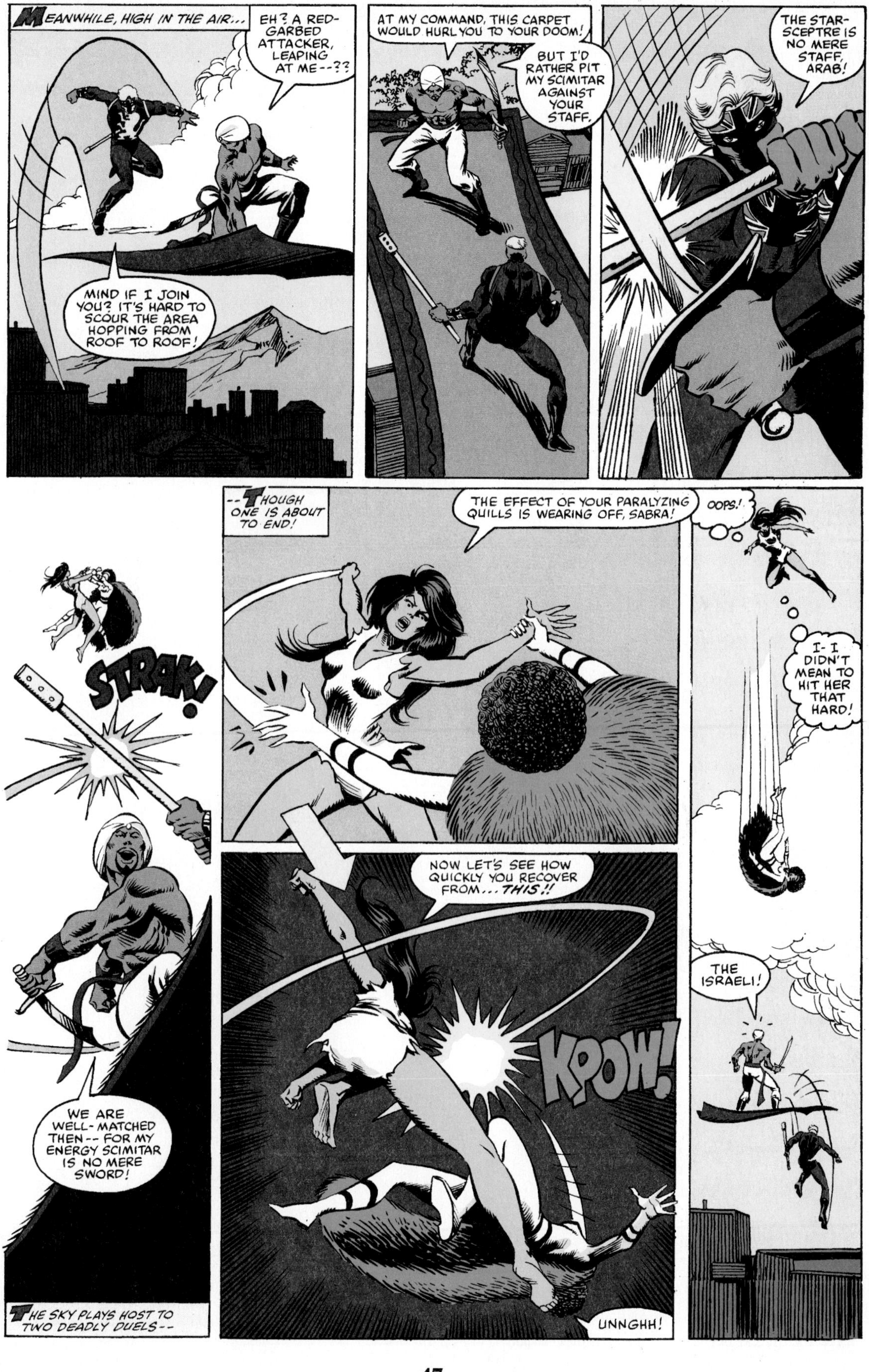
MEANWHILE, HIGH IN THE AIR...
EH? A RED-GARBED ATTACKER, LEAPING AT ME--??
MIND IF I JOIN YOU? IT'S HARD TO SCOUR THE AREA HOPPING FROM ROOF TO ROOF!
AT MY COMMAND, THIS CARPET WOULD HURL YOU TO YOUR DOOM!
BUT I'D RATHER PIT MY SCIMITAR AGAINST YOUR STAFF.
THE STAR-SCEPTRE IS NO MERE STAFF, ARAB!
STRAK!
WE ARE WELL-MATCHED THEN-- FOR MY ENERGY SCIMITAR IS NO MERE SWORD!
THE SKY PLAYS HOST TO TWO DEADLY DUELS--
--THOUGH ONE IS ABOUT TO END!
THE EFFECT OF YOUR PARALYZING QUILLS IS WEARING OFF, SABRA!
NOW LET'S SEE HOW QUICKLY YOU RECOVER FROM... THIS!!
KPOW!
UNNGHH!
OOPS!
I- I DIDN'T MEAN TO HIT HER THAT HARD!
THE ISRAELI!

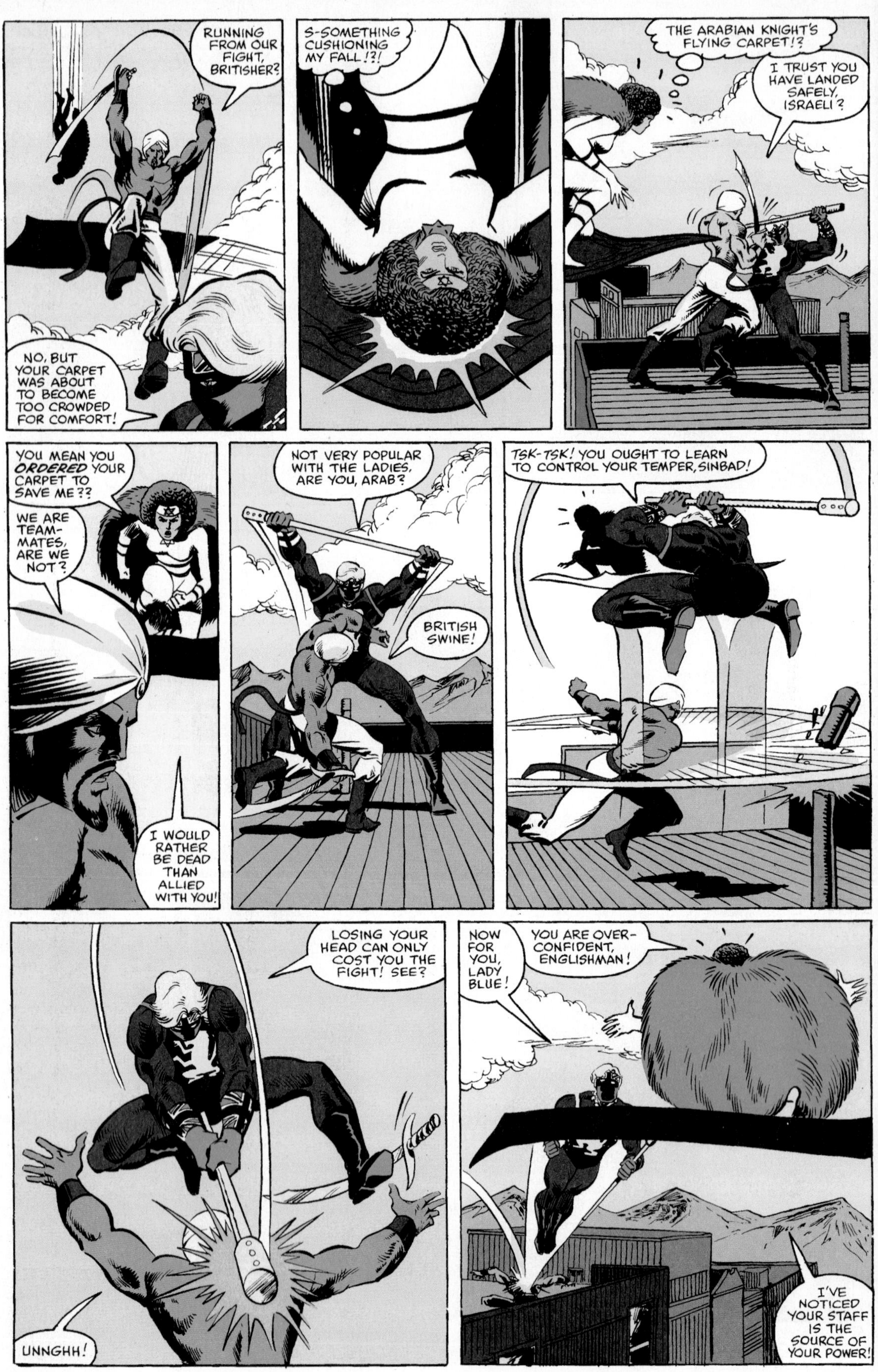

RUNNING FROM OUR FIGHT, BRITISHER?
NO, BUT YOUR CARPET WAS ABOUT TO BECOME TOO CROWDED FOR COMFORT!
S-SOMETHING CUSHIONING MY FALL!?!
THE ARABIAN KNIGHT'S FLYING CARPET!?
I TRUST YOU HAVE LANDED SAFELY, ISRAELI?
YOU MEAN YOU ORDERED YOUR CARPET TO SAVE ME??
WE ARE TEAM-MATES, ARE WE NOT?
I WOULD RATHER BE DEAD THAN ALLIED WITH YOU!
NOT VERY POPULAR WITH THE LADIES, ARE YOU, ARAB?
BRITISH SWINE!
TSK-TSK! YOU OUGHT TO LEARN TO CONTROL YOUR TEMPER, SINBAD!
LOSING YOUR HEAD CAN ONLY COST YOU THE FIGHT! SEE?
UNNGHH!
NOW FOR YOU, LADY BLUE!
YOU ARE OVER-CONFIDENT, ENGLISHMAN!
I'VE NOTICED YOUR STAFF IS THE SOURCE OF YOUR POWER!

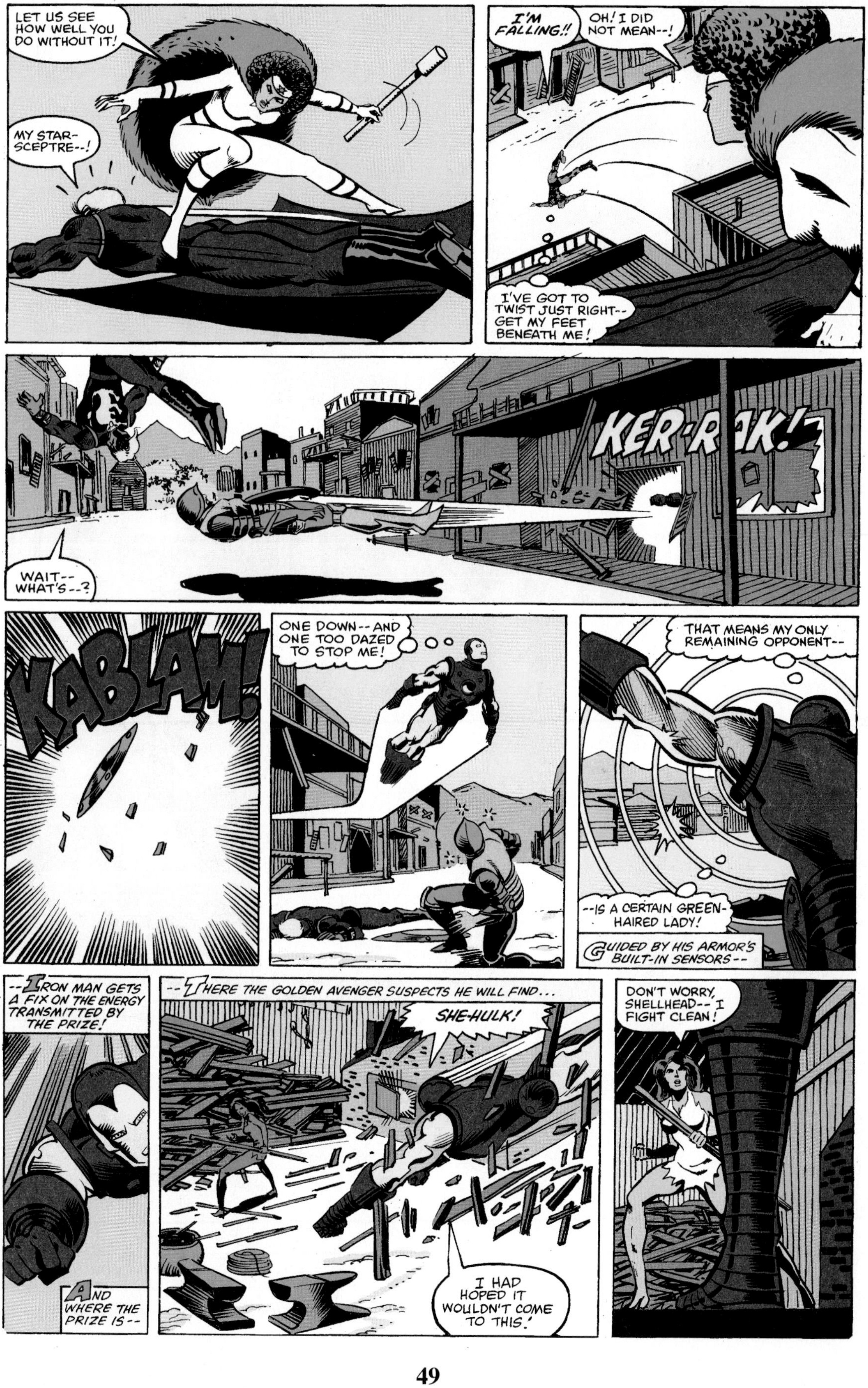

LET US SEE HOW WELL YOU DO WITHOUT IT!
MY STAR-SCEPTRE--!
I'M FALLING!!
OH! I DID NOT MEAN--!
I'VE GOT TO TWIST JUST RIGHT--GET MY FEET BENEATH ME!
KER-RAK!
WAIT--WHAT'S--?
KABLAM!
ONE DOWN--AND ONE TOO DAZED TO STOP ME!
THAT MEANS MY ONLY REMAINING OPPONENT--
--IS A CERTAIN GREEN-HAIRED LADY!
GUIDED BY HIS ARMOR'S BUILT-IN SENSORS--
--IRON MAN GETS A FIX ON THE ENERGY TRANSMITTED BY THE PRIZE!
AND WHERE THE PRIZE IS--
--THERE THE GOLDEN AVENGER SUSPECTS HE WILL FIND...
SHE-HULK!
I HAD HOPED IT WOULDN'T COME TO THIS!
DON'T WORRY, SHELLHEAD-- I FIGHT CLEAN!

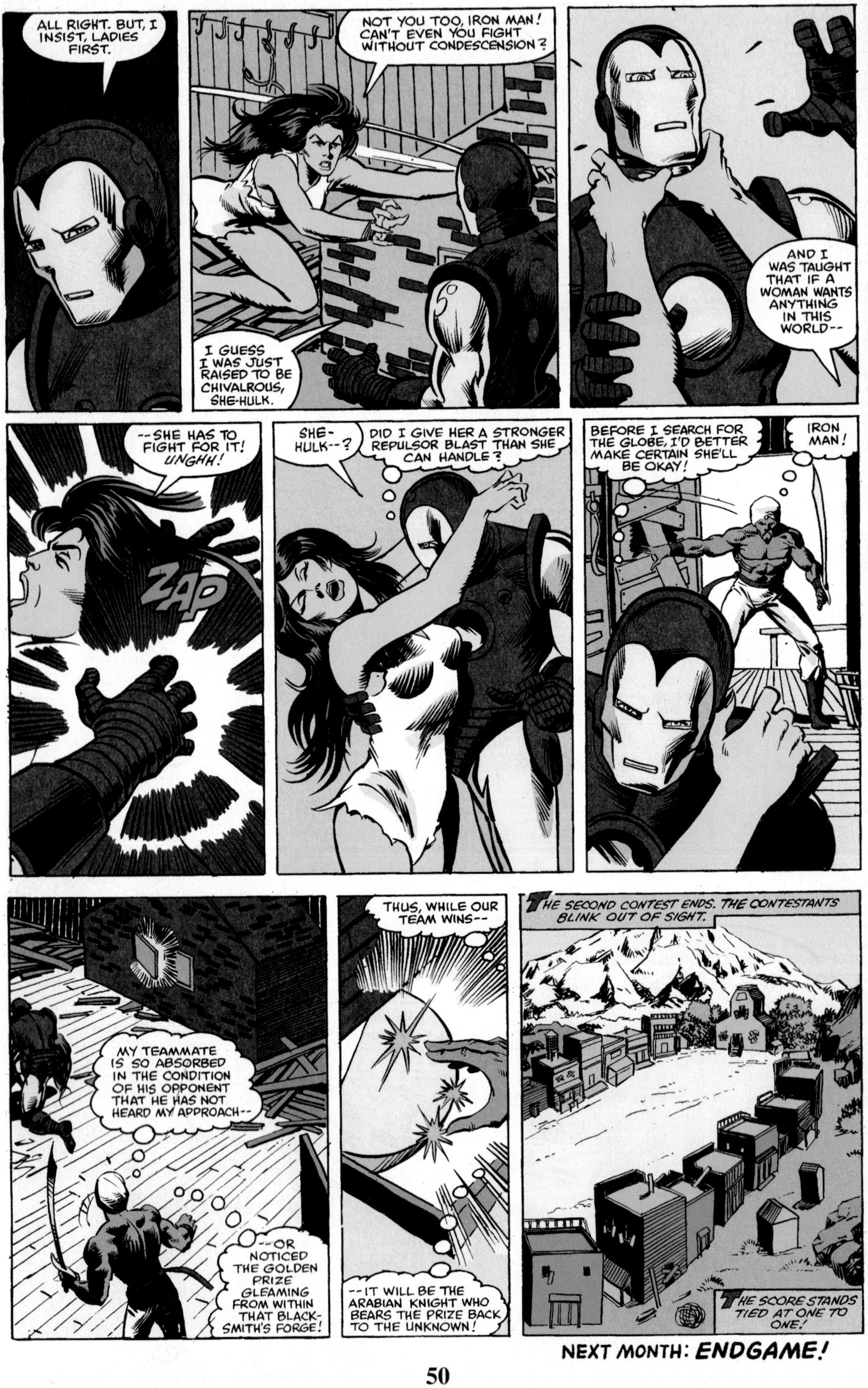
ALL RIGHT. BUT, I INSIST, LADIES FIRST.
NOT YOU TOO, IRON MAN! CAN'T EVEN YOU FIGHT WITHOUT CONDESCENSION?
I GUESS I WAS JUST RAISED TO BE CHIVALROUS, SHE-HULK.
AND I WAS TAUGHT THAT IF A WOMAN WANTS ANYTHING IN THIS WORLD--
--SHE HAS TO FIGHT FOR IT! UNGHH!
ZAP
SHE-HULK--?
DID I GIVE HER A STRONGER REPULSOR BLAST THAN SHE CAN HANDLE?
BEFORE I SEARCH FOR THE GLOBE, I'D BETTER MAKE CERTAIN SHE'LL BE OKAY!
IRON MAN!
MY TEAMMATE IS SO ABSORBED IN THE CONDITION OF HIS OPPONENT THAT HE HAS NOT HEARD MY APPROACH--
--OR NOTICED THE GOLDEN PRIZE GLEAMING FROM WITHIN THAT BLACK-SMITH'S FORGE!
THUS, WHILE OUR TEAM WINS--
--IT WILL BE THE ARABIAN KNIGHT WHO BEARS THE PRIZE BACK TO THE UNKNOWN!
THE SECOND CONTEST ENDS. THE CONTESTANTS BLINK OUT OF SIGHT.
THE SCORE STANDS TIED AT ONE TO ONE!

NEXT MONTH: **ENDGAME!**

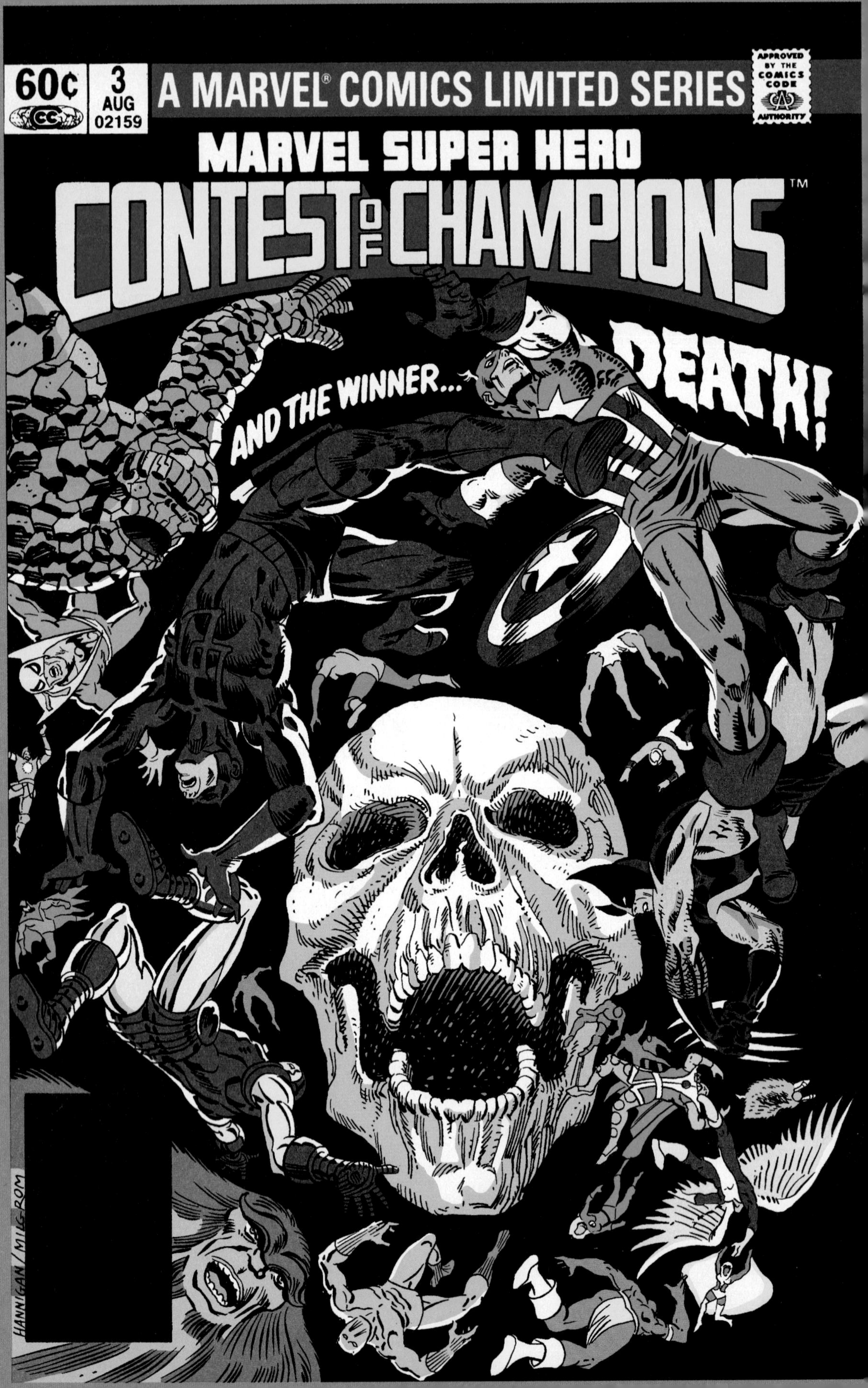
60¢
3
AUG
02159
A MARVEL® COMICS LIMITED SERIES
APPROVED BY THE COMICS CODE AUTHORITY
MARVEL SUPER HERO
CONTEST OF CHAMPIONS™
AND THE WINNER...
DEATH!
HANNIGAN / MILGROM

# MARVEL SUPER HERO
# CONTEST OF CHAMPIONS!

IN AN ORBITING ARENA ON THE THRESHOLD OF SPACE, EVERY SINGLE SUPER HERO ON EARTH HAS BEEN GATHERED...

...TO HELPLESSLY AWAIT THE OUTCOME OF THE MOST FANTASTIC CONTEST OF ALL TIME!

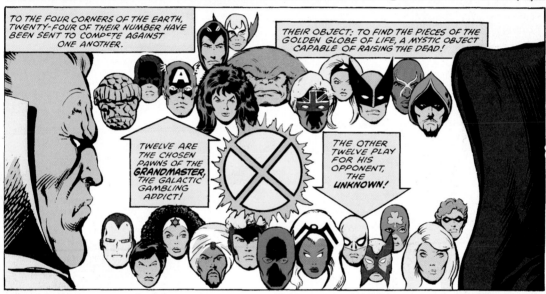

TO THE FOUR CORNERS OF THE EARTH, TWENTY-FOUR OF THEIR NUMBER HAVE BEEN SENT TO COMPETE AGAINST ONE ANOTHER.

THEIR OBJECT: TO FIND THE PIECES OF THE GOLDEN GLOBE OF LIFE, A MYSTIC OBJECT CAPABLE OF RAISING THE DEAD!

TWELVE ARE THE CHOSEN PAWNS OF THE GRANDMASTER, THE GALACTIC GAMBLING ADDICT!

THE OTHER TWELVE PLAY FOR HIS OPPONENT, THE UNKNOWN!

TWO CONTESTS HAVE ALREADY BEEN WAGED.

THE WINNERS WERE DAREDEVIL, AGENT OF THE GRANDMASTER...AND THE ARABIAN KNIGHT, AGENT OF THE UNKNOWN.

TWO CONTESTS REMAIN YET TO BE PLAYED. THE GRANDMASTER NEEDS TO WIN BOTH OF THEM IN ORDER TO ACQUIRE THE GOLDEN GLOBE TO RESTORE LIFE TO HIS IMMORTAL BROTHER.

AS FOR THE HEROES, MANY HAVE THE FEELING THAT NO MATTER WHICH OMNIPOTENT WINS, THE EARTH WILL LOSE...

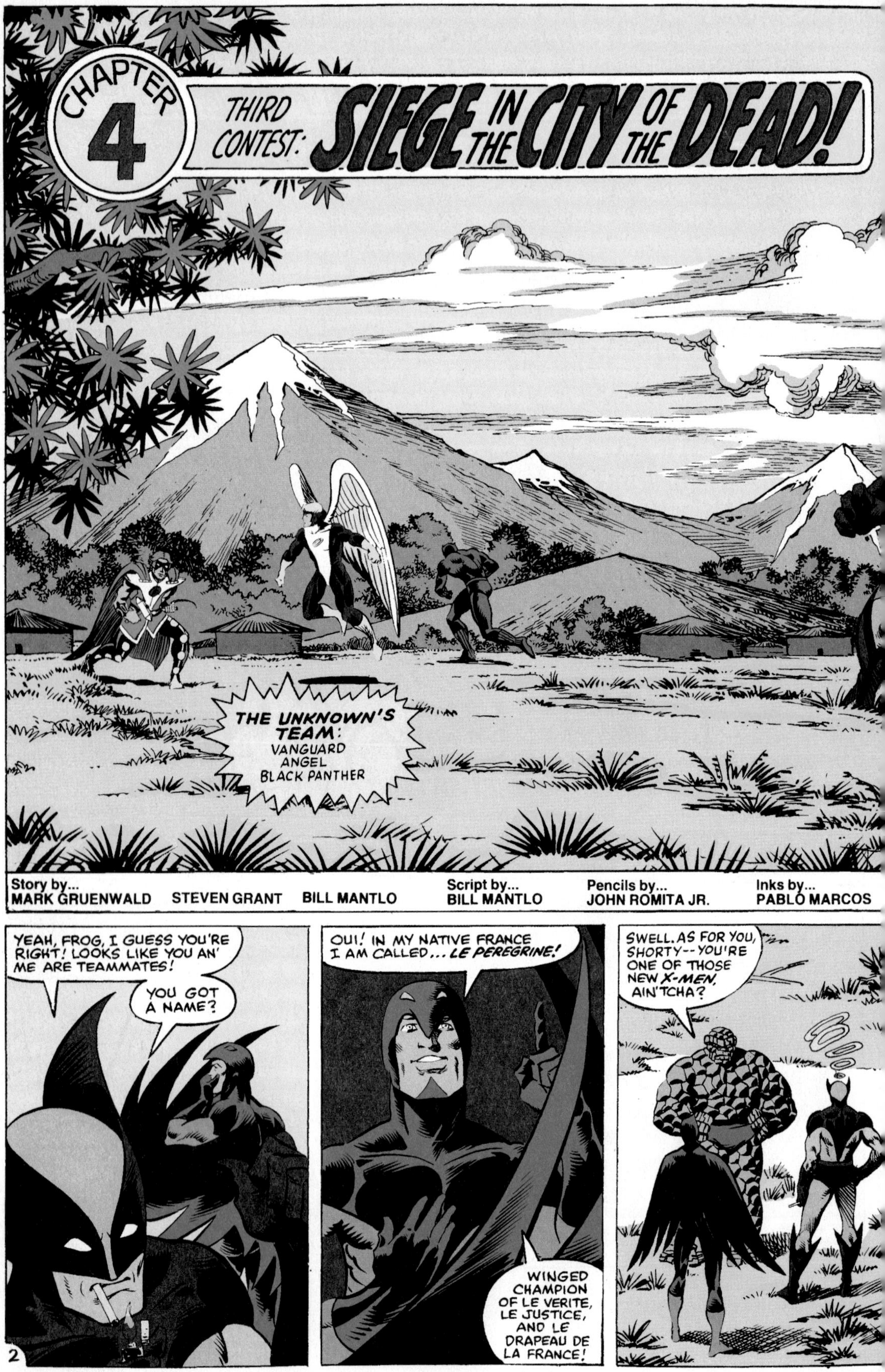
CHAPTER 4
THIRD CONTEST: SIEGE IN THE CITY OF THE DEAD!
THE UNKNOWN'S TEAM: VANGUARD ANGEL BLACK PANTHER
Story by... MARK GRUENWALD STEVEN GRANT BILL MANTLO
Script by... BILL MANTLO
Pencils by... JOHN ROMITA JR.
Inks by... PABLO MARCOS
YEAH, FROG, I GUESS YOU'RE RIGHT! LOOKS LIKE YOU AN' ME ARE TEAMMATES!
YOU GOT A NAME?
OUI! IN MY NATIVE FRANCE I AM CALLED... LE PEREGRINE!
WINGED CHAMPION OF LE VERITE, LE JUSTICE, AND LE DRAPEAU DE LA FRANCE!
SWELL. AS FOR YOU, SHORTY--YOU'RE ONE OF THOSE NEW X-MEN, AIN'TCHA?
2

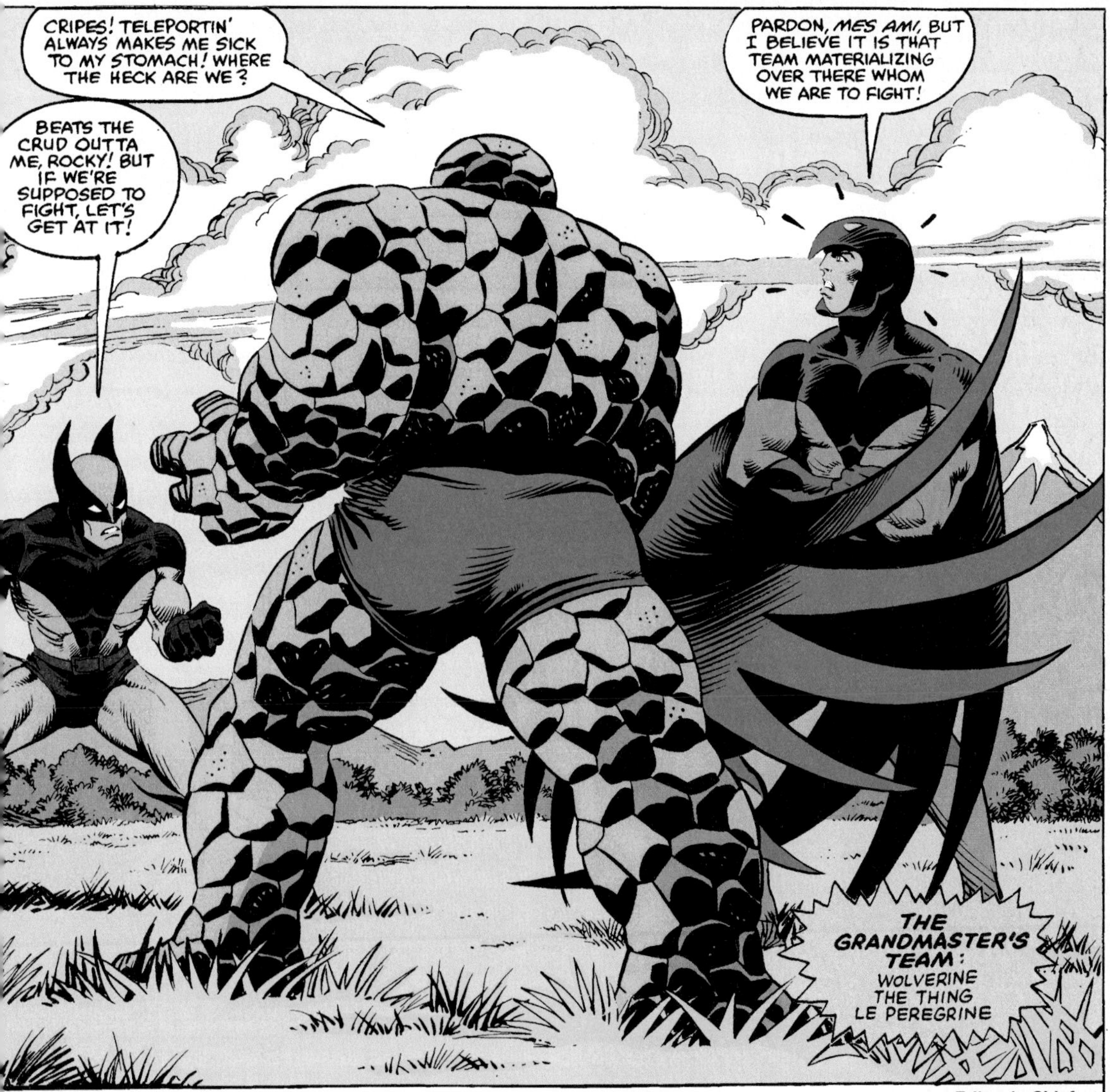
CRIPES! TELEPORTIN' ALWAYS MAKES ME SICK TO MY STOMACH! WHERE THE HECK ARE WE?
PARDON, *MES AMI*, BUT I BELIEVE IT IS THAT TEAM MATERIALIZING OVER THERE WHOM WE ARE TO FIGHT!
BEATS THE CRUD OUTTA ME, ROCKY! BUT IF WE'RE SUPPOSED TO FIGHT, LET'S GET AT IT!
THE GRANDMASTER'S TEAM: WOLVERINE THE THING LE PEREGRINE

Letters by... JOE ROSEN | Colors by... DON WARFIELD CARL GAFFORD | Edited by... MARK GRUENWALD TOM DEFALCO | Editor In Chief... JIM SHOOTER

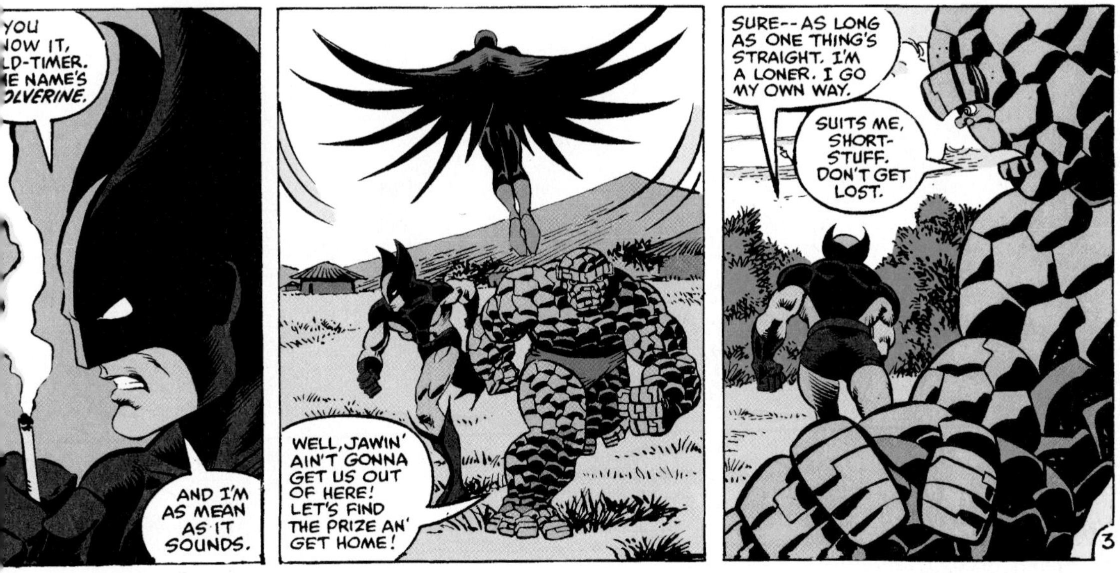
YOU NOW IT, LD-TIMER. IE NAME'S *OLVERINE.*
AND I'M AS MEAN AS IT SOUNDS.
WELL, JAWIN' AIN'T GONNA GET US OUT OF HERE! LET'S FIND THE PRIZE AN' GET HOME!
SURE--AS LONG AS ONE THING'S STRAIGHT. I'M A LONER. I GO MY OWN WAY.
SUITS ME, SHORT-STUFF. DON'T GET LOST.
3

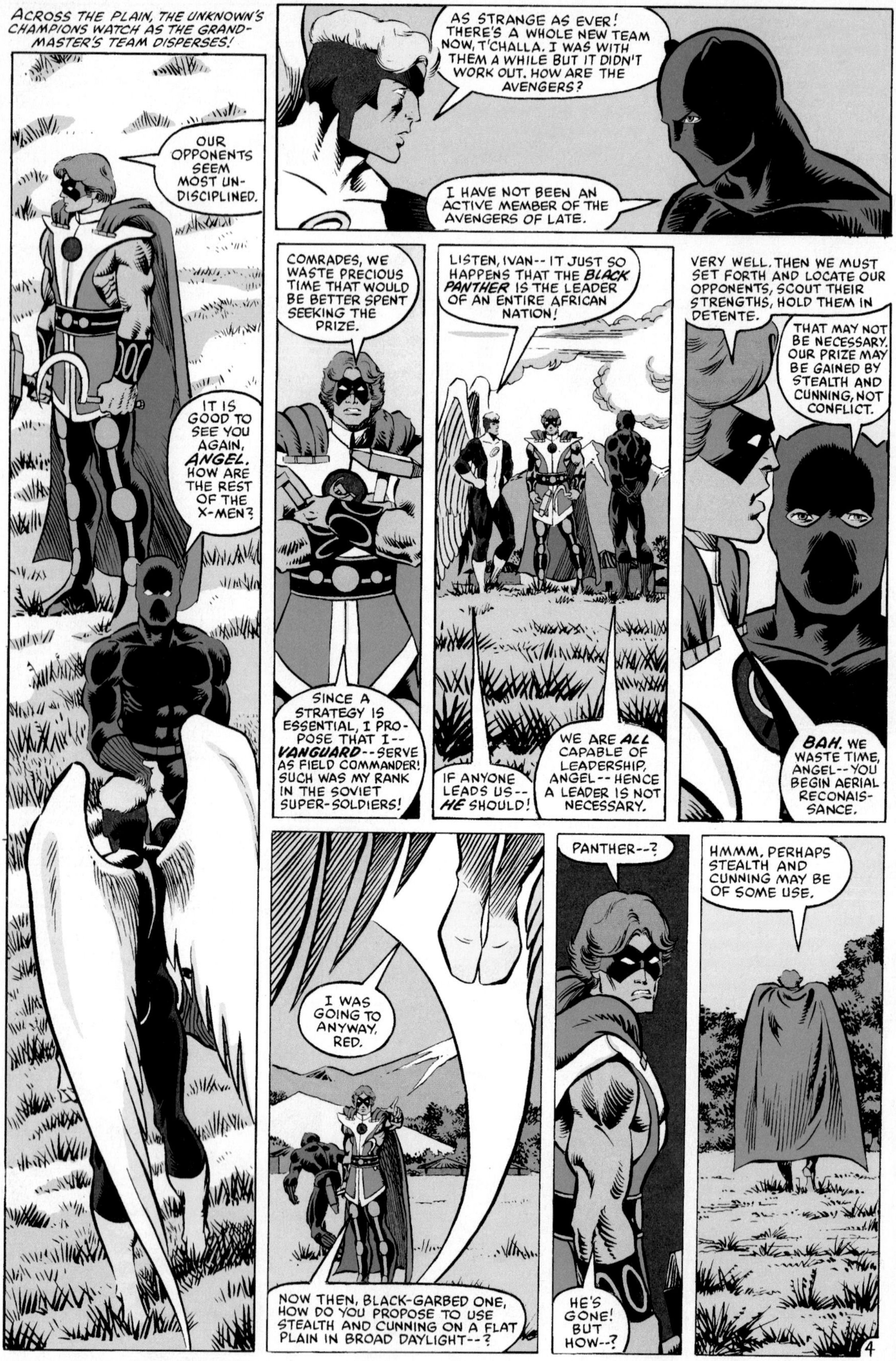
ACROSS THE PLAIN, THE UNKNOWN'S CHAMPIONS WATCH AS THE GRAND-MASTER'S TEAM DISPERSES!
OUR OPPONENTS SEEM MOST UN-DISCIPLINED.
IT IS GOOD TO SEE YOU AGAIN, ANGEL. HOW ARE THE REST OF THE X-MEN?
AS STRANGE AS EVER! THERE'S A WHOLE NEW TEAM NOW, T'CHALLA. I WAS WITH THEM A WHILE BUT IT DIDN'T WORK OUT. HOW ARE THE AVENGERS?
I HAVE NOT BEEN AN ACTIVE MEMBER OF THE AVENGERS OF LATE.
COMRADES, WE WASTE PRECIOUS TIME THAT WOULD BE BETTER SPENT SEEKING THE PRIZE.
SINCE A STRATEGY IS ESSENTIAL, I PRO-POSE THAT I-- VANGUARD--SERVE AS FIELD COMMANDER! SUCH WAS MY RANK IN THE SOVIET SUPER-SOLDIERS!
LISTEN, IVAN-- IT JUST SO HAPPENS THAT THE BLACK PANTHER IS THE LEADER OF AN ENTIRE AFRICAN NATION!
IF ANYONE LEADS US-- HE SHOULD!
WE ARE ALL CAPABLE OF LEADERSHIP, ANGEL-- HENCE A LEADER IS NOT NECESSARY.
VERY WELL. THEN WE MUST SET FORTH AND LOCATE OUR OPPONENTS, SCOUT THEIR STRENGTHS, HOLD THEM IN DETENTE.
THAT MAY NOT BE NECESSARY. OUR PRIZE MAY BE GAINED BY STEALTH AND CUNNING, NOT CONFLICT.
BAH. WE WASTE TIME. ANGEL--YOU BEGIN AERIAL RECONAIS-SANCE.
I WAS GOING TO ANYWAY, RED.
NOW THEN, BLACK-GARBED ONE, HOW DO YOU PROPOSE TO USE STEALTH AND CUNNING ON A FLAT PLAIN IN BROAD DAYLIGHT--?
PANTHER--?
HE'S GONE! BUT HOW--?
HMMM. PERHAPS STEALTH AND CUNNING MAY BE OF SOME USE.
4

ALREADY HUNDREDS OF METERS AHEAD OF VANGUARD, THE BLACK PANTHER IS THE FIRST TO SET EYES ON...

A CITY...OF THE DEAD?!

NO -- A VAST ARCHAEOLOGICAL EXCAVATION REVEALING HUNDREDS OF *CERAMIC WARRIORS!*

EVEN IN WAKANDA -- WHERE WONDERS ARE COMMONPLACE -- NEWS OF THIS DISCOVERY WAS GREETED WITH ASTONISHMENT!

LEGEND HAS IT THAT A CHINESE EMPEROR SOUGHT IMMORTALITY IN MUCH THE SAME WAY AS THE PHAROAHS OF ANCIENT EGYPT--

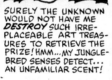

--BY BUILDING A MASSIVE TEMPLE TO HOUSE HIM IN HIS AFTERLIFE, COMPLETE WITH LIFESIZE REPLICAS OF HIS IMPERIAL ARMY!

SURELY THE UNKNOWN WOULD NOT HAVE ME *DESTROY* SUCH IRREPLACEABLE ART TREASURES TO RETRIEVE THE PRIZE! HMM...MY JUNGLE-BRED SENSES DETECT... AN UNFAMILIAR SCENT!

HUH--? HE *DUCKED!*

NICE MOVES, CAT-MAN. I'M NOT EASILY EVADED.

BUT YOU'RE OUTTA YOUR MIND IF YOU THINK I'M GONNA LET A LITTLE THING LIKE SPEED COME BETWEEN ME AND THE PRIZE.

YOU SEE, I'VE GOT SOMETHING *MORE* THAN JUST SPEED...

SNIKT

ADAMANTIUM CLAWS FLASH FROM THE BACK OF WOLVERINE'S HAND AT COMMAND...

MEANWHILE, HIGH ABOVE THE ANCIENT CITY...

UH-OH! LOOKS LIKE I'M NOT THE ONLY HERO WITH WINGS!

LE ANGEL! LONG 'AVE I READ OF YOU, MON AMI!

NOW LET US SEE IF YOU ARE AS FORMIDABLE AS I'VE READ.

5

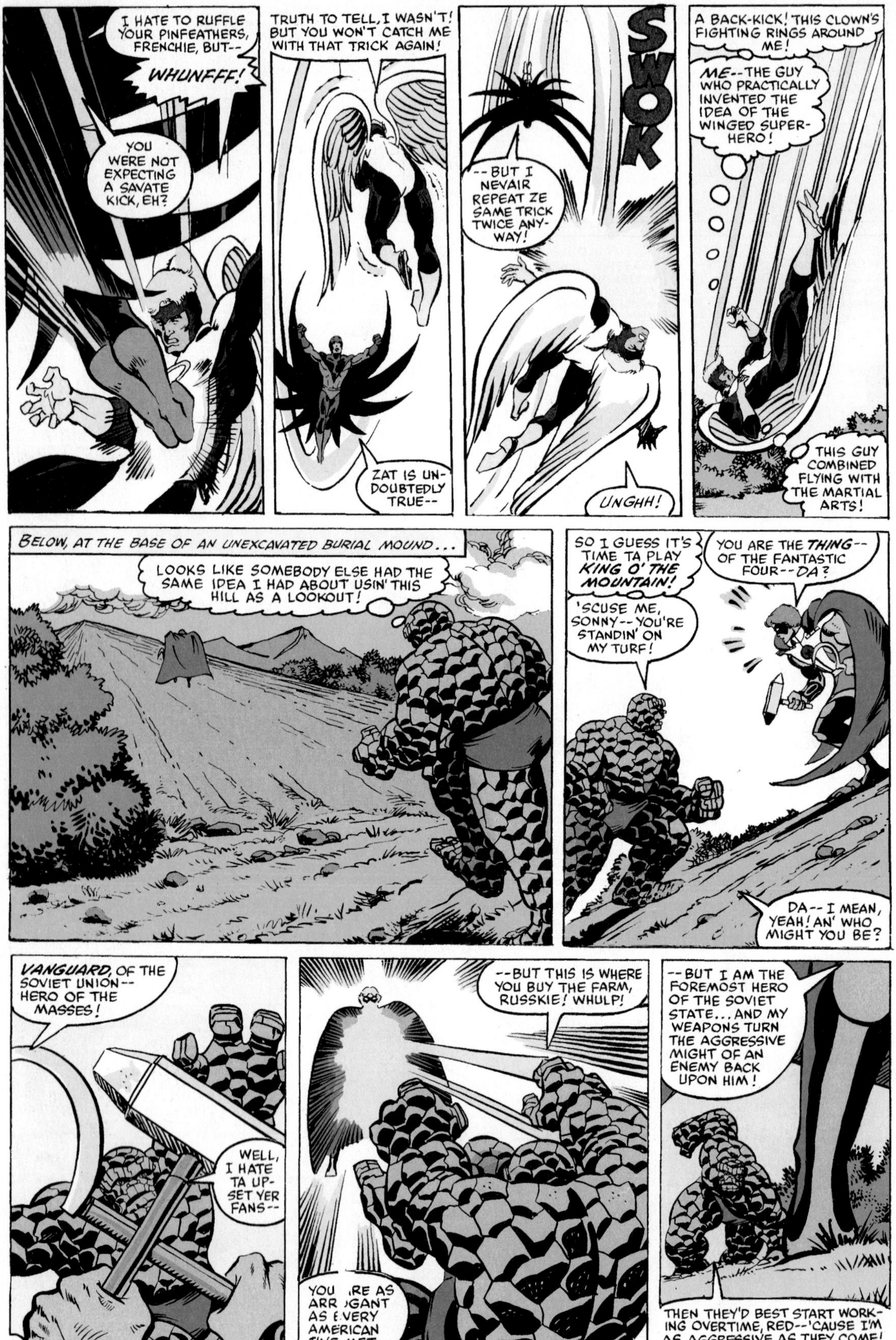
I HATE TO RUFFLE YOUR PINFEATHERS, FRENCHIE, BUT--
WHUNFFF!
YOU WERE NOT EXPECTING A SAVATE KICK, EH?
TRUTH TO TELL, I WASN'T! BUT YOU WON'T CATCH ME WITH THAT TRICK AGAIN!
ZAT IS UNDOUBTEDLY TRUE--
SWOK
--BUT I NEVAIR REPEAT ZE SAME TRICK TWICE ANYWAY!
UNGHH!
A BACK-KICK! THIS CLOWN'S FIGHTING RINGS AROUND ME!
ME--THE GUY WHO PRACTICALLY INVENTED THE IDEA OF THE WINGED SUPER-HERO!
THIS GUY COMBINED FLYING WITH THE MARTIAL ARTS!
BELOW, AT THE BASE OF AN UNEXCAVATED BURIAL MOUND...
LOOKS LIKE SOMEBODY ELSE HAD THE SAME IDEA I HAD ABOUT USIN' THIS HILL AS A LOOKOUT!
SO I GUESS IT'S TIME TA PLAY KING O' THE MOUNTAIN!
'SCUSE ME, SONNY--YOU'RE STANDIN' ON MY TURF!
YOU ARE THE THING--OF THE FANTASTIC FOUR--DA?
DA--I MEAN, YEAH! AN' WHO MIGHT YOU BE?
VANGUARD, OF THE SOVIET UNION--HERO OF THE MASSES!
WELL, I HATE TA UPSET YER FANS--
6
--BUT THIS IS WHERE YOU BUY THE FARM, RUSSKIE! WHULP!
YOU ARE AS ARROGANT AS EVERY AMERICAN I'VE MET--
--BUT I AM THE FOREMOST HERO OF THE SOVIET STATE... AND MY WEAPONS TURN THE AGGRESSIVE MIGHT OF AN ENEMY BACK UPON HIM!
THEN THEY'D BEST START WORKING OVERTIME, RED--'CAUSE I'M AS AGGRESSIVE AS THEY COME!

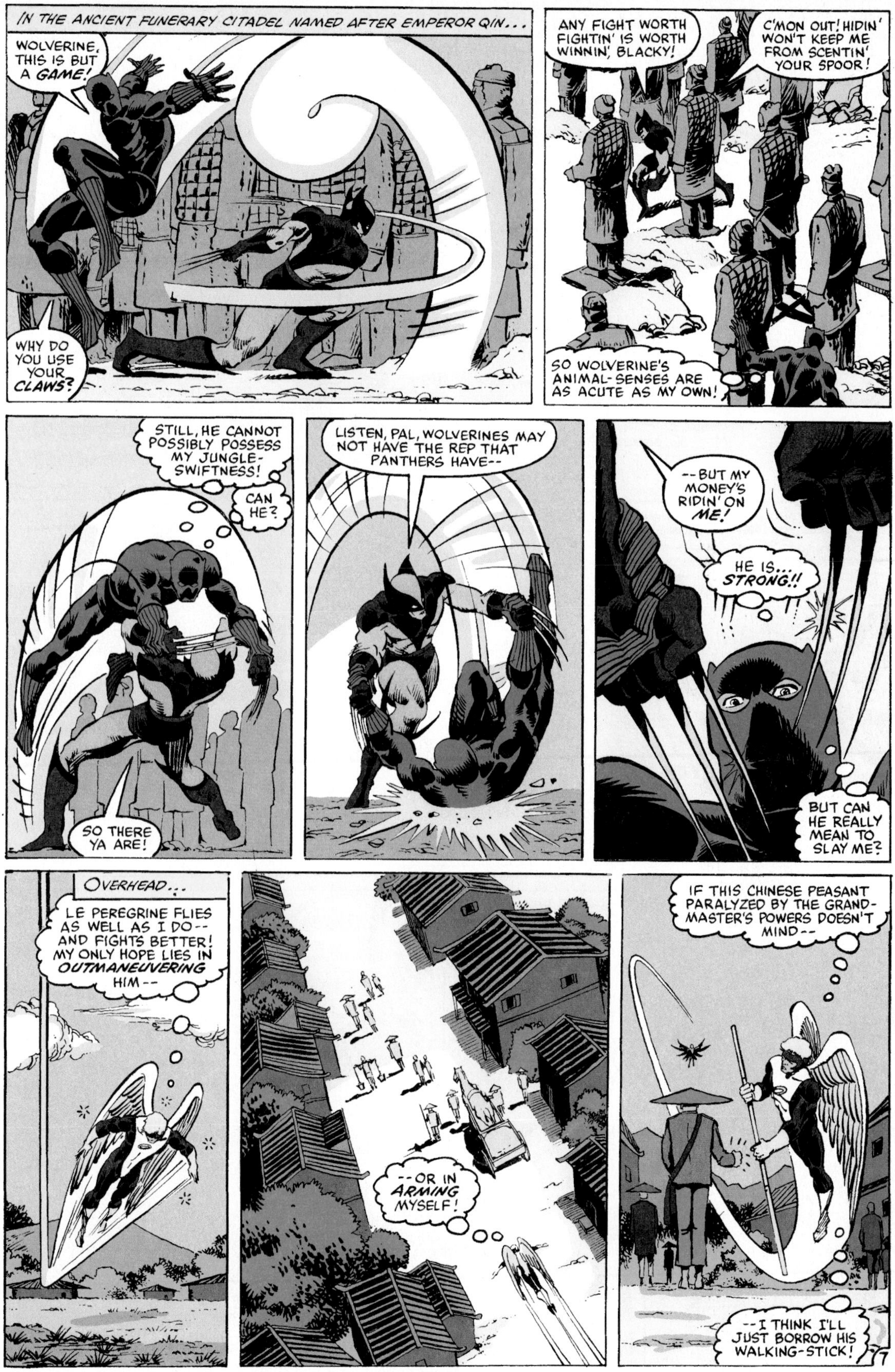
IN THE ANCIENT FUNERARY CITADEL NAMED AFTER EMPEROR QIN...
WOLVERINE, THIS IS BUT A GAME!
WHY DO YOU USE YOUR CLAWS?
ANY FIGHT WORTH FIGHTIN' IS WORTH WINNIN', BLACKY!
C'MON OUT! HIDIN' WON'T KEEP ME FROM SCENTIN' YOUR SPOOR!
SO WOLVERINE'S ANIMAL-SENSES ARE AS ACUTE AS MY OWN!
STILL, HE CANNOT POSSIBLY POSSESS MY JUNGLE-SWIFTNESS!
CAN HE?
SO THERE YA ARE!
LISTEN, PAL, WOLVERINES MAY NOT HAVE THE REP THAT PANTHERS HAVE--
--BUT MY MONEY'S RIDIN' ON ME!
HE IS... STRONG!!
BUT CAN HE REALLY MEAN TO SLAY ME?
OVERHEAD...
LE PEREGRINE FLIES AS WELL AS I DO-- AND FIGHTS BETTER! MY ONLY HOPE LIES IN OUTMANEUVERING HIM--
--OR IN ARMING MYSELF!
IF THIS CHINESE PEASANT PARALYZED BY THE GRAND-MASTER'S POWERS DOESN'T MIND--
--I THINK I'LL JUST BORROW HIS WALKING-STICK!
7

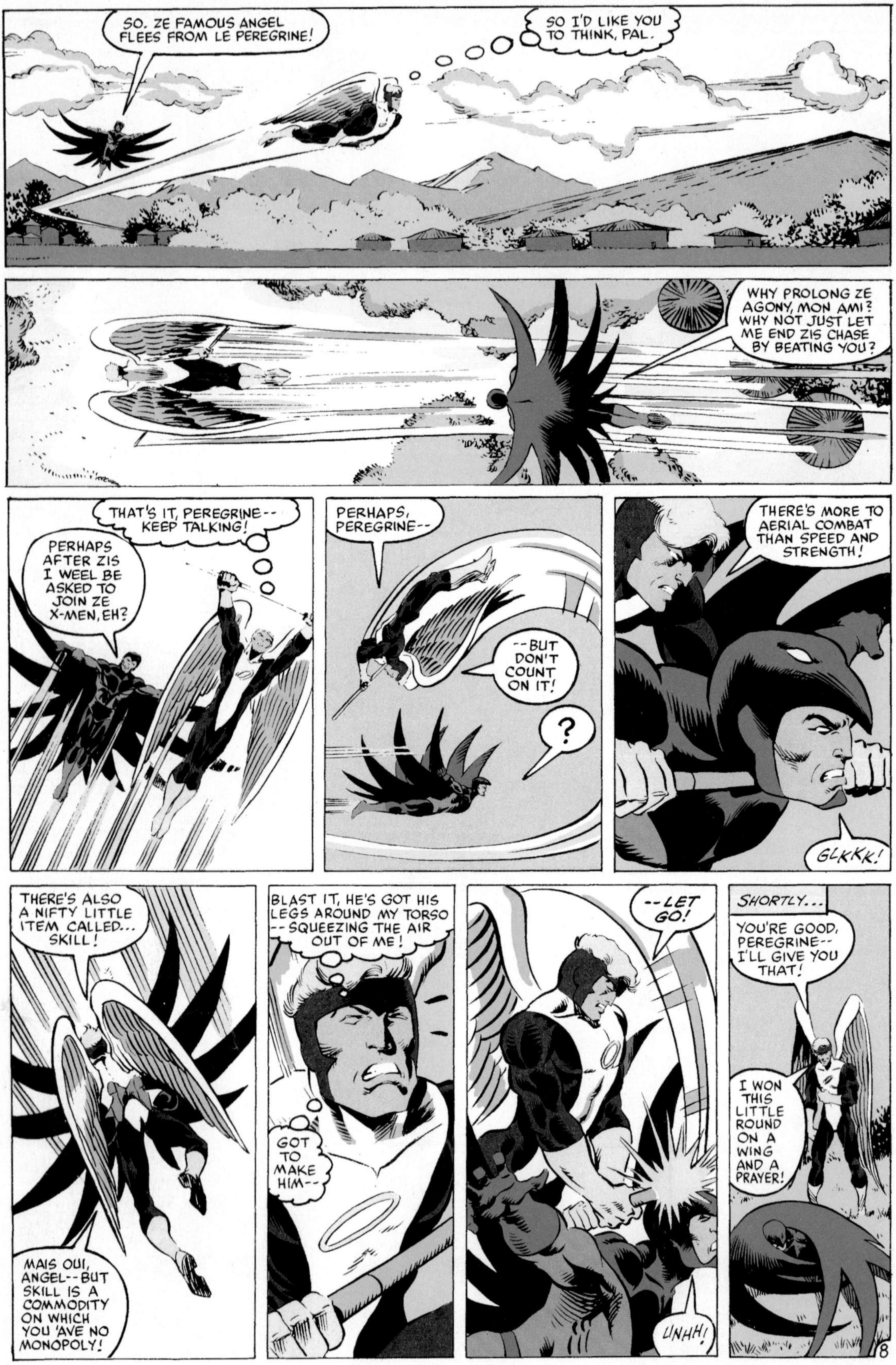
SO. ZE FAMOUS ANGEL FLEES FROM LE PEREGRINE!
SO I'D LIKE YOU TO THINK, PAL.
WHY PROLONG ZE AGONY, MON AMI? WHY NOT JUST LET ME END ZIS CHASE BY BEATING YOU?
THAT'S IT, PEREGRINE-- KEEP TALKING!
PERHAPS AFTER ZIS I WEEL BE ASKED TO JOIN ZE X-MEN, EH?
PERHAPS, PEREGRINE--
--BUT DON'T COUNT ON IT!
?
THERE'S MORE TO AERIAL COMBAT THAN SPEED AND STRENGTH!
GLKKK!
THERE'S ALSO A NIFTY LITTLE ITEM CALLED... SKILL!
MAIS OUI, ANGEL--BUT SKILL IS A COMMODITY ON WHICH YOU 'AVE NO MONOPOLY!
BLAST IT, HE'S GOT HIS LEGS AROUND MY TORSO --SQUEEZING THE AIR OUT OF ME!
GOT TO MAKE HIM--
--LET GO!
UNHH!
SHORTLY...
YOU'RE GOOD, PEREGRINE-- I'LL GIVE YOU THAT!
I WON THIS LITTLE ROUND ON A WING AND A PRAYER!
8

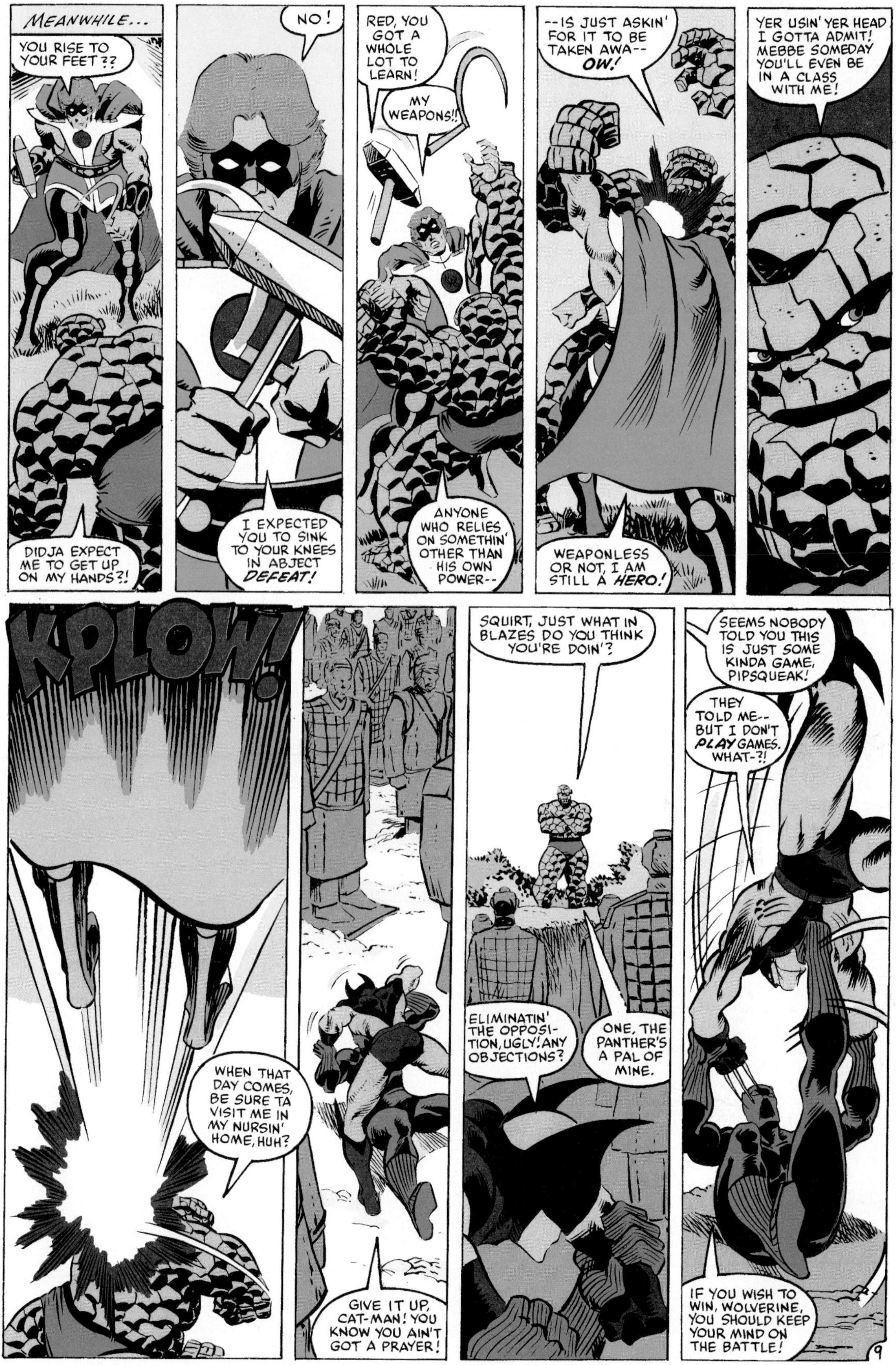
MEANWHILE...
YOU RISE TO YOUR FEET??
DIDJA EXPECT ME TO GET UP ON MY HANDS?!
NO!
I EXPECTED YOU TO SINK TO YOUR KNEES IN ABJECT DEFEAT!
RED, YOU GOT A WHOLE LOT TO LEARN!
MY WEAPONS!!
ANYONE WHO RELIES ON SOMETHIN' OTHER THAN HIS OWN POWER--
--IS JUST ASKIN' FOR IT TO BE TAKEN AWA-- OW!
WEAPONLESS OR NOT, I AM STILL A HERO!
YER USIN' YER HEAD I GOTTA ADMIT! MEBBE SOMEDAY YOU'LL EVEN BE IN A CLASS WITH ME!
KPLOW!
WHEN THAT DAY COMES, BE SURE TA VISIT ME IN MY NURSIN' HOME, HUH?
GIVE IT UP, CAT-MAN! YOU KNOW YOU AIN'T GOT A PRAYER!
SQUIRT, JUST WHAT IN BLAZES DO YOU THINK YOU'RE DOIN'?
ELIMINATIN' THE OPPOSITION, UGLY! ANY OBJECTIONS?
ONE, THE PANTHER'S A PAL OF MINE.
SEEMS NOBODY TOLD YOU THIS IS JUST SOME KINDA GAME, PIPSQUEAK!
THEY TOLD ME-- BUT I DON'T PLAY GAMES. WHAT-?!
IF YOU WISH TO WIN, WOLVERINE, YOU SHOULD KEEP YOUR MIND ON THE BATTLE!
9

YOU TAKE THE CAKE, SHORTY! YOU REALLY WERE SET TA ICE THE PANTHER, WEREN'T YA?

HE HAD NOT BEATEN ME YET, BEN.

I HAD YA LICKED SIX WAYS TO SUNDAY, BLACKY!

HALF-PINT, IT'S TOO BAD YOU AN' ME ARE TEAMMATES! YOURS IS ONE BUTT I'D LIKE TA BOOT FROM HERE TO BOISE!

ANYTIME YOU'D LIKE TO TRY IT, ROCKHEAD...!

HEY! HOLD ON-- I SMELL SOMETHIN'!

AS DO I! SOMETHING ALIEN TO THIS ANCIENT CITY!

IT CAN ONLY BE--

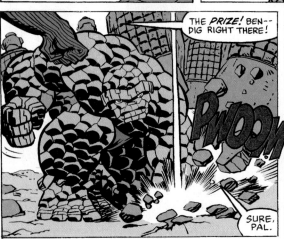

THE PRIZE! BEN-- DIG RIGHT THERE!

PWOOM

SURE, PAL.

I'D JUST AS SOON GET THIS COCKAMAMIE CONTEST OVER WITH.

I THINK I'VE GOT IT...

THIS IS IT, PLAYMATES! PARTY'S OVER-- AN' I GOT OUR BUS-PASS HOME!

THE TWO TEAMS FADE FROM SIGHT!

THE SCORE IS NOW GRANDMASTER-- TWO, THE UNKNOWN-- ONE!

10

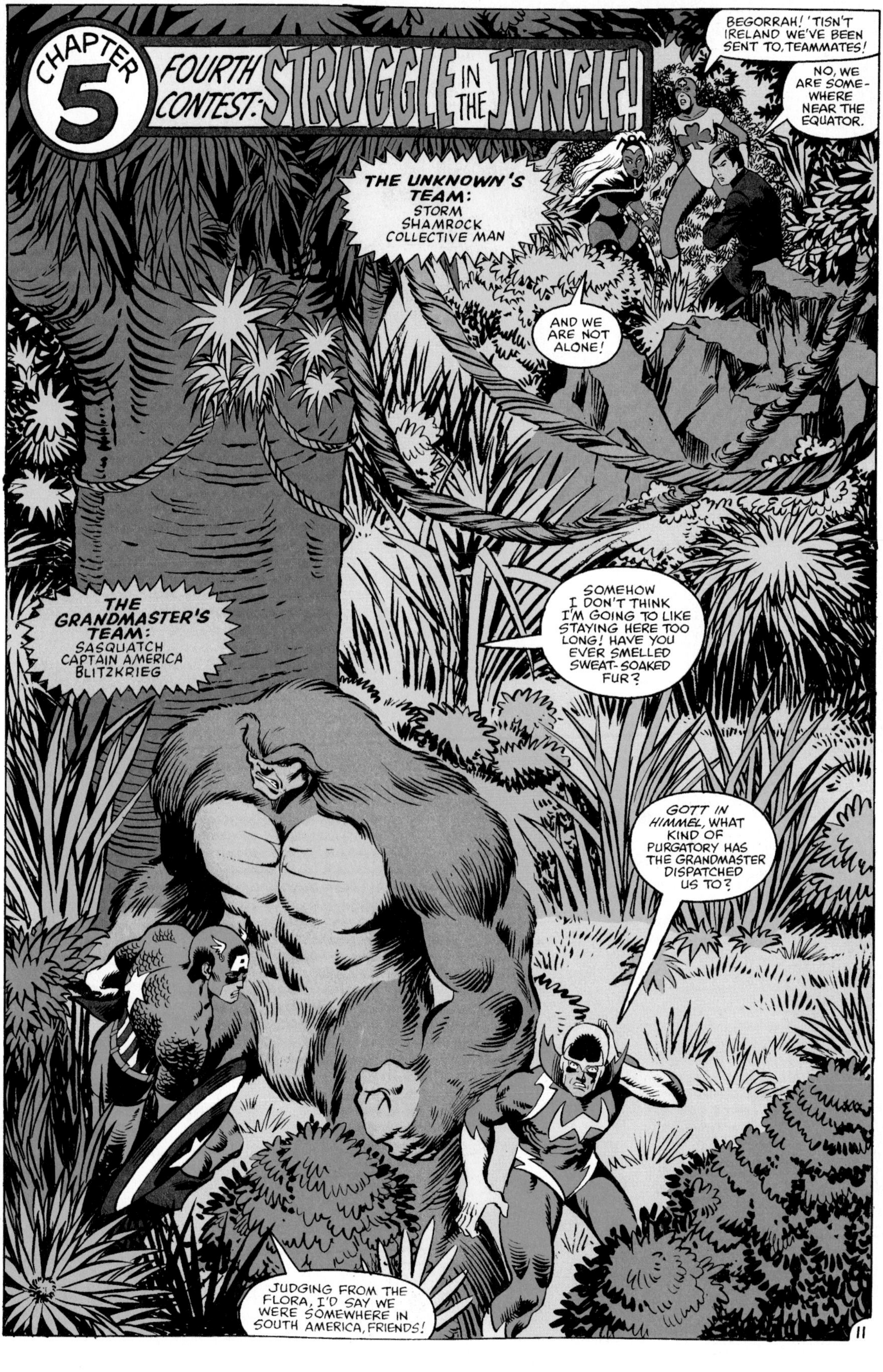
CHAPTER 5
FOURTH CONTEST: STRUGGLE IN THE JUNGLE!
BEGORRAH! 'TISN'T IRELAND WE'VE BEEN SENT TO, TEAMMATES!
NO, WE ARE SOMEWHERE NEAR THE EQUATOR.
THE UNKNOWN'S TEAM: STORM SHAMROCK COLLECTIVE MAN
AND WE ARE NOT ALONE!
THE GRANDMASTER'S TEAM: SASQUATCH CAPTAIN AMERICA BLITZKRIEG
SOMEHOW I DON'T THINK I'M GOING TO LIKE STAYING HERE TOO LONG! HAVE YOU EVER SMELLED SWEAT-SOAKED FUR?
GOTT IN HIMMEL, WHAT KIND OF PURGATORY HAS THE GRANDMASTER DISPATCHED US TO?
JUDGING FROM THE FLORA, I'D SAY WE WERE SOMEWHERE IN SOUTH AMERICA, FRIENDS!
11

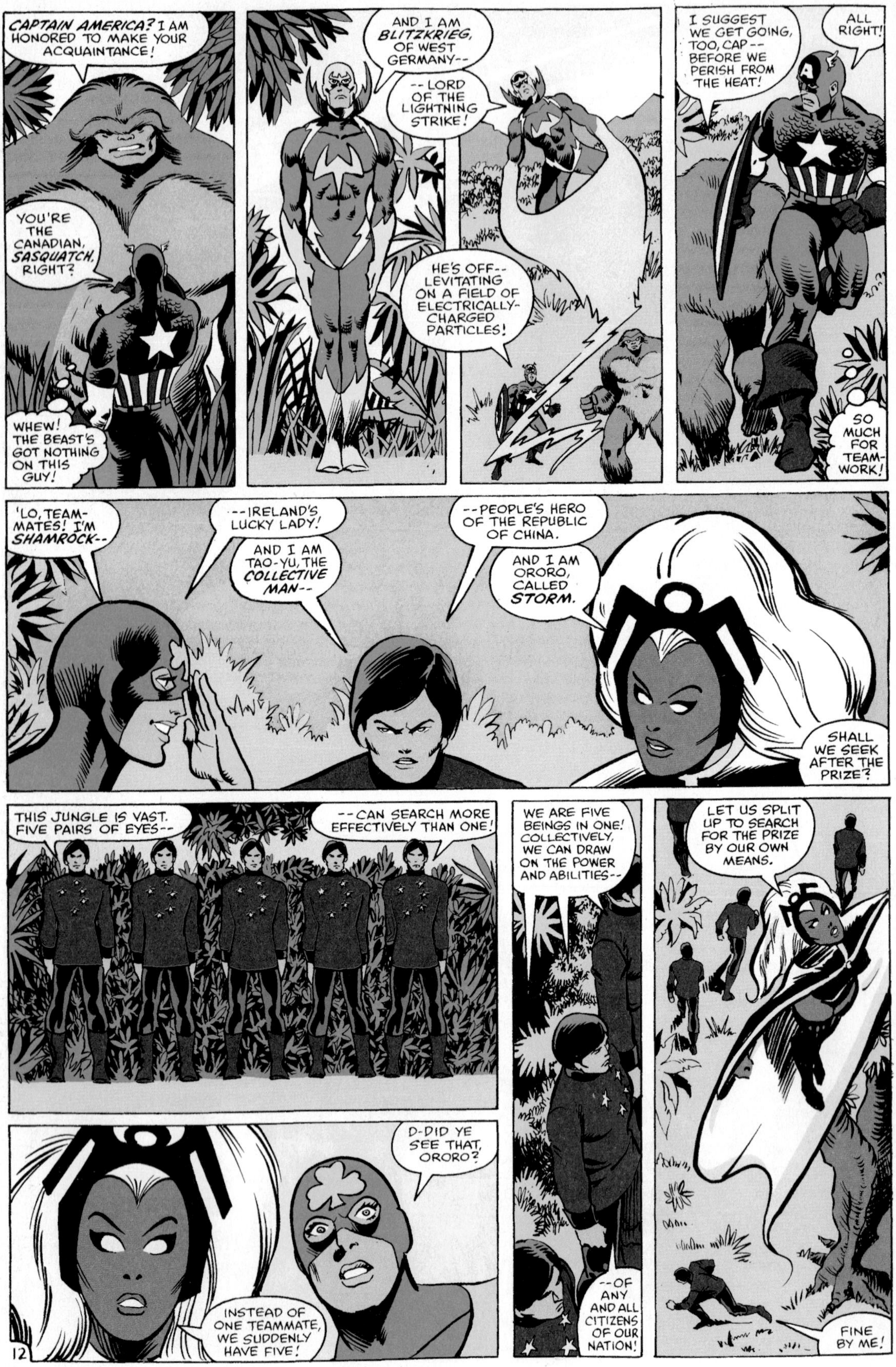
CAPTAIN AMERICA? I AM HONORED TO MAKE YOUR ACQUAINTANCE!
YOU'RE THE CANADIAN, SASQUATCH, RIGHT?
WHEW! THE BEAST'S GOT NOTHING ON THIS GUY!
AND I AM BLITZKRIEG, OF WEST GERMANY--
--LORD OF THE LIGHTNING STRIKE!
HE'S OFF-- LEVITATING ON A FIELD OF ELECTRICALLY-CHARGED PARTICLES!
I SUGGEST WE GET GOING, TOO, CAP-- BEFORE WE PERISH FROM THE HEAT!
ALL RIGHT!
SO MUCH FOR TEAM-WORK!
'LO, TEAM-MATES! I'M SHAMROCK--
--IRELAND'S LUCKY LADY!
AND I AM TAO-YU, THE COLLECTIVE MAN--
--PEOPLE'S HERO OF THE REPUBLIC OF CHINA.
AND I AM ORORO, CALLED STORM.
SHALL WE SEEK AFTER THE PRIZE?
THIS JUNGLE IS VAST. FIVE PAIRS OF EYES--
--CAN SEARCH MORE EFFECTIVELY THAN ONE!
D-DID YE SEE THAT, ORORO?
INSTEAD OF ONE TEAMMATE, WE SUDDENLY HAVE FIVE!
12
WE ARE FIVE BEINGS IN ONE! COLLECTIVELY, WE CAN DRAW ON THE POWER AND ABILITIES--
--OF ANY AND ALL CITIZENS OF OUR NATION!
LET US SPLIT UP TO SEARCH FOR THE PRIZE BY OUR OWN MEANS.
FINE BY ME!

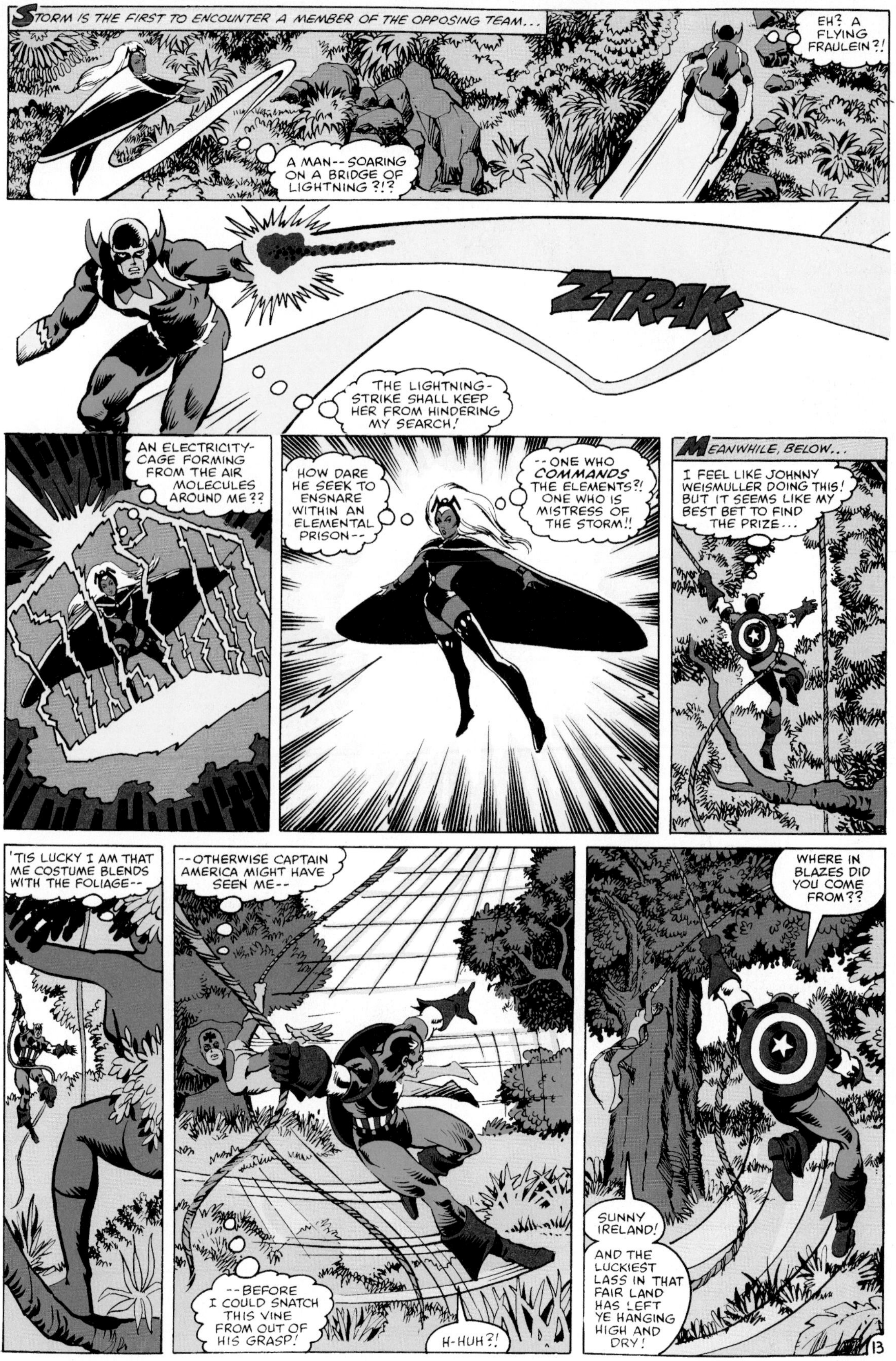
STORM IS THE FIRST TO ENCOUNTER A MEMBER OF THE OPPOSING TEAM...
A MAN--SOARING ON A BRIDGE OF LIGHTNING?!?
EH? A FLYING FRAULEIN?!
ZTRAK
THE LIGHTNING-STRIKE SHALL KEEP HER FROM HINDERING MY SEARCH!
AN ELECTRICITY-CAGE FORMING FROM THE AIR MOLECULES AROUND ME??
HOW DARE HE SEEK TO ENSNARE WITHIN AN ELEMENTAL PRISON--
--ONE WHO COMMANDS THE ELEMENTS?! ONE WHO IS MISTRESS OF THE STORM!!
MEANWHILE, BELOW...
I FEEL LIKE JOHNNY WEISMULLER DOING THIS! BUT IT SEEMS LIKE MY BEST BET TO FIND THE PRIZE...
'TIS LUCKY I AM THAT ME COSTUME BLENDS WITH THE FOLIAGE--
--OTHERWISE CAPTAIN AMERICA MIGHT HAVE SEEN ME--
--BEFORE I COULD SNATCH THIS VINE FROM OUT OF HIS GRASP!
H-HUH?!
WHERE IN BLAZES DID YOU COME FROM??
SUNNY IRELAND!
AND THE LUCKIEST LASS IN THAT FAIR LAND HAS LEFT YE HANGING HIGH AND DRY!
13

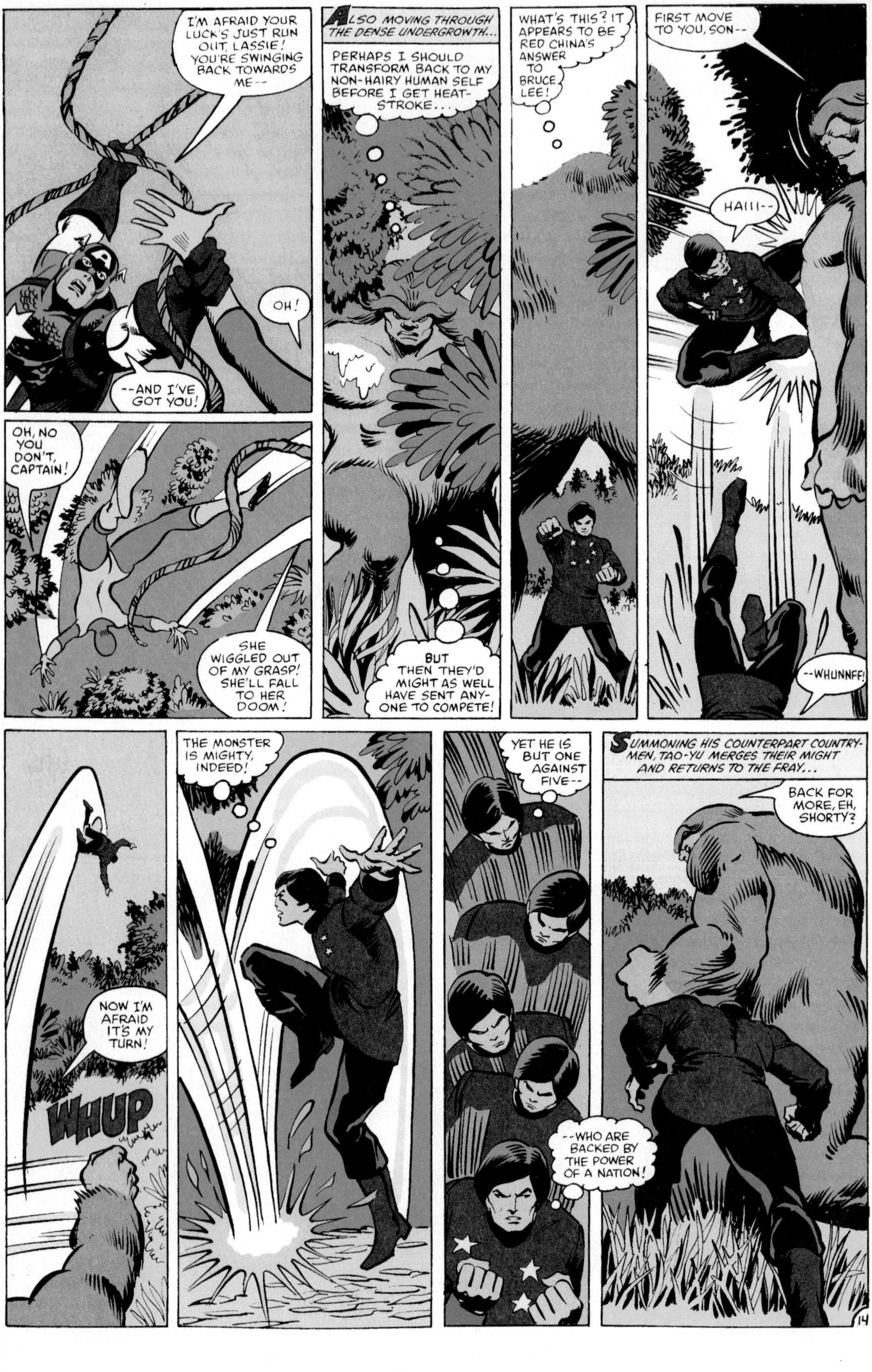
I'M AFRAID YOUR LUCK'S JUST RUN OUT, LASSIE! YOU'RE SWINGING BACK TOWARDS ME--
OH!
--AND I'VE GOT YOU!
OH, NO YOU DON'T, CAPTAIN!
SHE WIGGLED OUT OF MY GRASP! SHE'LL FALL TO HER DOOM!
ALSO MOVING THROUGH THE DENSE UNDERGROWTH...
PERHAPS I SHOULD TRANSFORM BACK TO MY NON-HAIRY HUMAN SELF BEFORE I GET HEAT-STROKE...
BUT THEN THEY'D MIGHT AS WELL HAVE SENT ANY-ONE TO COMPETE!
WHAT'S THIS? IT APPEARS TO BE RED CHINA'S ANSWER TO BRUCE LEE!
FIRST MOVE TO YOU, SON--
HAIII--
--WHUNNFF!
NOW I'M AFRAID IT'S MY TURN!
WHUP
THE MONSTER IS MIGHTY, INDEED!
YET HE IS BUT ONE AGAINST FIVE--
--WHO ARE BACKED BY THE POWER OF A NATION!
SUMMONING HIS COUNTERPART COUNTRY-MEN, TAO-YU MERGES THEIR MIGHT AND RETURNS TO THE FRAY...
BACK FOR MORE, EH, SHORTY?
14

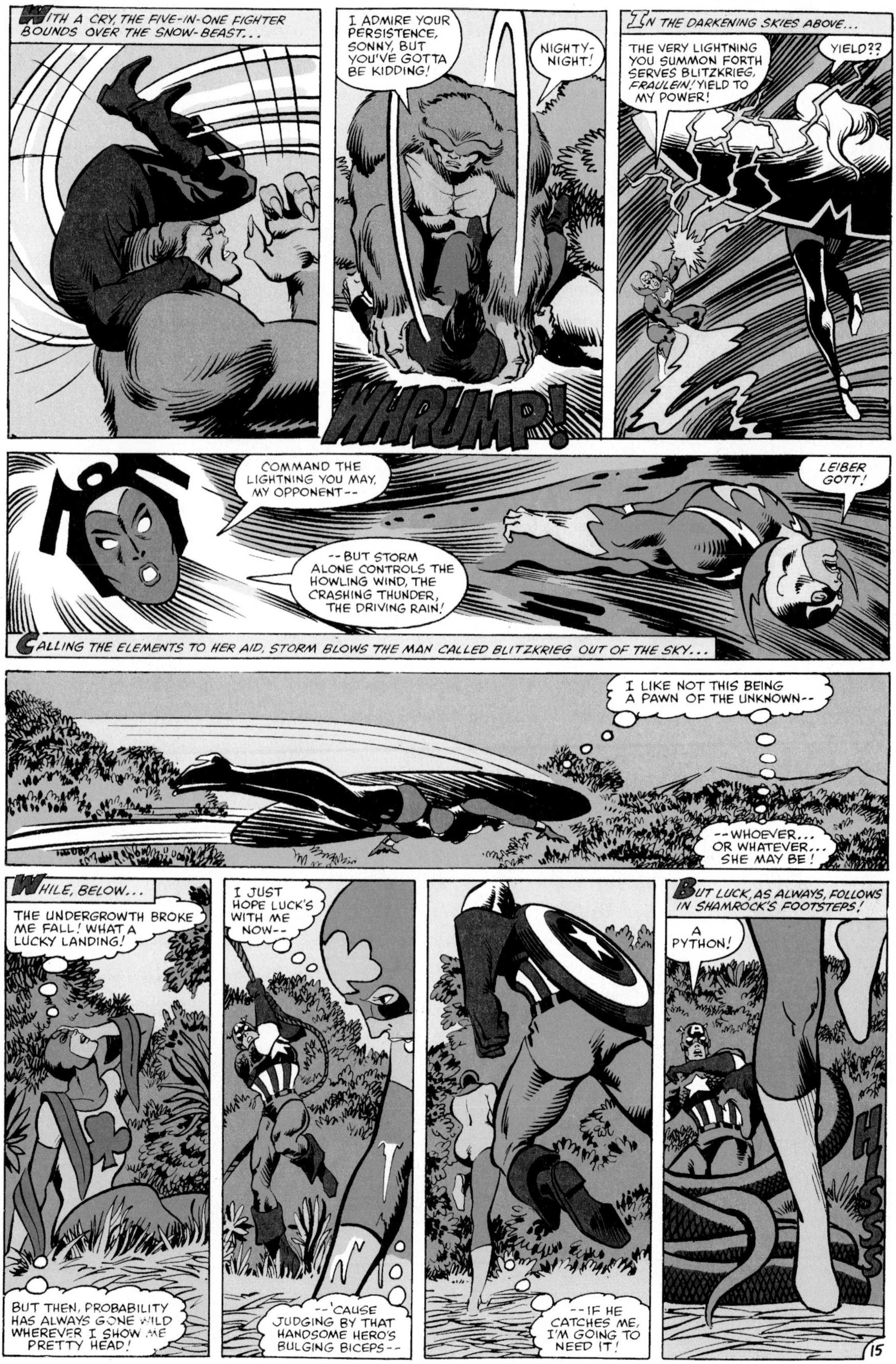
WITH A CRY, THE FIVE-IN-ONE FIGHTER BOUNDS OVER THE SNOW-BEAST...
I ADMIRE YOUR PERSISTENCE, SONNY, BUT YOU'VE GOTTA BE KIDDING!
NIGHTY-NIGHT!
WHRUMP!
IN THE DARKENING SKIES ABOVE...
THE VERY LIGHTNING YOU SUMMON FORTH SERVES BLITZKRIEG, FRAULEIN! YIELD TO MY POWER!
YIELD??
COMMAND THE LIGHTNING YOU MAY, MY OPPONENT--
--BUT STORM ALONE CONTROLS THE HOWLING WIND, THE CRASHING THUNDER, THE DRIVING RAIN!
LEIBER GOTT!
CALLING THE ELEMENTS TO HER AID, STORM BLOWS THE MAN CALLED BLITZKRIEG OUT OF THE SKY...
I LIKE NOT THIS BEING A PAWN OF THE UNKNOWN--
--WHOEVER... OR WHATEVER... SHE MAY BE!
WHILE, BELOW...
THE UNDERGROWTH BROKE ME FALL! WHAT A LUCKY LANDING!
BUT THEN, PROBABILITY HAS ALWAYS GONE WILD WHEREVER I SHOW ME PRETTY HEAD!
I JUST HOPE LUCK'S WITH ME NOW--
--'CAUSE JUDGING BY THAT HANDSOME HERO'S BULGING BICEPS--
--IF HE CATCHES ME, I'M GOING TO NEED IT!
BUT LUCK, AS ALWAYS, FOLLOWS IN SHAMROCK'S FOOTSTEPS!
A PYTHON!
HISSS
15

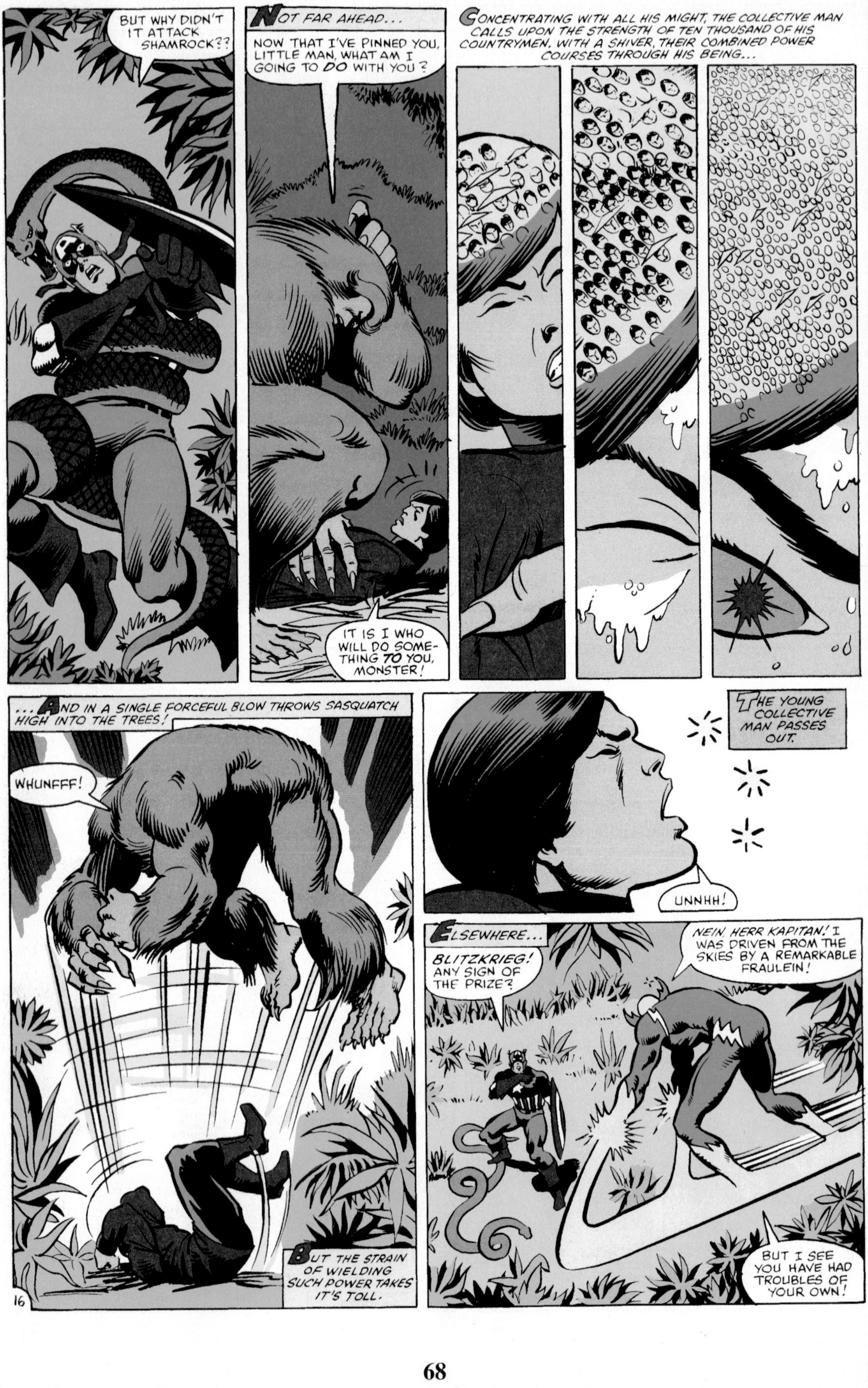
BUT WHY DIDN'T IT ATTACK SHAMROCK??
NOT FAR AHEAD...
NOW THAT I'VE PINNED YOU, LITTLE MAN, WHAT AM I GOING TO DO WITH YOU?
IT IS I WHO WILL DO SOMETHING TO YOU, MONSTER!
CONCENTRATING WITH ALL HIS MIGHT, THE COLLECTIVE MAN CALLS UPON THE STRENGTH OF TEN THOUSAND OF HIS COUNTRYMEN. WITH A SHIVER, THEIR COMBINED POWER COURSES THROUGH HIS BEING...
...AND IN A SINGLE FORCEFUL BLOW THROWS SASQUATCH HIGH INTO THE TREES!
WHUNFFF!
BUT THE STRAIN OF WIELDING SUCH POWER TAKES IT'S TOLL.
THE YOUNG COLLECTIVE MAN PASSES OUT.
UNNHH!
ELSEWHERE...
BLITZKRIEG! ANY SIGN OF THE PRIZE?
NEIN, HERR KAPITAN! I WAS DRIVEN FROM THE SKIES BY A REMARKABLE FRAULEIN!
BUT I SEE YOU HAVE HAD TROUBLES OF YOUR OWN!
16

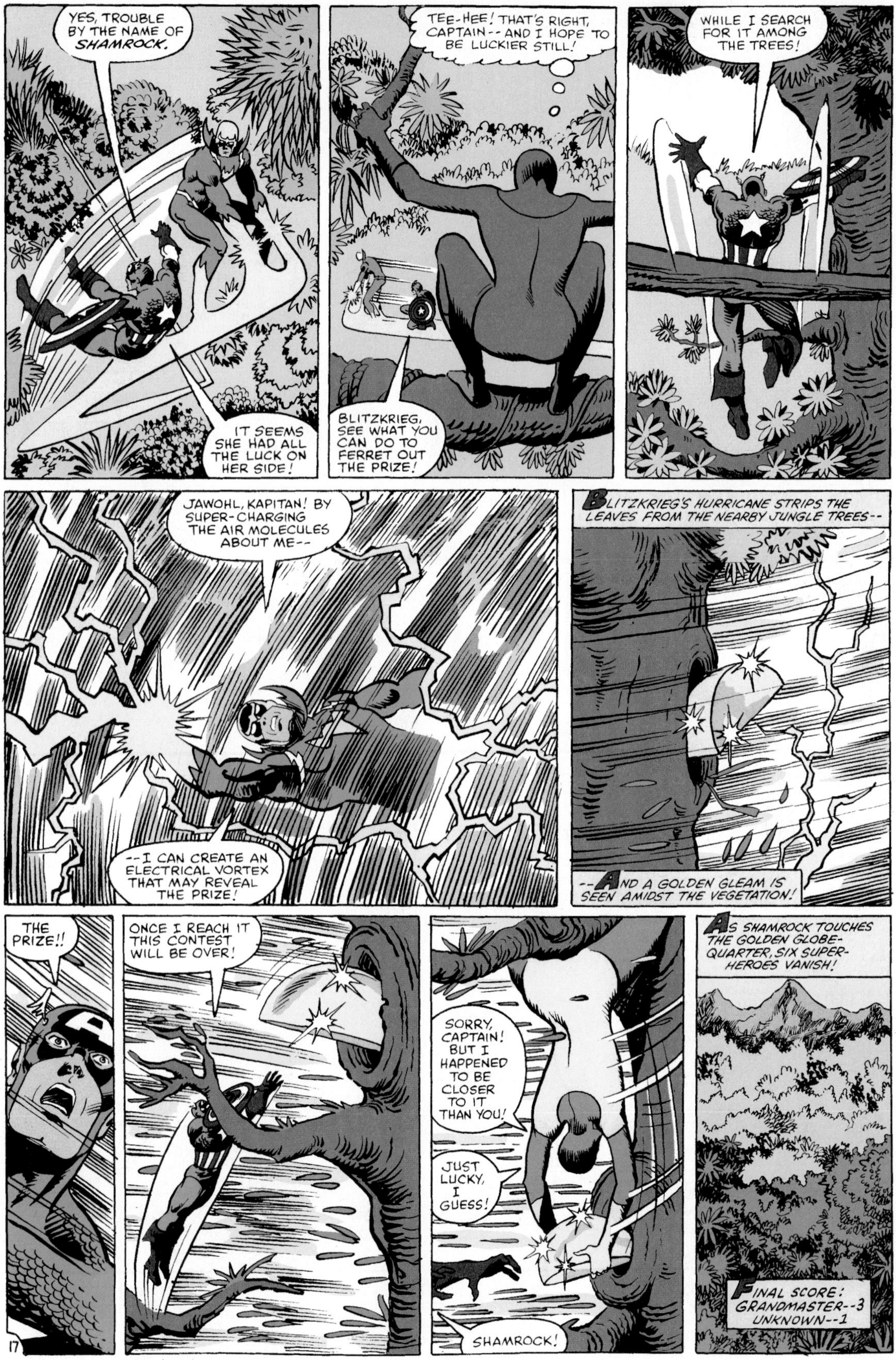
YES, TROUBLE BY THE NAME OF SHAMROCK.
IT SEEMS SHE HAD ALL THE LUCK ON HER SIDE!
TEE-HEE! THAT'S RIGHT, CAPTAIN--AND I HOPE TO BE LUCKIER STILL!
BLITZKRIEG, SEE WHAT YOU CAN DO TO FERRET OUT THE PRIZE!
WHILE I SEARCH FOR IT AMONG THE TREES!
JAWOHL, KAPITAN! BY SUPER-CHARGING THE AIR MOLECULES ABOUT ME--
--I CAN CREATE AN ELECTRICAL VORTEX THAT MAY REVEAL THE PRIZE!
BLITZKRIEG'S HURRICANE STRIPS THE LEAVES FROM THE NEARBY JUNGLE TREES--
--AND A GOLDEN GLEAM IS SEEN AMIDST THE VEGETATION!
THE PRIZE!!
17
ONCE I REACH IT THIS CONTEST WILL BE OVER!
SORRY, CAPTAIN! BUT I HAPPENED TO BE CLOSER TO IT THAN YOU!
JUST LUCKY, I GUESS!
SHAMROCK!
AS SHAMROCK TOUCHES THE GOLDEN GLOBE-QUARTER, SIX SUPER-HEROES VANISH!
FINAL SCORE: GRANDMASTER--3 UNKNOWN--1

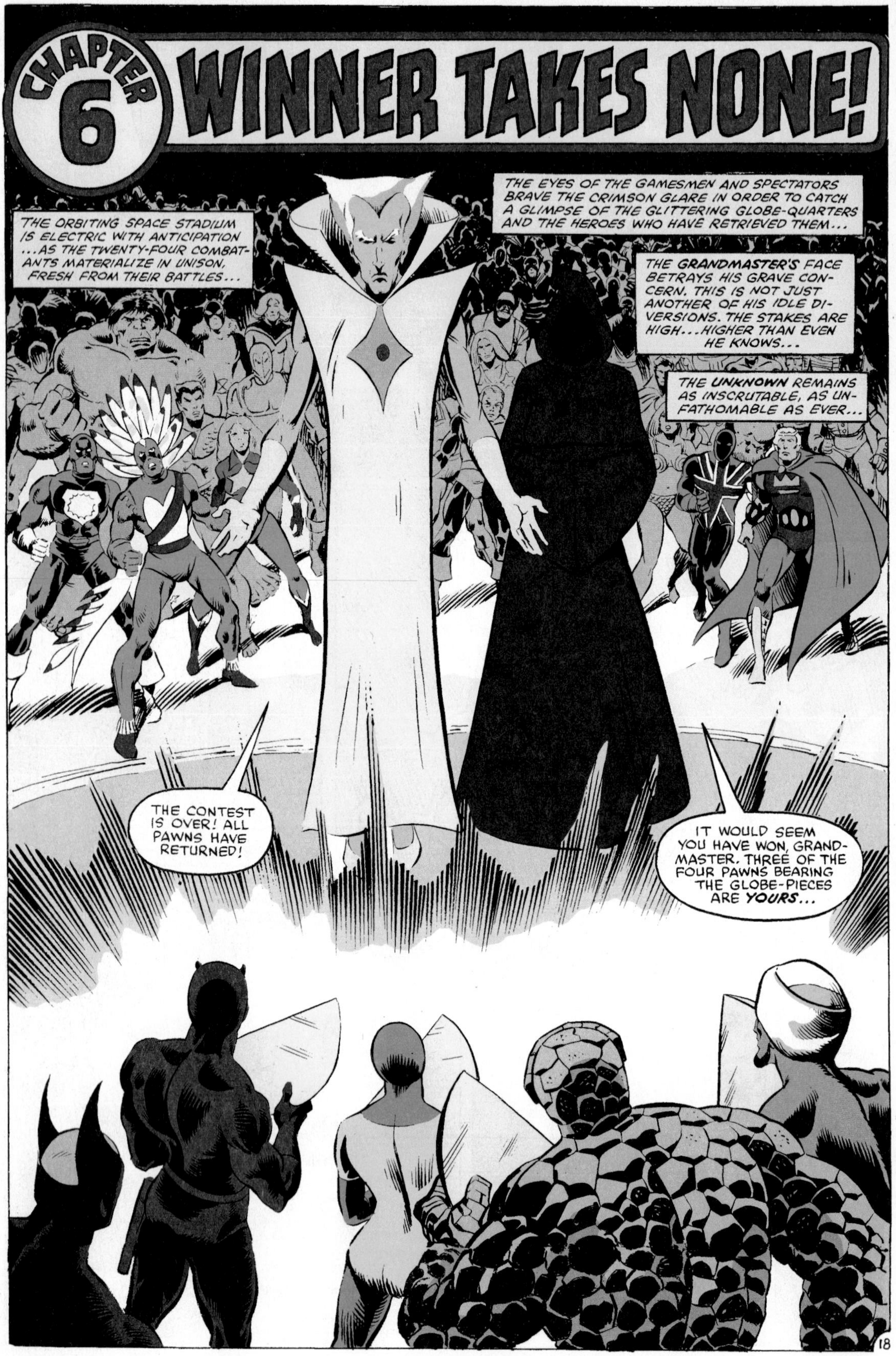
CHAPTER 6
WINNER TAKES NONE!
THE ORBITING SPACE STADIUM IS ELECTRIC WITH ANTICIPATION ...AS THE TWENTY-FOUR COMBATANTS MATERIALIZE IN UNISON, FRESH FROM THEIR BATTLES...
THE EYES OF THE GAMESMEN AND SPECTATORS BRAVE THE CRIMSON GLARE IN ORDER TO CATCH A GLIMPSE OF THE GLITTERING GLOBE-QUARTERS AND THE HEROES WHO HAVE RETRIEVED THEM...
THE GRANDMASTER'S FACE BETRAYS HIS GRAVE CONCERN. THIS IS NOT JUST ANOTHER OF HIS IDLE DIVERSIONS. THE STAKES ARE HIGH...HIGHER THAN EVEN HE KNOWS...
THE UNKNOWN REMAINS AS INSCRUTABLE, AS UNFATHOMABLE AS EVER...
THE CONTEST IS OVER! ALL PAWNS HAVE RETURNED!
IT WOULD SEEM YOU HAVE WON, GRANDMASTER. THREE OF THE FOUR PAWNS BEARING THE GLOBE-PIECES ARE YOURS...
18

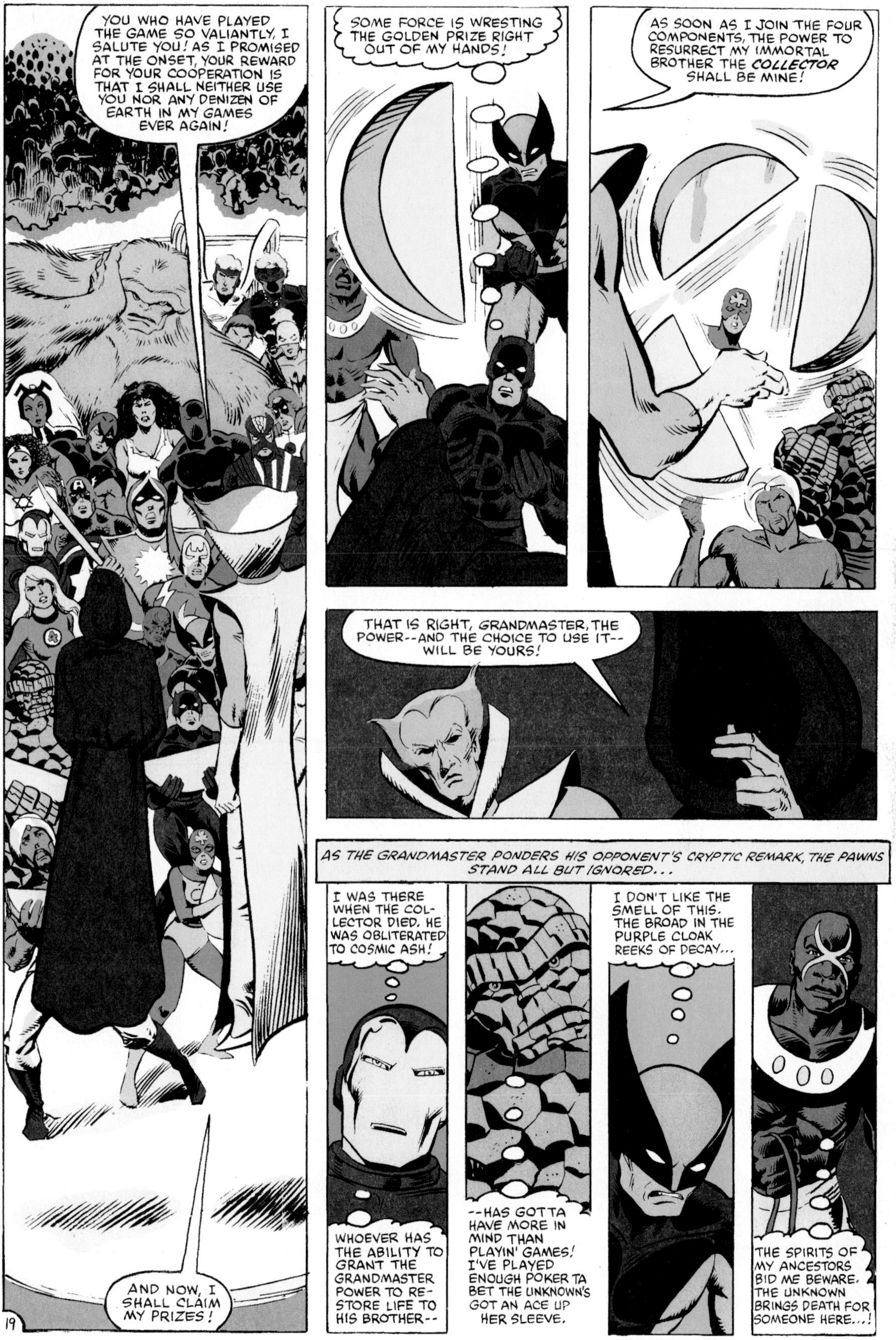
YOU WHO HAVE PLAYED THE GAME SO VALIANTLY, I SALUTE YOU! AS I PROMISED AT THE ONSET, YOUR REWARD FOR YOUR COOPERATION IS THAT I SHALL NEITHER USE YOU NOR ANY DENIZEN OF EARTH IN MY GAMES EVER AGAIN!
AND NOW, I SHALL CLAIM MY PRIZES!
19
SOME FORCE IS WRESTING THE GOLDEN PRIZE RIGHT OUT OF MY HANDS!
AS SOON AS I JOIN THE FOUR COMPONENTS, THE POWER TO RESURRECT MY IMMORTAL BROTHER THE COLLECTOR SHALL BE MINE!
THAT IS RIGHT, GRANDMASTER, THE POWER--AND THE CHOICE TO USE IT--WILL BE YOURS!
AS THE GRANDMASTER PONDERS HIS OPPONENT'S CRYPTIC REMARK, THE PAWNS STAND ALL BUT IGNORED...
I WAS THERE WHEN THE COLLECTOR DIED. HE WAS OBLITERATED TO COSMIC ASH!
WHOEVER HAS THE ABILITY TO GRANT THE GRANDMASTER POWER TO RESTORE LIFE TO HIS BROTHER--
--HAS GOTTA HAVE MORE IN MIND THAN PLAYIN' GAMES! I'VE PLAYED ENOUGH POKER TA BET THE UNKNOWN'S GOT AN ACE UP HER SLEEVE.
I DON'T LIKE THE SMELL OF THIS. THE BROAD IN THE PURPLE CLOAK REEKS OF DECAY...
THE SPIRITS OF MY ANCESTORS BID ME BEWARE. THE UNKNOWN BRINGS DEATH FOR SOMEONE HERE...!

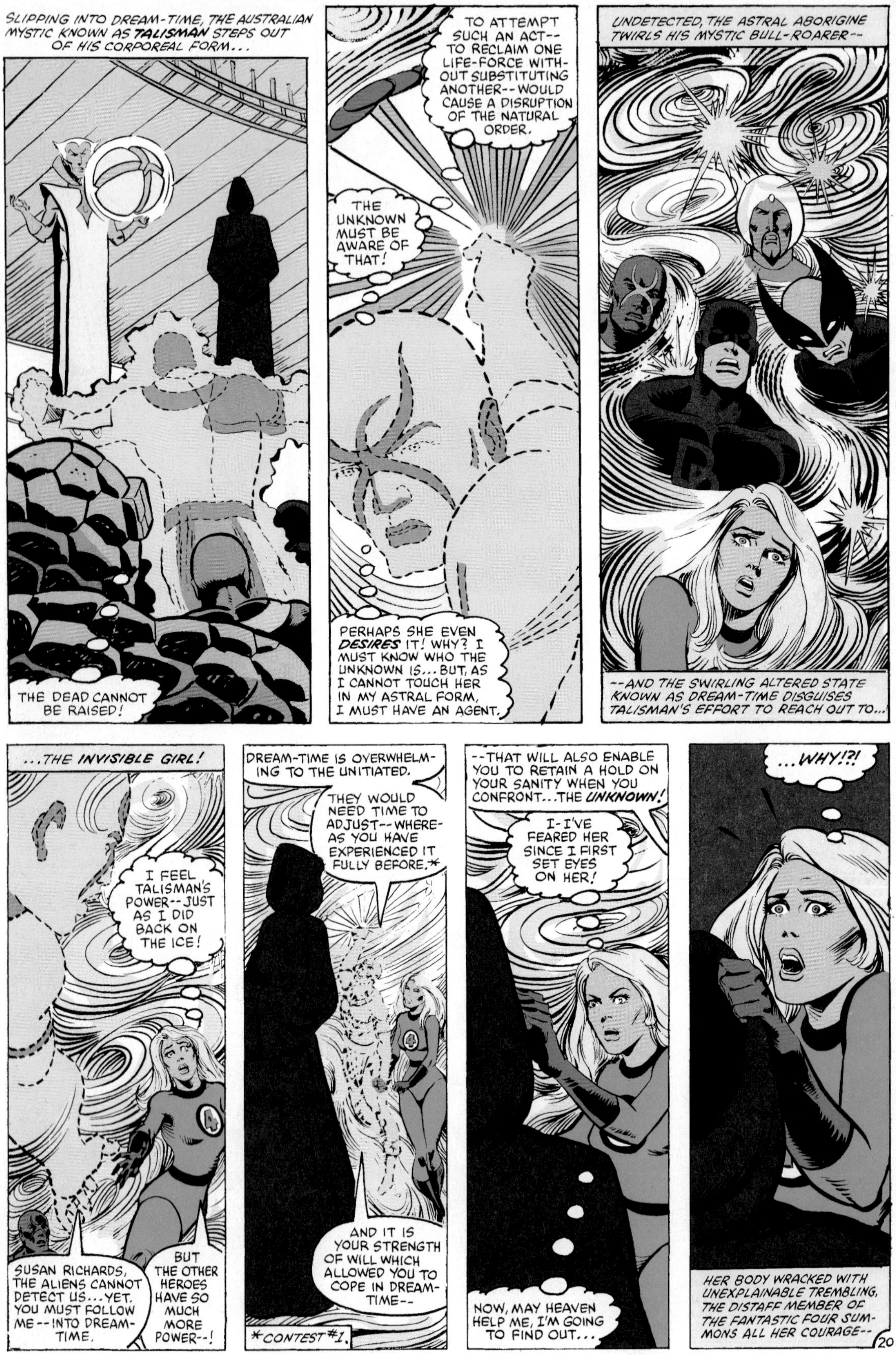
SLIPPING INTO DREAM-TIME, THE AUSTRALIAN MYSTIC KNOWN AS TALISMAN STEPS OUT OF HIS CORPOREAL FORM...
THE DEAD CANNOT BE RAISED!
TO ATTEMPT SUCH AN ACT--TO RECLAIM ONE LIFE-FORCE WITHOUT SUBSTITUTING ANOTHER--WOULD CAUSE A DISRUPTION OF THE NATURAL ORDER.
THE UNKNOWN MUST BE AWARE OF THAT!
PERHAPS SHE EVEN DESIRES IT! WHY? I MUST KNOW WHO THE UNKNOWN IS... BUT, AS I CANNOT TOUCH HER IN MY ASTRAL FORM, I MUST HAVE AN AGENT.
UNDETECTED, THE ASTRAL ABORIGINE TWIRLS HIS MYSTIC BULL-ROARER--
--AND THE SWIRLING ALTERED STATE KNOWN AS DREAM-TIME DISGUISES TALISMAN'S EFFORT TO REACH OUT TO...
...THE INVISIBLE GIRL!
I FEEL TALISMAN'S POWER--JUST AS I DID BACK ON THE ICE!
SUSAN RICHARDS, THE ALIENS CANNOT DETECT US...YET. YOU MUST FOLLOW ME--INTO DREAM-TIME.
BUT THE OTHER HEROES HAVE SO MUCH MORE POWER--!
DREAM-TIME IS OVERWHELMING TO THE UNITIATED.
THEY WOULD NEED TIME TO ADJUST--WHEREAS YOU HAVE EXPERIENCED IT FULLY BEFORE.*
AND IT IS YOUR STRENGTH OF WILL WHICH ALLOWED YOU TO COPE IN DREAM-TIME--
*CONTEST #1.
--THAT WILL ALSO ENABLE YOU TO RETAIN A HOLD ON YOUR SANITY WHEN YOU CONFRONT...THE UNKNOWN!
I-I'VE FEARED HER SINCE I FIRST SET EYES ON HER!
NOW, MAY HEAVEN HELP ME, I'M GOING TO FIND OUT...
...WHY!?!
HER BODY WRACKED WITH UNEXPLAINABLE TREMBLING, THE DISTAFF MEMBER OF THE FANTASTIC FOUR SUMMONS ALL HER COURAGE--
20

--AND, TEARING BACK THE UNKNOWN'S COWL, REVEALS THE GRINNING FEATURES OF... *DEATH!*

COLD-- SO COLD!

HER HORRIFIC APPEARANCE MAGNIFIED BY THE HALLUCINOGENIC EFFECTS OF DREAM-TIME, DEATH FILLS THE ASSEMBLED HEROES WITH FEAR OF HER PRESENCE!

THE UNKNOWN IS NOW KNOWN.

YES, THE UNKNOWN IS *DEATH.* WHO ELSE COULD HOLD ALL YOU HEROES--AND YOUR WORLD--IN THRALL...

--THAN ONE WHOSE DOMINION EXTENDS OVER ALL?

AND *YOU,* GRANDMASTER-- DID YOU KNOW YOUR OPPONENT TO BE THE GRIMMEST *GAMESMAN* OF THEM ALL?

OF COURSE! WHO ELSE COULD POSSESS THE POWER TO RESURRECT AN IMMORTAL?

STILL, THE HUMAN'S FEARS ARE WARRANTED.

I NEGLECTED TO TELL YOU, GRANDMASTER, THAT THE GOLDEN GLOBE IS BUT AN EMPTY INSTRUMENT. IT NEEDS A LIFE-FORCE TO ENERGIZE IT.

YES, IT CAN RESTORE THE COLLECTOR TO LIFE, PROVIDING THAT ONE OF EQUAL POWER *DIES* IN HIS PLACE. ONE SUCH AS *YOU,* GRANDMASTER.

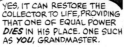

THEN YOU HAVE MISREPRESENTED THE TERMS OF OUR CONTEST. YOU HAVE *CHEATED!*

DEATH NEVER CHEATS. MY RULES ARE MY OWN, AND ALL THE UNIVERSE MUST OBEY THEM.

21

73

YOU HAVE WON THE POWER TO RESTORE YOUR BROTHER, GRANDMASTER-- THERE IS NO ONE TO SAY YOU MUST *USE* IT.

YET... SUCH WAS THE PURPOSE OF THE GAME! I AM THE *GRANDMASTER!* NEVER-- IN A THOUSAND GAMES ON A THOUSAND WORLDS-- HAVE I QUIT THE TABLE ERE THE GAME WAS THROUGH!

THERE IS AN ALTERNATIVE, GRANDMASTER, AS I SAID, THE GOLDEN GLOBE *EXCHANGES* LIFE FOR LIFE.

IF YOU ARE UNWILLING TO SACRIFICE *YOURS,* THE COMBINED LIFE ENERGIES OF THESE ASSEMBLED EARTH HEROES SHOULD SUFFICE.

SUCH WAS NOT THE TERMS OF MY BARGAIN!

IN WINNING FOR ME, THEY HAVE ENSURED THAT NEVER AGAIN SHALL THE GRANDMASTER USE THEM OR THEIR WORLD AS PAWNS!

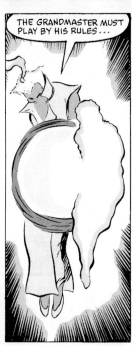

THE GRANDMASTER MUST PLAY BY HIS RULES...

...TO THE END!

THERE IS A RIPPLE IN SPACE, A FLUX IN THE FLOW OF THE UNIVERSE...

...AND ONE ELDER GOD DIES TO BRING ABOUT THE REBIRTH OF ANOTHER!

I... LIVE!?! WHAT HAS TRANSPIRED HERE?!

THAT IS THE UNIFORM OF MY BROTHER IN THAT SMOLDERING PILE OF ASHES!

'TWAS YOUR DOING, DEATH! I'M CERTAIN! I WILL FORCE YOU TO RESTORE HIM... EVEN IF I MUST COLLECT EVERY HERO IN THE COSMOS TO FIGHT YOU!

YOU WOULD LOSE.

22

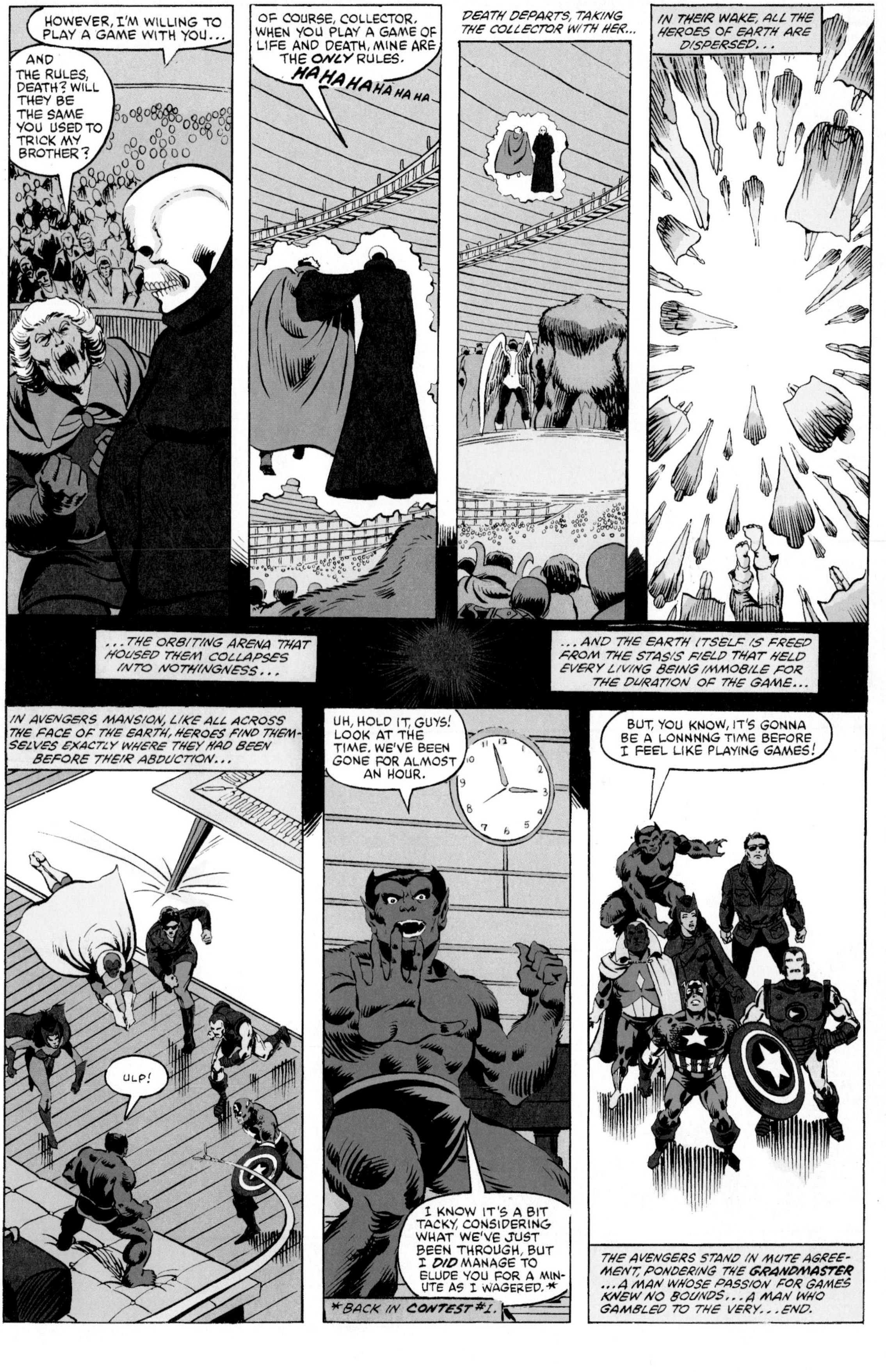

HOWEVER, I'M WILLING TO PLAY A GAME WITH YOU...
AND THE RULES, DEATH? WILL THEY BE THE SAME YOU USED TO TRICK MY BROTHER?
OF COURSE, COLLECTOR. WHEN YOU PLAY A GAME OF LIFE AND DEATH, MINE ARE THE ONLY RULES.
HAHAHAHAHAHAHA
DEATH DEPARTS, TAKING THE COLLECTOR WITH HER...
IN THEIR WAKE, ALL THE HEROES OF EARTH ARE DISPERSED...
...THE ORBITING ARENA THAT HOUSED THEM COLLAPSES INTO NOTHINGNESS...
...AND THE EARTH ITSELF IS FREED FROM THE STASIS FIELD THAT HELD EVERY LIVING BEING IMMOBILE FOR THE DURATION OF THE GAME...
IN AVENGERS MANSION, LIKE ALL ACROSS THE FACE OF THE EARTH, HEROES FIND THEMSELVES EXACTLY WHERE THEY HAD BEEN BEFORE THEIR ABDUCTION...
ULP!
UH, HOLD IT, GUYS! LOOK AT THE TIME. WE'VE BEEN GONE FOR ALMOST AN HOUR.
I KNOW IT'S A BIT TACKY, CONSIDERING WHAT WE'VE JUST BEEN THROUGH, BUT I DID MANAGE TO ELUDE YOU FOR A MINUTE AS I WAGERED.*
*BACK IN CONTEST #1.
BUT, YOU KNOW, IT'S GONNA BE A LONNNNG TIME BEFORE I FEEL LIKE PLAYING GAMES!
THE AVENGERS STAND IN MUTE AGREEMENT, PONDERING THE GRANDMASTER ...A MAN WHOSE PASSION FOR GAMES KNEW NO BOUNDS...A MAN WHO GAMBLED TO THE VERY...END.

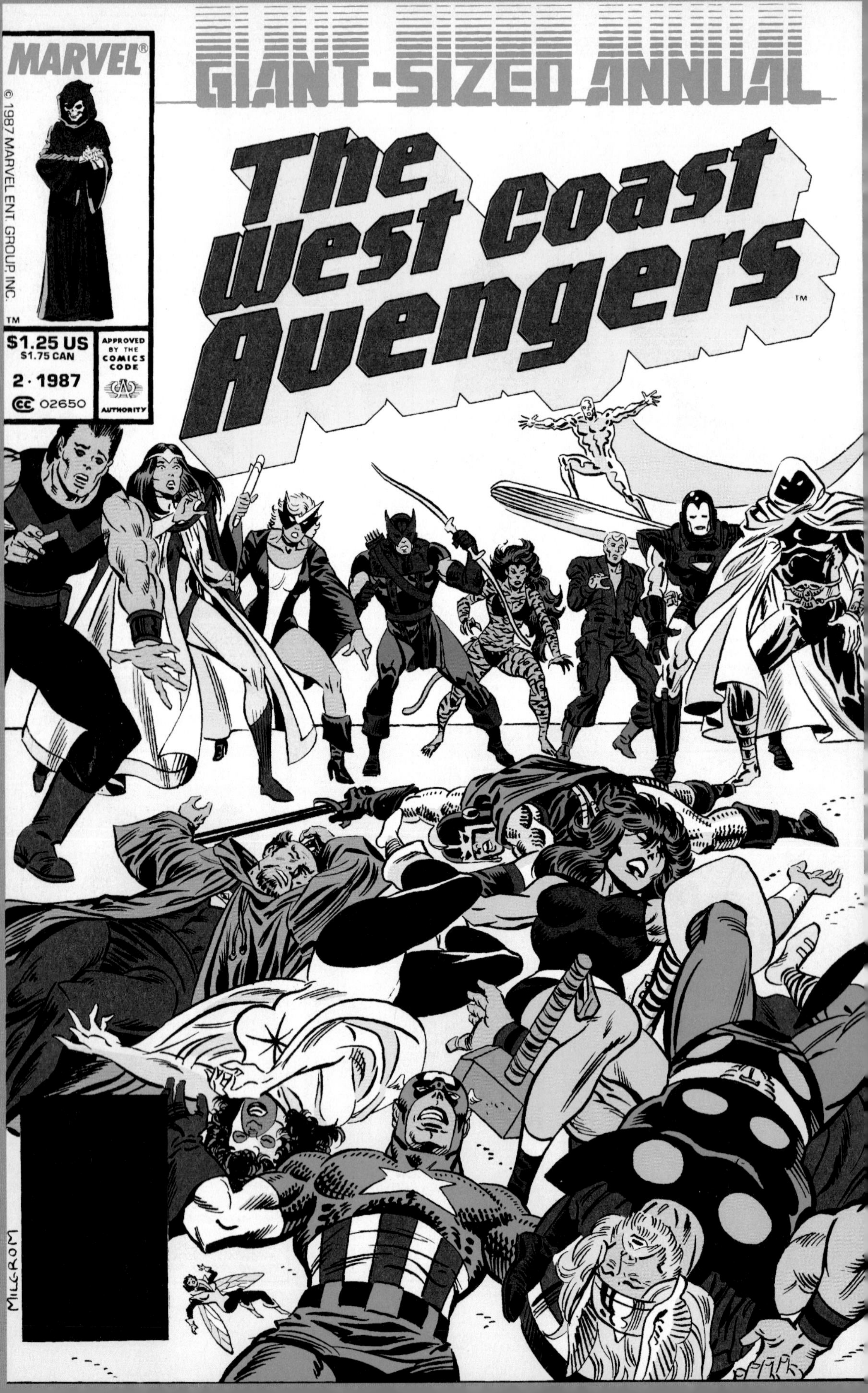

GIANT-SIZED ANNUAL
The West Coast Avengers™
MARVEL®
© 1987 MARVEL ENT. GROUP, INC.
TM
$1.25 US
$1.75 CAN
2 · 1987
CC 02650
APPROVED BY THE COMICS CODE AUTHORITY
MILGROM

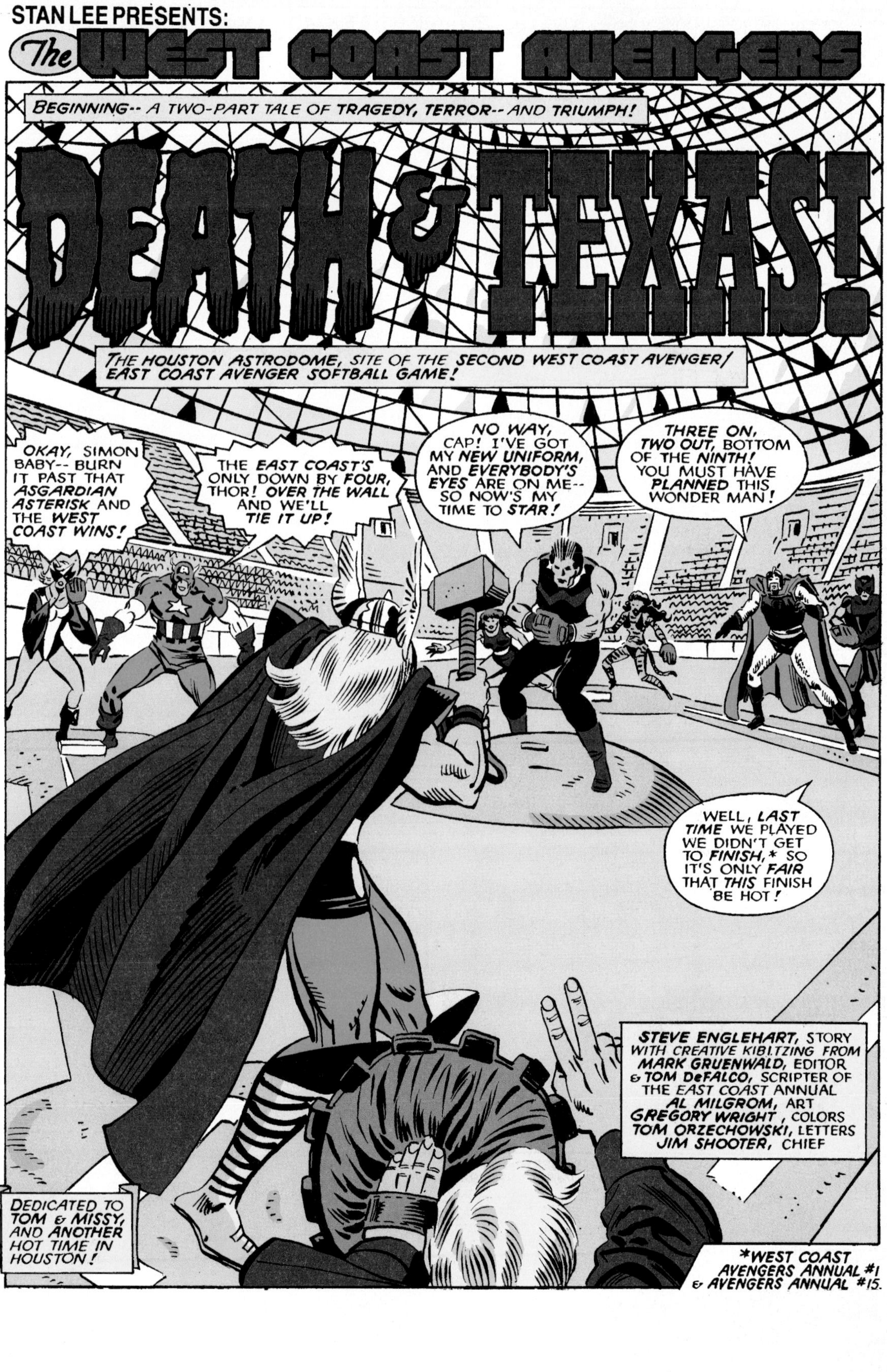

STAN LEE PRESENTS:
The WEST COAST AVENGERS
BEGINNING-- A TWO-PART TALE OF TRAGEDY, TERROR-- AND TRIUMPH!
DEATH & TEXAS!
THE HOUSTON ASTRODOME, SITE OF THE SECOND WEST COAST AVENGER/ EAST COAST AVENGER SOFTBALL GAME!
OKAY, SIMON BABY-- BURN IT PAST THAT ASGARDIAN ASTERISK AND THE WEST COAST WINS!
THE EAST COAST'S ONLY DOWN BY FOUR, THOR! OVER THE WALL AND WE'LL TIE IT UP!
NO WAY, CAP! I'VE GOT MY NEW UNIFORM, AND EVERYBODY'S EYES ARE ON ME-- SO NOW'S MY TIME TO STAR!
THREE ON, TWO OUT, BOTTOM OF THE NINTH! YOU MUST HAVE PLANNED THIS, WONDER MAN!
WELL, LAST TIME WE PLAYED WE DIDN'T GET TO FINISH,* SO IT'S ONLY FAIR THAT THIS FINISH BE HOT!
STEVE ENGLEHART, STORY WITH CREATIVE KIBITZING FROM MARK GRUENWALD, EDITOR & TOM DeFALCO, SCRIPTER OF THE EAST COAST ANNUAL AL MILGROM, ART GREGORY WRIGHT, COLORS TOM ORZECHOWSKI, LETTERS JIM SHOOTER, CHIEF
DEDICATED TO TOM & MISSY, AND ANOTHER HOT TIME IN HOUSTON!
*WEST COAST AVENGERS ANNUAL #1 & AVENGERS ANNUAL #15.

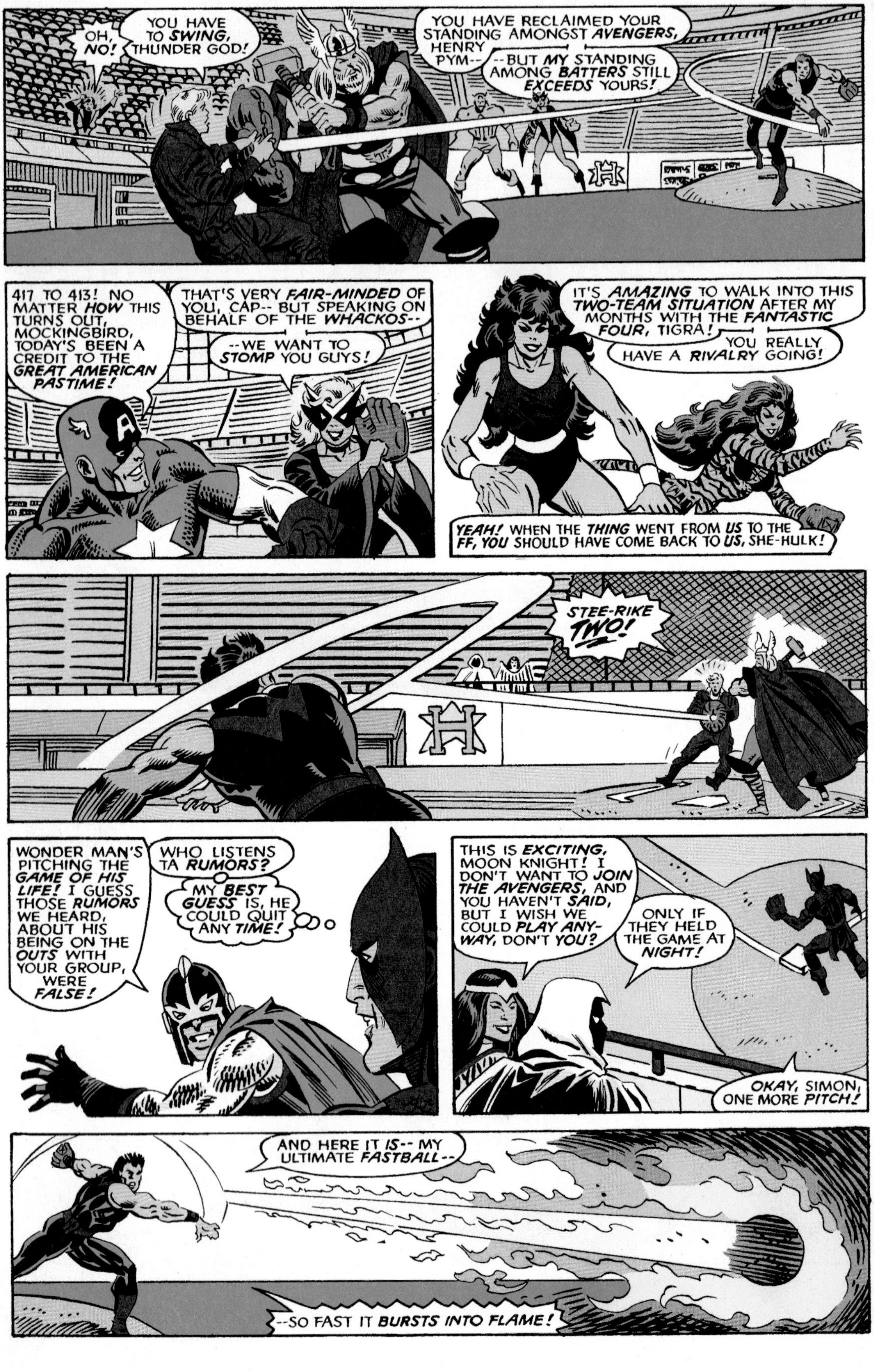
OH, NO!
YOU HAVE TO SWING, THUNDER GOD!
YOU HAVE RECLAIMED YOUR STANDING AMONGST AVENGERS, HENRY PYM--
--BUT MY STANDING AMONG BATTERS STILL EXCEEDS YOURS!
417 TO 413! NO MATTER HOW THIS TURNS OUT, MOCKINGBIRD, TODAY'S BEEN A CREDIT TO THE GREAT AMERICAN PASTIME!
THAT'S VERY FAIR-MINDED OF YOU, CAP-- BUT SPEAKING ON BEHALF OF THE WHACKOS--
--WE WANT TO STOMP YOU GUYS!
IT'S AMAZING TO WALK INTO THIS TWO-TEAM SITUATION AFTER MY MONTHS WITH THE FANTASTIC FOUR, TIGRA!
YOU REALLY HAVE A RIVALRY GOING!
YEAH! WHEN THE THING WENT FROM US TO THE FF, YOU SHOULD HAVE COME BACK TO US, SHE-HULK!
STEE-RIKE TWO!
WONDER MAN'S PITCHING THE GAME OF HIS LIFE! I GUESS THOSE RUMORS WE HEARD, ABOUT HIS BEING ON THE OUTS WITH YOUR GROUP, WERE FALSE!
WHO LISTENS TA RUMORS?
MY BEST GUESS IS, HE COULD QUIT ANY TIME!
THIS IS EXCITING, MOON KNIGHT! I DON'T WANT TO JOIN THE AVENGERS, AND YOU HAVEN'T SAID, BUT I WISH WE COULD PLAY ANY-WAY, DON'T YOU?
ONLY IF THEY HELD THE GAME AT NIGHT!
OKAY, SIMON, ONE MORE PITCH!
AND HERE IT IS-- MY ULTIMATE FASTBALL--
--SO FAST IT BURSTS INTO FLAME!

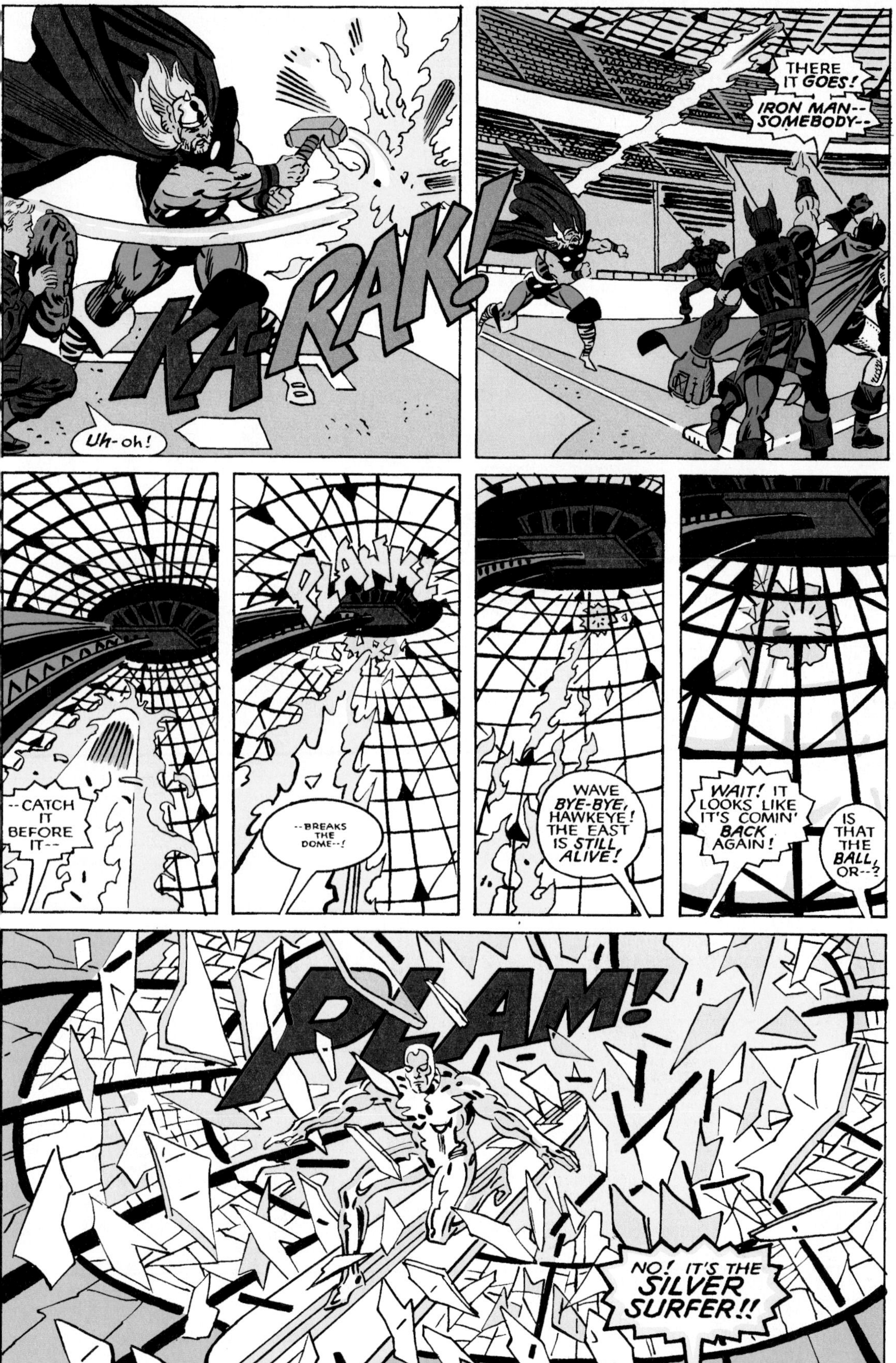
KA-RAK!
Uh-oh!
THERE IT GOES!
IRON MAN-- SOMEBODY--
--CATCH IT BEFORE IT--
PLANK!
--BREAKS THE DOME--!
WAVE BYE-BYE, HAWKEYE! THE EAST IS STILL ALIVE!
WAIT! IT LOOKS LIKE IT'S COMIN' BACK AGAIN!
IS THAT THE BALL, OR--?
PLLAM!
NO! IT'S THE SILVER SURFER!!

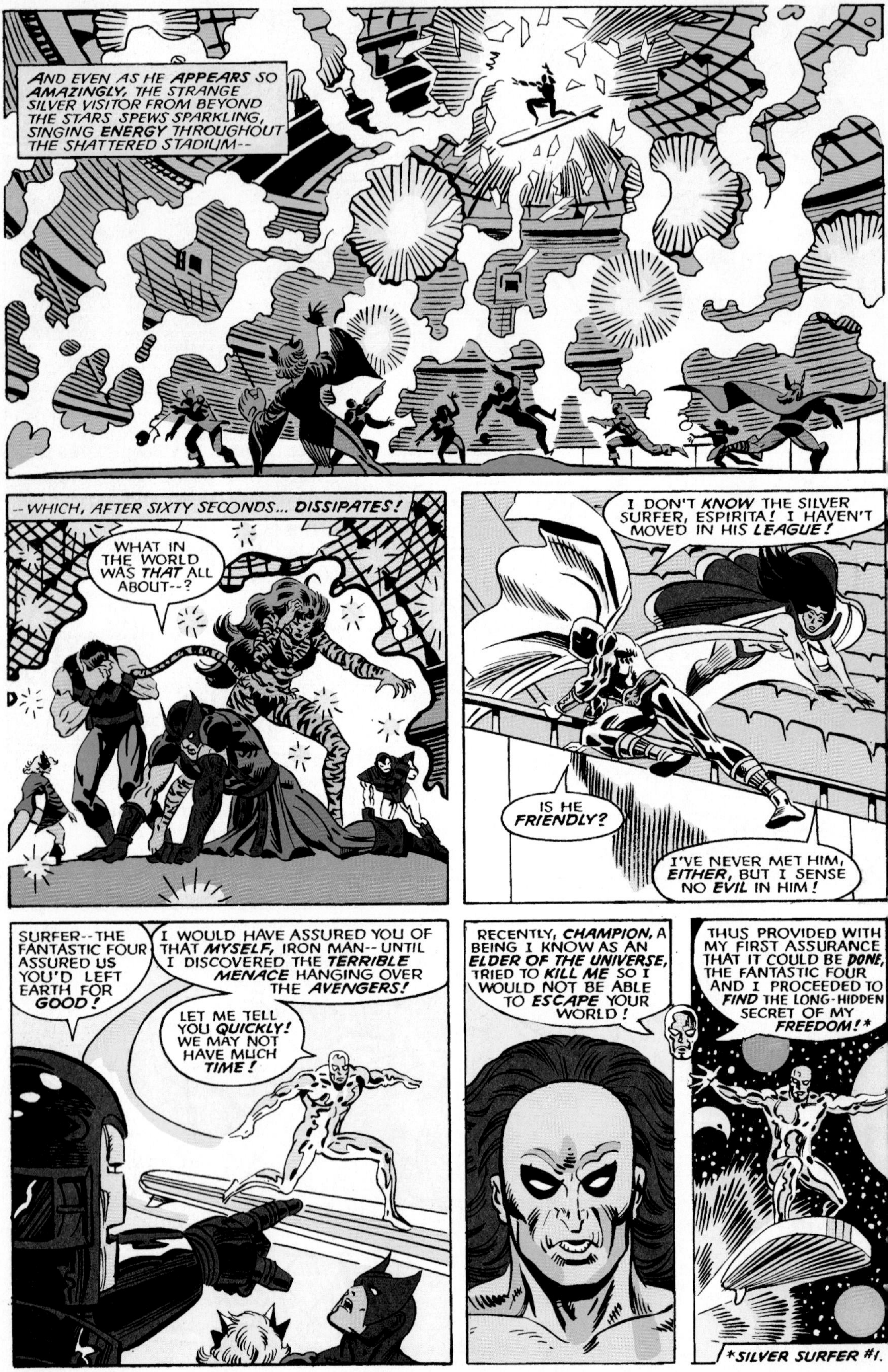
AND EVEN AS HE APPEARS SO AMAZINGLY, THE STRANGE SILVER VISITOR FROM BEYOND THE STARS SPEWS SPARKLING, SINGING ENERGY THROUGHOUT THE SHATTERED STADIUM--
--WHICH, AFTER SIXTY SECONDS... DISSIPATES!
WHAT IN THE WORLD WAS THAT ALL ABOUT--?
I DON'T KNOW THE SILVER SURFER, ESPIRITA! I HAVEN'T MOVED IN HIS LEAGUE!
IS HE FRIENDLY?
I'VE NEVER MET HIM, EITHER, BUT I SENSE NO EVIL IN HIM!
SURFER--THE FANTASTIC FOUR ASSURED US YOU'D LEFT EARTH FOR GOOD!
I WOULD HAVE ASSURED YOU OF THAT MYSELF, IRON MAN-- UNTIL I DISCOVERED THE TERRIBLE MENACE HANGING OVER THE AVENGERS!
LET ME TELL YOU QUICKLY! WE MAY NOT HAVE MUCH TIME!
RECENTLY, CHAMPION, A BEING I KNOW AS AN ELDER OF THE UNIVERSE, TRIED TO KILL ME SO I WOULD NOT BE ABLE TO ESCAPE YOUR WORLD!
THUS PROVIDED WITH MY FIRST ASSURANCE THAT IT COULD BE DONE, THE FANTASTIC FOUR AND I PROCEEDED TO FIND THE LONG-HIDDEN SECRET OF MY FREEDOM!*
*SILVER SURFER #1.

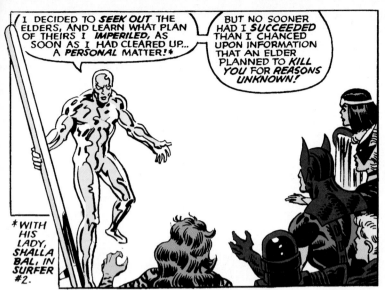

I DECIDED TO *SEEK OUT* THE ELDERS, AND LEARN WHAT PLAN OF THEIRS I *IMPERILED*, AS SOON AS I HAD CLEARED UP... A *PERSONAL MATTER!**

BUT NO SOONER HAD I *SUCCEEDED* THAN I CHANCED UPON INFORMATION THAT AN ELDER PLANNED TO *KILL* YOU FOR *REASONS UNKNOWN!*

*WITH HIS LADY, SHALLA BAL, IN SURFER #2.

I RACED *BACK* ACROSS THE COSMOS WITH ALL THE SPEED MY *POWER COSMIC* COULD *PROVIDE!* AS I *NEARED* YOUR WORLD, I SAW THE ELDER'S ELDRITCH ENERGY BOLT *ALSO* APPROACHING--!

AND IT WAS A *PHOTO FINISH,* JUST LIKE OUR *GAME--RIGHT,* EAKOS?*

*EAST COAST AVENGERS.

EAKOS--?

HAWKEYE! THE *WASP--* IN THE *STANDS--!*

OH, *NO!* CAN I HAVE BEEN *TOO LATE,* AFTER ALL--?

*NO!* IT *CAN'T* BE! IT---

--IT *IS!*

THE *EAST COAST* AVENGERS--

--THEY'RE *ALL DEAD!*

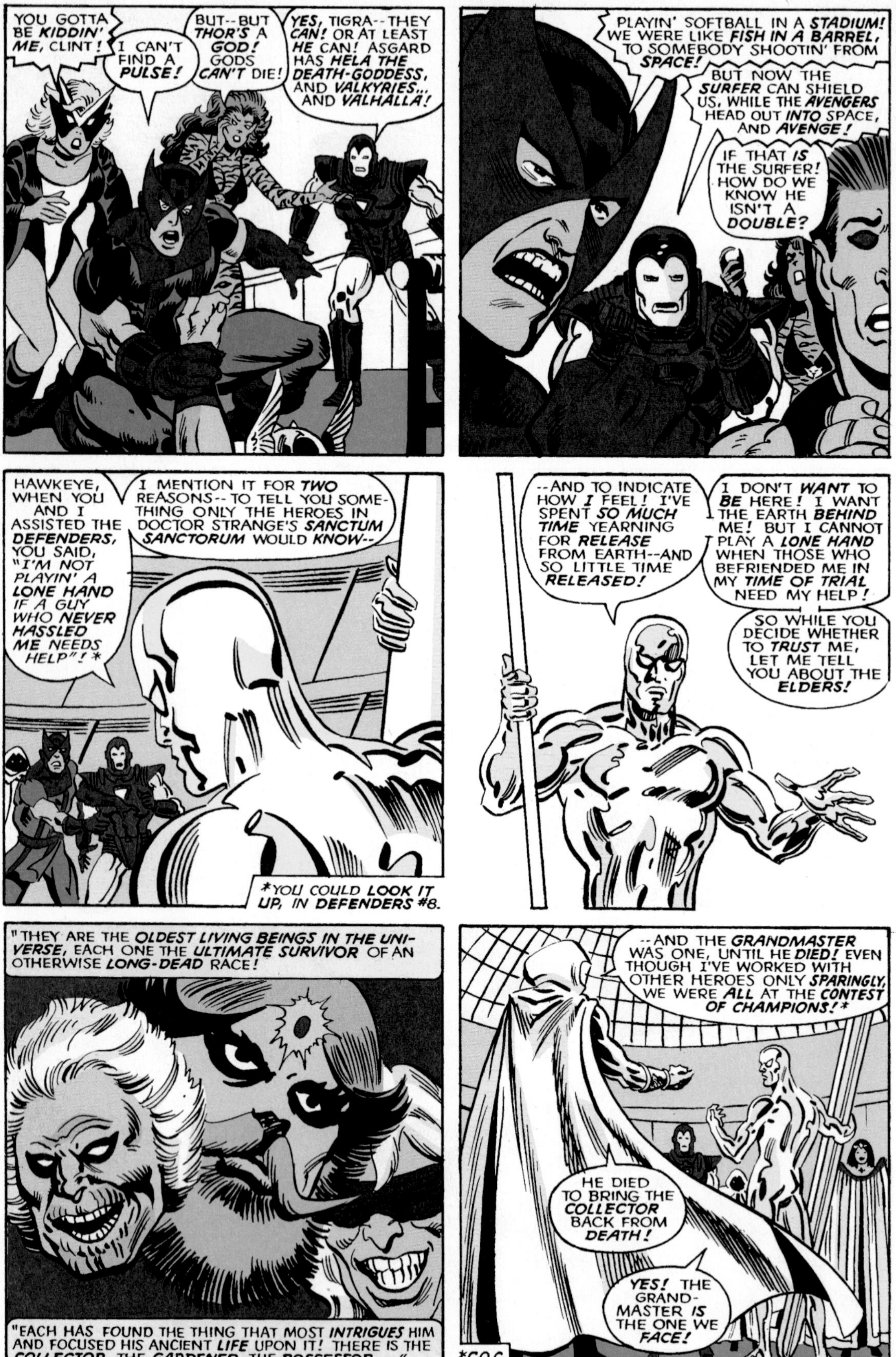
YOU GOTTA BE KIDDIN' ME, CLINT!
I CAN'T FIND A PULSE!
BUT--BUT THOR'S A GOD! GODS CAN'T DIE!
YES, TIGRA--THEY CAN! OR AT LEAST HE CAN! ASGARD HAS HELA THE DEATH-GODDESS, AND VALKYRIES... AND VALHALLA!
PLAYIN' SOFTBALL IN A STADIUM! WE WERE LIKE FISH IN A BARREL, TO SOMEBODY SHOOTIN' FROM SPACE!
BUT NOW THE SURFER CAN SHIELD US, WHILE THE AVENGERS HEAD OUT INTO SPACE, AND AVENGE!
IF THAT IS THE SURFER! HOW DO WE KNOW HE ISN'T A DOUBLE?
HAWKEYE, WHEN YOU AND I ASSISTED THE DEFENDERS, YOU SAID, "I'M NOT PLAYIN' A LONE HAND IF A GUY WHO NEVER HASSLED ME NEEDS HELP"!*
I MENTION IT FOR TWO REASONS-- TO TELL YOU SOMETHING ONLY THE HEROES IN DOCTOR STRANGE'S SANCTUM SANCTORUM WOULD KNOW--
*YOU COULD LOOK IT UP, IN DEFENDERS #8.
--AND TO INDICATE HOW I FEEL! I'VE SPENT SO MUCH TIME YEARNING FOR RELEASE FROM EARTH--AND SO LITTLE TIME RELEASED!
I DON'T WANT TO BE HERE! I WANT THE EARTH BEHIND ME! BUT I CANNOT PLAY A LONE HAND WHEN THOSE WHO BEFRIENDED ME IN MY TIME OF TRIAL NEED MY HELP!
SO WHILE YOU DECIDE WHETHER TO TRUST ME, LET ME TELL YOU ABOUT THE ELDERS!
"THEY ARE THE OLDEST LIVING BEINGS IN THE UNIVERSE, EACH ONE THE ULTIMATE SURVIVOR OF AN OTHERWISE LONG-DEAD RACE!
"EACH HAS FOUND THE THING THAT MOST INTRIGUES HIM AND FOCUSED HIS ANCIENT LIFE UPON IT! THERE IS THE COLLECTOR, THE GARDENER, THE POSSESSOR---"
--AND THE GRANDMASTER WAS ONE, UNTIL HE DIED! EVEN THOUGH I'VE WORKED WITH OTHER HEROES ONLY SPARINGLY, WE WERE ALL AT THE CONTEST OF CHAMPIONS!*
HE DIED TO BRING THE COLLECTOR BACK FROM DEATH!
YES! THE GRANDMASTER IS THE ONE WE FACE!
*C.O.C. #1-3.

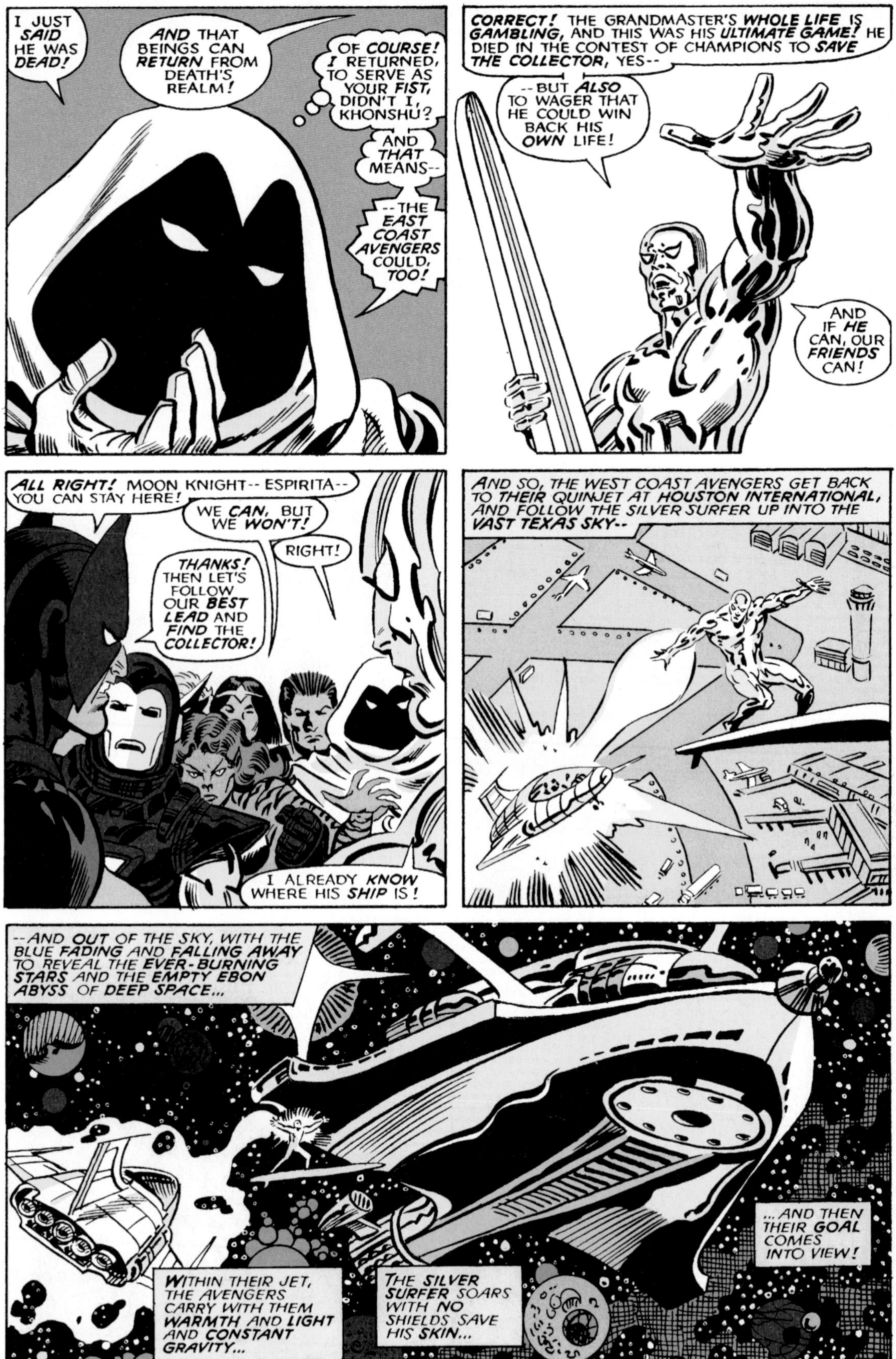

I JUST SAID HE WAS DEAD!
AND THAT BEINGS CAN RETURN FROM DEATH'S REALM!
OF COURSE! I RETURNED, TO SERVE AS YOUR FIST, DIDN'T I, KHONSHU?
AND THAT MEANS--
--THE EAST COAST AVENGERS COULD, TOO!
CORRECT! THE GRANDMASTER'S WHOLE LIFE IS GAMBLING, AND THIS WAS HIS ULTIMATE GAME! HE DIED IN THE CONTEST OF CHAMPIONS TO SAVE THE COLLECTOR, YES--
--BUT ALSO TO WAGER THAT HE COULD WIN BACK HIS OWN LIFE!
AND IF HE CAN, OUR FRIENDS CAN!
ALL RIGHT! MOON KNIGHT-- ESPIRITA-- YOU CAN STAY HERE!
WE CAN, BUT WE WON'T!
RIGHT!
THANKS! THEN LET'S FOLLOW OUR BEST LEAD AND FIND THE COLLECTOR!
I ALREADY KNOW WHERE HIS SHIP IS!
AND SO, THE WEST COAST AVENGERS GET BACK TO THEIR QUINJET AT HOUSTON INTERNATIONAL, AND FOLLOW THE SILVER SURFER UP INTO THE VAST TEXAS SKY--
--AND OUT OF THE SKY, WITH THE BLUE FADING AND FALLING AWAY TO REVEAL THE EVER-BURNING STARS AND THE EMPTY EBON ABYSS OF DEEP SPACE...
WITHIN THEIR JET, THE AVENGERS CARRY WITH THEM WARMTH AND LIGHT AND CONSTANT GRAVITY...
THE SILVER SURFER SOARS WITH NO SHIELDS SAVE HIS SKIN...
...AND THEN THEIR GOAL COMES INTO VIEW!

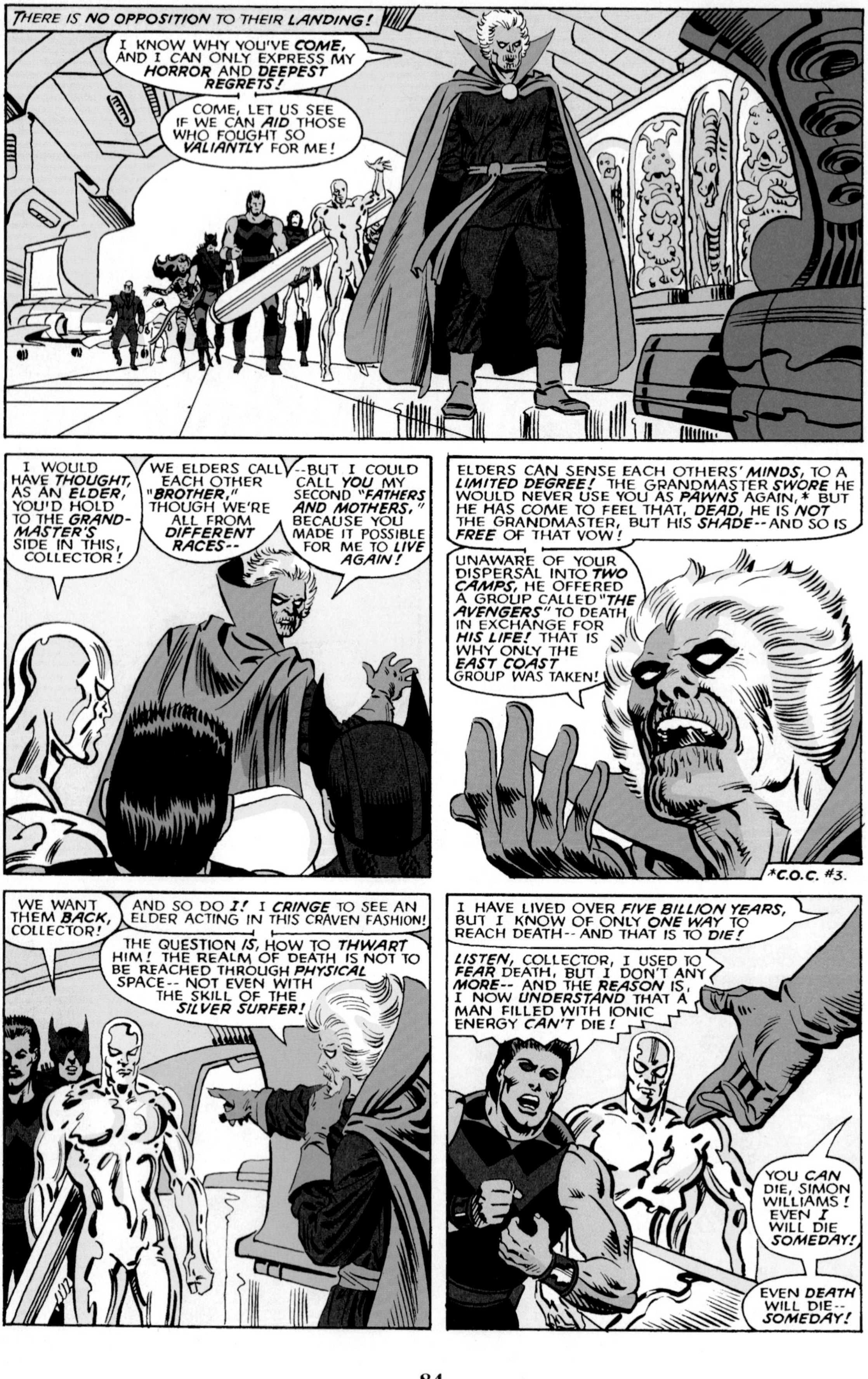
THERE IS NO OPPOSITION TO THEIR LANDING!
I KNOW WHY YOU'VE COME, AND I CAN ONLY EXPRESS MY HORROR AND DEEPEST REGRETS!
COME, LET US SEE IF WE CAN AID THOSE WHO FOUGHT SO VALIANTLY FOR ME!
I WOULD HAVE THOUGHT, AS AN ELDER, YOU'D HOLD TO THE GRAND-MASTER'S SIDE IN THIS, COLLECTOR!
WE ELDERS CALL EACH OTHER "BROTHER," THOUGH WE'RE ALL FROM DIFFERENT RACES--
--BUT I COULD CALL YOU MY SECOND "FATHERS AND MOTHERS," BECAUSE YOU MADE IT POSSIBLE FOR ME TO LIVE AGAIN!
ELDERS CAN SENSE EACH OTHERS' MINDS, TO A LIMITED DEGREE! THE GRANDMASTER SWORE HE WOULD NEVER USE YOU AS PAWNS AGAIN,* BUT HE HAS COME TO FEEL THAT, DEAD, HE IS NOT THE GRANDMASTER, BUT HIS SHADE--AND SO IS FREE OF THAT VOW!
UNAWARE OF YOUR DISPERSAL INTO TWO CAMPS, HE OFFERED A GROUP CALLED "THE AVENGERS" TO DEATH IN EXCHANGE FOR HIS LIFE! THAT IS WHY ONLY THE EAST COAST GROUP WAS TAKEN!
*C.O.C. #3.
WE WANT THEM BACK, COLLECTOR!
AND SO DO I! I CRINGE TO SEE AN ELDER ACTING IN THIS CRAVEN FASHION!
THE QUESTION IS, HOW TO THWART HIM! THE REALM OF DEATH IS NOT TO BE REACHED THROUGH PHYSICAL SPACE-- NOT EVEN WITH THE SKILL OF THE SILVER SURFER!
I HAVE LIVED OVER FIVE BILLION YEARS, BUT I KNOW OF ONLY ONE WAY TO REACH DEATH-- AND THAT IS TO DIE!
LISTEN, COLLECTOR, I USED TO FEAR DEATH, BUT I DON'T ANY MORE-- AND THE REASON IS, I NOW UNDERSTAND THAT A MAN FILLED WITH IONIC ENERGY CAN'T DIE!
YOU CAN DIE, SIMON WILLIAMS! EVEN I WILL DIE SOMEDAY!
EVEN DEATH WILL DIE-- SOMEDAY!

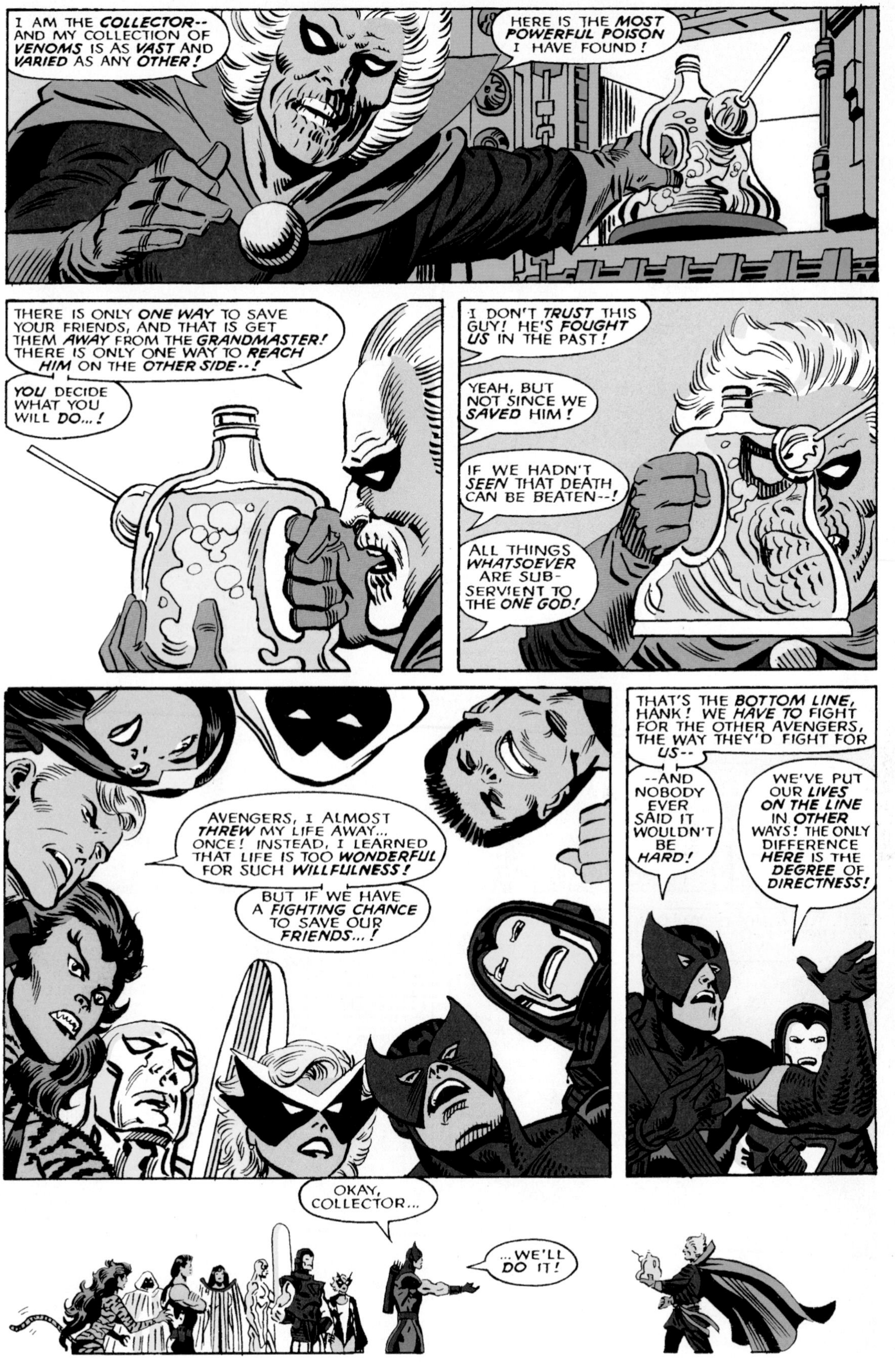
I AM THE COLLECTOR-- AND MY COLLECTION OF VENOMS IS AS VAST AND VARIED AS ANY OTHER!
HERE IS THE MOST POWERFUL POISON I HAVE FOUND!
THERE IS ONLY ONE WAY TO SAVE YOUR FRIENDS, AND THAT IS GET THEM AWAY FROM THE GRANDMASTER! THERE IS ONLY ONE WAY TO REACH HIM ON THE OTHER SIDE--!
YOU DECIDE WHAT YOU WILL DO...!
I DON'T TRUST THIS GUY! HE'S FOUGHT US IN THE PAST!
YEAH, BUT NOT SINCE WE SAVED HIM!
IF WE HADN'T SEEN THAT DEATH CAN BE BEATEN--!
ALL THINGS WHATSOEVER ARE SUB-SERVIENT TO THE ONE GOD!
AVENGERS, I ALMOST THREW MY LIFE AWAY... ONCE! INSTEAD, I LEARNED THAT LIFE IS TOO WONDERFUL FOR SUCH WILLFULNESS!
BUT IF WE HAVE A FIGHTING CHANCE TO SAVE OUR FRIENDS...!
THAT'S THE BOTTOM LINE, HANK! WE HAVE TO FIGHT FOR THE OTHER AVENGERS, THE WAY THEY'D FIGHT FOR US--
--AND NOBODY EVER SAID IT WOULDN'T BE HARD!
WE'VE PUT OUR LIVES ON THE LINE IN OTHER WAYS! THE ONLY DIFFERENCE HERE IS THE DEGREE OF DIRECTNESS!
OKAY, COLLECTOR...
...WE'LL DO IT!

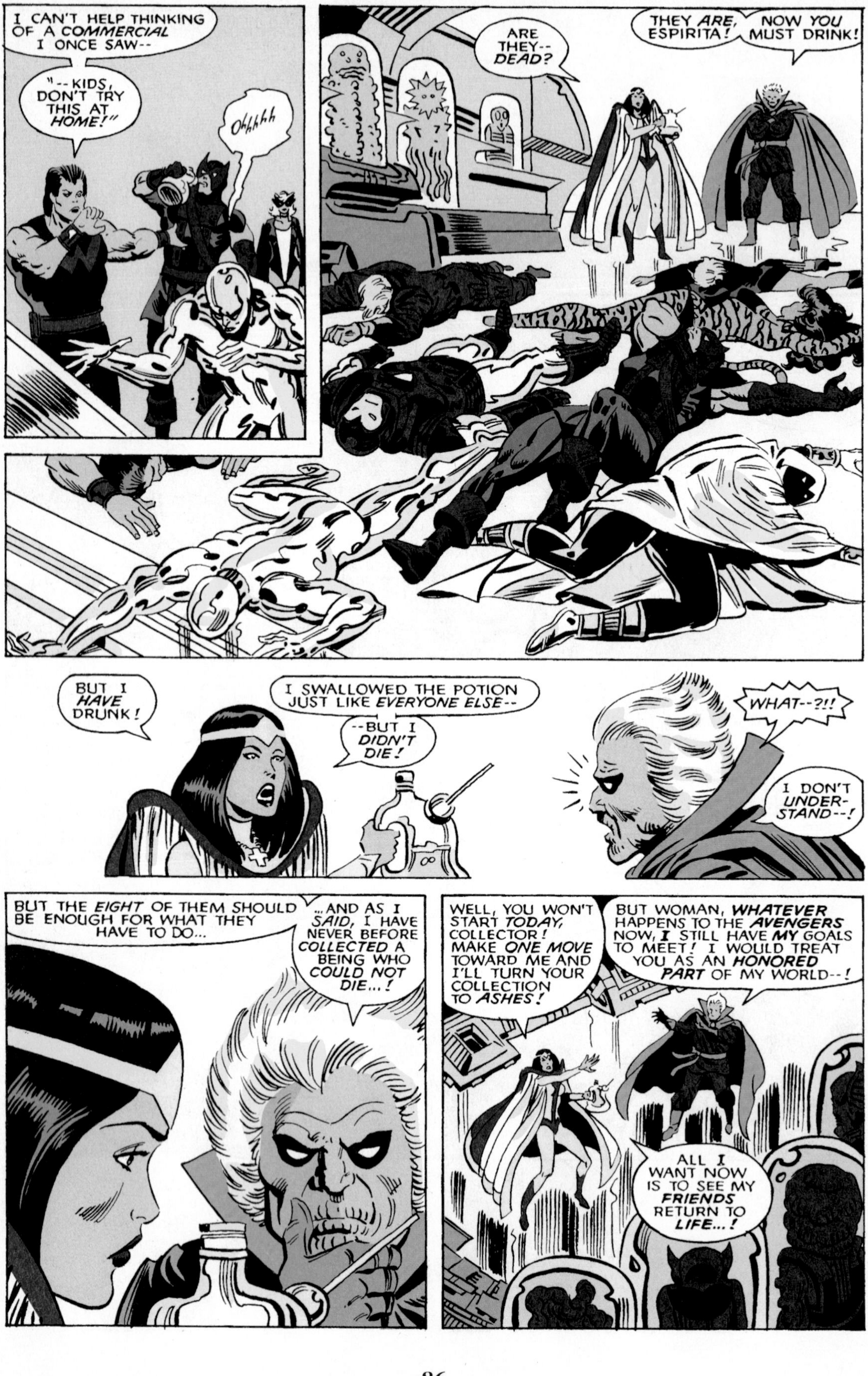
I CAN'T HELP THINKING OF A COMMERCIAL I ONCE SAW--
"--KIDS, DON'T TRY THIS AT HOME!"
Ohhhhh
ARE THEY--DEAD?
THEY ARE, ESPIRITA!
NOW YOU MUST DRINK!
BUT I HAVE DRUNK!
I SWALLOWED THE POTION JUST LIKE EVERYONE ELSE--
--BUT I DIDN'T DIE!
WHAT--?!!
I DON'T UNDER-STAND--!
BUT THE EIGHT OF THEM SHOULD BE ENOUGH FOR WHAT THEY HAVE TO DO...
...AND AS I SAID, I HAVE NEVER BEFORE COLLECTED A BEING WHO COULD NOT DIE...!
WELL, YOU WON'T START TODAY, COLLECTOR! MAKE ONE MOVE TOWARD ME AND I'LL TURN YOUR COLLECTION TO ASHES!
BUT WOMAN, WHATEVER HAPPENS TO THE AVENGERS NOW, I STILL HAVE MY GOALS TO MEET! I WOULD TREAT YOU AS AN HONORED PART OF MY WORLD--!
ALL I WANT NOW IS TO SEE MY FRIENDS RETURN TO LIFE...!

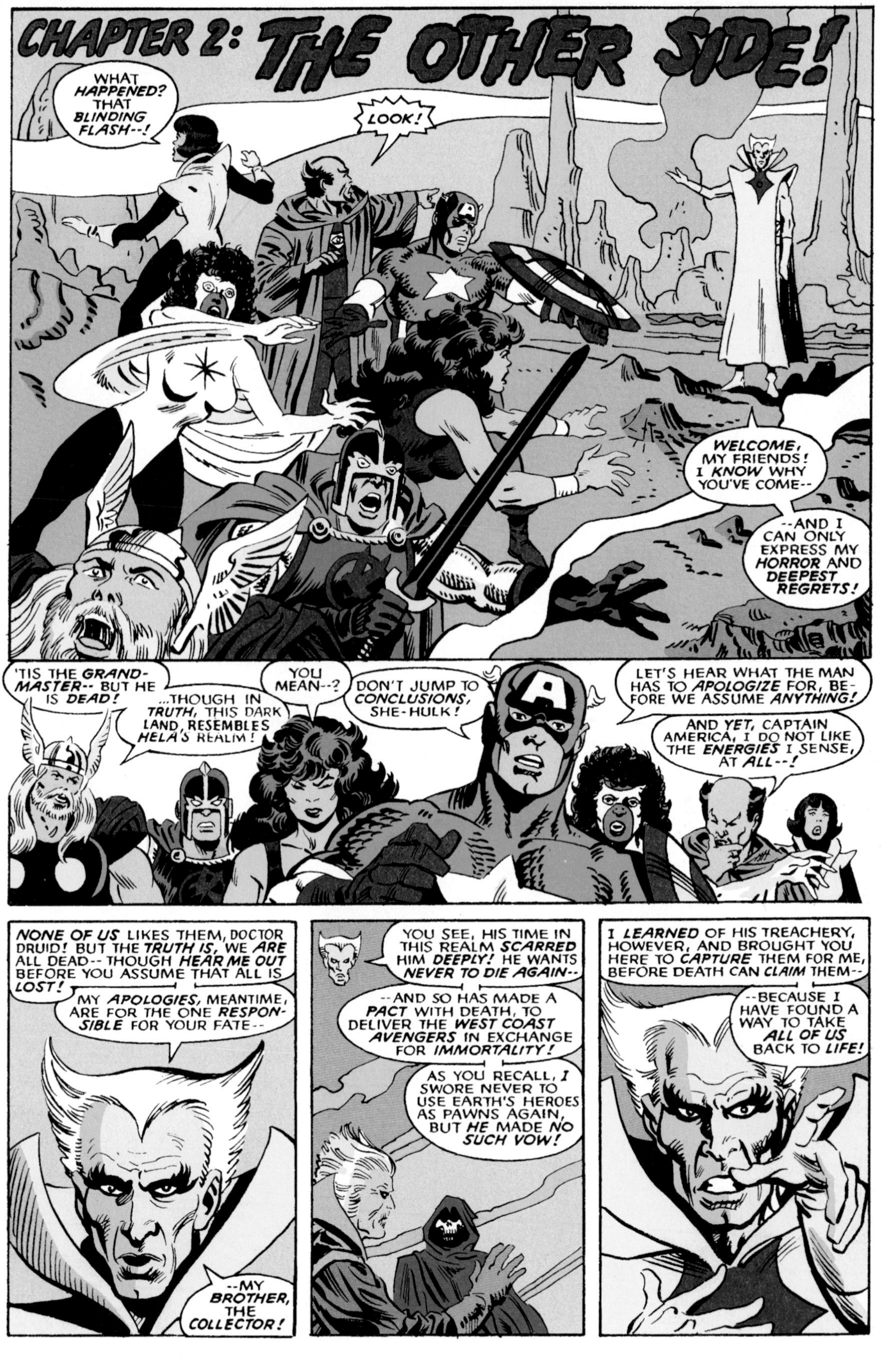
CHAPTER 2: THE OTHER SIDE!
WHAT HAPPENED? THAT BLINDING FLASH--!
LOOK!
WELCOME, MY FRIENDS! I KNOW WHY YOU'VE COME--
--AND I CAN ONLY EXPRESS MY HORROR AND DEEPEST REGRETS!
'TIS THE GRAND-MASTER-- BUT HE IS DEAD!
...THOUGH IN TRUTH, THIS DARK LAND, RESEMBLES HELA'S REALM!
YOU MEAN--?
DON'T JUMP TO CONCLUSIONS, SHE-HULK!
LET'S HEAR WHAT THE MAN HAS TO APOLOGIZE FOR, BEFORE WE ASSUME ANYTHING!
AND YET, CAPTAIN AMERICA, I DO NOT LIKE THE ENERGIES I SENSE, AT ALL--!
NONE OF US LIKES THEM, DOCTOR DRUID! BUT THE TRUTH IS, WE ARE ALL DEAD-- THOUGH HEAR ME OUT BEFORE YOU ASSUME THAT ALL IS LOST!
MY APOLOGIES, MEANTIME, ARE FOR THE ONE RESPONSIBLE FOR YOUR FATE--
--MY BROTHER, THE COLLECTOR!
YOU SEE, HIS TIME IN THIS REALM SCARRED HIM DEEPLY! HE WANTS NEVER TO DIE AGAIN--
--AND SO HAS MADE A PACT WITH DEATH, TO DELIVER THE WEST COAST AVENGERS IN EXCHANGE FOR IMMORTALITY!
AS YOU RECALL, I SWORE NEVER TO USE EARTH'S HEROES AS PAWNS AGAIN, BUT HE MADE NO SUCH VOW!
I LEARNED OF HIS TREACHERY, HOWEVER, AND BROUGHT YOU HERE TO CAPTURE THEM FOR ME, BEFORE DEATH CAN CLAIM THEM--
--BECAUSE I HAVE FOUND A WAY TO TAKE ALL OF US BACK TO LIFE!

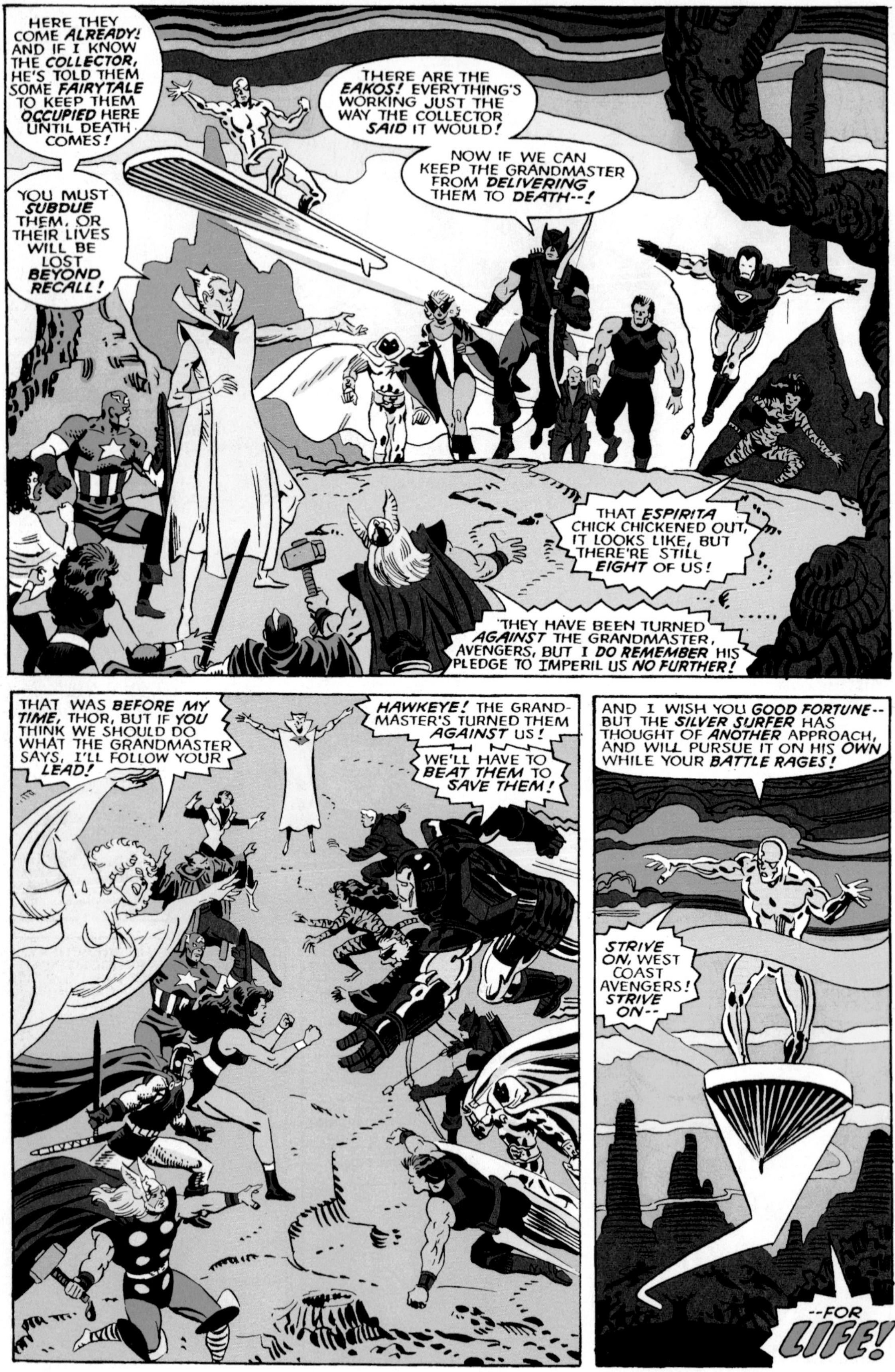
HERE THEY COME ALREADY! AND IF I KNOW THE COLLECTOR, HE'S TOLD THEM SOME FAIRYTALE TO KEEP THEM OCCUPIED HERE UNTIL DEATH COMES!
YOU MUST SUBDUE THEM, OR THEIR LIVES WILL BE LOST BEYOND RECALL!
THERE ARE THE EAKOS! EVERYTHING'S WORKING JUST THE WAY THE COLLECTOR SAID IT WOULD!
NOW IF WE CAN KEEP THE GRANDMASTER FROM DELIVERING THEM TO DEATH--!
THAT ESPIRITA CHICK CHICKENED OUT, IT LOOKS LIKE, BUT THERE'RE STILL EIGHT OF US!
THEY HAVE BEEN TURNED AGAINST THE GRANDMASTER, AVENGERS, BUT I DO REMEMBER HIS PLEDGE TO IMPERIL US NO FURTHER!
THAT WAS BEFORE MY TIME, THOR, BUT IF YOU THINK WE SHOULD DO WHAT THE GRANDMASTER SAYS, I'LL FOLLOW YOUR LEAD!
HAWKEYE! THE GRANDMASTER'S TURNED THEM AGAINST US!
WE'LL HAVE TO BEAT THEM TO SAVE THEM!
AND I WISH YOU GOOD FORTUNE-- BUT THE SILVER SURFER HAS THOUGHT OF ANOTHER APPROACH, AND WILL PURSUE IT ON HIS OWN WHILE YOUR BATTLE RAGES!
STRIVE ON, WEST COAST AVENGERS! STRIVE ON--
--FOR LIFE!

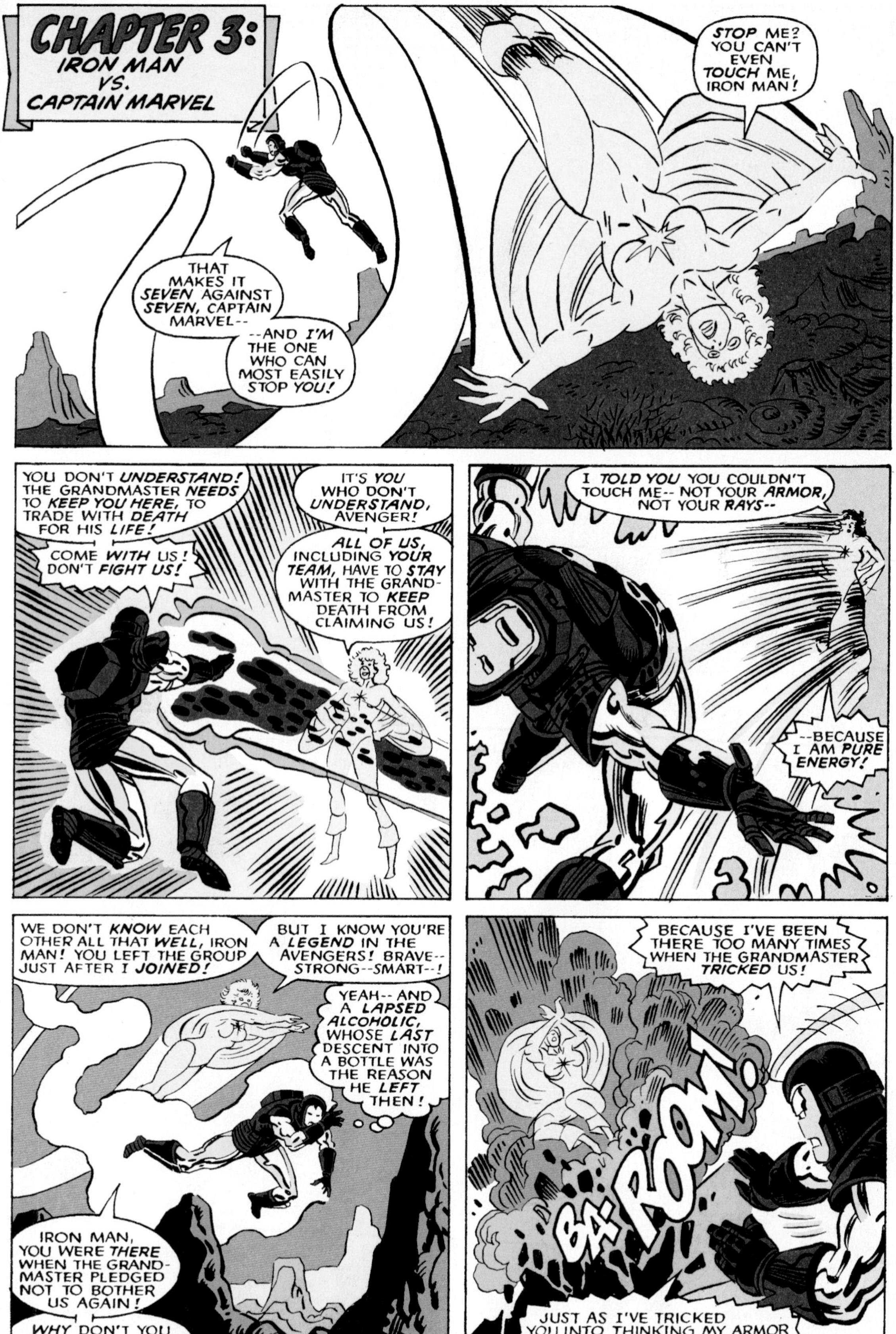
CHAPTER 3: IRON MAN VS. CAPTAIN MARVEL
THAT MAKES IT SEVEN AGAINST SEVEN, CAPTAIN MARVEL--
--AND I'M THE ONE WHO CAN MOST EASILY STOP YOU!
STOP ME? YOU CAN'T EVEN TOUCH ME, IRON MAN!
YOU DON'T UNDERSTAND! THE GRANDMASTER NEEDS TO KEEP YOU HERE, TO TRADE WITH DEATH FOR HIS LIFE!
COME WITH US! DON'T FIGHT US!
IT'S YOU WHO DON'T UNDERSTAND, AVENGER!
ALL OF US, INCLUDING YOUR TEAM, HAVE TO STAY WITH THE GRANDMASTER TO KEEP DEATH FROM CLAIMING US!
I TOLD YOU YOU COULDN'T TOUCH ME-- NOT YOUR ARMOR, NOT YOUR RAYS--
--BECAUSE I AM PURE ENERGY!
WE DON'T KNOW EACH OTHER ALL THAT WELL, IRON MAN! YOU LEFT THE GROUP JUST AFTER I JOINED!
BUT I KNOW YOU'RE A LEGEND IN THE AVENGERS! BRAVE-- STRONG--SMART--!
YEAH-- AND A LAPSED ALCOHOLIC, WHOSE LAST DESCENT INTO A BOTTLE WAS THE REASON HE LEFT THEN!
IRON MAN, YOU WERE THERE WHEN THE GRANDMASTER PLEDGED NOT TO BOTHER US AGAIN!
WHY DON'T YOU BELIEVE HIS STORY?
BECAUSE I'VE BEEN THERE TOO MANY TIMES WHEN THE GRANDMASTER TRICKED US!
BA-ROOM!
JUST AS I'VE TRICKED YOU INTO THINKING MY ARMOR WAS SERIOUSLY DAMAGED.

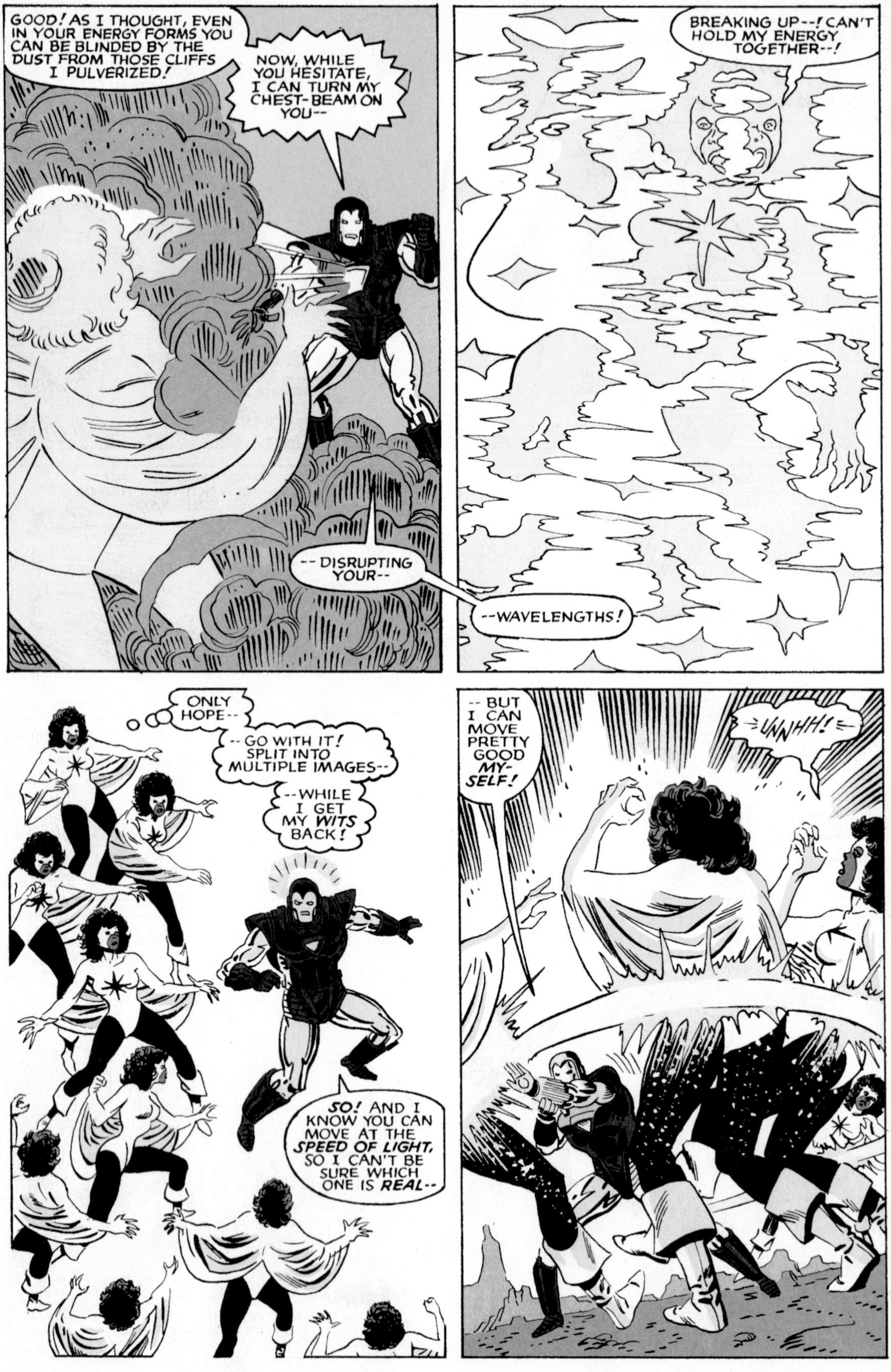
GOOD! AS I THOUGHT, EVEN IN YOUR ENERGY FORMS YOU CAN BE BLINDED BY THE DUST FROM THOSE CLIFFS I PULVERIZED!
NOW, WHILE YOU HESITATE, I CAN TURN MY CHEST-BEAM ON YOU--
--DISRUPTING YOUR--
--WAVELENGTHS!
BREAKING UP--! CAN'T HOLD MY ENERGY TOGETHER--!
ONLY HOPE--
--GO WITH IT! SPLIT INTO MULTIPLE IMAGES--
--WHILE I GET MY WITS BACK!
SO! AND I KNOW YOU CAN MOVE AT THE SPEED OF LIGHT, SO I CAN'T BE SURE WHICH ONE IS REAL--
--BUT I CAN MOVE PRETTY GOOD MY-SELF!
UNNHH!

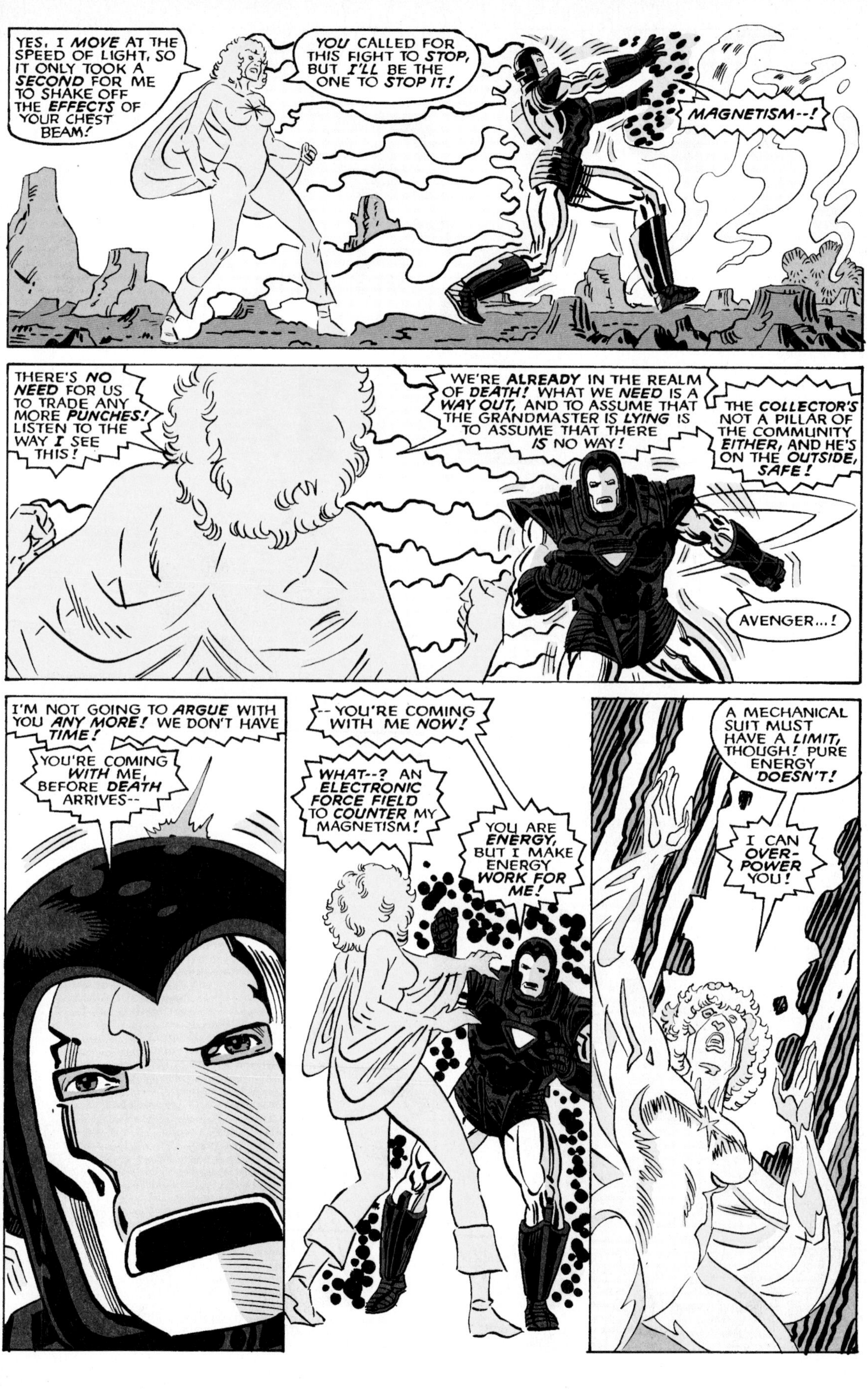
YES, I MOVE AT THE SPEED OF LIGHT, SO IT ONLY TOOK A SECOND FOR ME TO SHAKE OFF THE EFFECTS OF YOUR CHEST BEAM!
YOU CALLED FOR THIS FIGHT TO STOP, BUT I'LL BE THE ONE TO STOP IT!
MAGNETISM--!
THERE'S NO NEED FOR US TO TRADE ANY MORE PUNCHES! LISTEN TO THE WAY I SEE THIS!
WE'RE ALREADY IN THE REALM OF DEATH! WHAT WE NEED IS A WAY OUT, AND TO ASSUME THAT THE GRANDMASTER IS LYING IS TO ASSUME THAT THERE IS NO WAY!
THE COLLECTOR'S NOT A PILLAR OF THE COMMUNITY EITHER, AND HE'S ON THE OUTSIDE, SAFE!
AVENGER...!
I'M NOT GOING TO ARGUE WITH YOU ANY MORE! WE DON'T HAVE TIME!
YOU'RE COMING WITH ME, BEFORE DEATH ARRIVES--
--YOU'RE COMING WITH ME NOW!
WHAT--? AN ELECTRONIC FORCE FIELD TO COUNTER MY MAGNETISM!
YOU ARE ENERGY, BUT I MAKE ENERGY WORK FOR ME!
A MECHANICAL SUIT MUST HAVE A LIMIT, THOUGH! PURE ENERGY DOESN'T!
I CAN OVER-POWER YOU!

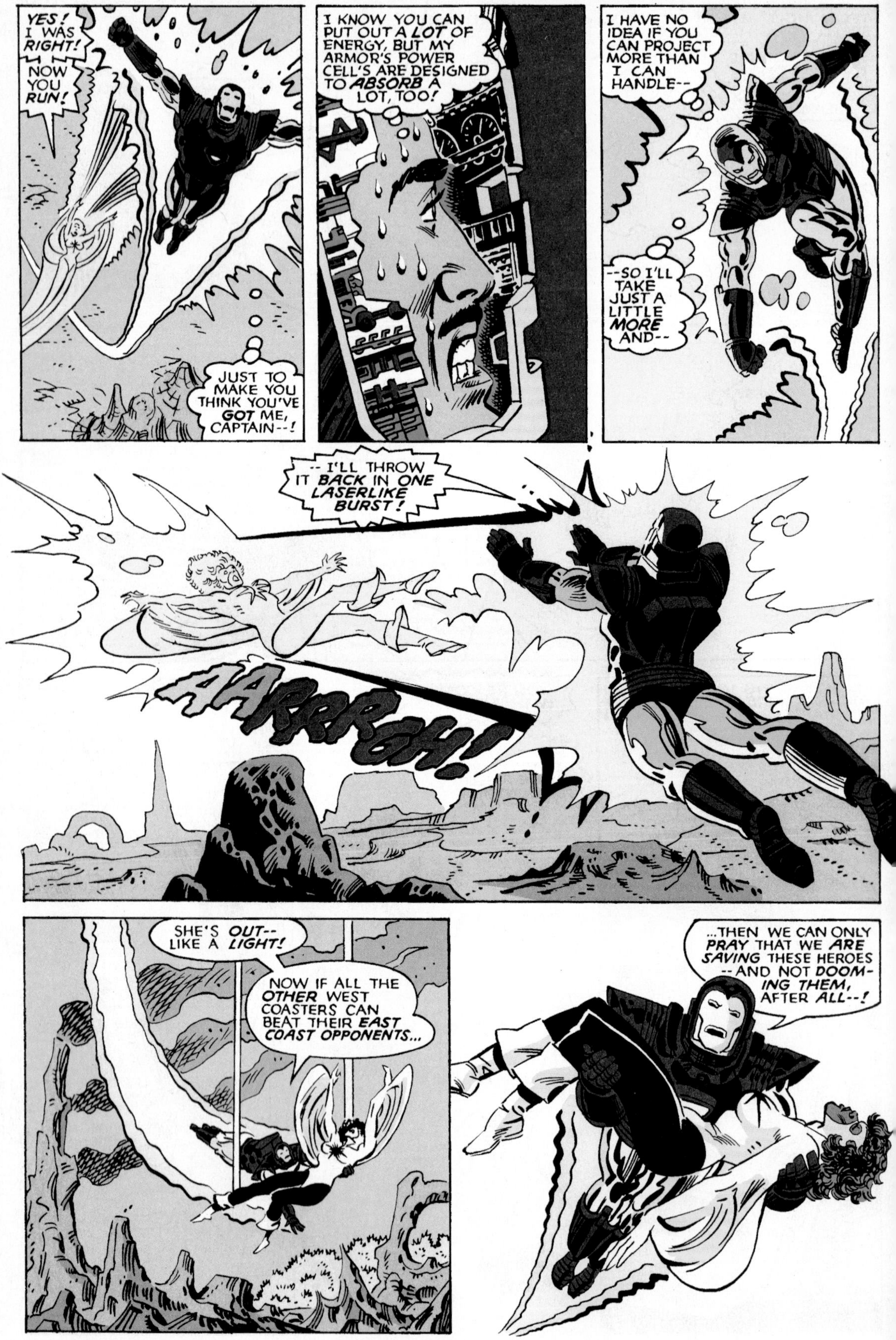
YES! I WAS RIGHT!
NOW YOU RUN!
JUST TO MAKE YOU THINK YOU'VE GOT ME, CAPTAIN--!
I KNOW YOU CAN PUT OUT A LOT OF ENERGY, BUT MY ARMOR'S POWER CELL'S ARE DESIGNED TO ABSORB A LOT, TOO!
I HAVE NO IDEA IF YOU CAN PROJECT MORE THAN I CAN HANDLE--
--SO I'LL TAKE JUST A LITTLE MORE AND--
-- I'LL THROW IT BACK IN ONE LASERLIKE BURST!
AARRRGH!!
SHE'S OUT-- LIKE A LIGHT!
NOW IF ALL THE OTHER WEST COASTERS CAN BEAT THEIR EAST COAST OPPONENTS...
...THEN WE CAN ONLY PRAY THAT WE ARE SAVING THESE HEROES --AND NOT DOOMING THEM, AFTER ALL--!

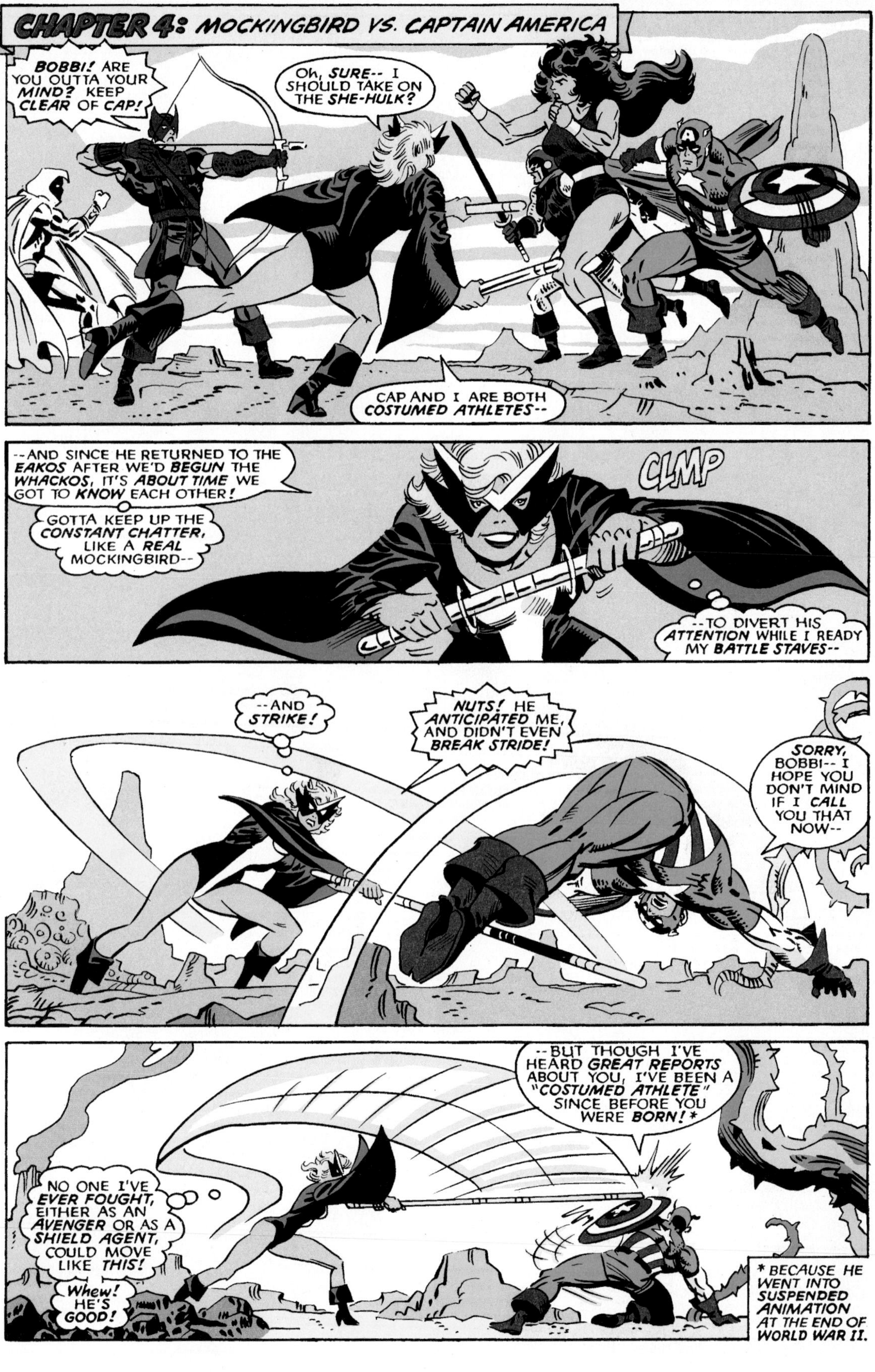
CHAPTER 4: MOCKINGBIRD VS. CAPTAIN AMERICA
BOBBI! ARE YOU OUTTA YOUR MIND? KEEP CLEAR OF CAP!
Oh, SURE-- I SHOULD TAKE ON THE SHE-HULK?
CAP AND I ARE BOTH COSTUMED ATHLETES--
--AND SINCE HE RETURNED TO THE EAKOS AFTER WE'D BEGUN THE WHACKOS, IT'S ABOUT TIME WE GOT TO KNOW EACH OTHER!
GOTTA KEEP UP THE CONSTANT CHATTER, LIKE A REAL MOCKINGBIRD--
CLMP
--TO DIVERT HIS ATTENTION WHILE I READY MY BATTLE STAVES--
--AND STRIKE!
NUTS! HE ANTICIPATED ME, AND DIDN'T EVEN BREAK STRIDE!
SORRY, BOBBI-- I HOPE YOU DON'T MIND IF I CALL YOU THAT NOW--
--BUT THOUGH I'VE HEARD GREAT REPORTS ABOUT YOU, I'VE BEEN A "COSTUMED ATHLETE" SINCE BEFORE YOU WERE BORN! *
NO ONE I'VE EVER FOUGHT, EITHER AS AN AVENGER OR AS A SHIELD AGENT, COULD MOVE LIKE THIS!
Whew! HE'S GOOD!
* BECAUSE HE WENT INTO SUSPENDED ANIMATION AT THE END OF WORLD WAR II.

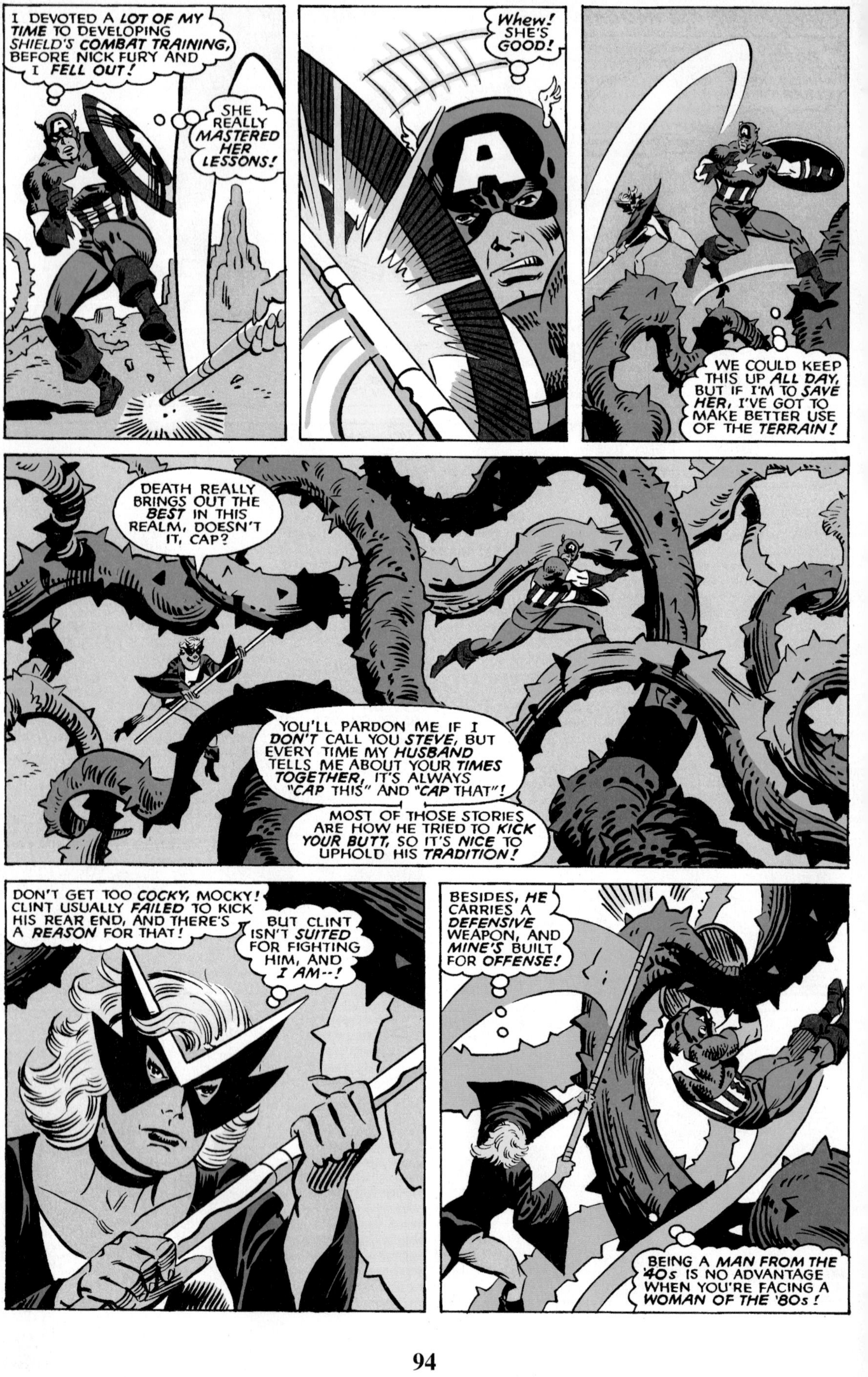
I DEVOTED A LOT OF MY TIME TO DEVELOPING SHIELD'S COMBAT TRAINING, BEFORE NICK FURY AND I FELL OUT!
SHE REALLY MASTERED HER LESSONS!
Whew! SHE'S GOOD!
WE COULD KEEP THIS UP ALL DAY, BUT IF I'M TO SAVE HER, I'VE GOT TO MAKE BETTER USE OF THE TERRAIN!
DEATH REALLY BRINGS OUT THE BEST IN THIS REALM, DOESN'T IT, CAP?
YOU'LL PARDON ME IF I DON'T CALL YOU STEVE, BUT EVERY TIME MY HUSBAND TELLS ME ABOUT YOUR TIMES TOGETHER, IT'S ALWAYS "CAP THIS" AND "CAP THAT"!
MOST OF THOSE STORIES ARE HOW HE TRIED TO KICK YOUR BUTT, SO IT'S NICE TO UPHOLD HIS TRADITION!
DON'T GET TOO COCKY, MOCKY! CLINT USUALLY FAILED TO KICK HIS REAR END, AND THERE'S A REASON FOR THAT!
BUT CLINT ISN'T SUITED FOR FIGHTING HIM, AND I AM--!
BESIDES, HE CARRIES A DEFENSIVE WEAPON, AND MINE'S BUILT FOR OFFENSE!
BEING A MAN FROM THE '40s IS NO ADVANTAGE WHEN YOU'RE FACING A WOMAN OF THE '80s!

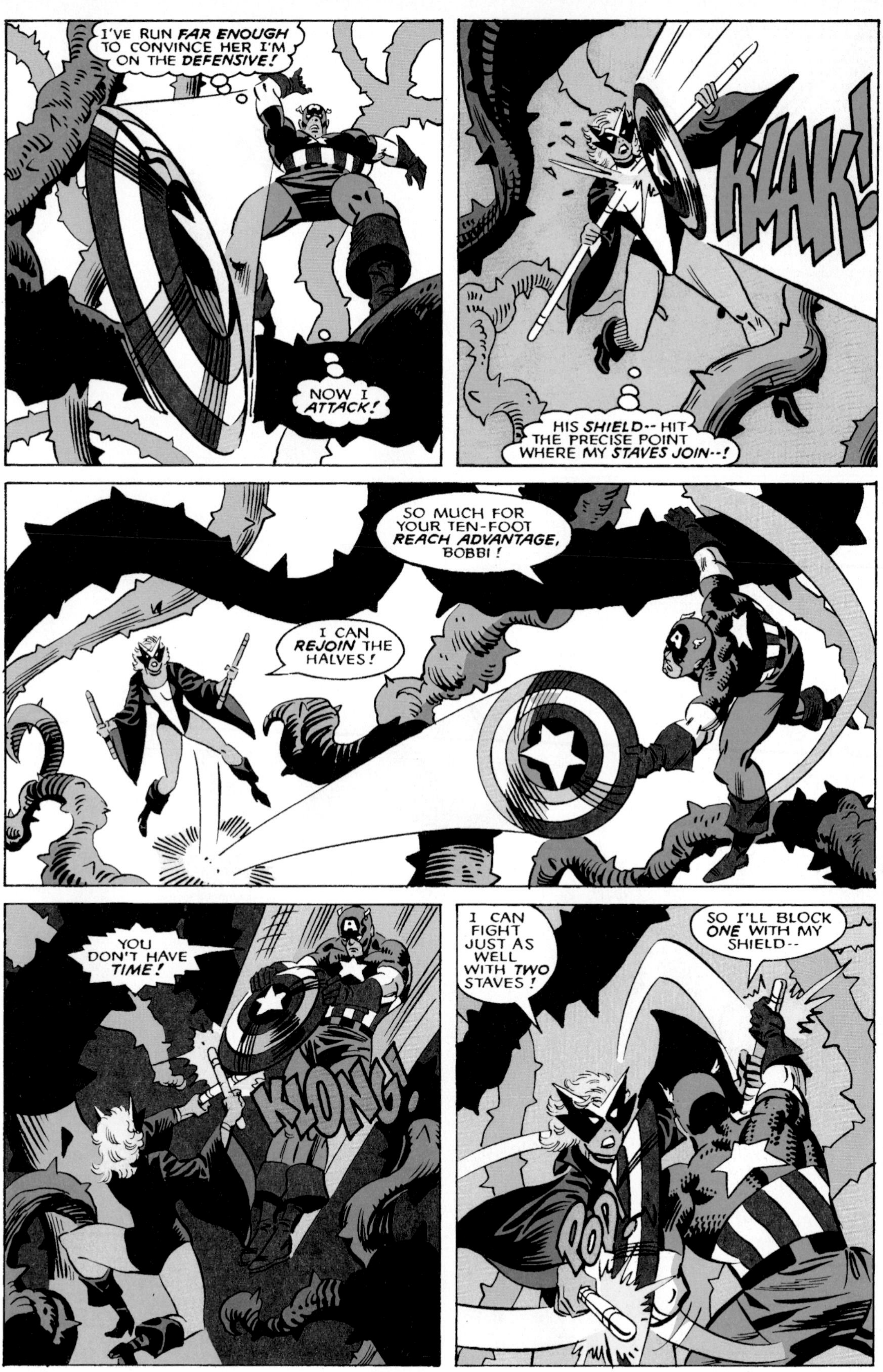
I'VE RUN FAR ENOUGH TO CONVINCE HER I'M ON THE DEFENSIVE!
NOW I ATTACK!
KLAK!
HIS SHIELD-- HIT THE PRECISE POINT WHERE MY STAVES JOIN--!
SO MUCH FOR YOUR TEN-FOOT REACH ADVANTAGE, BOBBI!
I CAN REJOIN THE HALVES!
YOU DON'T HAVE TIME!
KLONG!
I CAN FIGHT JUST AS WELL WITH TWO STAVES!
SO I'LL BLOCK ONE WITH MY SHIELD--

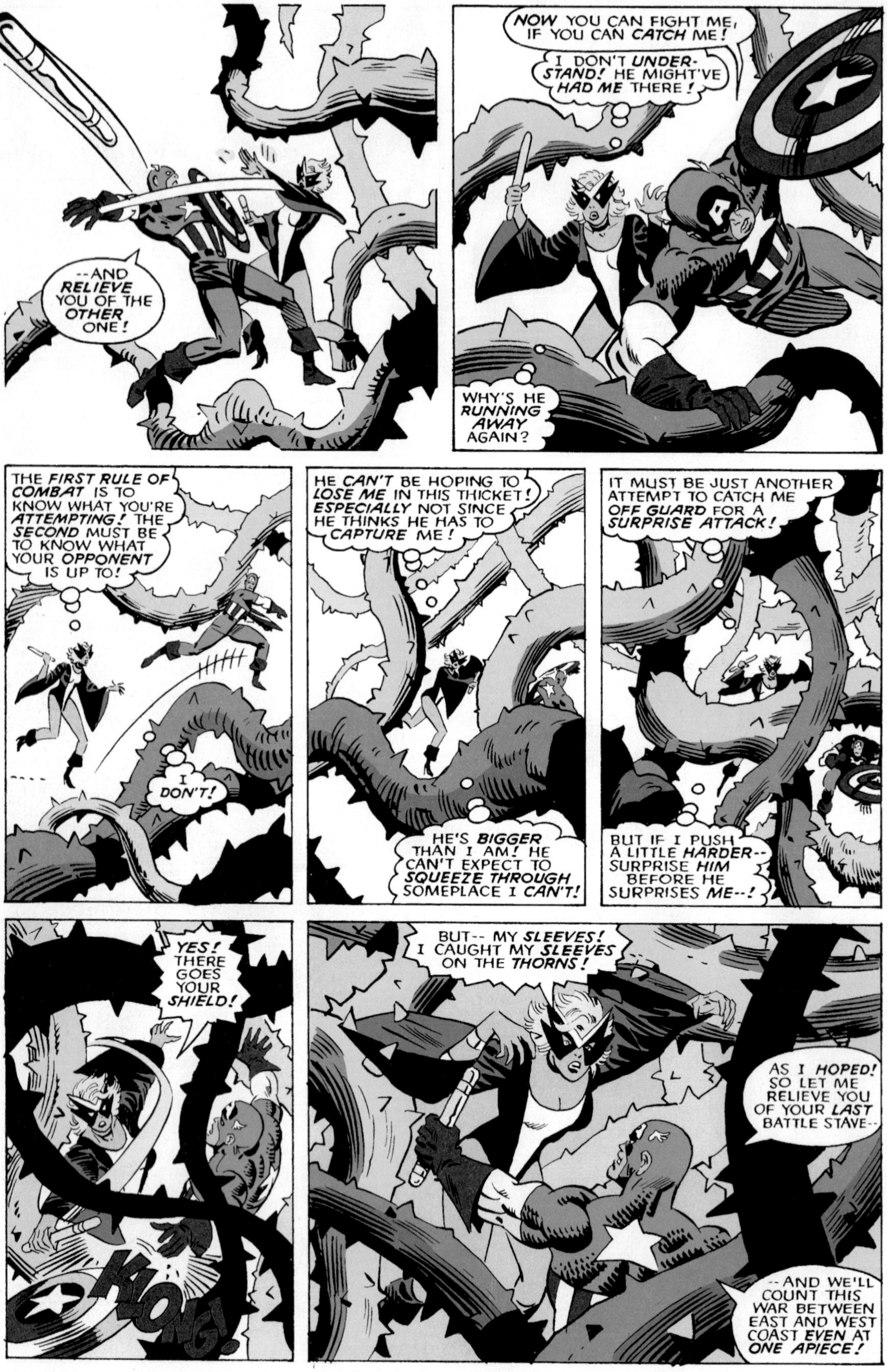
--AND RELIEVE YOU OF THE OTHER ONE!
NOW YOU CAN FIGHT ME, IF YOU CAN CATCH ME!
I DON'T UNDER-STAND! HE MIGHT'VE HAD ME THERE!
WHY'S HE RUNNING AWAY AGAIN?
THE FIRST RULE OF COMBAT IS TO KNOW WHAT YOU'RE ATTEMPTING! THE SECOND MUST BE TO KNOW WHAT YOUR OPPONENT IS UP TO!
I DON'T!
HE CAN'T BE HOPING TO LOSE ME IN THIS THICKET! ESPECIALLY NOT SINCE HE THINKS HE HAS TO CAPTURE ME!
HE'S BIGGER THAN I AM! HE CAN'T EXPECT TO SQUEEZE THROUGH SOMEPLACE I CAN'T!
IT MUST BE JUST ANOTHER ATTEMPT TO CATCH ME OFF GUARD FOR A SURPRISE ATTACK!
BUT IF I PUSH A LITTLE HARDER-- SURPRISE HIM BEFORE HE SURPRISES ME--!
YES! THERE GOES YOUR SHIELD!
KLONG!
BUT-- MY SLEEVES! I CAUGHT MY SLEEVES ON THE THORNS!
AS I HOPED! SO LET ME RELIEVE YOU OF YOUR LAST BATTLE STAVE--
--AND WE'LL COUNT THIS WAR BETWEEN EAST AND WEST COAST EVEN AT ONE APIECE!

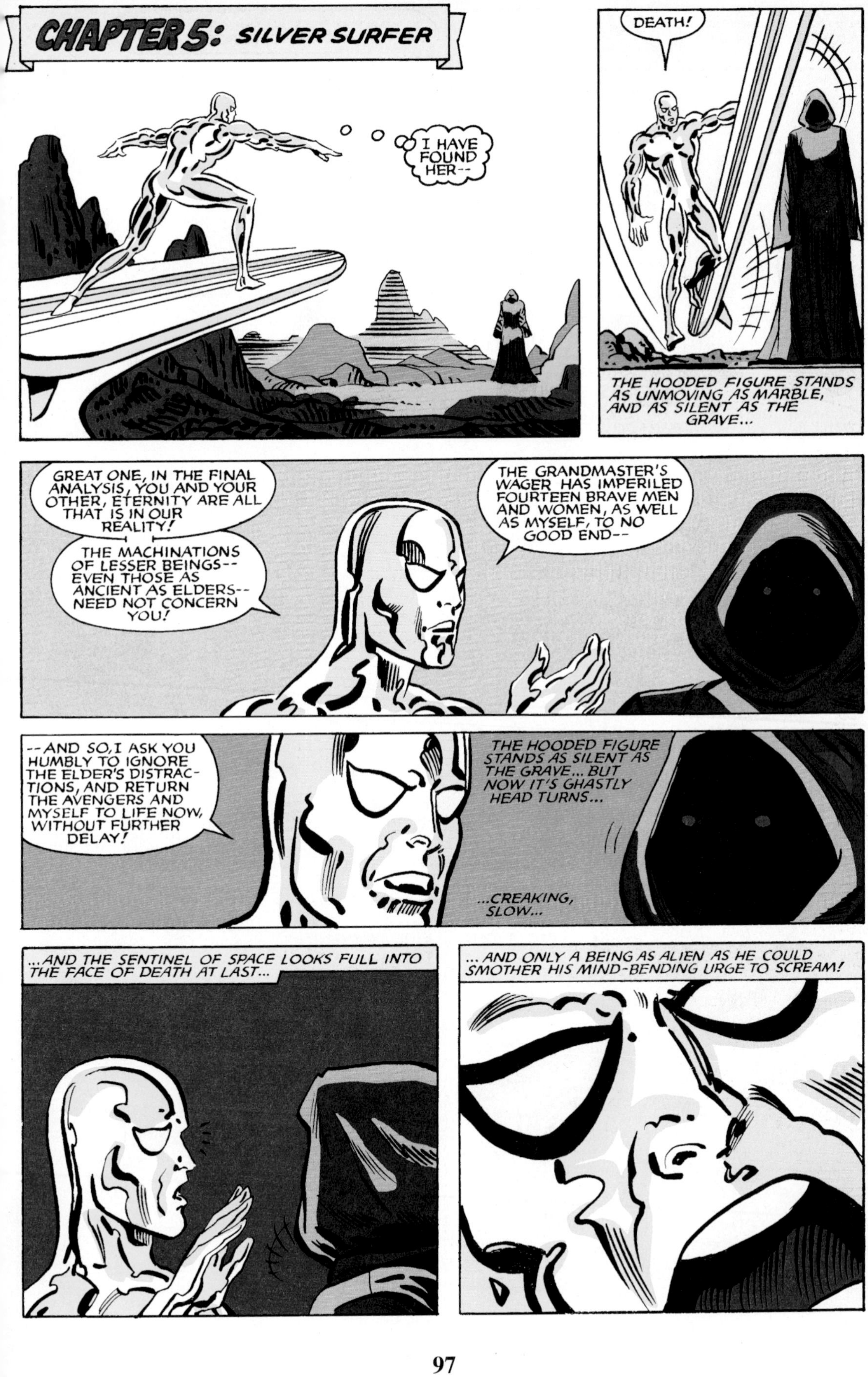
CHAPTER 5: SILVER SURFER
I HAVE FOUND HER--
DEATH!
THE HOODED FIGURE STANDS AS UNMOVING AS MARBLE, AND AS SILENT AS THE GRAVE...
GREAT ONE, IN THE FINAL ANALYSIS, YOU AND YOUR OTHER, ETERNITY ARE ALL THAT IS IN OUR REALITY!
THE MACHINATIONS OF LESSER BEINGS-- EVEN THOSE AS ANCIENT AS ELDERS-- NEED NOT CONCERN YOU!
THE GRANDMASTER'S WAGER HAS IMPERILED FOURTEEN BRAVE MEN AND WOMEN, AS WELL AS MYSELF, TO NO GOOD END--
--AND SO, I ASK YOU HUMBLY TO IGNORE THE ELDER'S DISTRACTIONS, AND RETURN THE AVENGERS AND MYSELF TO LIFE NOW, WITHOUT FURTHER DELAY!
THE HOODED FIGURE STANDS AS SILENT AS THE GRAVE... BUT NOW IT'S GHASTLY HEAD TURNS...
...CREAKING, SLOW...
...AND THE SENTINEL OF SPACE LOOKS FULL INTO THE FACE OF DEATH AT LAST...
...AND ONLY A BEING AS ALIEN AS HE COULD SMOTHER HIS MIND-BENDING URGE TO SCREAM!

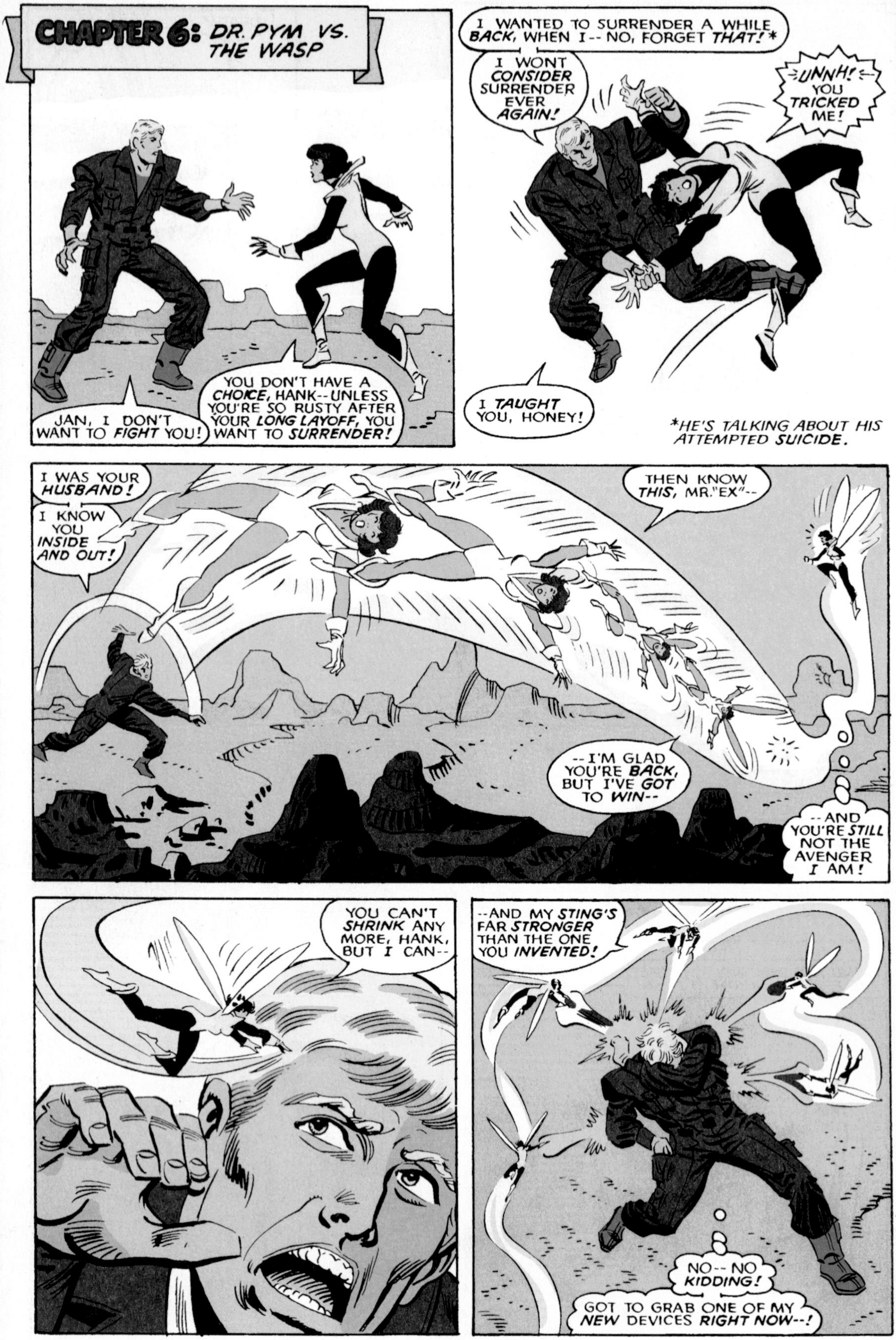
CHAPTER 6: DR. PYM VS. THE WASP
JAN, I DON'T WANT TO FIGHT YOU!
YOU DON'T HAVE A CHOICE, HANK--UNLESS YOU'RE SO RUSTY AFTER YOUR LONG LAYOFF, YOU WANT TO SURRENDER!
I WANTED TO SURRENDER A WHILE BACK, WHEN I-- NO, FORGET THAT!*
I WONT CONSIDER SURRENDER EVER AGAIN!
UNNH! YOU TRICKED ME!
I TAUGHT YOU, HONEY!
*HE'S TALKING ABOUT HIS ATTEMPTED SUICIDE.
I WAS YOUR HUSBAND!
I KNOW YOU INSIDE AND OUT!
THEN KNOW THIS, MR."EX"--
--I'M GLAD YOU'RE BACK, BUT I'VE GOT TO WIN--
--AND YOU'RE STILL NOT THE AVENGER I AM!
YOU CAN'T SHRINK ANY MORE, HANK, BUT I CAN--
--AND MY STING'S FAR STRONGER THAN THE ONE YOU INVENTED!
NO-- NO KIDDING!
GOT TO GRAB ONE OF MY NEW DEVICES RIGHT NOW--!

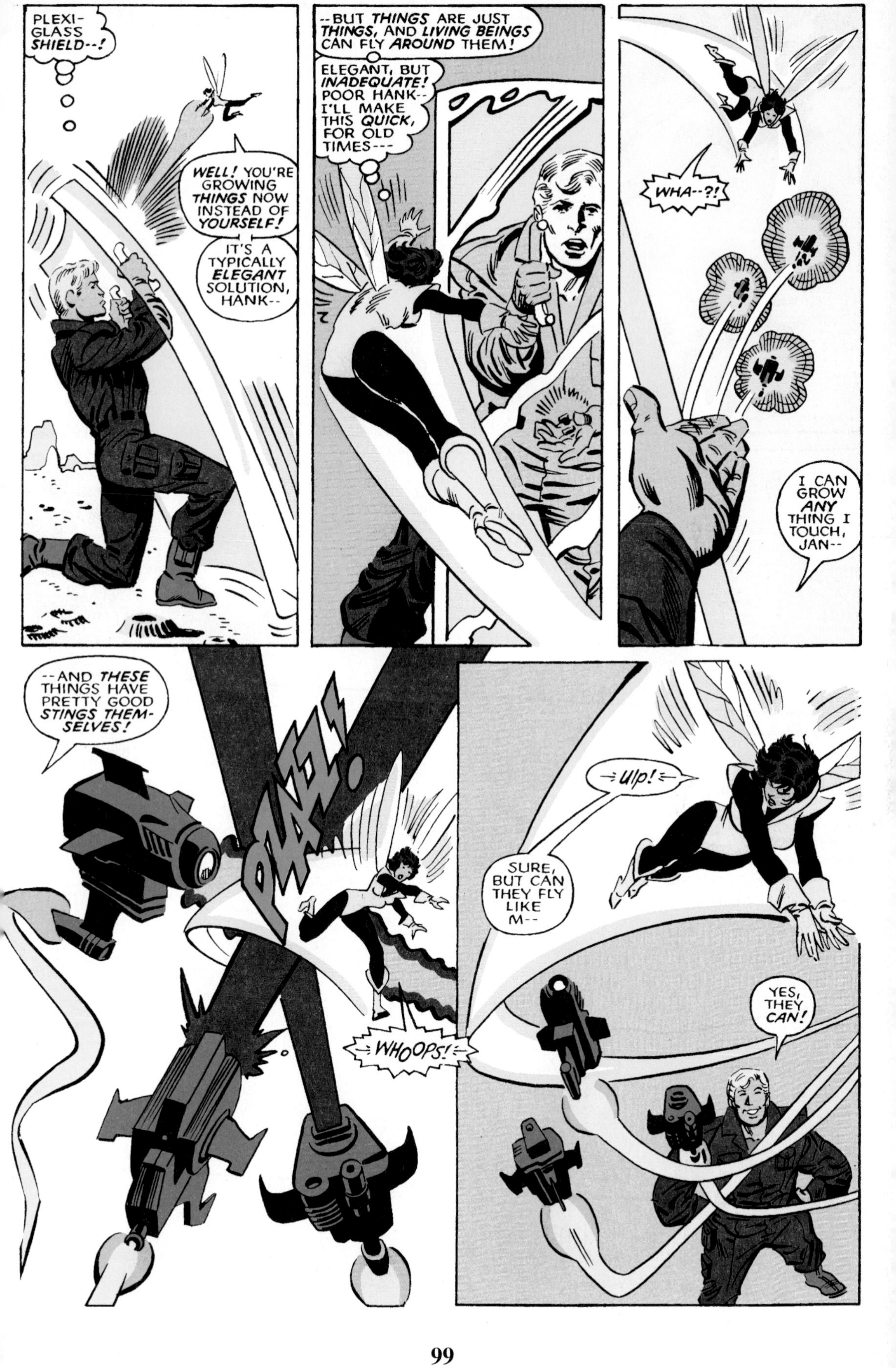
PLEXI-GLASS SHIELD--!
WELL! YOU'RE GROWING THINGS NOW INSTEAD OF YOURSELF!
IT'S A TYPICALLY ELEGANT SOLUTION, HANK--
--BUT THINGS ARE JUST THINGS, AND LIVING BEINGS CAN FLY AROUND THEM!
ELEGANT, BUT INADEQUATE! POOR HANK-- I'LL MAKE THIS QUICK, FOR OLD TIMES---
WHA--?!
I CAN GROW ANY THING I TOUCH, JAN--
--AND THESE THINGS HAVE PRETTY GOOD STINGS THEM-SELVES!
PZAZZ!
WHOOPS!
ULP!
SURE, BUT CAN THEY FLY LIKE M--
YES, THEY CAN!

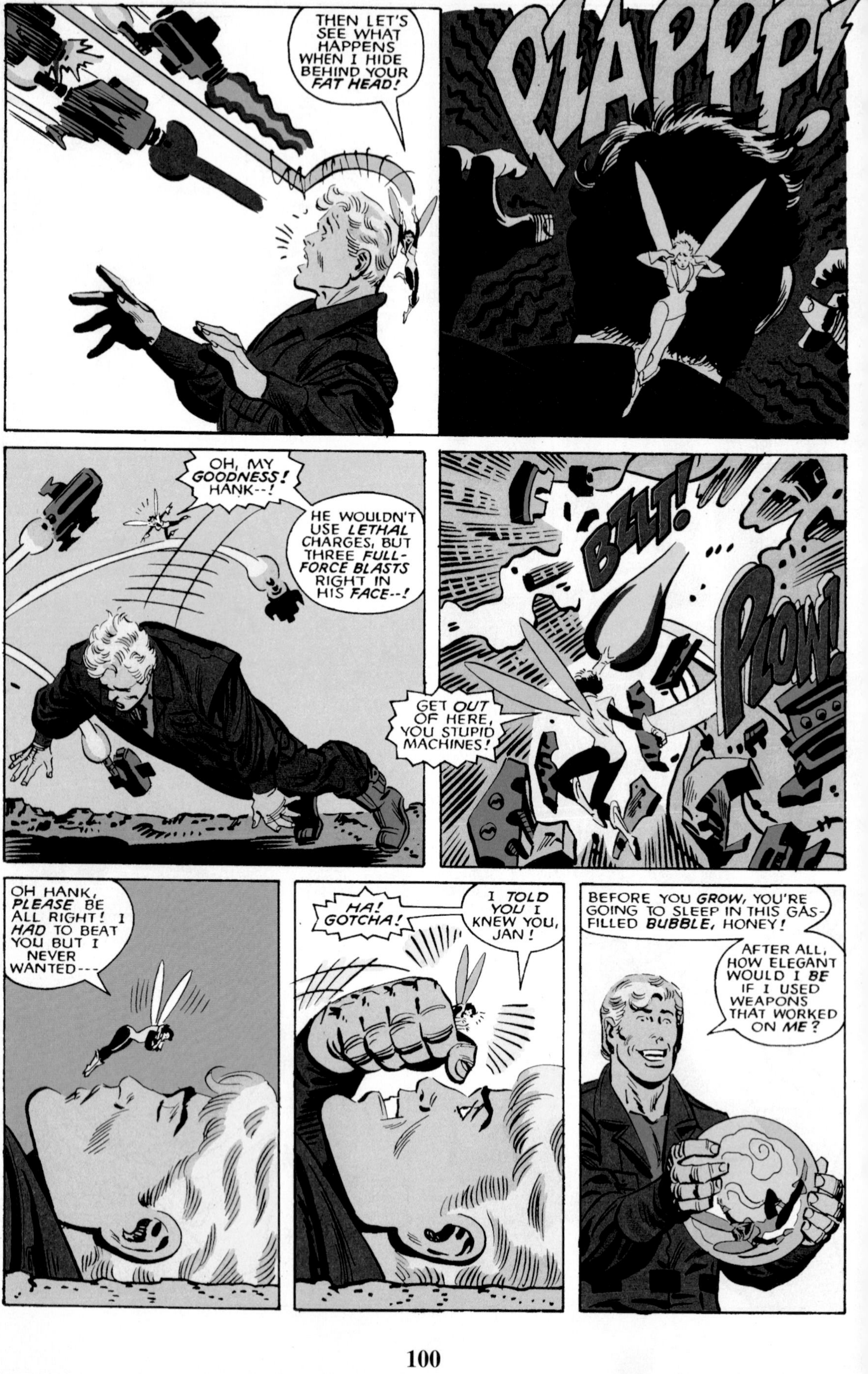
THEN LET'S SEE WHAT HAPPENS WHEN I HIDE BEHIND YOUR FAT HEAD!
OZAPPP!
OH, MY GOODNESS! HANK--!
HE WOULDN'T USE LETHAL CHARGES, BUT THREE FULL-FORCE BLASTS RIGHT IN HIS FACE--!
BZLT!
PLOW!
GET OUT OF HERE, YOU STUPID MACHINES!
OH HANK, PLEASE BE ALL RIGHT! I HAD TO BEAT YOU BUT I NEVER WANTED---
HA! GOTCHA!
I TOLD YOU I KNEW YOU, JAN!
BEFORE YOU GROW, YOU'RE GOING TO SLEEP IN THIS GAS-FILLED BUBBLE, HONEY!
AFTER ALL, HOW ELEGANT WOULD I BE IF I USED WEAPONS THAT WORKED ON ME?

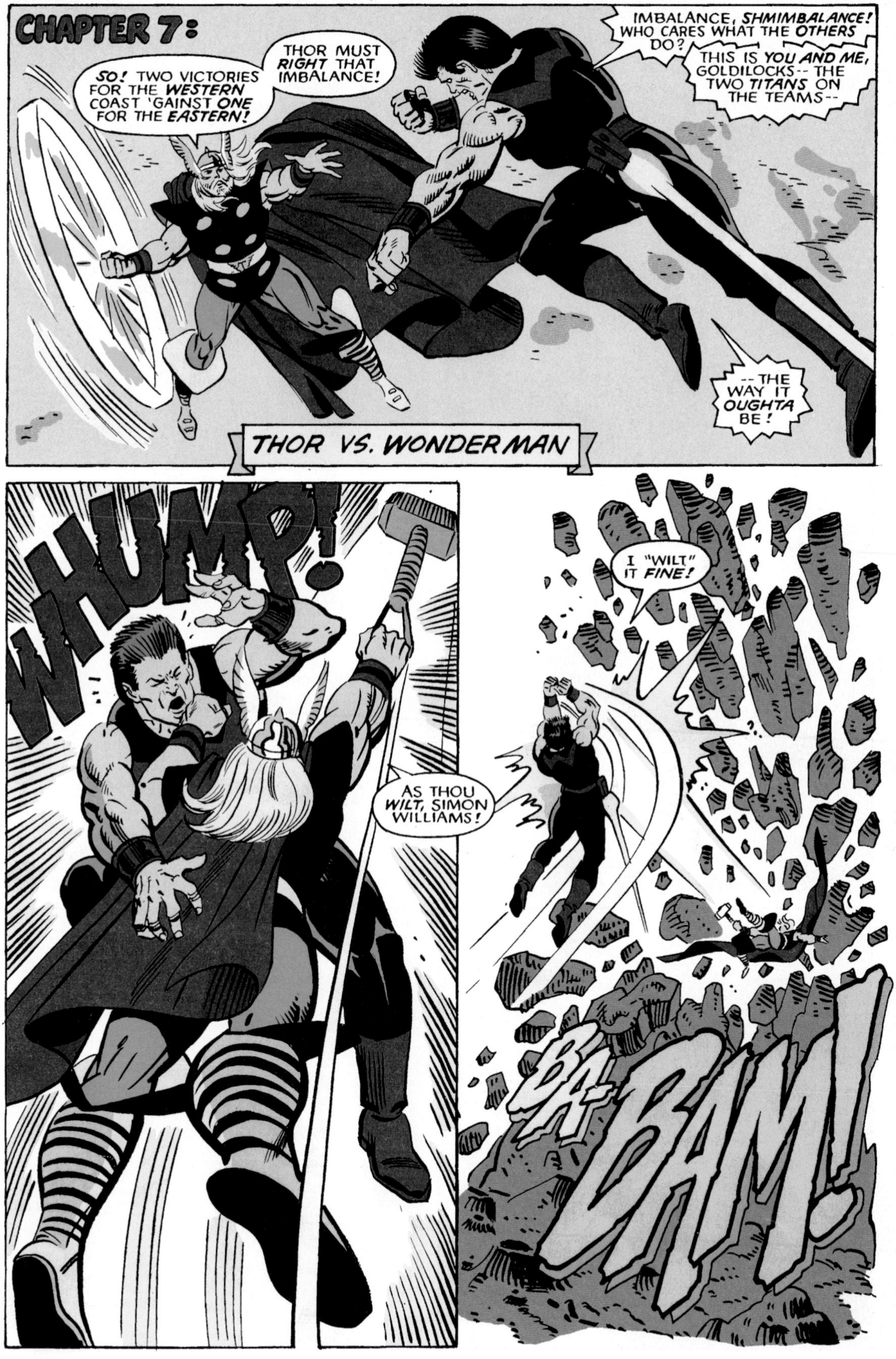
CHAPTER 7:
SO! TWO VICTORIES FOR THE WESTERN COAST 'GAINST ONE FOR THE EASTERN!
THOR MUST RIGHT THAT IMBALANCE!
IMBALANCE, SHMIMBALANCE! WHO CARES WHAT THE OTHERS DO?
THIS IS YOU AND ME, GOLDILOCKS-- THE TWO TITANS ON THE TEAMS--
--THE WAY IT OUGHTA BE!
THOR VS. WONDER MAN
WHUMP!
AS THOU WILT, SIMON WILLIAMS!
I "WILT" IT FINE!
BA-BAM!

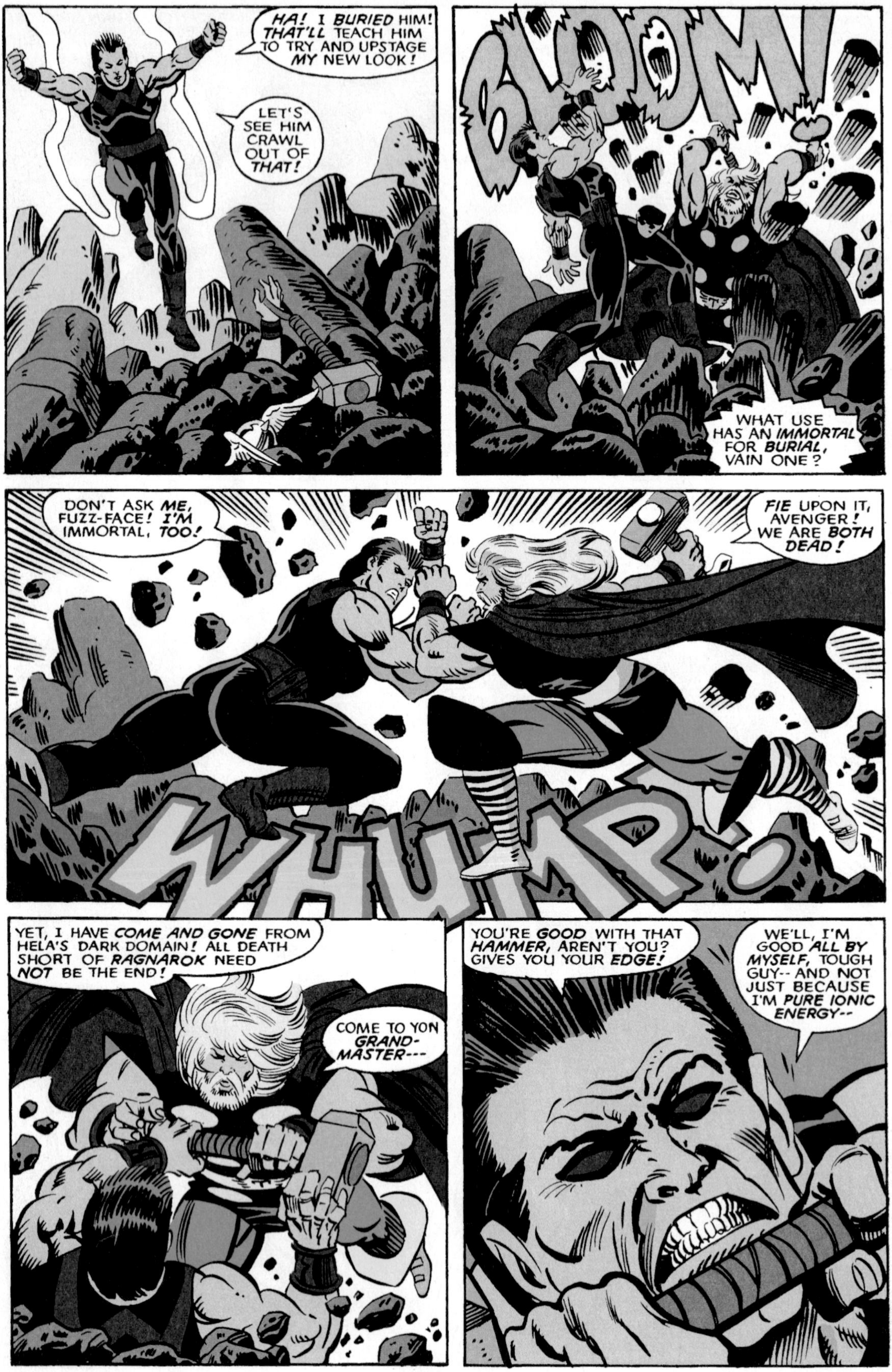
HA! I BURIED HIM! THAT'LL TEACH HIM TO TRY AND UPSTAGE MY NEW LOOK!
LET'S SEE HIM CRAWL OUT OF THAT!
BLOOM!
WHAT USE HAS AN IMMORTAL FOR BURIAL, VAIN ONE?
DON'T ASK ME, FUZZ-FACE! I'M IMMORTAL, TOO!
FIE UPON IT, AVENGER! WE ARE BOTH DEAD!
WHUMP!
YET, I HAVE COME AND GONE FROM HELA'S DARK DOMAIN! ALL DEATH SHORT OF RAGNAROK NEED NOT BE THE END!
COME TO YON GRAND-MASTER---
YOU'RE GOOD WITH THAT HAMMER, AREN'T YOU? GIVES YOU YOUR EDGE!
WE'LL, I'M GOOD ALL BY MYSELF, TOUGH GUY-- AND NOT JUST BECAUSE I'M PURE IONIC ENERGY--

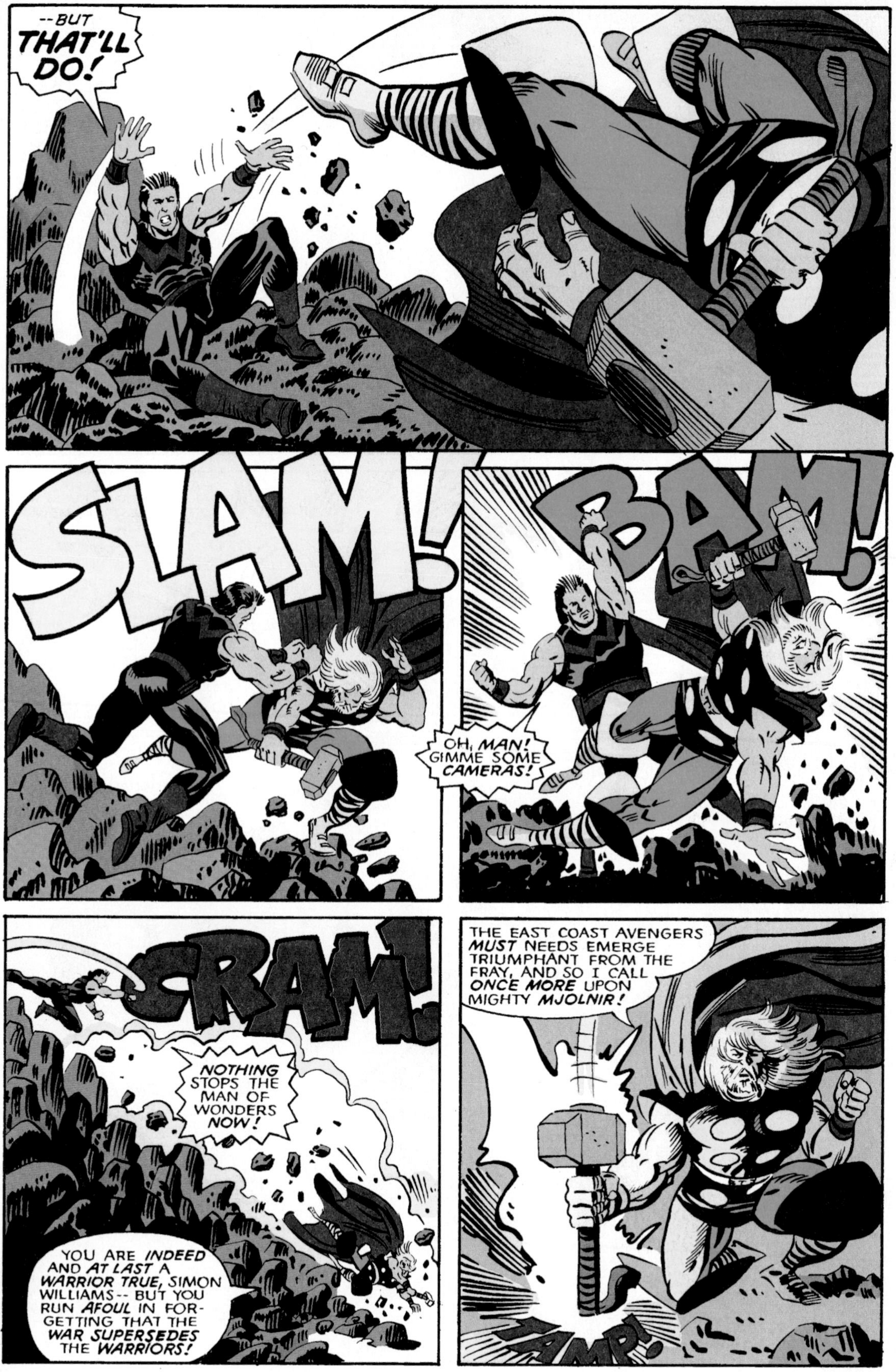

--BUT THAT'LL DO!
SLAM!
BAM!
OH, MAN! GIMME SOME CAMERAS!
CRAM!
NOTHING STOPS THE MAN OF WONDERS NOW!
YOU ARE INDEED AND AT LAST A WARRIOR TRUE, SIMON WILLIAMS-- BUT YOU RUN AFOUL IN FOR-GETTING THAT THE WAR SUPERSEDES THE WARRIORS!
THE EAST COAST AVENGERS MUST NEEDS EMERGE TRIUMPHANT FROM THE FRAY, AND SO I CALL ONCE MORE UPON MIGHTY MJOLNIR!
TAMP!

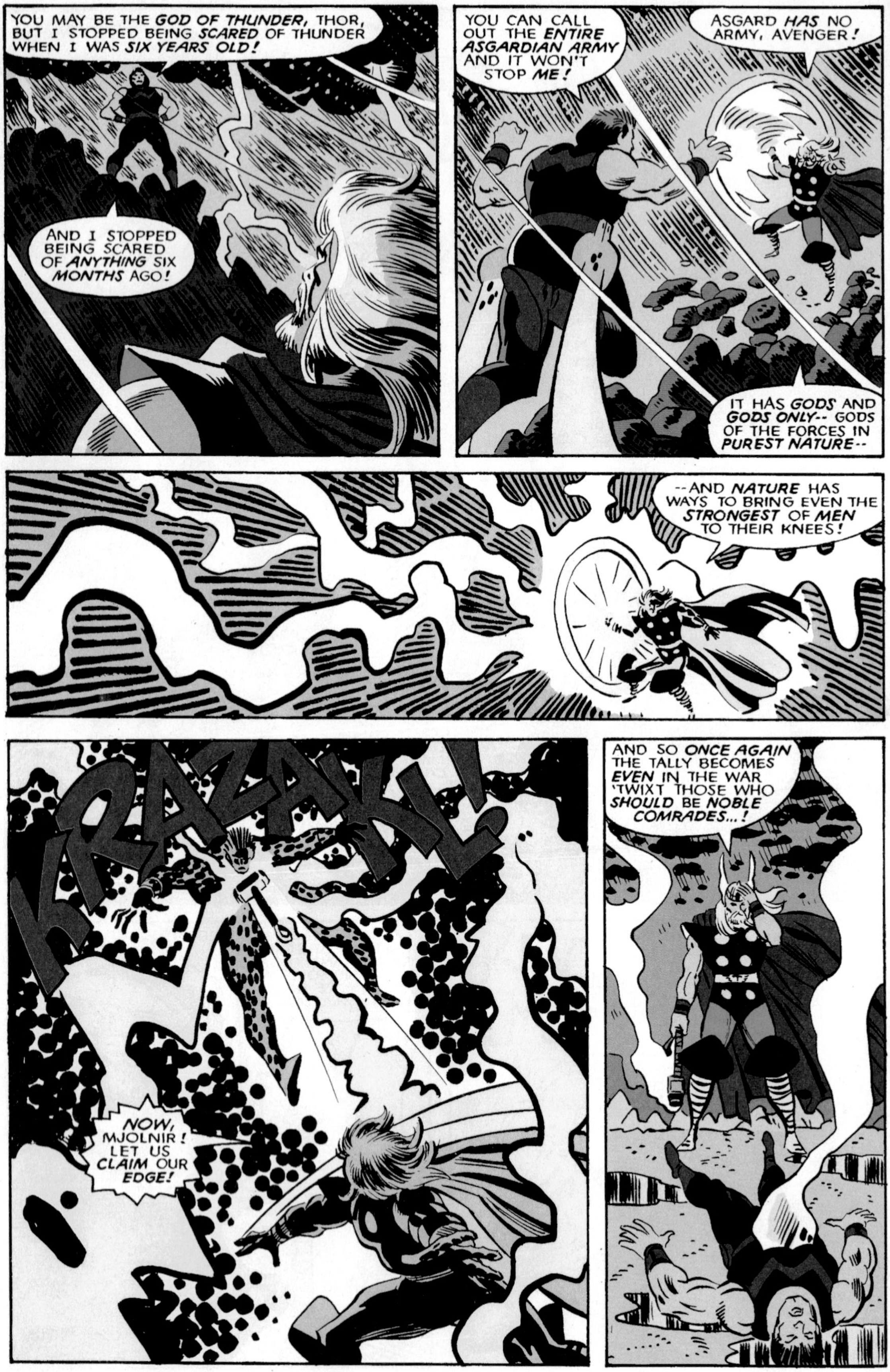
YOU MAY BE THE GOD OF THUNDER, THOR, BUT I STOPPED BEING SCARED OF THUNDER WHEN I WAS SIX YEARS OLD!
AND I STOPPED BEING SCARED OF ANYTHING SIX MONTHS AGO!
YOU CAN CALL OUT THE ENTIRE ASGARDIAN ARMY AND IT WON'T STOP ME!
ASGARD HAS NO ARMY, AVENGER!
IT HAS GODS AND GODS ONLY-- GODS OF THE FORCES IN PUREST NATURE--
--AND NATURE HAS WAYS TO BRING EVEN THE STRONGEST OF MEN TO THEIR KNEES!
KRAZAKL!
NOW, MJOLNIR! LET US CLAIM OUR EDGE!
AND SO ONCE AGAIN THE TALLY BECOMES EVEN IN THE WAR 'TWIXT THOSE WHO SHOULD BE NOBLE COMRADES...!

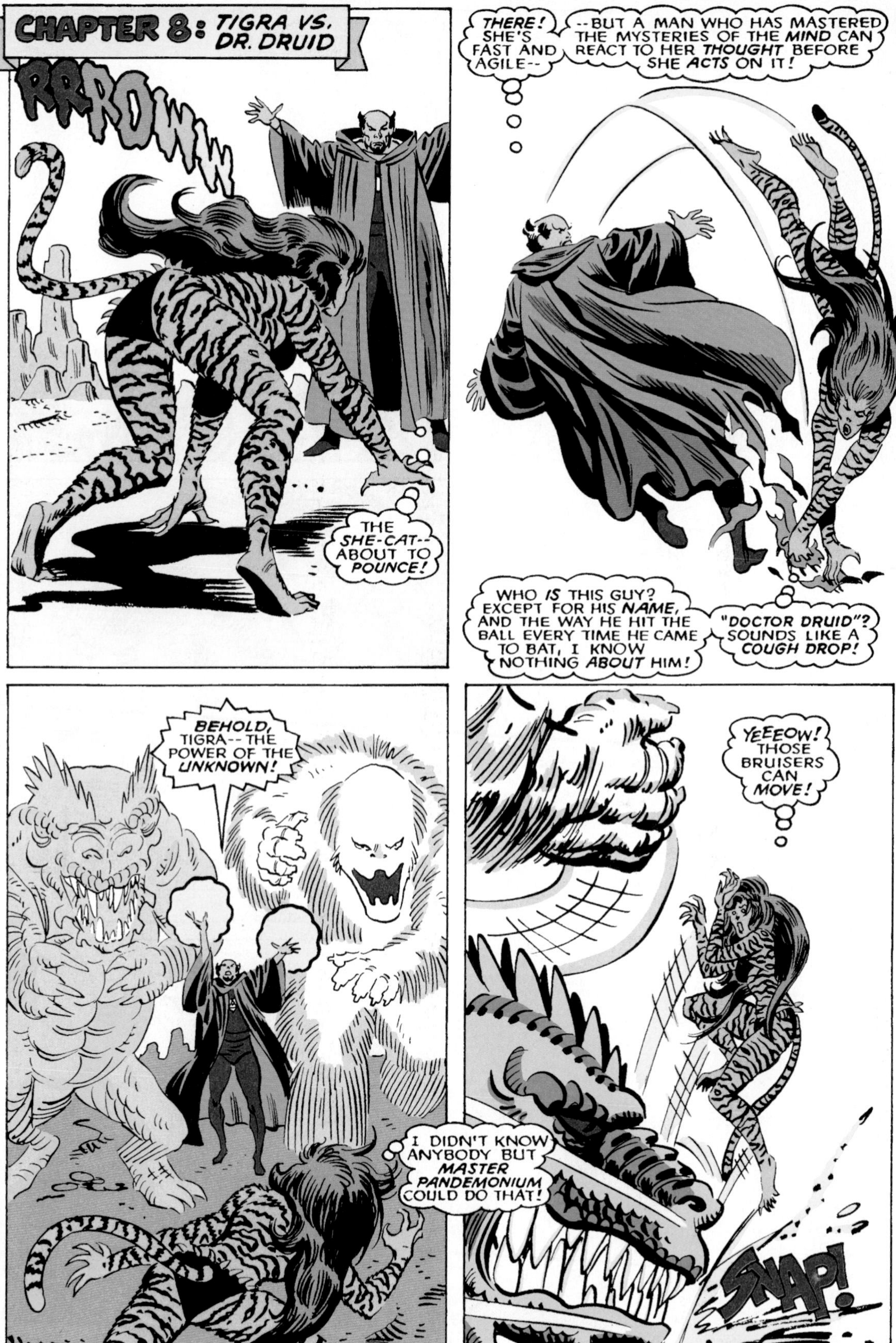
CHAPTER 8: TIGRA VS. DR. DRUID
RRROWW
THE SHE-CAT-- ABOUT TO POUNCE!
THERE! SHE'S FAST AND AGILE--
--BUT A MAN WHO HAS MASTERED THE MYSTERIES OF THE MIND CAN REACT TO HER THOUGHT BEFORE SHE ACTS ON IT!
WHO IS THIS GUY? EXCEPT FOR HIS NAME, AND THE WAY HE HIT THE BALL EVERY TIME HE CAME TO BAT, I KNOW NOTHING ABOUT HIM!
"DOCTOR DRUID"? SOUNDS LIKE A COUGH DROP!
BEHOLD, TIGRA-- THE POWER OF THE UNKNOWN!
I DIDN'T KNOW ANYBODY BUT MASTER PANDEMONIUM COULD DO THAT!
YEEEOW! THOSE BRUISERS CAN MOVE!
SNAP!

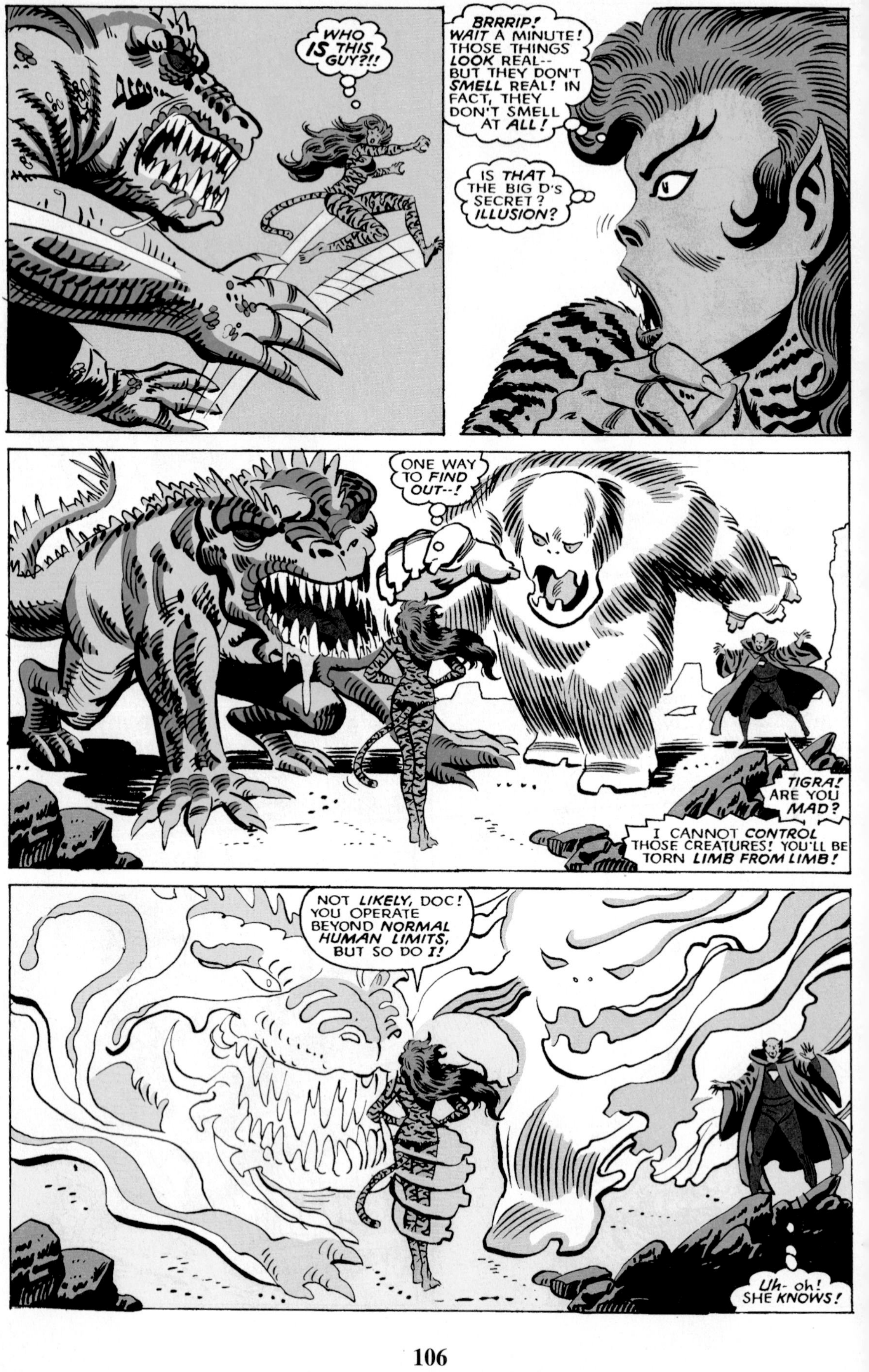
WHO IS THIS GUY?!!
BRRRIP! WAIT A MINUTE! THOSE THINGS LOOK REAL-- BUT THEY DON'T SMELL REAL! IN FACT, THEY DON'T SMELL AT ALL!
IS THAT THE BIG D'S SECRET? ILLUSION?
ONE WAY TO FIND OUT--!
TIGRA! ARE YOU MAD?
I CANNOT CONTROL THOSE CREATURES! YOU'LL BE TORN LIMB FROM LIMB!
NOT LIKELY, DOC! YOU OPERATE BEYOND NORMAL HUMAN LIMITS, BUT SO DO I!
Uh- oh! SHE KNOWS!

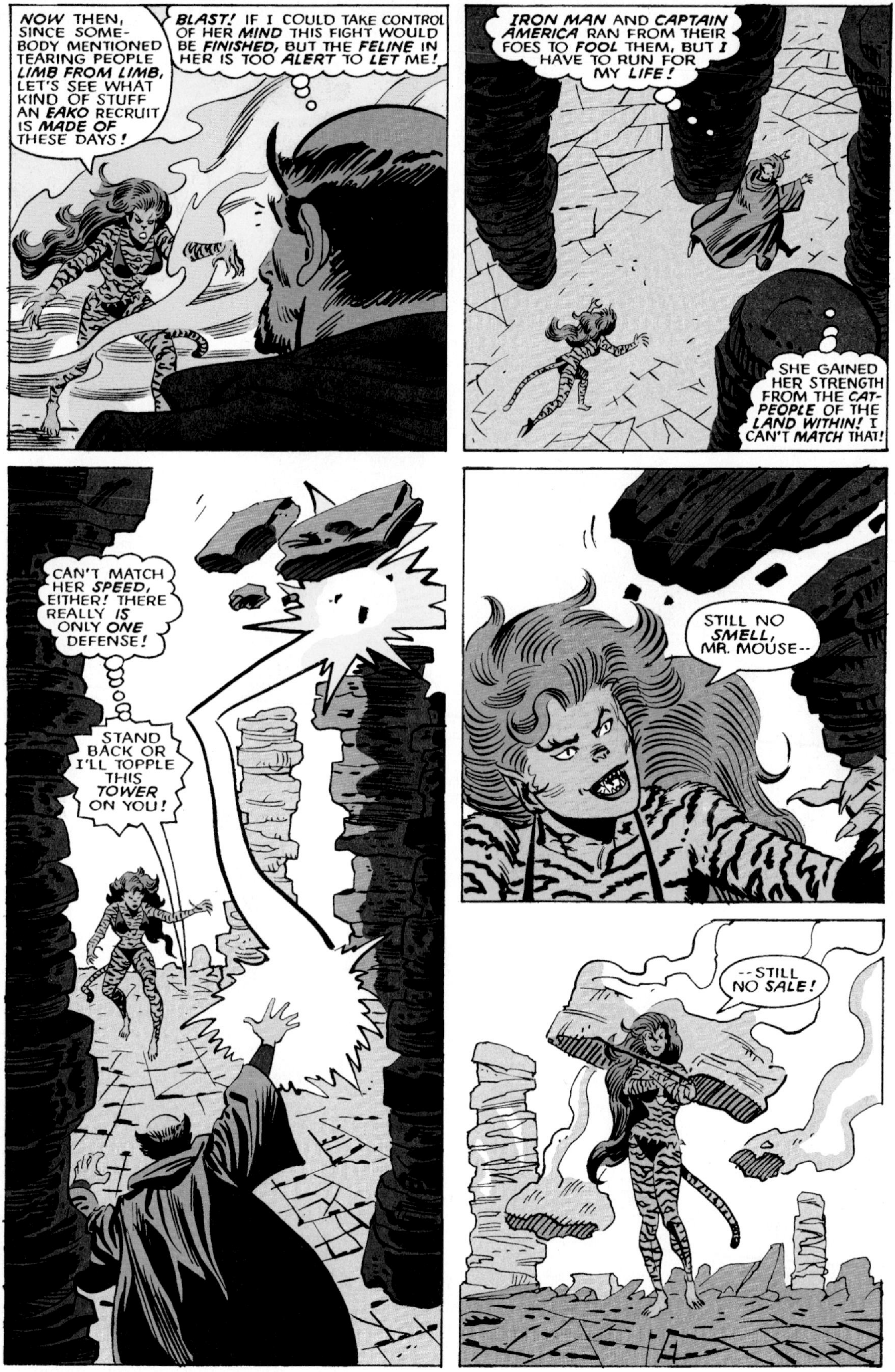
NOW THEN, SINCE SOMEBODY MENTIONED TEARING PEOPLE LIMB FROM LIMB, LET'S SEE WHAT KIND OF STUFF AN EAKO RECRUIT IS MADE OF THESE DAYS!
BLAST! IF I COULD TAKE CONTROL OF HER MIND THIS FIGHT WOULD BE FINISHED, BUT THE FELINE IN HER IS TOO ALERT TO LET ME!
IRON MAN AND CAPTAIN AMERICA RAN FROM THEIR FOES TO FOOL THEM, BUT I HAVE TO RUN FOR MY LIFE!
SHE GAINED HER STRENGTH FROM THE CAT-PEOPLE OF THE LAND WITHIN! I CAN'T MATCH THAT!
CAN'T MATCH HER SPEED, EITHER! THERE REALLY IS ONLY ONE DEFENSE!
STAND BACK OR I'LL TOPPLE THIS TOWER ON YOU!
STILL NO SMELL, MR. MOUSE--
--STILL NO SALE!

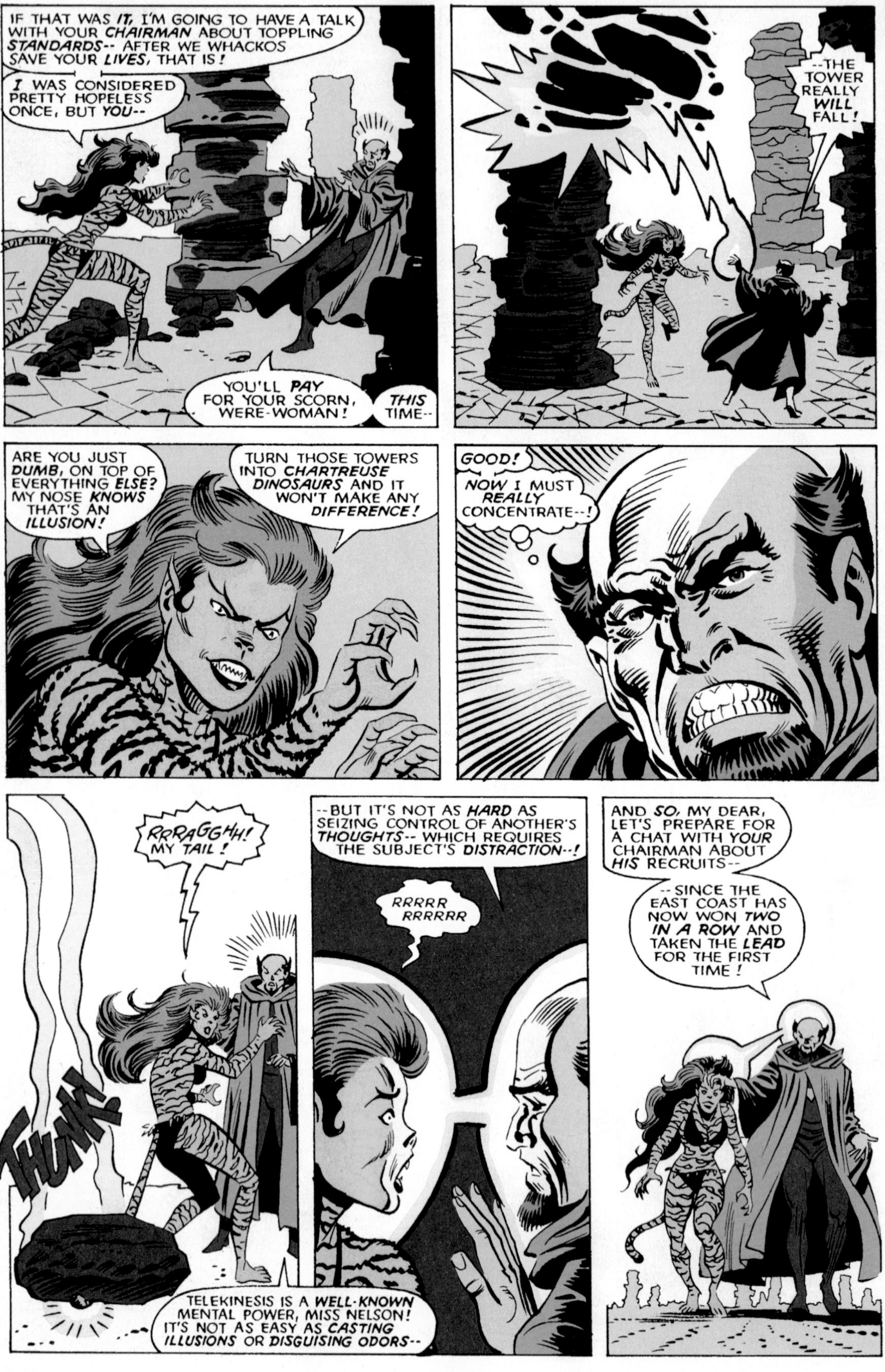

IF THAT WAS *IT*, I'M GOING TO HAVE A TALK WITH YOUR *CHAIRMAN* ABOUT TOPPLING *STANDARDS*-- AFTER WE WHACKOS SAVE YOUR *LIVES*, THAT IS!
*I* WAS CONSIDERED PRETTY HOPELESS ONCE, BUT *YOU*--
YOU'LL *PAY* FOR YOUR SCORN, WERE-WOMAN!
*THIS* TIME--
--THE TOWER REALLY *WILL* FALL!
ARE YOU JUST *DUMB*, ON TOP OF EVERYTHING *ELSE*? MY NOSE *KNOWS* THAT'S AN *ILLUSION*!
TURN THOSE TOWERS INTO *CHARTREUSE DINOSAURS* AND IT WON'T MAKE ANY *DIFFERENCE*!
*GOOD!*
*NOW* I MUST *REALLY* CONCENTRATE--!
*RRRAGGHH!* MY *TAIL*!
THUNK!
TELEKINESIS IS A *WELL-KNOWN* MENTAL POWER, MISS NELSON! IT'S NOT AS EASY AS *CASTING ILLUSIONS* OR *DISGUISING ODORS*--
--BUT IT'S NOT AS *HARD* AS SEIZING CONTROL OF ANOTHER'S *THOUGHTS*-- WHICH REQUIRES THE SUBJECT'S *DISTRACTION*--!
*RRRRR RRRRRR*
AND *SO*, MY DEAR, LET'S PREPARE FOR A CHAT WITH *YOUR* CHAIRMAN ABOUT *HIS* RECRUITS--
--SINCE THE EAST COAST HAS NOW WON *TWO IN A ROW* AND TAKEN THE *LEAD* FOR THE FIRST TIME!

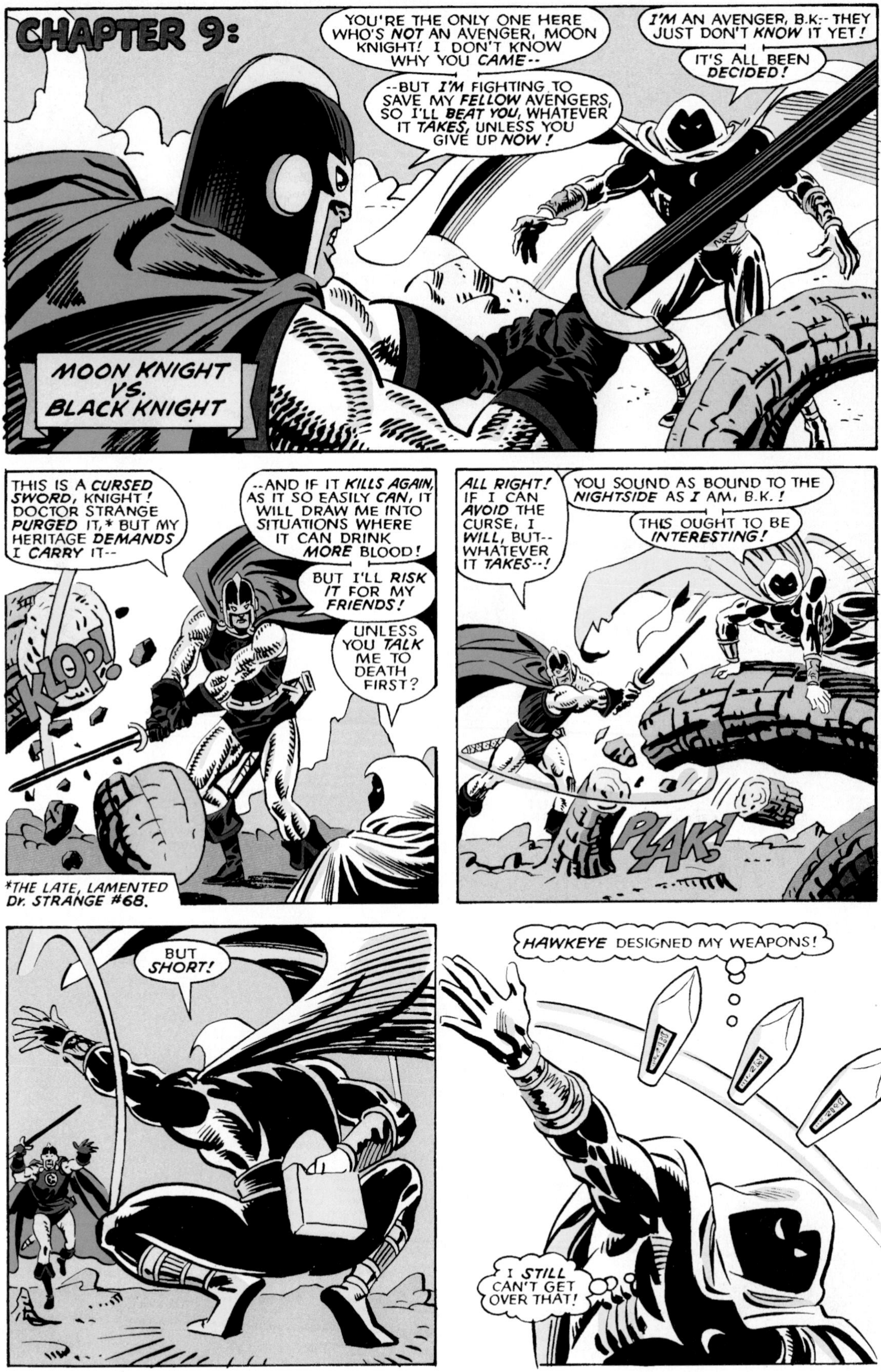

CHAPTER 9:
YOU'RE THE ONLY ONE HERE WHO'S NOT AN AVENGER, MOON KNIGHT! I DON'T KNOW WHY YOU CAME--
--BUT I'M FIGHTING TO SAVE MY FELLOW AVENGERS, SO I'LL BEAT YOU, WHATEVER IT TAKES, UNLESS YOU GIVE UP NOW!
I'M AN AVENGER, B.K.-- THEY JUST DON'T KNOW IT YET!
IT'S ALL BEEN DECIDED!
MOON KNIGHT VS. BLACK KNIGHT
THIS IS A CURSED SWORD, KNIGHT! DOCTOR STRANGE PURGED IT,* BUT MY HERITAGE DEMANDS I CARRY IT--
--AND IF IT KILLS AGAIN, AS IT SO EASILY CAN, IT WILL DRAW ME INTO SITUATIONS WHERE IT CAN DRINK MORE BLOOD!
BUT I'LL RISK IT FOR MY FRIENDS!
UNLESS YOU TALK ME TO DEATH FIRST?
KLOP!
*THE LATE, LAMENTED Dr. STRANGE #68.
ALL RIGHT! IF I CAN AVOID THE CURSE, I WILL, BUT-- WHATEVER IT TAKES--!
YOU SOUND AS BOUND TO THE NIGHTSIDE AS I AM, B.K.!
THIS OUGHT TO BE INTERESTING!
PLAK!
BUT SHORT!
HAWKEYE DESIGNED MY WEAPONS!
I STILL CAN'T GET OVER THAT!

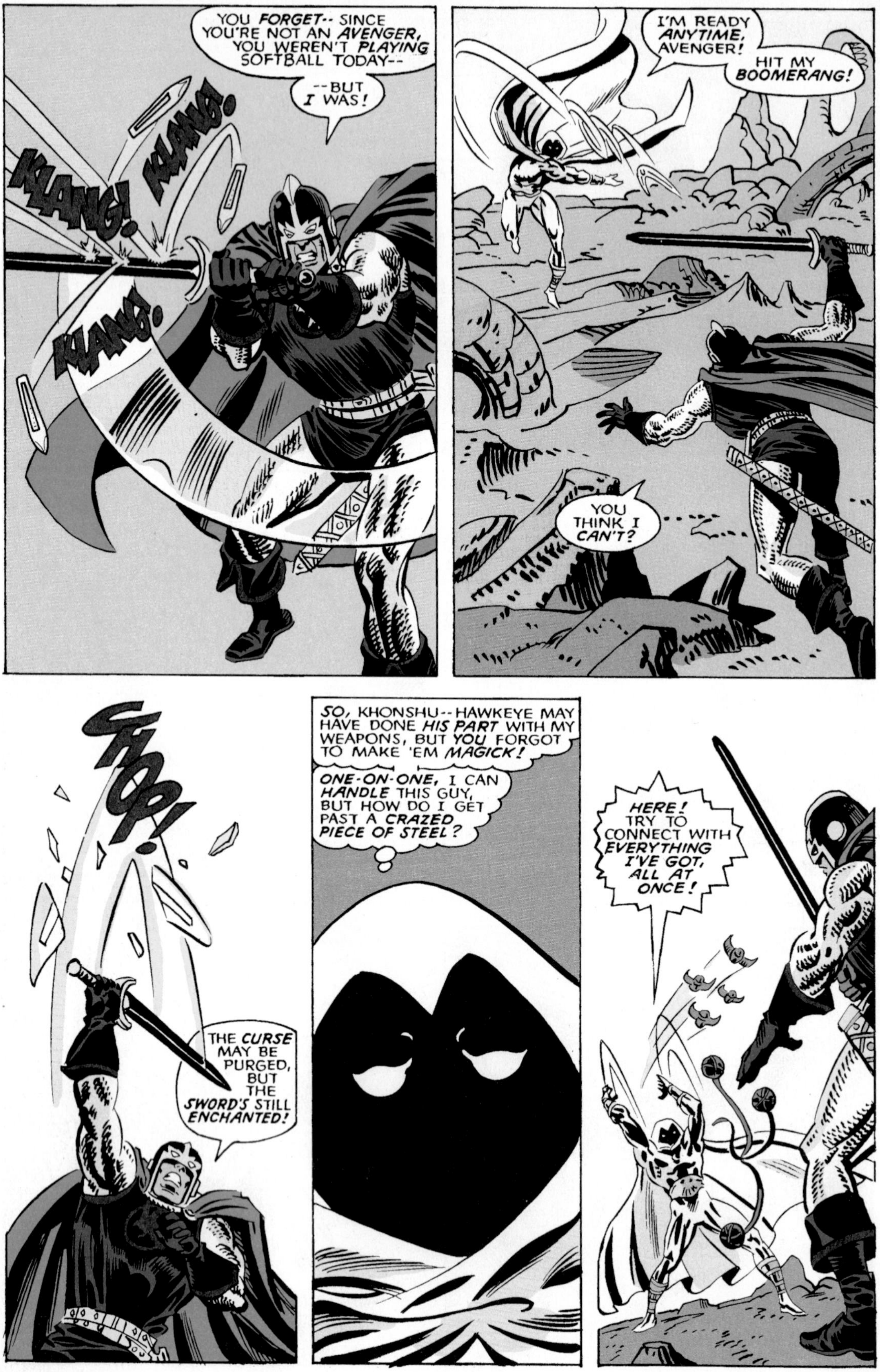

YOU FORGET-- SINCE YOU'RE NOT AN AVENGER, YOU WEREN'T PLAYING SOFTBALL TODAY--
--BUT I WAS!
KLANG!
KLANG!
KLANG!
I'M READY ANYTIME, AVENGER!
HIT MY BOOMERANG!
YOU THINK I CAN'T?
CHOP!
THE CURSE MAY BE PURGED, BUT THE SWORD'S STILL ENCHANTED!
SO, KHONSHU--HAWKEYE MAY HAVE DONE HIS PART WITH MY WEAPONS, BUT YOU FORGOT TO MAKE 'EM MAGICK!
ONE-ON-ONE, I CAN HANDLE THIS GUY, BUT HOW DO I GET PAST A CRAZED PIECE OF STEEL?
HERE! TRY TO CONNECT WITH EVERYTHING I'VE GOT, ALL AT ONCE!

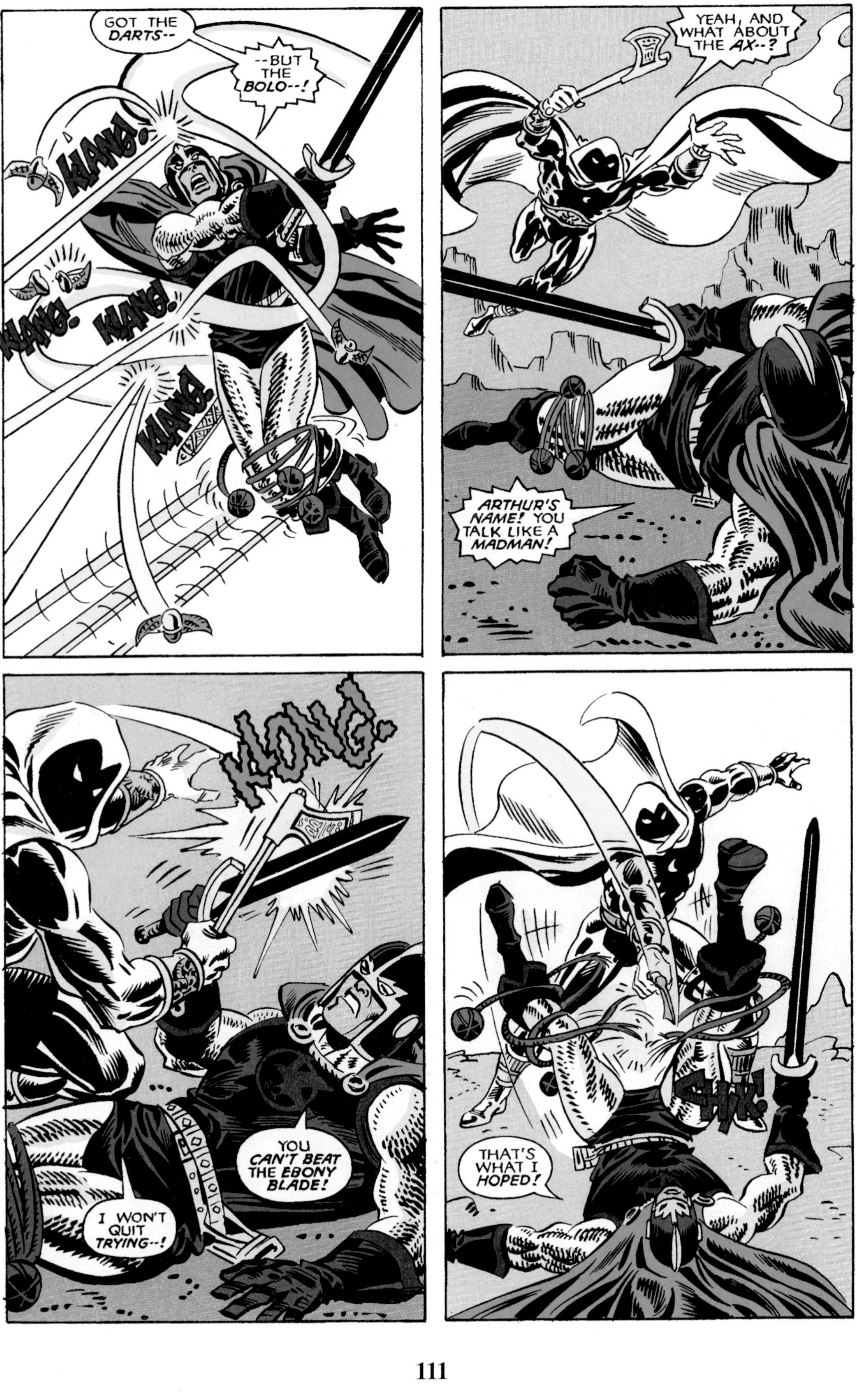
GOT THE *DARTS*--
--BUT THE *BOLO*--!
KLANG!
KLANG!
KLANG!
KLANG!
YEAH, AND WHAT ABOUT THE *AX*--?
*ARTHUR'S NAME!* YOU TALK LIKE A *MADMAN!*
KLONG!
YOU *CAN'T BEAT* THE *EBONY BLADE!*
I WON'T QUIT *TRYING*--!
THAT'S WHAT I *HOPED!*
CHK!

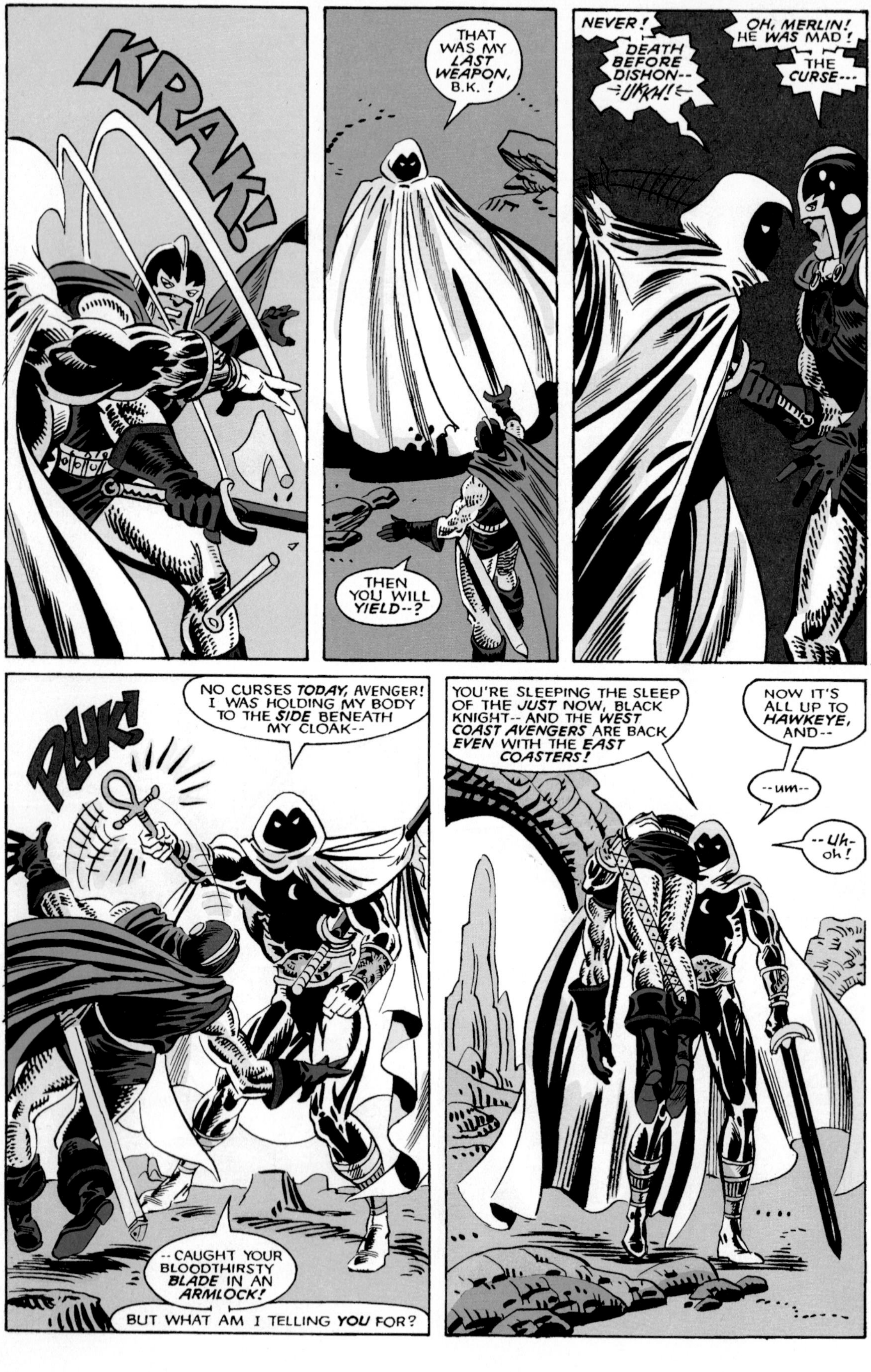
KRAK!
THAT WAS MY LAST WEAPON, B.K.!
THEN YOU WILL YIELD--?
NEVER!
DEATH BEFORE DISHON--
UKKH!
OH, MERLIN! HE WAS MAD!
THE CURSE---
PLUK!
NO CURSES TODAY, AVENGER! I WAS HOLDING MY BODY TO THE SIDE BENEATH MY CLOAK--
--CAUGHT YOUR BLOODTHIRSTY BLADE IN AN ARMLOCK!
BUT WHAT AM I TELLING YOU FOR?
YOU'RE SLEEPING THE SLEEP OF THE JUST NOW, BLACK KNIGHT-- AND THE WEST COAST AVENGERS ARE BACK EVEN WITH THE EAST COASTERS!
NOW IT'S ALL UP TO HAWKEYE, AND--
--um--
--Uh-oh!

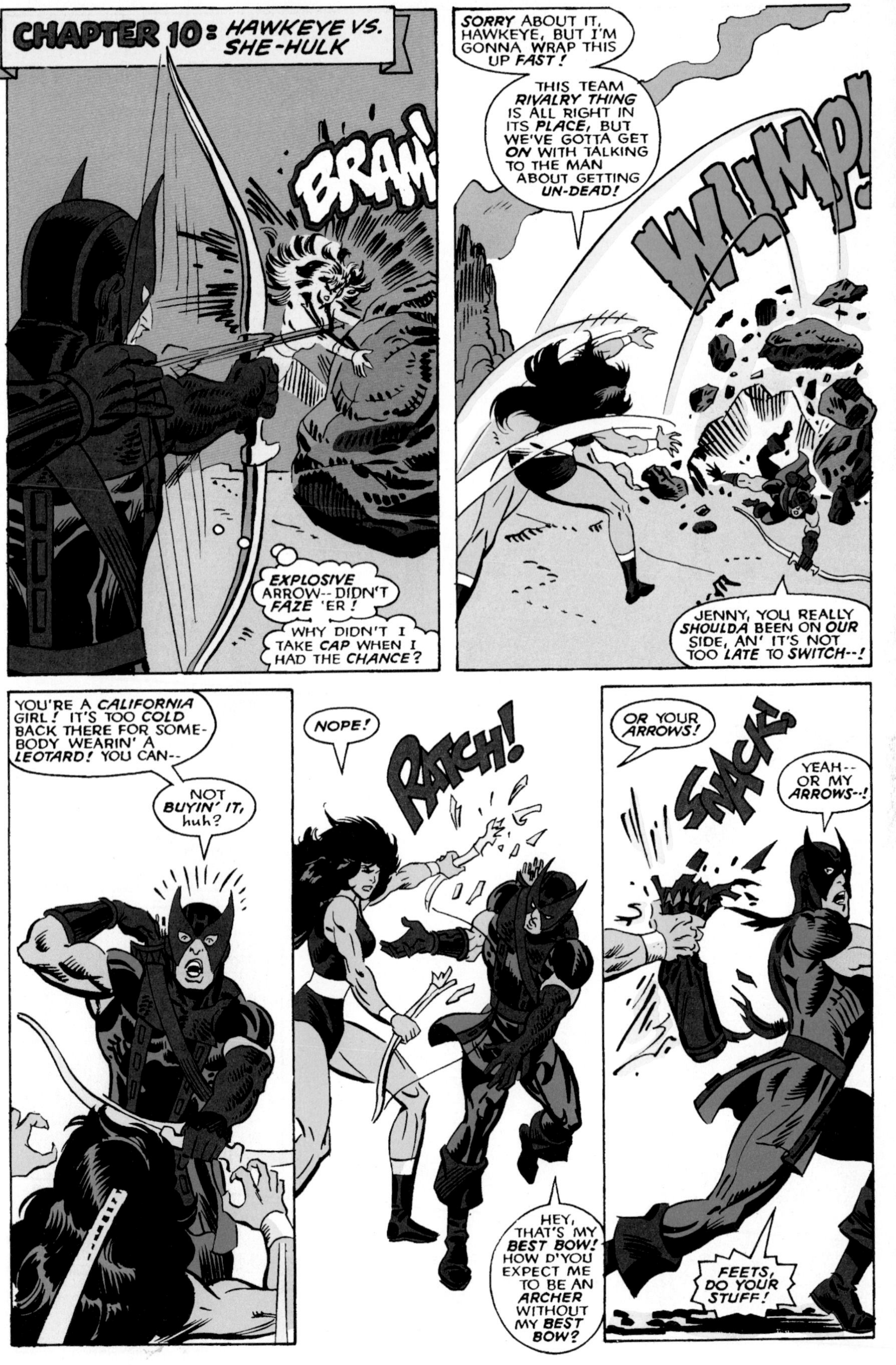
CHAPTER 10: HAWKEYE VS. SHE-HULK
BRAM!
EXPLOSIVE ARROW-- DIDN'T FAZE 'ER!
WHY DIDN'T I TAKE CAP WHEN I HAD THE CHANCE?
SORRY ABOUT IT, HAWKEYE, BUT I'M GONNA WRAP THIS UP FAST!
THIS TEAM RIVALRY THING IS ALL RIGHT IN ITS PLACE, BUT WE'VE GOTTA GET ON WITH TALKING TO THE MAN ABOUT GETTING UN-DEAD!
WUMP!
JENNY, YOU REALLY SHOULDA BEEN ON OUR SIDE, AN' IT'S NOT TOO LATE TO SWITCH--!
YOU'RE A CALIFORNIA GIRL! IT'S TOO COLD BACK THERE FOR SOMEBODY WEARIN' A LEOTARD! YOU CAN--
NOT BUYIN' IT, huh?
NOPE!
RATCH!
HEY, THAT'S MY BEST BOW! HOW D'YOU EXPECT ME TO BE AN ARCHER WITHOUT MY BEST BOW?
OR YOUR ARROWS!
SNACK!
YEAH-- OR MY ARROWS--!
FEETS, DO YOUR STUFF!

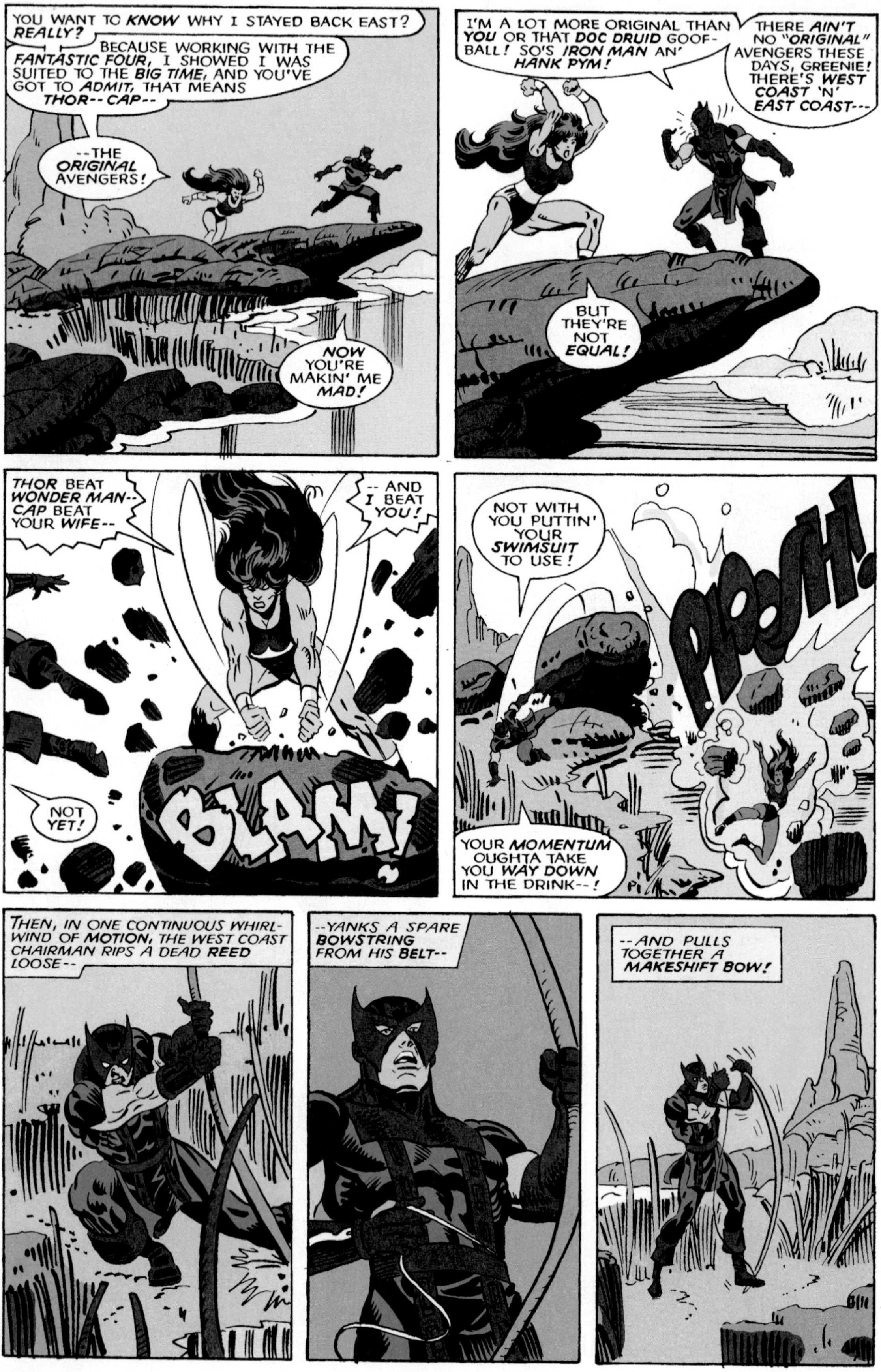
YOU WANT TO KNOW WHY I STAYED BACK EAST? REALLY?
BECAUSE WORKING WITH THE FANTASTIC FOUR, I SHOWED I WAS SUITED TO THE BIG TIME, AND YOU'VE GOT TO ADMIT, THAT MEANS THOR-- CAP--
--THE ORIGINAL AVENGERS!
NOW YOU'RE MAKIN' ME MAD!
I'M A LOT MORE ORIGINAL THAN YOU OR THAT DOC DRUID GOOF-BALL! SO'S IRON MAN AN' HANK PYM!
THERE AIN'T NO "ORIGINAL" AVENGERS THESE DAYS, GREENIE! THERE'S WEST COAST 'N' EAST COAST---
BUT THEY'RE NOT EQUAL!
THOR BEAT WONDER MAN-- CAP BEAT YOUR WIFE--
-- AND I BEAT YOU!
NOT YET!
BLAM!
NOT WITH YOU PUTTIN' YOUR SWIMSUIT TO USE!
PPPESH!
YOUR MOMENTUM OUGHTA TAKE YOU WAY DOWN IN THE DRINK--!
THEN, IN ONE CONTINUOUS WHIRL-WIND OF MOTION, THE WEST COAST CHAIRMAN RIPS A DEAD REED LOOSE--
--YANKS A SPARE BOWSTRING FROM HIS BELT--
--AND PULLS TOGETHER A MAKESHIFT BOW!

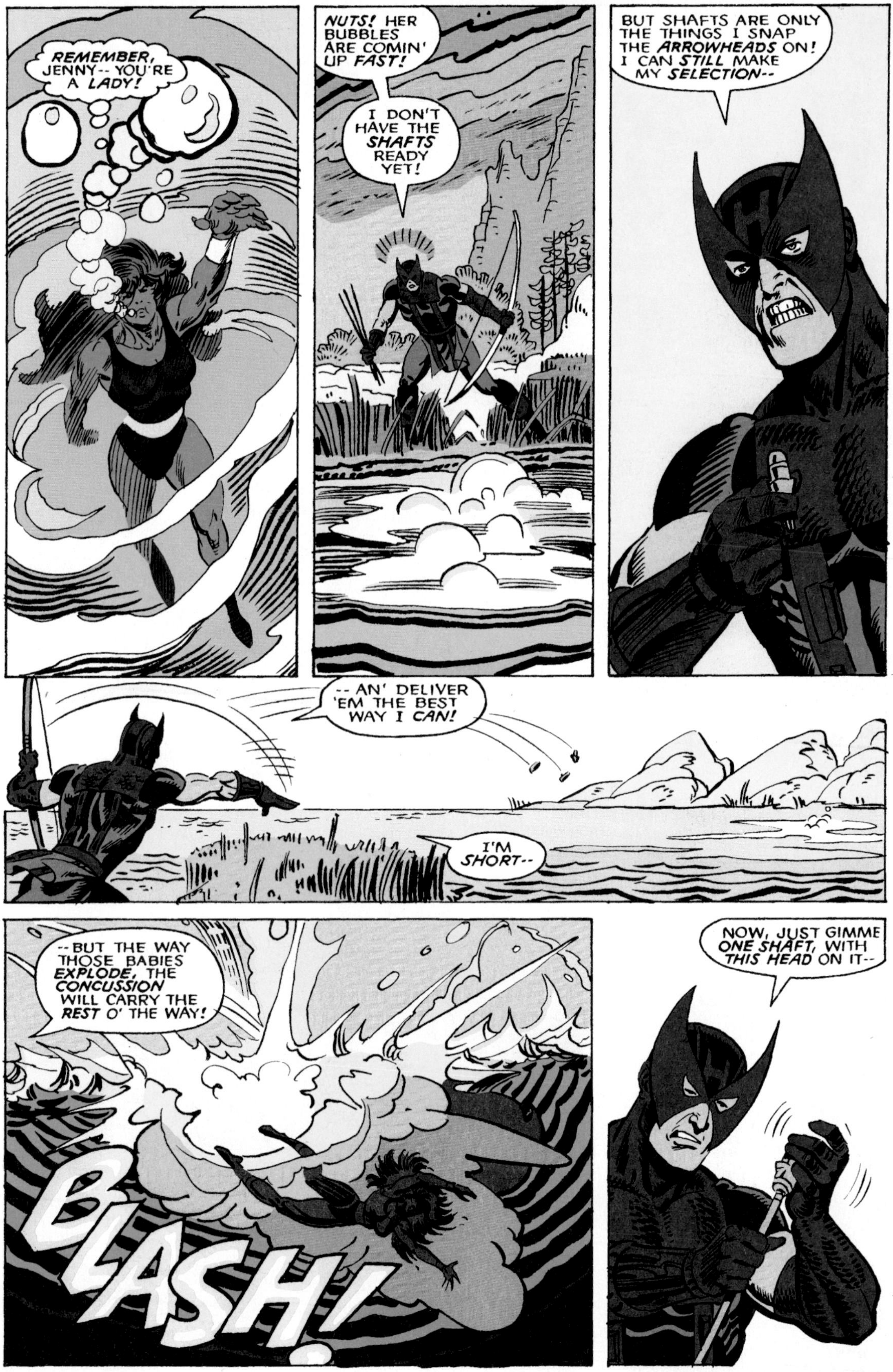
REMEMBER, JENNY-- YOU'RE A LADY!
NUTS! HER BUBBLES ARE COMIN' UP FAST!
I DON'T HAVE THE SHAFTS READY YET!
BUT SHAFTS ARE ONLY THE THINGS I SNAP THE ARROWHEADS ON! I CAN STILL MAKE MY SELECTION--
--AN' DELIVER 'EM THE BEST WAY I CAN!
I'M SHORT--
--BUT THE WAY THOSE BABIES EXPLODE, THE CONCUSSION WILL CARRY THE REST O' THE WAY!
BLASH!
NOW, JUST GIMME ONE SHAFT, WITH THIS HEAD ON IT--

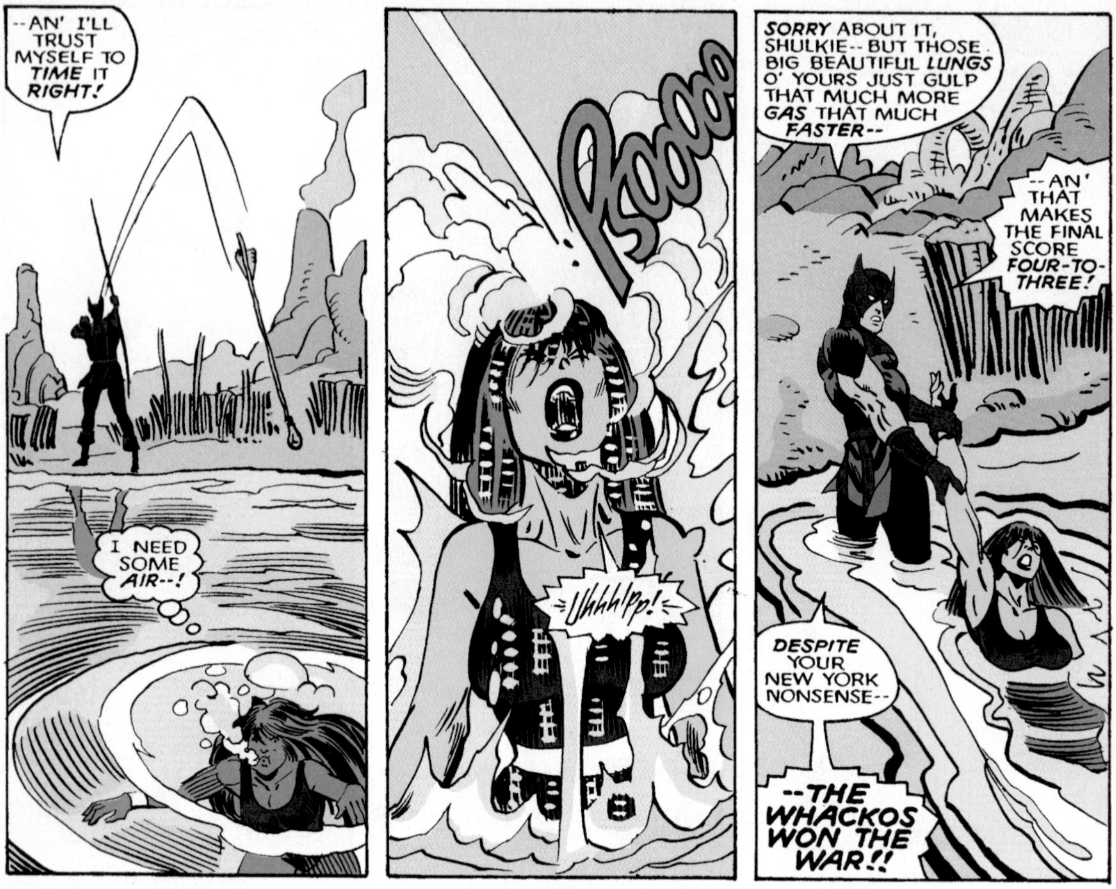
--AN' I'LL TRUST MYSELF TO TIME IT RIGHT!
I NEED SOME AIR--!
Poooo
Uhhhlpp!
SORRY ABOUT IT, SHULKIE-- BUT THOSE BIG BEAUTIFUL LUNGS O' YOURS JUST GULP THAT MUCH MORE GAS THAT MUCH FASTER--
--AN' THAT MAKES THE FINAL SCORE FOUR-TO-THREE!
DESPITE YOUR NEW YORK NONSENSE--
--THE WHACKOS WON THE WAR!!

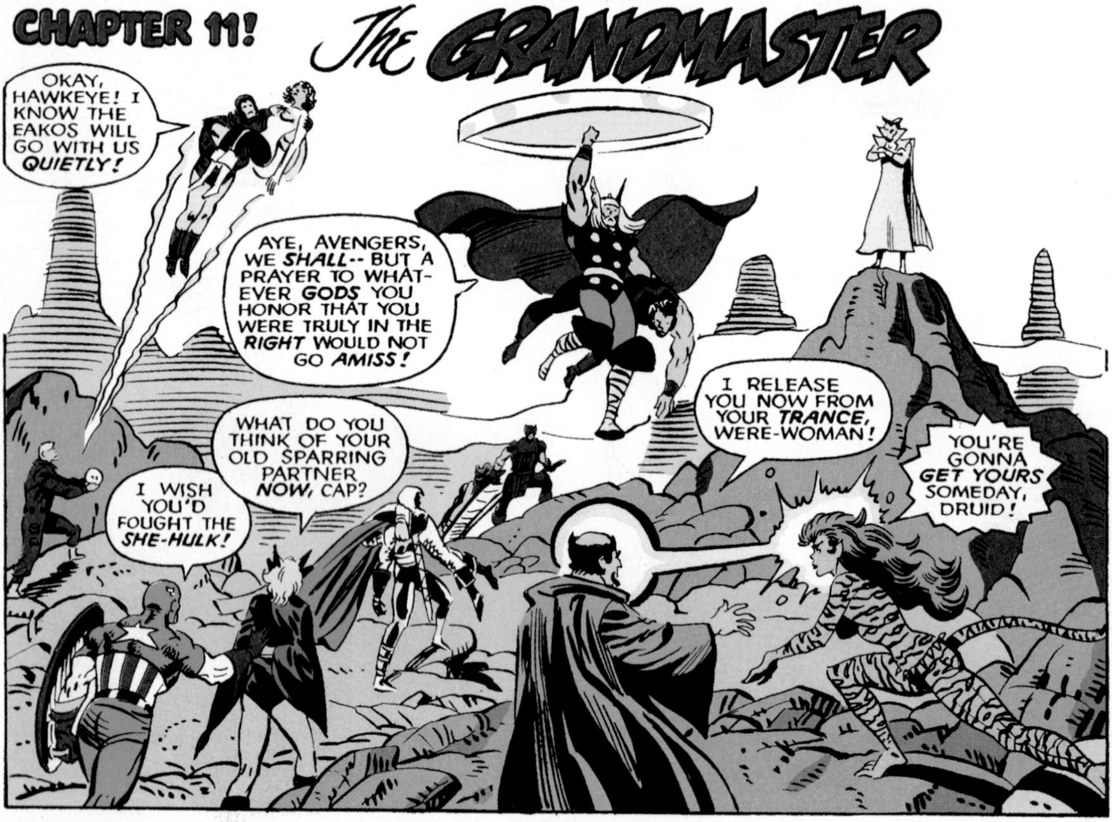
CHAPTER 11!
The GRANDMASTER
OKAY, HAWKEYE! I KNOW THE EAKOS WILL GO WITH US QUIETLY!
AYE, AVENGERS, WE SHALL-- BUT A PRAYER TO WHAT-EVER GODS YOU HONOR THAT YOU WERE TRULY IN THE RIGHT WOULD NOT GO AMISS!
I RELEASE YOU NOW FROM YOUR TRANCE, WERE-WOMAN!
YOU'RE GONNA GET YOURS SOMEDAY, DRUID!
WHAT DO YOU THINK OF YOUR OLD SPARRING PARTNER NOW, CAP?
I WISH YOU'D FOUGHT THE SHE-HULK!

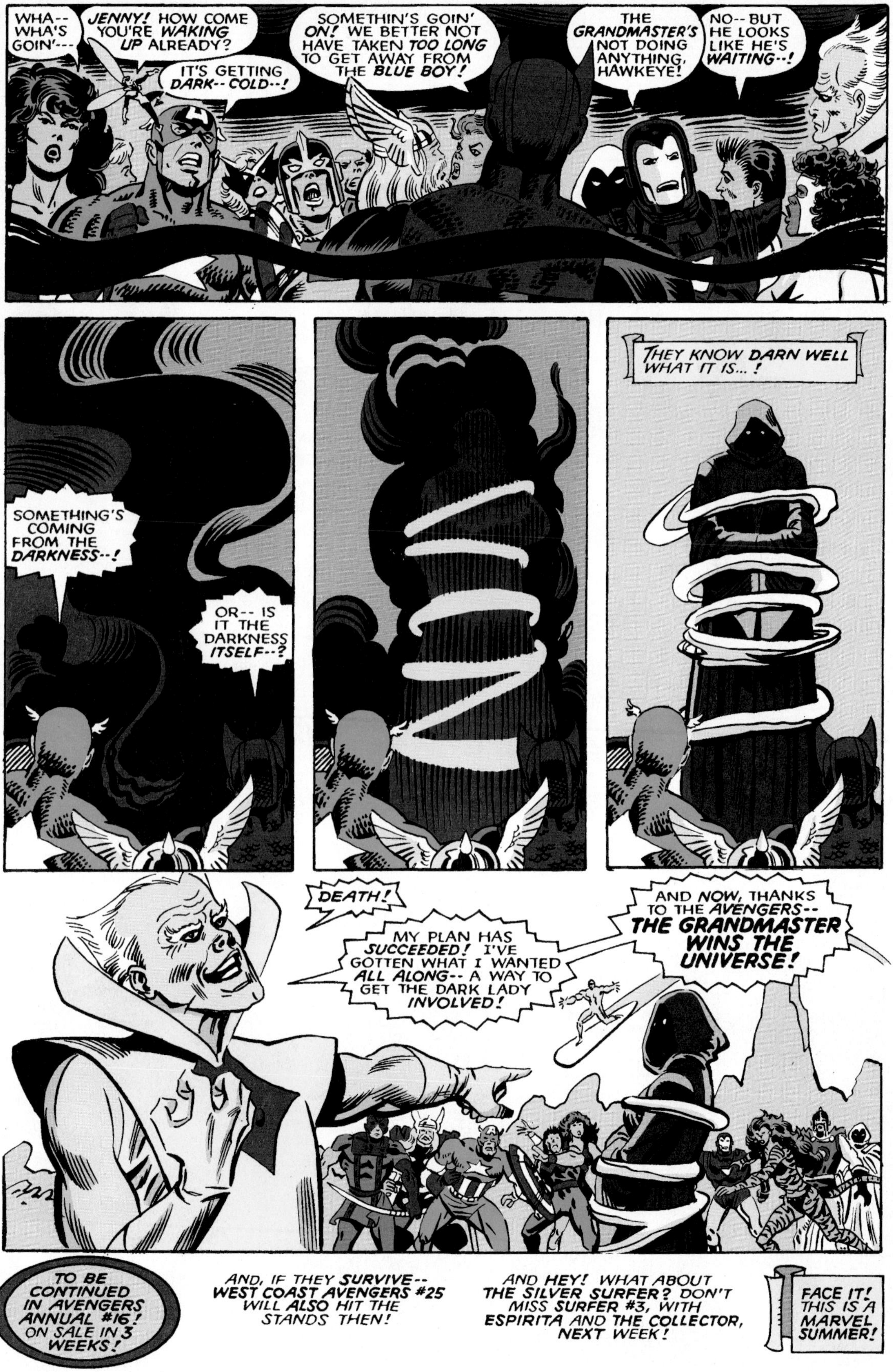
WHA-- WHA'S GOIN'---
JENNY! HOW COME YOU'RE WAKING UP ALREADY?
IT'S GETTING DARK-- COLD--!
SOMETHIN'S GOIN' ON! WE BETTER NOT HAVE TAKEN TOO LONG TO GET AWAY FROM THE BLUE BOY!
THE GRANDMASTER'S NOT DOING ANYTHING, HAWKEYE!
NO-- BUT HE LOOKS LIKE HE'S WAITING--!
SOMETHING'S COMING FROM THE DARKNESS--!
OR-- IS IT THE DARKNESS ITSELF--?
THEY KNOW DARN WELL WHAT IT IS...!
DEATH!
MY PLAN HAS SUCCEEDED! I'VE GOTTEN WHAT I WANTED ALL ALONG-- A WAY TO GET THE DARK LADY INVOLVED!
AND NOW, THANKS TO THE AVENGERS-- THE GRANDMASTER WINS THE UNIVERSE!
TO BE CONTINUED IN AVENGERS ANNUAL #16! ON SALE IN 3 WEEKS!
AND, IF THEY SURVIVE-- WEST COAST AVENGERS #25 WILL ALSO HIT THE STANDS THEN!
AND HEY! WHAT ABOUT THE SILVER SURFER? DON'T MISS SURFER #3, WITH ESPIRITA AND THE COLLECTOR, NEXT WEEK!
FACE IT! THIS IS A MARVEL SUMMER!

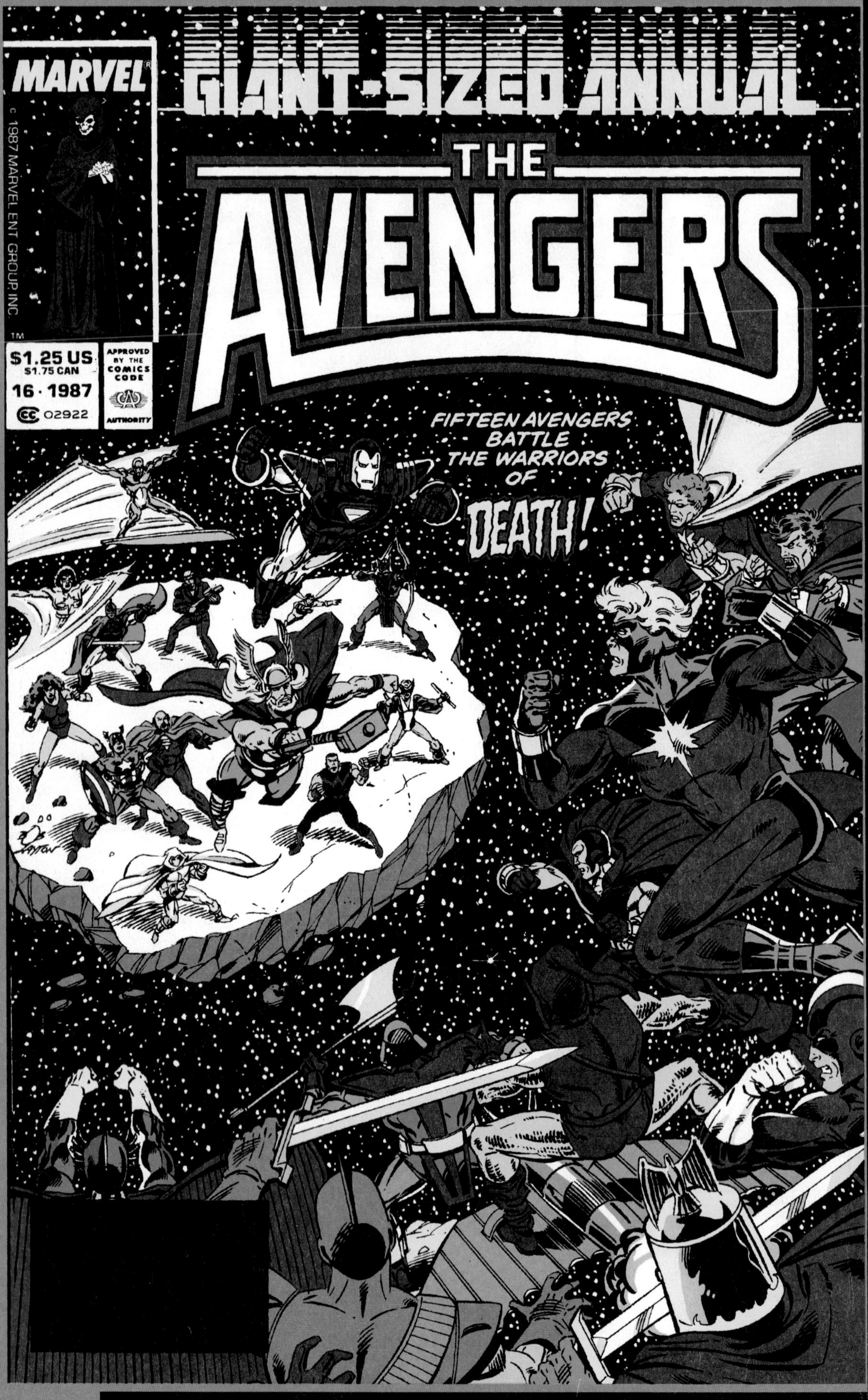
MARVEL
GIANT-SIZED ANNUAL
THE AVENGERS
c 1987 MARVEL ENT GROUP INC.
TM
$1.25 US
$1.75 CAN
16 · 1987
02922
APPROVED BY THE COMICS CODE AUTHORITY
FIFTEEN AVENGERS BATTLE THE WARRIORS OF DEATH!

STAN LEE PRESENTS:

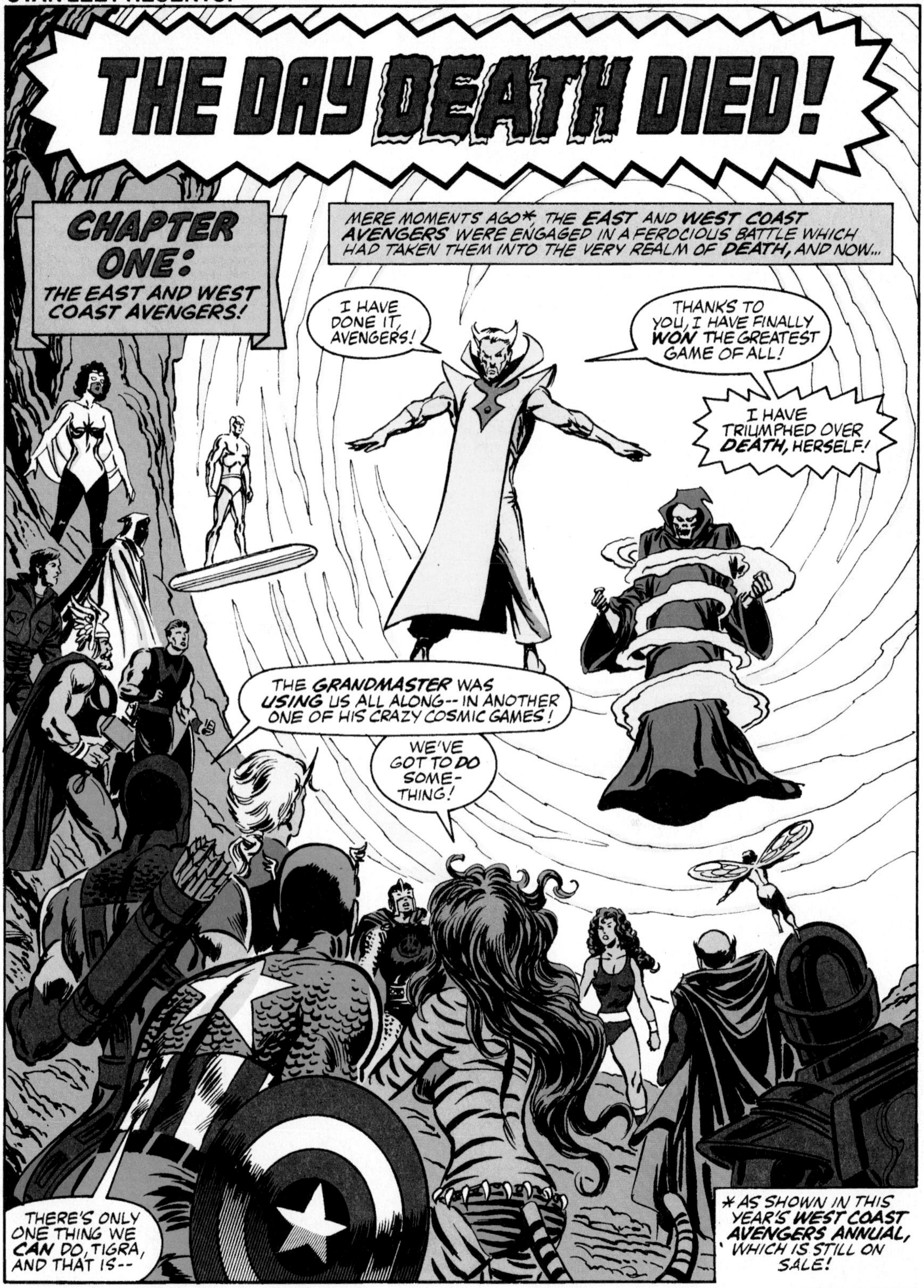

THE DAY DEATH DIED!
CHAPTER ONE: THE EAST AND WEST COAST AVENGERS!
MERE MOMENTS AGO* THE EAST AND WEST COAST AVENGERS WERE ENGAGED IN A FEROCIOUS BATTLE WHICH HAD TAKEN THEM INTO THE VERY REALM OF DEATH, AND NOW...
I HAVE DONE IT, AVENGERS!
THANKS TO YOU, I HAVE FINALLY WON THE GREATEST GAME OF ALL!
I HAVE TRIUMPHED OVER DEATH, HERSELF!
THE GRANDMASTER WAS USING US ALL ALONG-- IN ANOTHER ONE OF HIS CRAZY COSMIC GAMES!
WE'VE GOT TO DO SOME-THING!
THERE'S ONLY ONE THING WE CAN DO, TIGRA, AND THAT IS--
*AS SHOWN IN THIS YEAR'S WEST COAST AVENGERS ANNUAL, WHICH IS STILL ON SALE!


STORY TOM DeFALCO · BREAKDOWNS BOB HALL · FINISHES TOM PALMER · COLORS MAX SCHEELE · LETTERS KEN LOPEZ · EDITOR MARK GRUENWALD · EDITOR IN CHIEF JIM SHOOTER

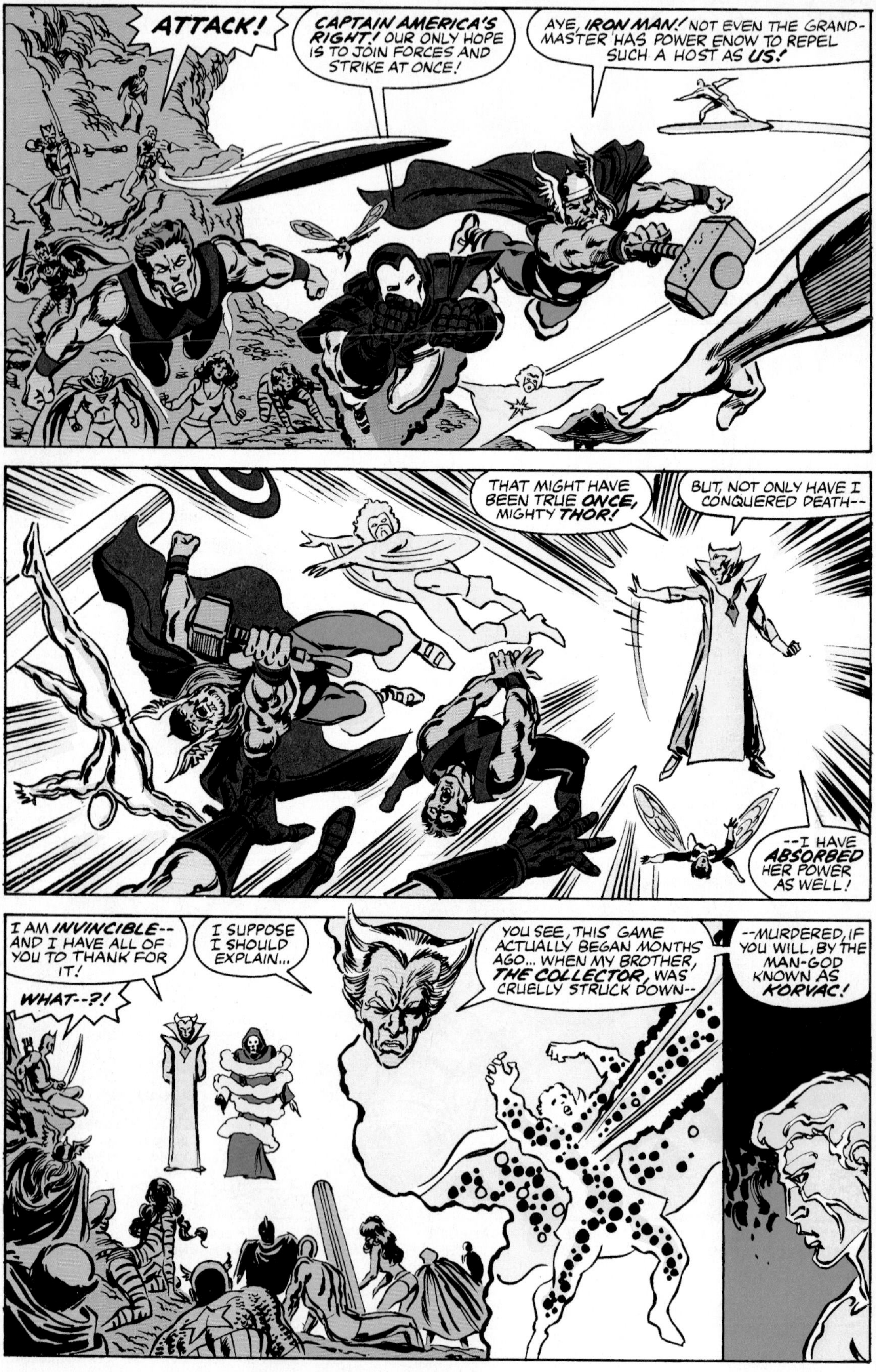
ATTACK!
CAPTAIN AMERICA'S RIGHT! OUR ONLY HOPE IS TO JOIN FORCES AND STRIKE AT ONCE!
AYE, IRON MAN! NOT EVEN THE GRANDMASTER HAS POWER ENOW TO REPEL SUCH A HOST AS US!
THAT MIGHT HAVE BEEN TRUE ONCE, MIGHTY THOR!
BUT, NOT ONLY HAVE I CONQUERED DEATH--
--I HAVE ABSORBED HER POWER AS WELL!
I AM INVINCIBLE-- AND I HAVE ALL OF YOU TO THANK FOR IT!
WHAT--?!
I SUPPOSE I SHOULD EXPLAIN...
YOU SEE, THIS GAME ACTUALLY BEGAN MONTHS AGO... WHEN MY BROTHER, THE COLLECTOR, WAS CRUELLY STRUCK DOWN--
--MURDERED, IF YOU WILL, BY THE MAN-GOD KNOWN AS KORVAC!

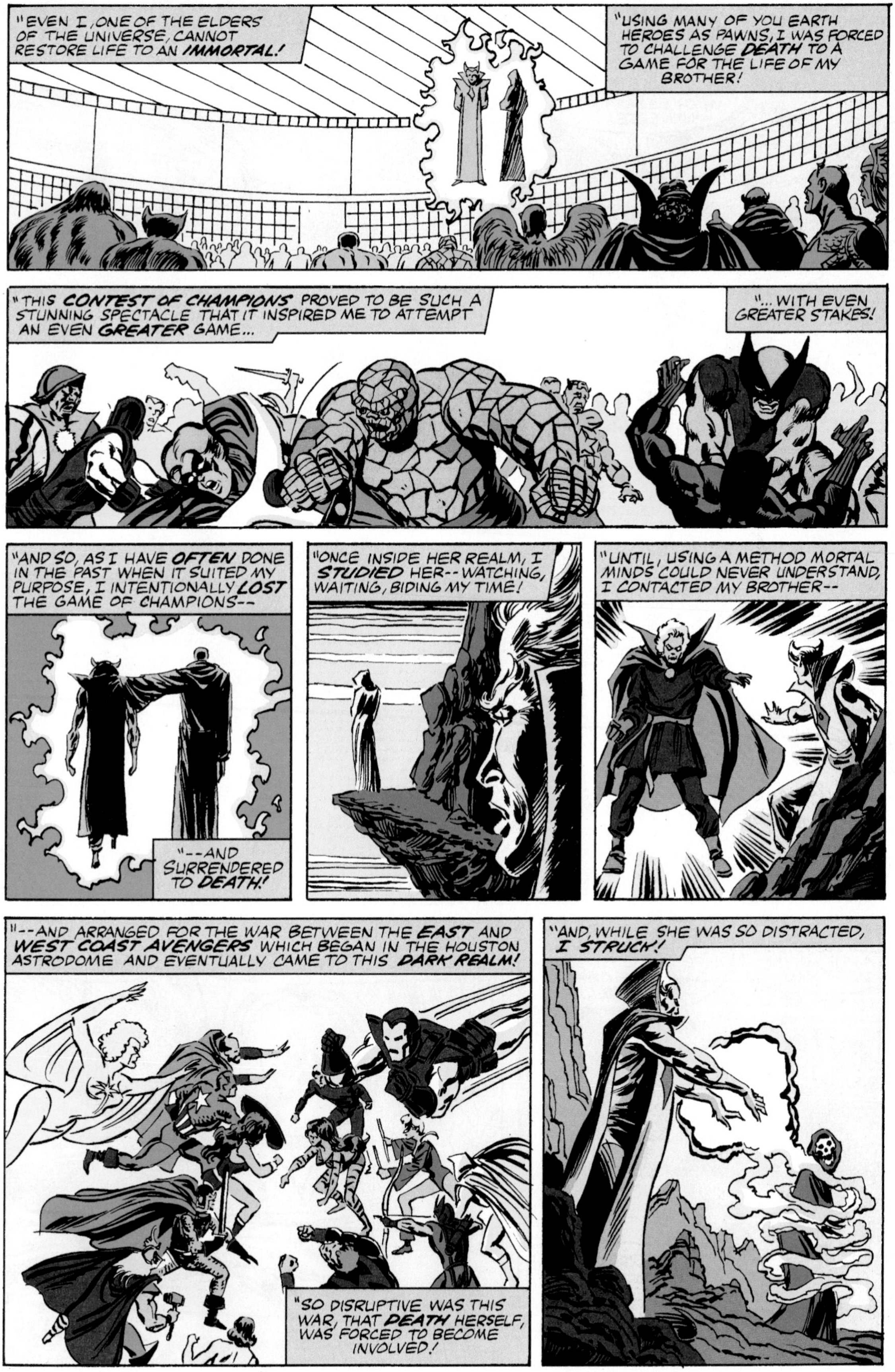
"EVEN I, ONE OF THE ELDERS OF THE UNIVERSE, CANNOT RESTORE LIFE TO AN IMMORTAL!
"USING MANY OF YOU EARTH HEROES AS PAWNS, I WAS FORCED TO CHALLENGE DEATH TO A GAME FOR THE LIFE OF MY BROTHER!
"THIS CONTEST OF CHAMPIONS PROVED TO BE SUCH A STUNNING SPECTACLE THAT IT INSPIRED ME TO ATTEMPT AN EVEN GREATER GAME...
"... WITH EVEN GREATER STAKES!
"AND SO, AS I HAVE OFTEN DONE IN THE PAST WHEN IT SUITED MY PURPOSE, I INTENTIONALLY LOST THE GAME OF CHAMPIONS--
"--AND SURRENDERED TO DEATH!
"ONCE INSIDE HER REALM, I STUDIED HER--WATCHING, WAITING, BIDING MY TIME!
"UNTIL, USING A METHOD MORTAL MINDS COULD NEVER UNDERSTAND, I CONTACTED MY BROTHER--
"--AND ARRANGED FOR THE WAR BETWEEN THE EAST AND WEST COAST AVENGERS WHICH BEGAN IN THE HOUSTON ASTRODOME AND EVENTUALLY CAME TO THIS DARK REALM!
"SO DISRUPTIVE WAS THIS WAR, THAT DEATH HERSELF, WAS FORCED TO BECOME INVOLVED!
"AND, WHILE SHE WAS SO DISTRACTED, I STRUCK!

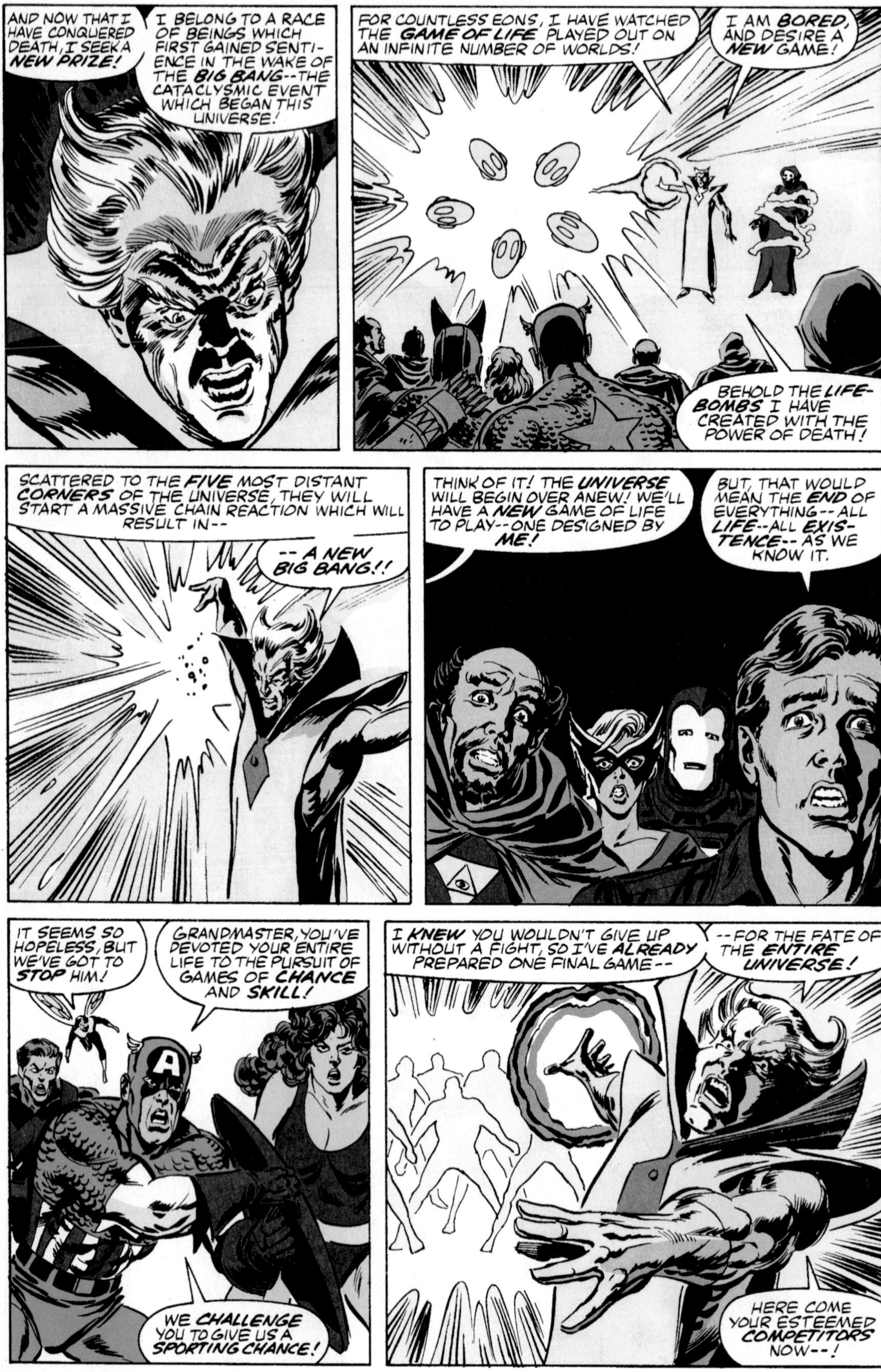
AND NOW THAT I HAVE CONQUERED DEATH, I SEEK A NEW PRIZE!
I BELONG TO A RACE OF BEINGS WHICH FIRST GAINED SENTI-ENCE IN THE WAKE OF THE BIG BANG--THE CATACLYSMIC EVENT WHICH BEGAN THIS UNIVERSE!
FOR COUNTLESS EONS, I HAVE WATCHED THE GAME OF LIFE PLAYED OUT ON AN INFINITE NUMBER OF WORLDS!
I AM BORED, AND DESIRE A NEW GAME!
BEHOLD THE LIFE-BOMBS I HAVE CREATED WITH THE POWER OF DEATH!
SCATTERED TO THE FIVE MOST DISTANT CORNERS OF THE UNIVERSE, THEY WILL START A MASSIVE CHAIN REACTION WHICH WILL RESULT IN--
-- A NEW BIG BANG!!
THINK OF IT! THE UNIVERSE WILL BEGIN OVER ANEW! WE'LL HAVE A NEW GAME OF LIFE TO PLAY--ONE DESIGNED BY ME!
BUT, THAT WOULD MEAN THE END OF EVERYTHING--ALL LIFE--ALL EXIS-TENCE--AS WE KNOW IT.
IT SEEMS SO HOPELESS, BUT WE'VE GOT TO STOP HIM!
GRANDMASTER, YOU'VE DEVOTED YOUR ENTIRE LIFE TO THE PURSUIT OF GAMES OF CHANCE AND SKILL!
WE CHALLENGE YOU TO GIVE US A SPORTING CHANCE!
I KNEW YOU WOULDN'T GIVE UP WITHOUT A FIGHT, SO I'VE ALREADY PREPARED ONE FINAL GAME--
--FOR THE FATE OF THE ENTIRE UNIVERSE!
HERE COME YOUR ESTEEMED COMPETITORS NOW--!

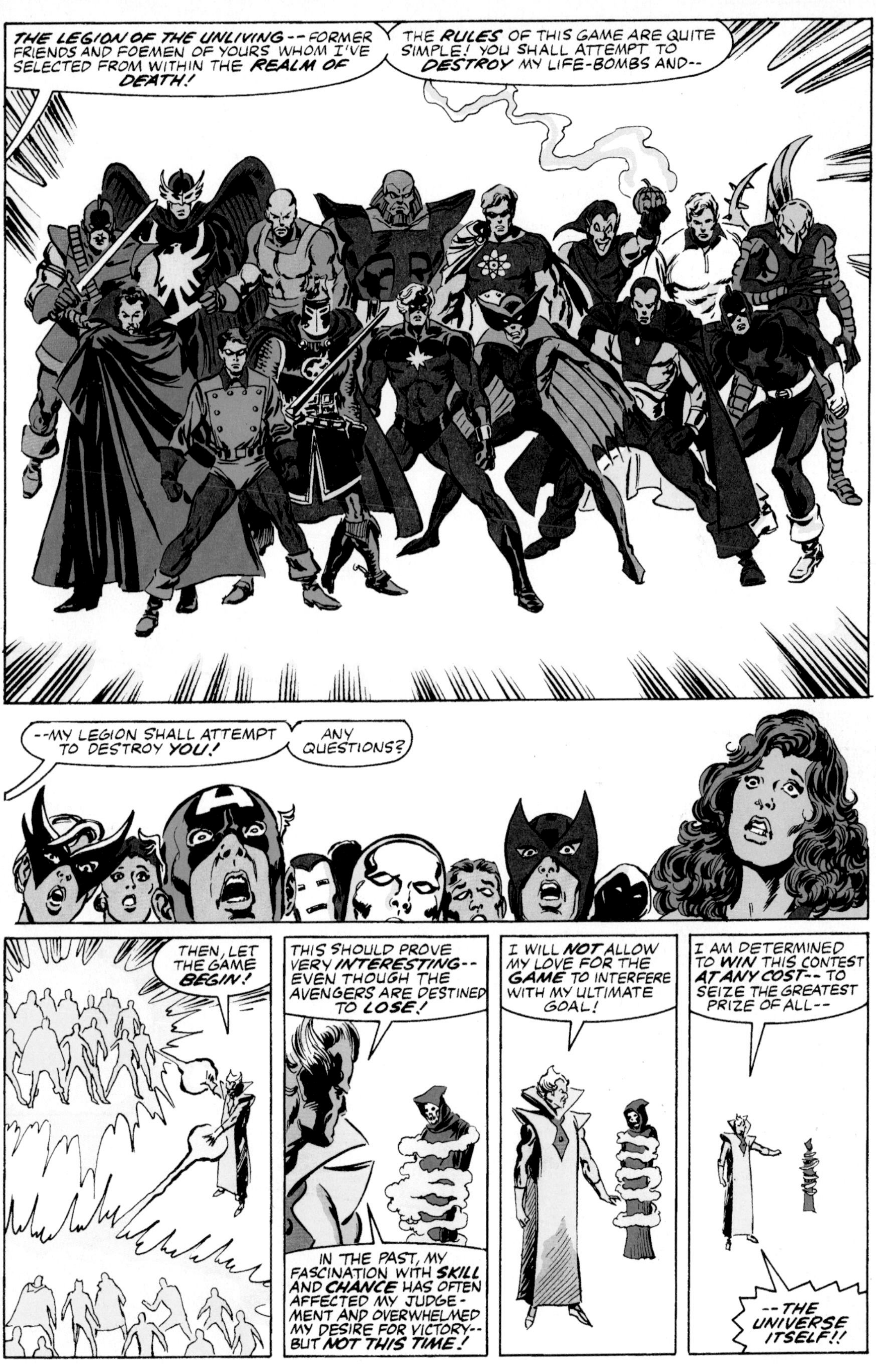
THE LEGION OF THE UNLIVING -- FORMER FRIENDS AND FOEMEN OF YOURS WHOM I'VE SELECTED FROM WITHIN THE REALM OF DEATH!
THE RULES OF THIS GAME ARE QUITE SIMPLE! YOU SHALL ATTEMPT TO DESTROY MY LIFE-BOMBS AND--
--MY LEGION SHALL ATTEMPT TO DESTROY YOU!
ANY QUESTIONS?
THEN, LET THE GAME BEGIN!
THIS SHOULD PROVE VERY INTERESTING-- EVEN THOUGH THE AVENGERS ARE DESTINED TO LOSE!
IN THE PAST, MY FASCINATION WITH SKILL AND CHANCE HAS OFTEN AFFECTED MY JUDGE-MENT AND OVERWHELMED MY DESIRE FOR VICTORY-- BUT NOT THIS TIME!
I WILL NOT ALLOW MY LOVE FOR THE GAME TO INTERFERE WITH MY ULTIMATE GOAL!
I AM DETERMINED TO WIN THIS CONTEST AT ANY COST-- TO SEIZE THE GREATEST PRIZE OF ALL--
--THE UNIVERSE ITSELF!!

## CHAPTER TWO:
### HAWKEYE! THOR! DOCTOR PYM!

**Pym:** WHAT THE--?! WE'VE SUDDENLY MATERIALIZED WITHIN SOME KIND OF *UNDERWORLD!*

**Thor:** AYE, FRIEND *PYM,* AND THE STENCH OF THIS PLACE IS NOT *UNFAMILIAR* TO ME! I FEAR THAT THE GRANDMASTER HAS BANISHED US TO A DISTANT CORNER OF *HADES!*

**Hawkeye:** LOOKS LIKE HE ALSO BROKE US INTO TEAMS, *THOR!*

I WONDER HOW HE DECIDED WHO GOES *WHERE,* AND WITH *WHOM?*

**Thor:** DOES IT TRULY MATTER, *HAWKEYE?*

**Hawkeye:** NAH, I GUESS NOT!

**Thor:** ALTHOUGH I REALLY WISH MY WIFE, MOCKINGBIRD, WERE HERE SO THAT I COULD WATCH OVER HER.

**Hawkeye:** FACE FRONT, GUYS! WE'VE GOT--

"-- COMPANY!"

**Executioner:** I BID THEE GREETINGS, THUNDER GOD! THE *EXECUTIONER* HATH RETURNED FROM THE ETERNAL LAND OF SHADE--AND I'VE COME FOR *THEE!*

**Nighthawk:** WELCOME, AVENGERS! I'M CERTAIN YOU *RECOGNIZE* ALL OF US!

THEY COULD NEVER FORGET ME, *NIGHTHAWK!*

THE *SWORDSMAN* USED TO BE A MEMBER OF THEIR STUPID TEAM!

TRIGGERING HIS JET-POWERED WINGS, NIGHTHAWK SUDDENLY SOARS FORWARD...

**Nighthawk:** YOU DON'T *BELONG* HERE, PYM! YOU DON'T POSSESS ANY *POWERS!* YOU DON'T WEAR A *COSTUME!*

YOU'RE ONLY AN *ORDINARY MAN!*

**Pym:** I MAY ONLY BE A MAN, FEATHER-FACE--

BREAKDOWNS: JOHN ROMITA JR.

FINISHES: BILL SIENKIEWICZ

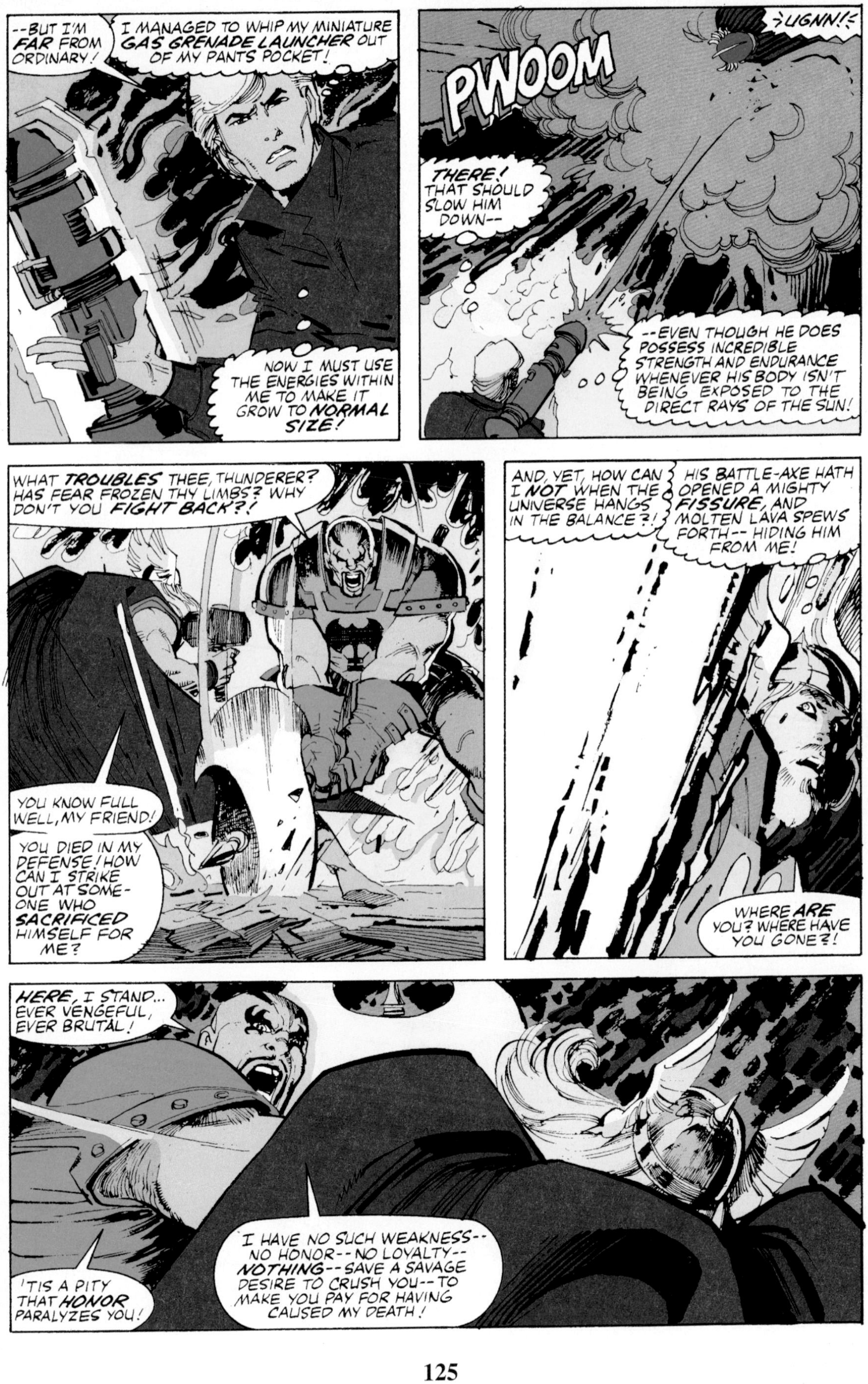
--BUT I'M FAR FROM ORDINARY!
I MANAGED TO WHIP MY MINIATURE GAS GRENADE LAUNCHER OUT OF MY PANTS POCKET!
NOW I MUST USE THE ENERGIES WITHIN ME TO MAKE IT GROW TO NORMAL SIZE!
PWOOM
UGNN!
THERE! THAT SHOULD SLOW HIM DOWN--
--EVEN THOUGH HE DOES POSSESS INCREDIBLE STRENGTH AND ENDURANCE WHENEVER HIS BODY ISN'T BEING EXPOSED TO THE DIRECT RAYS OF THE SUN!
WHAT TROUBLES THEE, THUNDERER? HAS FEAR FROZEN THY LIMBS? WHY DON'T YOU FIGHT BACK?!
YOU KNOW FULL WELL, MY FRIEND!
YOU DIED IN MY DEFENSE! HOW CAN I STRIKE OUT AT SOMEONE WHO SACRIFICED HIMSELF FOR ME?
AND, YET, HOW CAN I NOT WHEN THE UNIVERSE HANGS IN THE BALANCE?!
HIS BATTLE-AXE HATH OPENED A MIGHTY FISSURE, AND MOLTEN LAVA SPEWS FORTH-- HIDING HIM FROM ME!
WHERE ARE YOU? WHERE HAVE YOU GONE?!
HERE, I STAND... EVER VENGEFUL, EVER BRUTAL!
'TIS A PITY THAT HONOR PARALYZES YOU!
I HAVE NO SUCH WEAKNESS-- NO HONOR--NO LOYALTY-- NOTHING--SAVE A SAVAGE DESIRE TO CRUSH YOU--TO MAKE YOU PAY FOR HAVING CAUSED MY DEATH!

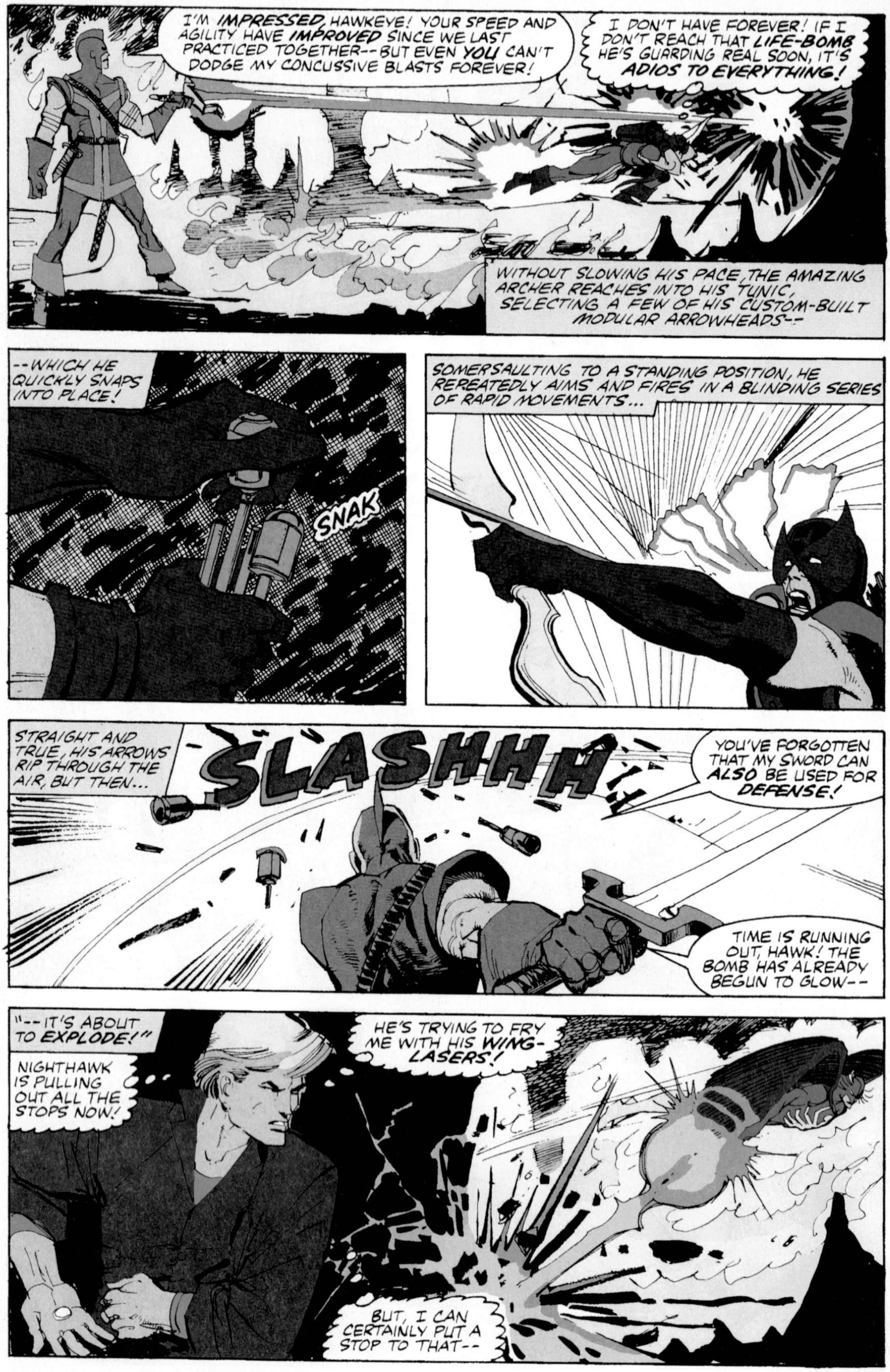
I'M IMPRESSED, HAWKEYE! YOUR SPEED AND AGILITY HAVE IMPROVED SINCE WE LAST PRACTICED TOGETHER--BUT EVEN YOU CAN'T DODGE MY CONCUSSIVE BLASTS FOREVER!
I DON'T HAVE FOREVER! IF I DON'T REACH THAT LIFE-BOMB HE'S GUARDING REAL SOON, IT'S ADIOS TO EVERYTHING!
WITHOUT SLOWING HIS PACE, THE AMAZING ARCHER REACHES INTO HIS TUNIC, SELECTING A FEW OF HIS CUSTOM-BUILT MODULAR ARROWHEADS--
--WHICH HE QUICKLY SNAPS INTO PLACE!
SNAK
SOMERSAULTING TO A STANDING POSITION, HE REPEATEDLY AIMS AND FIRES IN A BLINDING SERIES OF RAPID MOVEMENTS...
STRAIGHT AND TRUE, HIS ARROWS RIP THROUGH THE AIR, BUT THEN...
SLASHHH
YOU'VE FORGOTTEN THAT MY SWORD CAN ALSO BE USED FOR DEFENSE!
TIME IS RUNNING OUT, HAWK! THE BOMB HAS ALREADY BEGUN TO GLOW--
"--IT'S ABOUT TO EXPLODE!"
NIGHTHAWK IS PULLING OUT ALL THE STOPS NOW!
HE'S TRYING TO FRY ME WITH HIS WING-LASERS!
BUT, I CAN CERTAINLY PUT A STOP TO THAT--

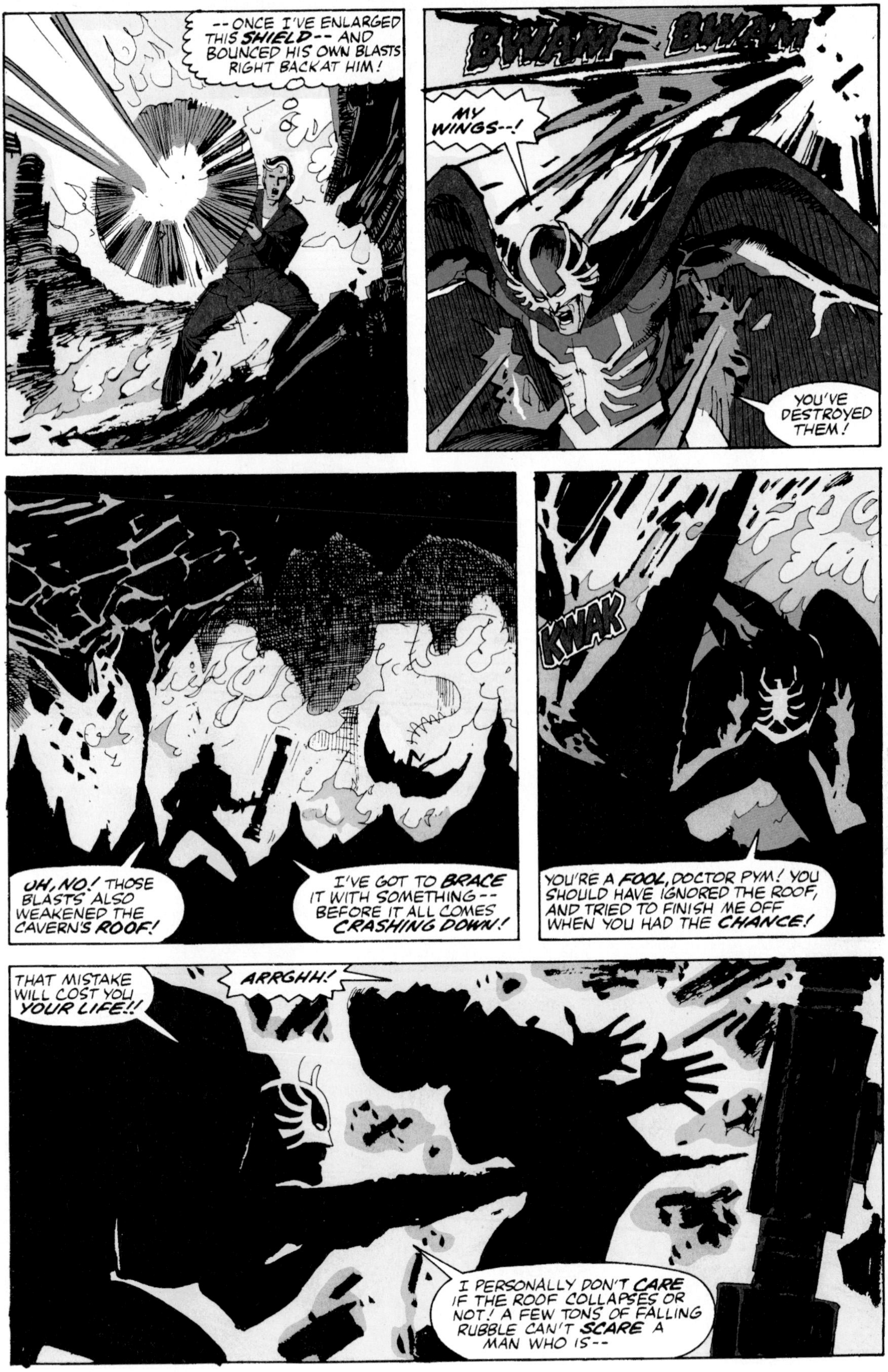
--ONCE I'VE ENLARGED THIS SHIELD-- AND BOUNCED HIS OWN BLASTS RIGHT BACK AT HIM!
BWAM BWAM
MY WINGS--!
YOU'VE DESTROYED THEM!
UH, NO! THOSE BLASTS ALSO WEAKENED THE CAVERN'S ROOF!
I'VE GOT TO BRACE IT WITH SOMETHING-- BEFORE IT ALL COMES CRASHING DOWN!
KWAK
YOU'RE A FOOL, DOCTOR PYM! YOU SHOULD HAVE IGNORED THE ROOF, AND TRIED TO FINISH ME OFF WHEN YOU HAD THE CHANCE!
THAT MISTAKE WILL COST YOU YOUR LIFE!!
ARRGHH!
I PERSONALLY DON'T CARE IF THE ROOF COLLAPSES OR NOT! A FEW TONS OF FALLING RUBBLE CAN'T SCARE A MAN WHO IS--

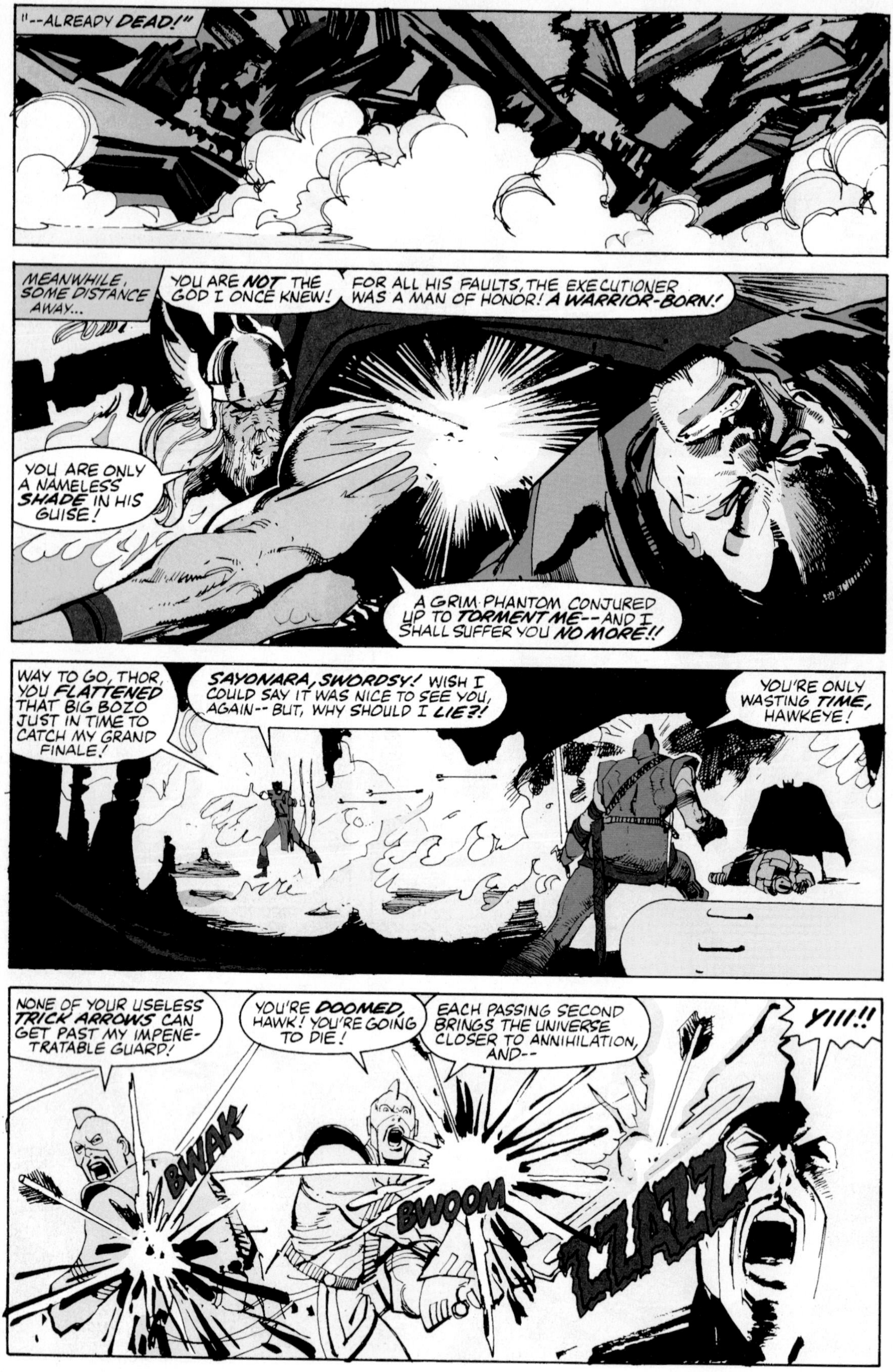
"--ALREADY DEAD!"
MEANWHILE, SOME DISTANCE AWAY...
YOU ARE NOT THE GOD I ONCE KNEW!
FOR ALL HIS FAULTS, THE EXECUTIONER WAS A MAN OF HONOR! A WARRIOR-BORN!
YOU ARE ONLY A NAMELESS SHADE IN HIS GUISE!
A GRIM PHANTOM CONJURED UP TO TORMENT ME--AND I SHALL SUFFER YOU NO MORE!!
WAY TO GO, THOR, YOU FLATTENED THAT BIG BOZO JUST IN TIME TO CATCH MY GRAND FINALE!
SAYONARA, SWORDSY! WISH I COULD SAY IT WAS NICE TO SEE YOU, AGAIN-- BUT, WHY SHOULD I LIE?!
YOU'RE ONLY WASTING TIME, HAWKEYE!
NONE OF YOUR USELESS TRICK ARROWS CAN GET PAST MY IMPENE-TRATABLE GUARD!
YOU'RE DOOMED, HAWK! YOU'RE GOING TO DIE!
EACH PASSING SECOND BRINGS THE UNIVERSE CLOSER TO ANNIHILATION, AND--
YIII!!
BWAK
BWOOM
ZZAZZ

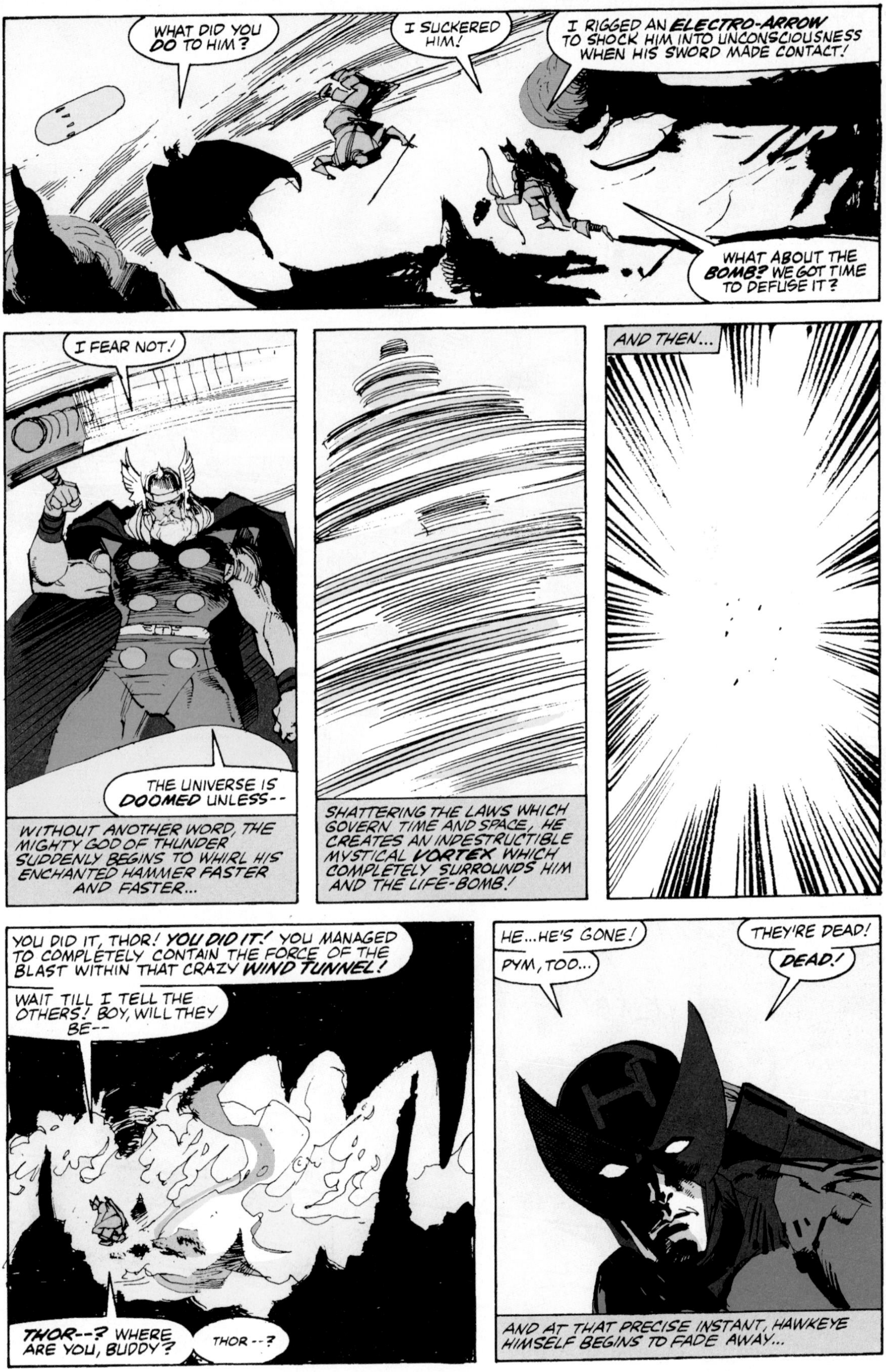

WHAT DID YOU DO TO HIM?
I SUCKERED HIM!
I RIGGED AN ELECTRO-ARROW TO SHOCK HIM INTO UNCONSCIOUSNESS WHEN HIS SWORD MADE CONTACT!
WHAT ABOUT THE BOMB? WE GOT TIME TO DEFUSE IT?
I FEAR NOT!
THE UNIVERSE IS DOOMED UNLESS--
WITHOUT ANOTHER WORD, THE MIGHTY GOD OF THUNDER SUDDENLY BEGINS TO WHIRL HIS ENCHANTED HAMMER FASTER AND FASTER...
SHATTERING THE LAWS WHICH GOVERN TIME AND SPACE, HE CREATES AN INDESTRUCTIBLE MYSTICAL VORTEX WHICH COMPLETELY SURROUNDS HIM AND THE LIFE-BOMB!
AND THEN...
YOU DID IT, THOR! YOU DID IT! YOU MANAGED TO COMPLETELY CONTAIN THE FORCE OF THE BLAST WITHIN THAT CRAZY WIND TUNNEL!
WAIT TILL I TELL THE OTHERS! BOY, WILL THEY BE--
THOR--? WHERE ARE YOU, BUDDY?
THOR--?
HE...HE'S GONE!
PYM, TOO...
THEY'RE DEAD!
DEAD!
AND AT THAT PRECISE INSTANT, HAWKEYE HIMSELF BEGINS TO FADE AWAY...

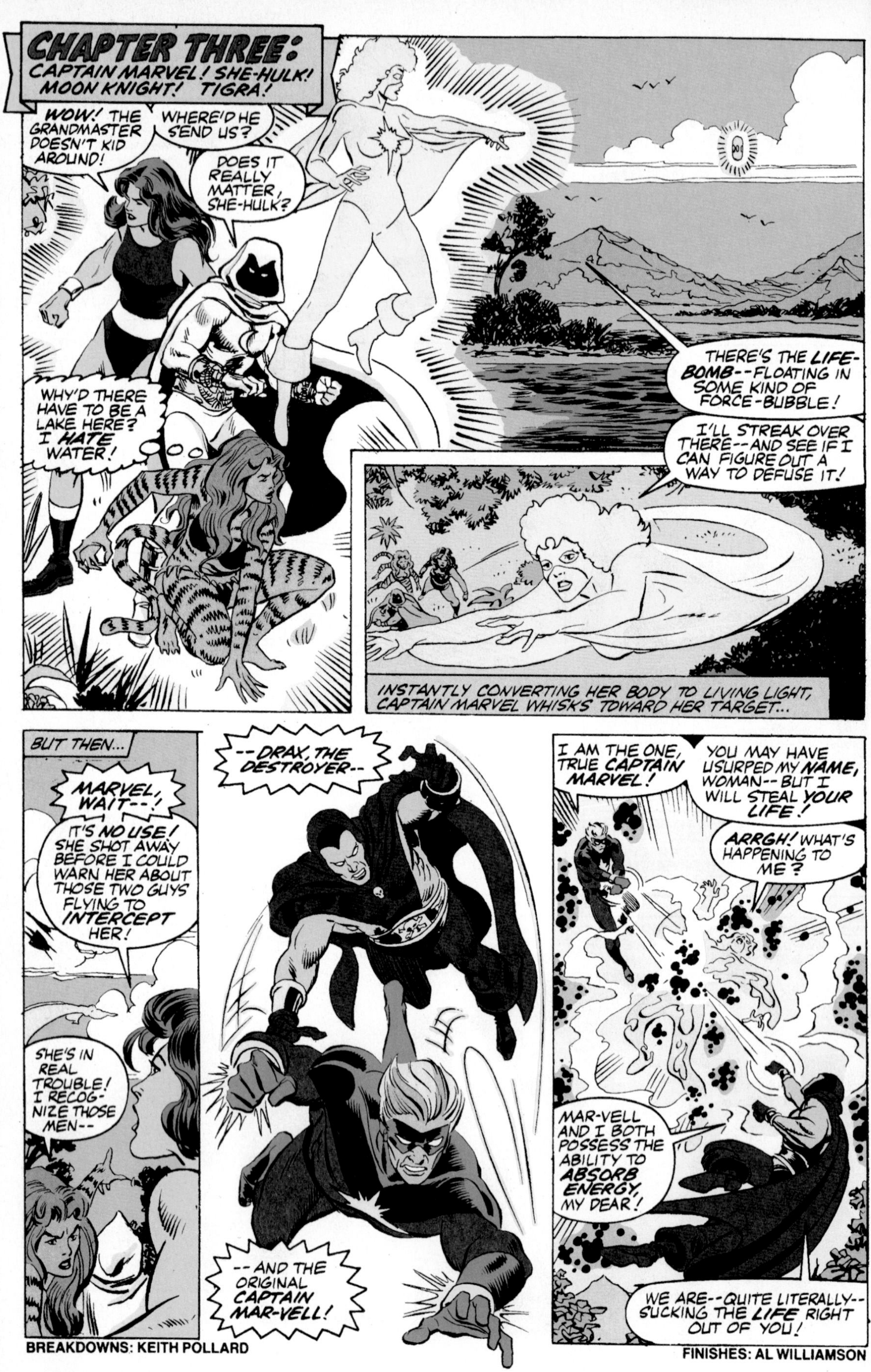
CHAPTER THREE:
CAPTAIN MARVEL! SHE-HULK! MOON KNIGHT! TIGRA!
WOW! THE GRANDMASTER DOESN'T KID AROUND!
WHERE'D HE SEND US?
DOES IT REALLY MATTER, SHE-HULK?
WHY'D THERE HAVE TO BE A LAKE HERE? I HATE WATER!
THERE'S THE LIFE-BOMB--FLOATING IN SOME KIND OF FORCE-BUBBLE!
I'LL STREAK OVER THERE--AND SEE IF I CAN FIGURE OUT A WAY TO DEFUSE IT!
INSTANTLY CONVERTING HER BODY TO LIVING LIGHT, CAPTAIN MARVEL WHISKS TOWARD HER TARGET...
BUT THEN...
MARVEL, WAIT--!
IT'S NO USE! SHE SHOT AWAY BEFORE I COULD WARN HER ABOUT THOSE TWO GUYS FLYING TO INTERCEPT HER!
SHE'S IN REAL TROUBLE! I RECOGNIZE THOSE MEN--
--DRAX, THE DESTROYER--
--AND THE ORIGINAL CAPTAIN MAR-VELL!
I AM THE ONE, TRUE CAPTAIN MARVEL!
YOU MAY HAVE USURPED MY NAME, WOMAN--BUT I WILL STEAL YOUR LIFE!
ARRGH! WHAT'S HAPPENING TO ME?
MAR-VELL AND I BOTH POSSESS THE ABILITY TO ABSORB ENERGY, MY DEAR!
WE ARE--QUITE LITERALLY--SUCKING THE LIFE RIGHT OUT OF YOU!

BREAKDOWNS: KEITH POLLARD

FINISHES: AL WILLIAMSON

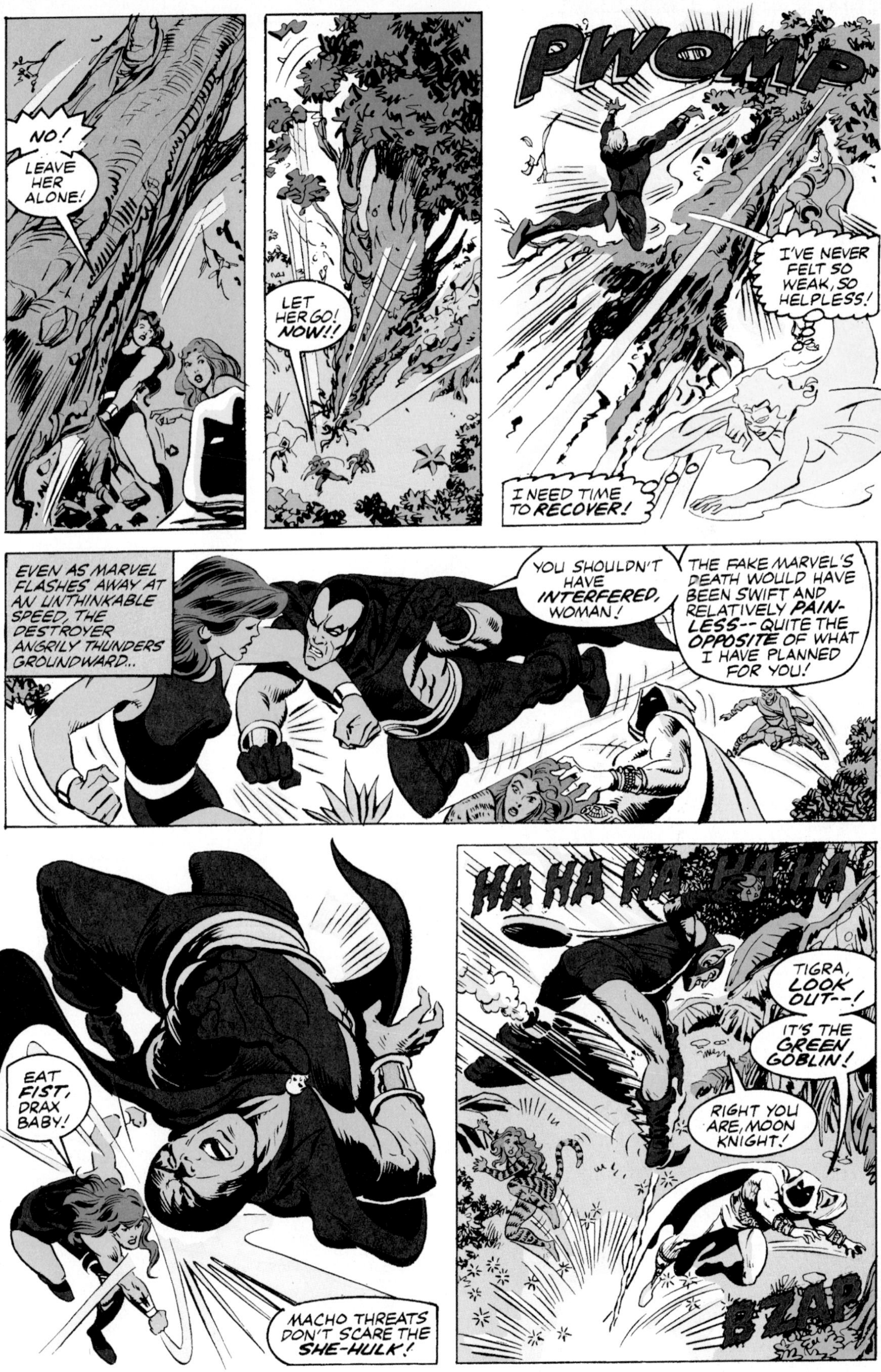
NO! LEAVE HER ALONE!
LET HER GO! NOW!!
PWOMP
I'VE NEVER FELT SO WEAK, SO HELPLESS!
I NEED TIME TO RECOVER!
EVEN AS MARVEL FLASHES AWAY AT AN UNTHINKABLE SPEED, THE DESTROYER ANGRILY THUNDERS GROUNDWARD...
YOU SHOULDN'T HAVE INTERFERED, WOMAN!
THE FAKE MARVEL'S DEATH WOULD HAVE BEEN SWIFT AND RELATIVELY PAINLESS--QUITE THE OPPOSITE OF WHAT I HAVE PLANNED FOR YOU!
EAT FIST, DRAX BABY!
MACHO THREATS DON'T SCARE THE SHE-HULK!
HA HA HA HA HA
TIGRA, LOOK OUT--!
IT'S THE GREEN GOBLIN!
RIGHT YOU ARE, MOON KNIGHT!
B ZAP

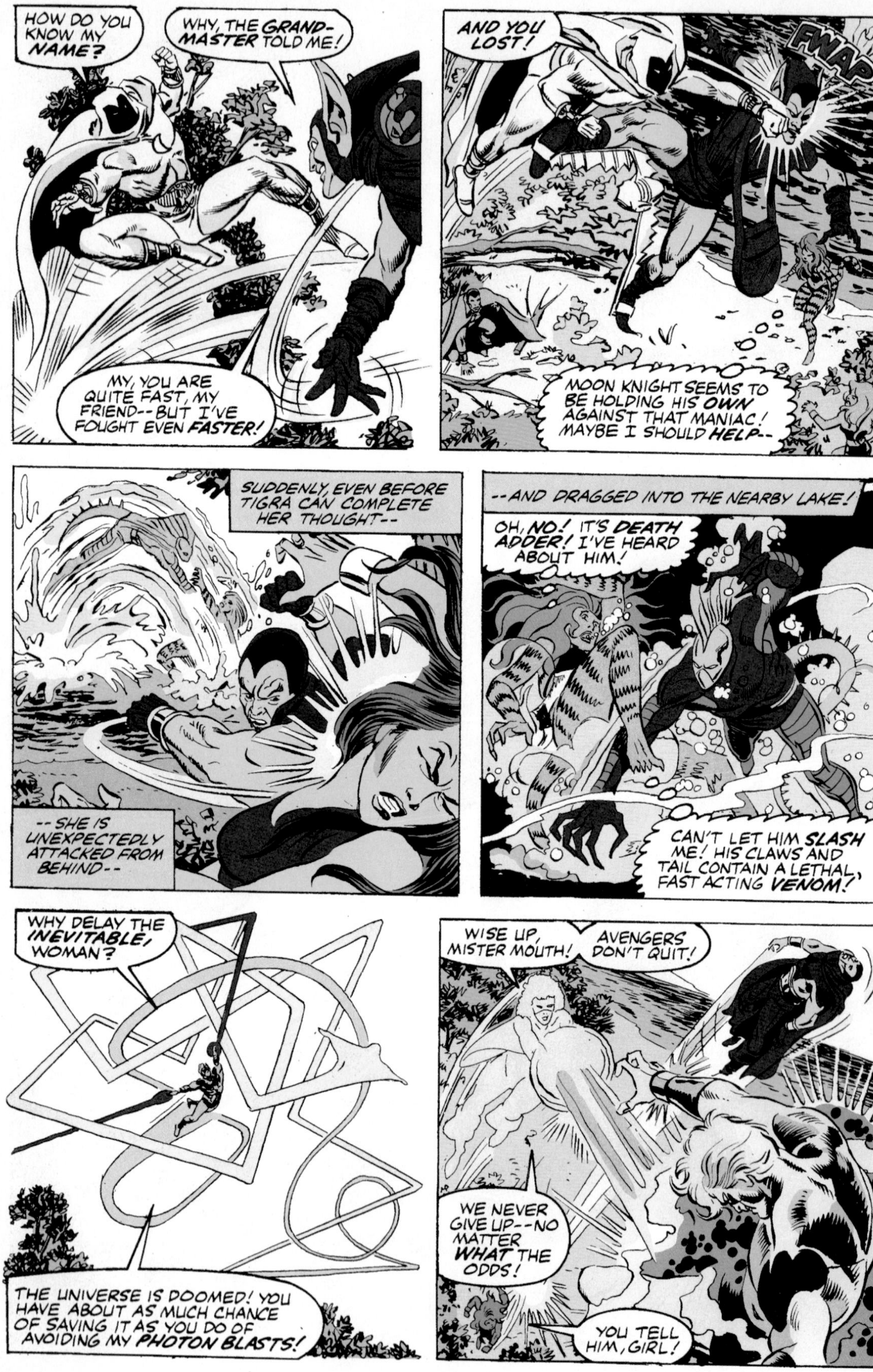
HOW DO YOU KNOW MY NAME?
WHY, THE GRAND-MASTER TOLD ME!
MY, YOU ARE QUITE FAST, MY FRIEND--BUT I'VE FOUGHT EVEN FASTER!
AND YOU LOST!
FWAP
MOON KNIGHT SEEMS TO BE HOLDING HIS OWN AGAINST THAT MANIAC! MAYBE I SHOULD HELP--
SUDDENLY, EVEN BEFORE TIGRA CAN COMPLETE HER THOUGHT--
--SHE IS UNEXPECTEDLY ATTACKED FROM BEHIND--
--AND DRAGGED INTO THE NEARBY LAKE!
OH, NO! IT'S DEATH ADDER! I'VE HEARD ABOUT HIM!
CAN'T LET HIM SLASH ME! HIS CLAWS AND TAIL CONTAIN A LETHAL, FAST ACTING VENOM!
WHY DELAY THE INEVITABLE, WOMAN?
THE UNIVERSE IS DOOMED! YOU HAVE ABOUT AS MUCH CHANCE OF SAVING IT AS YOU DO OF AVOIDING MY PHOTON BLASTS!
WISE UP, MISTER MOUTH!
AVENGERS DON'T QUIT!
WE NEVER GIVE UP--NO MATTER WHAT THE ODDS!
YOU TELL HIM, GIRL!

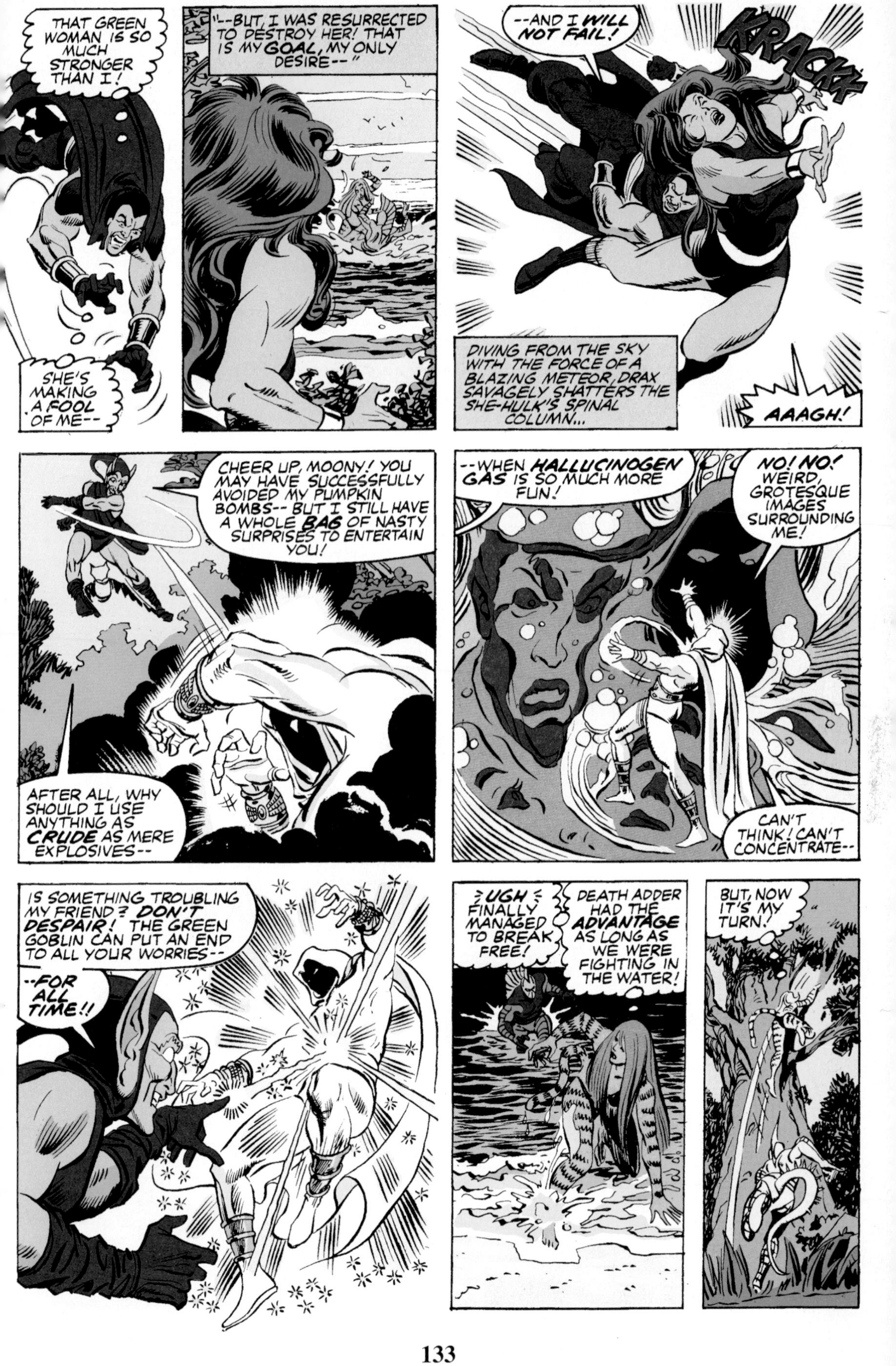
THAT GREEN WOMAN IS SO MUCH STRONGER THAN I!
SHE'S MAKING A FOOL OF ME--
"--BUT, I WAS RESURRECTED TO DESTROY HER! THAT IS MY GOAL, MY ONLY DESIRE--"
--AND I WILL NOT FAIL!
KRACKK
DIVING FROM THE SKY WITH THE FORCE OF A BLAZING METEOR, DRAX SAVAGELY SHATTERS THE SHE-HULK'S SPINAL COLUMN...
AAAGH!
CHEER UP, MOONY! YOU MAY HAVE SUCCESSFULLY AVOIDED MY PUMPKIN BOMBS-- BUT I STILL HAVE A WHOLE BAG OF NASTY SURPRISES TO ENTERTAIN YOU!
AFTER ALL, WHY SHOULD I USE ANYTHING AS CRUDE AS MERE EXPLOSIVES--
--WHEN HALLUCINOGEN GAS IS SO MUCH MORE FUN!
NO! NO! WEIRD, GROTESQUE IMAGES SURROUNDING ME!
CAN'T THINK! CAN'T CONCENTRATE--
IS SOMETHING TROUBLING MY FRIEND? DON'T DESPAIR! THE GREEN GOBLIN CAN PUT AN END TO ALL YOUR WORRIES--
--FOR ALL TIME!!
UGH
FINALLY MANAGED TO BREAK FREE!
DEATH ADDER HAD THE ADVANTAGE AS LONG AS WE WERE FIGHTING IN THE WATER!
BUT, NOW IT'S MY TURN!

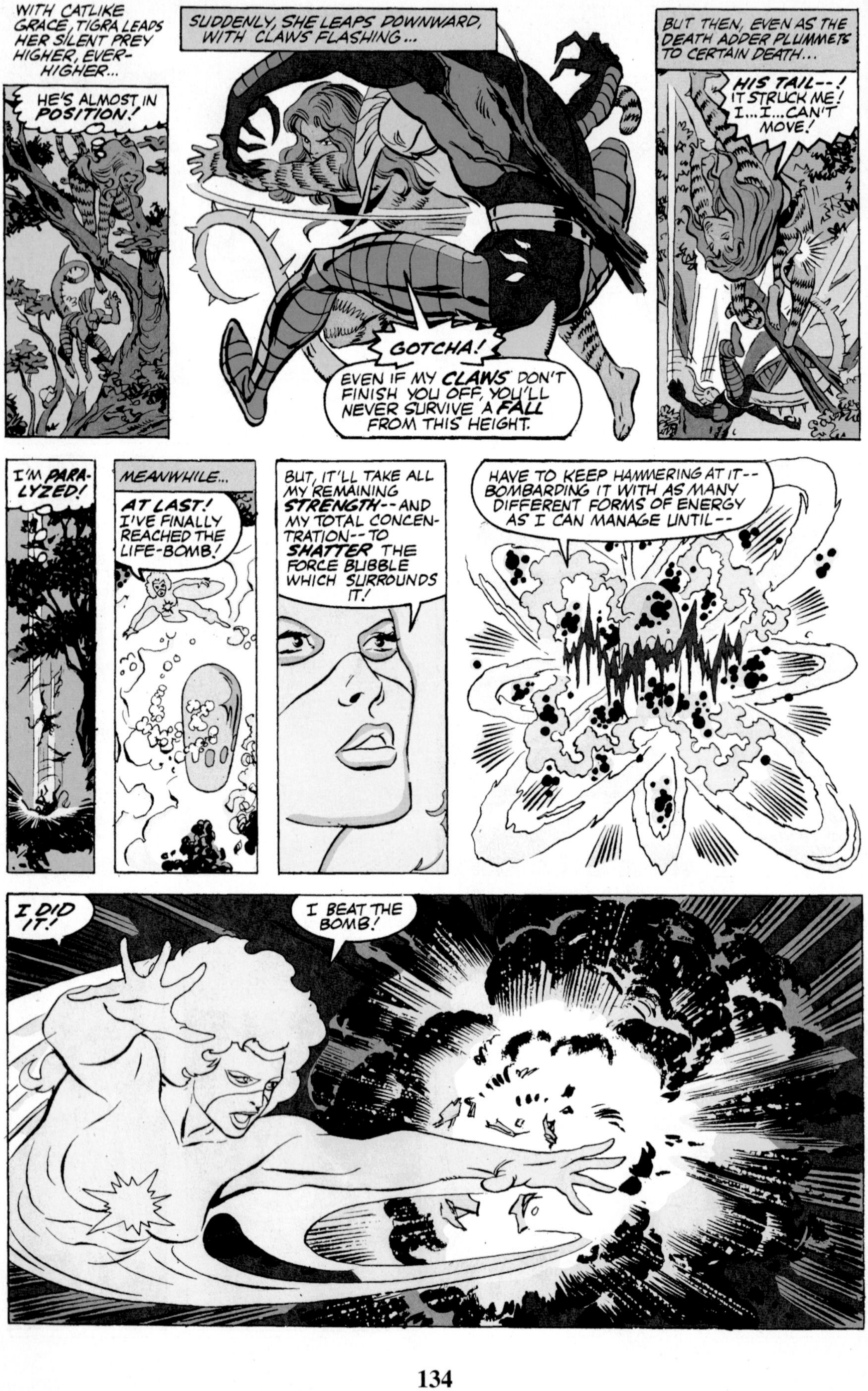
WITH CATLIKE GRACE, TIGRA LEADS HER SILENT PREY HIGHER, EVER-HIGHER...
HE'S ALMOST IN POSITION!
SUDDENLY, SHE LEAPS DOWNWARD, WITH CLAWS FLASHING...
GOTCHA!
EVEN IF MY CLAWS DON'T FINISH YOU OFF, YOU'LL NEVER SURVIVE A FALL FROM THIS HEIGHT.
BUT THEN, EVEN AS THE DEATH ADDER PLUMMETS TO CERTAIN DEATH...
HIS TAIL--! IT STRUCK ME! I...I...CAN'T MOVE!
I'M PARALYZED!
MEANWHILE...
AT LAST! I'VE FINALLY REACHED THE LIFE-BOMB!
BUT, IT'LL TAKE ALL MY REMAINING STRENGTH--AND MY TOTAL CONCENTRATION--TO SHATTER THE FORCE BUBBLE WHICH SURROUNDS IT!
HAVE TO KEEP HAMMERING AT IT--BOMBARDING IT WITH AS MANY DIFFERENT FORMS OF ENERGY AS I CAN MANAGE UNTIL--
I DID IT!
I BEAT THE BOMB!

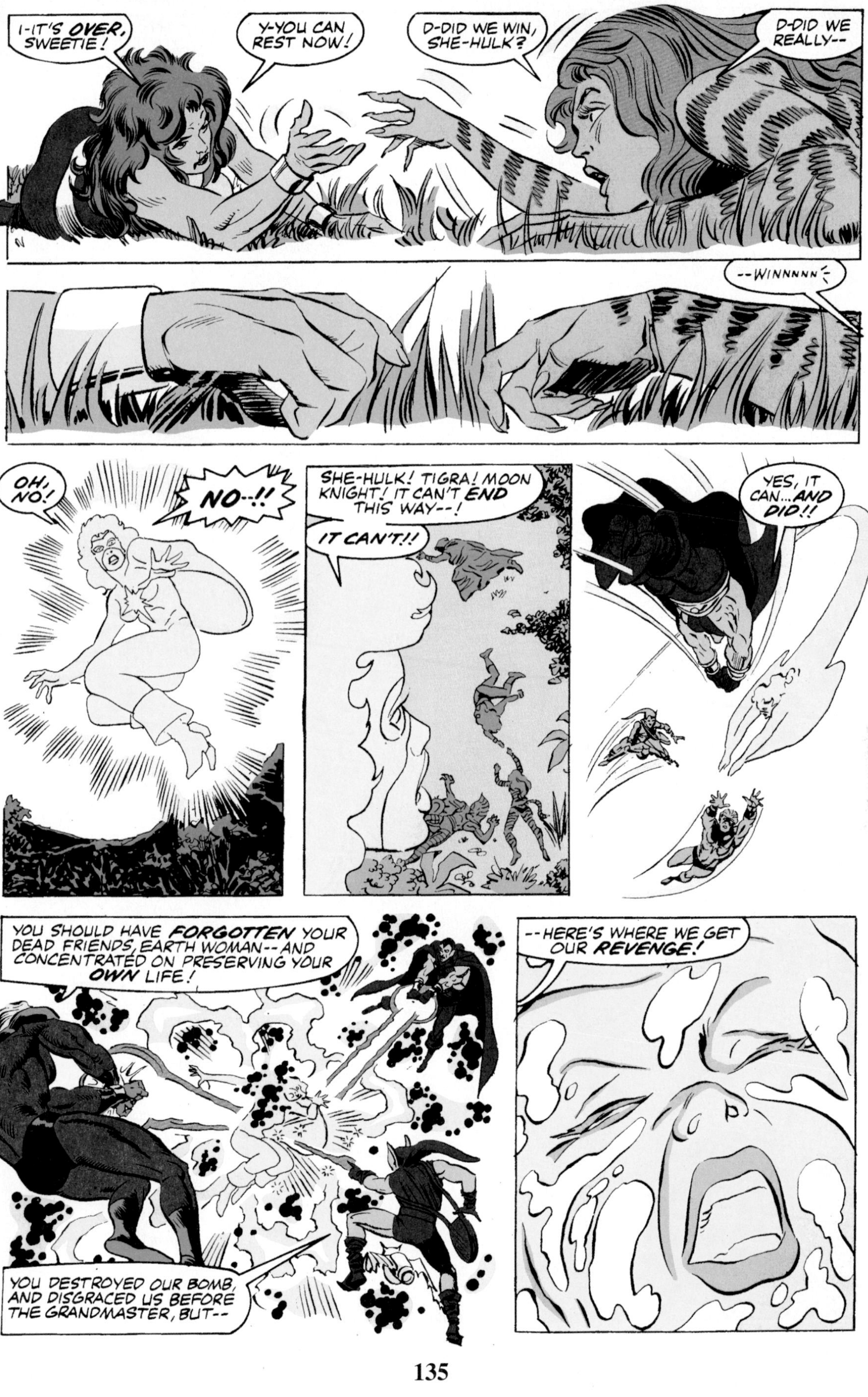

I-IT'S OVER, SWEETIE!
Y-YOU CAN REST NOW!
D-DID WE WIN, SHE-HULK?
D-DID WE REALLY--
--WINNNNN
OH, NO!
NO--!!
SHE-HULK! TIGRA! MOON KNIGHT! IT CAN'T END THIS WAY--!
IT CAN'T!!
YES, IT CAN...AND DID!!
YOU SHOULD HAVE FORGOTTEN YOUR DEAD FRIENDS, EARTH WOMAN--AND CONCENTRATED ON PRESERVING YOUR OWN LIFE!
YOU DESTROYED OUR BOMB, AND DISGRACED US BEFORE THE GRANDMASTER, BUT--
--HERE'S WHERE WE GET OUR REVENGE!

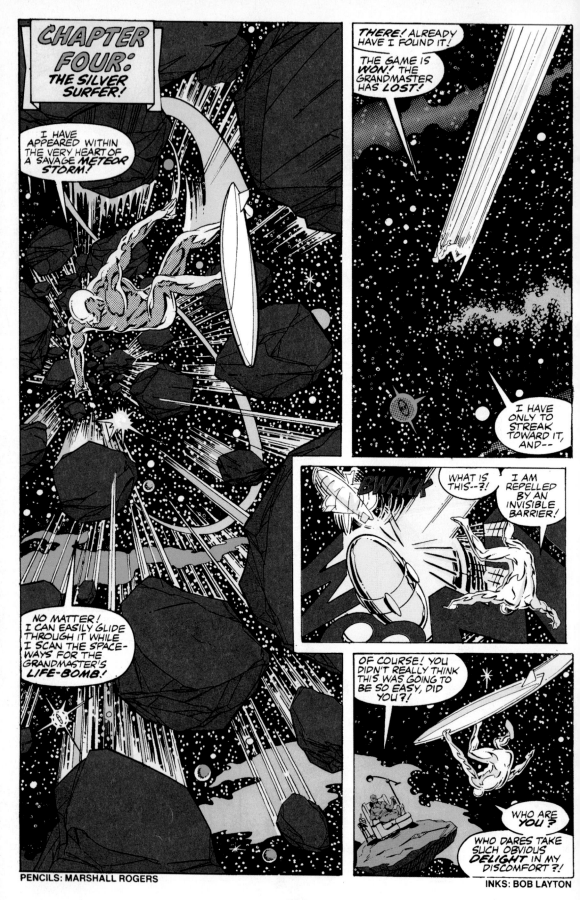

CHAPTER FOUR:
THE SILVER SURFER!

I HAVE APPEARED WITHIN THE VERY HEART OF A SAVAGE *METEOR STORM!*

THERE! ALREADY HAVE I FOUND IT!

THE GAME IS *WON!* THE GRANDMASTER HAS *LOST!*

I HAVE ONLY TO STREAK TOWARD IT, AND--

BWAKK

WHAT IS THIS--?!

I AM REPELLED BY AN INVISIBLE BARRIER!

NO MATTER! I CAN EASILY *GLIDE* THROUGH IT WHILE I SCAN THE SPACE-WAYS FOR THE GRANDMASTER'S *LIFE-BOMB!*

OF COURSE! YOU DIDN'T REALLY THINK THIS WAS GOING TO BE SO EASY, DID YOU?!

WHO ARE *YOU?*

WHO DARES TAKE SUCH OBVIOUS *DELIGHT* IN MY DISCOMFORT?!

PENCILS: MARSHALL ROGERS

INKS: BOB LAYTON

I AM *MICHAEL KORVAC.*

THERE WAS A TIME WHEN MY NAME WAS KNOWN AND FEARED THROUGHOUT THE ENTIRE UNIVERSE.

YOU SEE, I POSSESS THE *POWER COSMIC* ON A SCALE FAR GREATER THAN EVEN YOU CAN IMAGINE.

LET'S BE *CIVILIZED,* SHALL WE?

SINCE THERE'S NO POSSIBLE *WAY* FOR YOU TO *DEFEAT* ME, WE MIGHT AS WELL ENJOY A *DRINK* TOGETHER WHILE THE UNIVERSE GOES 'BYE-BYE.

WHAT'S THE MATTER? DON'T YOU CARE FOR CHAMPAGNE? MAYBE YOU'D PREFER A NICE, HOT--

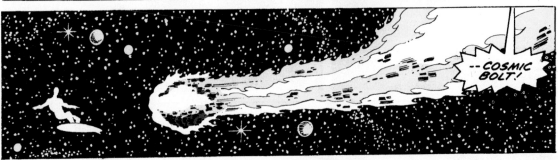

-- COSMIC BOLT!

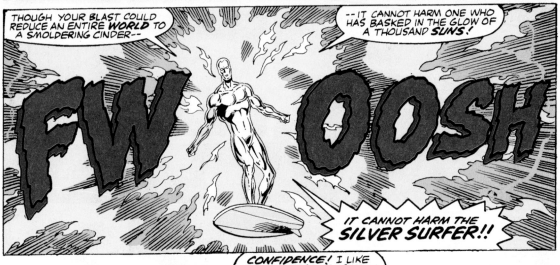

THOUGH YOUR BLAST COULD REDUCE AN ENTIRE *WORLD* TO A SMOLDERING CINDER--

-- IT CANNOT HARM ONE WHO HAS BASKED IN THE GLOW OF A THOUSAND *SUNS!*

FW OOSH

IT CANNOT HARM THE *SILVER SURFER!!*

CONFIDENCE! I LIKE THAT IN A FOE. IT USUALLY MAKES A BATTLE SO MUCH MORE INTERESTING.

UNFORTUNATELY, THOUGH, I'M WORKING UNDER A RATHER HARSH DEADLINE, AND CAN'T SPEND A LOT OF *TIME* WITH YOU.

AND SO, IN THE INTERESTS OF EXPEDIENCY, I'VE DECIDED TO *MAGNETIZE* THE SILVER SHELL WHICH COVERS YOU--

--SO THAT IT DRAWS ALL OF THE METEORS IN THE IMMEDIATE AREA TO YOU--

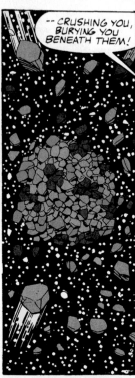

-- CRUSHING YOU, BURYING YOU BENEATH THEM!

CONGRATULATIONS, SURFER!

YOU'VE JUST BECOME THE INNERMOST *CORE* OF YOUR VERY OWN PLANET!

A PAINFUL, BUT *MEMORABLE* DEATH!

AT LEAST, IT WILL BE MEMORABLE UNTIL THE WHOLE UNIVERSE GOES *BANG...*

...WHICH SHOULD OCCUR IN THE NEXT FEW *SECONDS!*

BUT THEN, SUDDENLY, UNEXPECTEDLY, THE PLANET SURROUNDING THE SURFER BEGINS TO QUIVER, TO QUAKE...

AND THEN...

WHAT THE--?!

I AM FREE!

FREE!!

YOU HAVE FAILED, KORVAC!

NOT EVEN YOUR LIMITLESS POWER COULD CONTAIN ME!

I, TOO, WIELD THE POWER COSMIC!

LET THE LIFE-BOMB NOW FEEL MY FULL FURY!

IN THE NAME OF ALL LIFE ITSELF, I STRIKE--

--AND I WILL NOT BE DENIED!

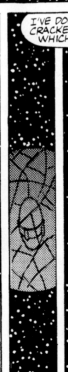

I'VE DONE IT! I'VE CRACKED THE BARRIER WHICH PROTECTS IT!

ONE MORE PASS IS ALL THAT'S NEEDED TO DESTROY IT!

NO!

NO!!

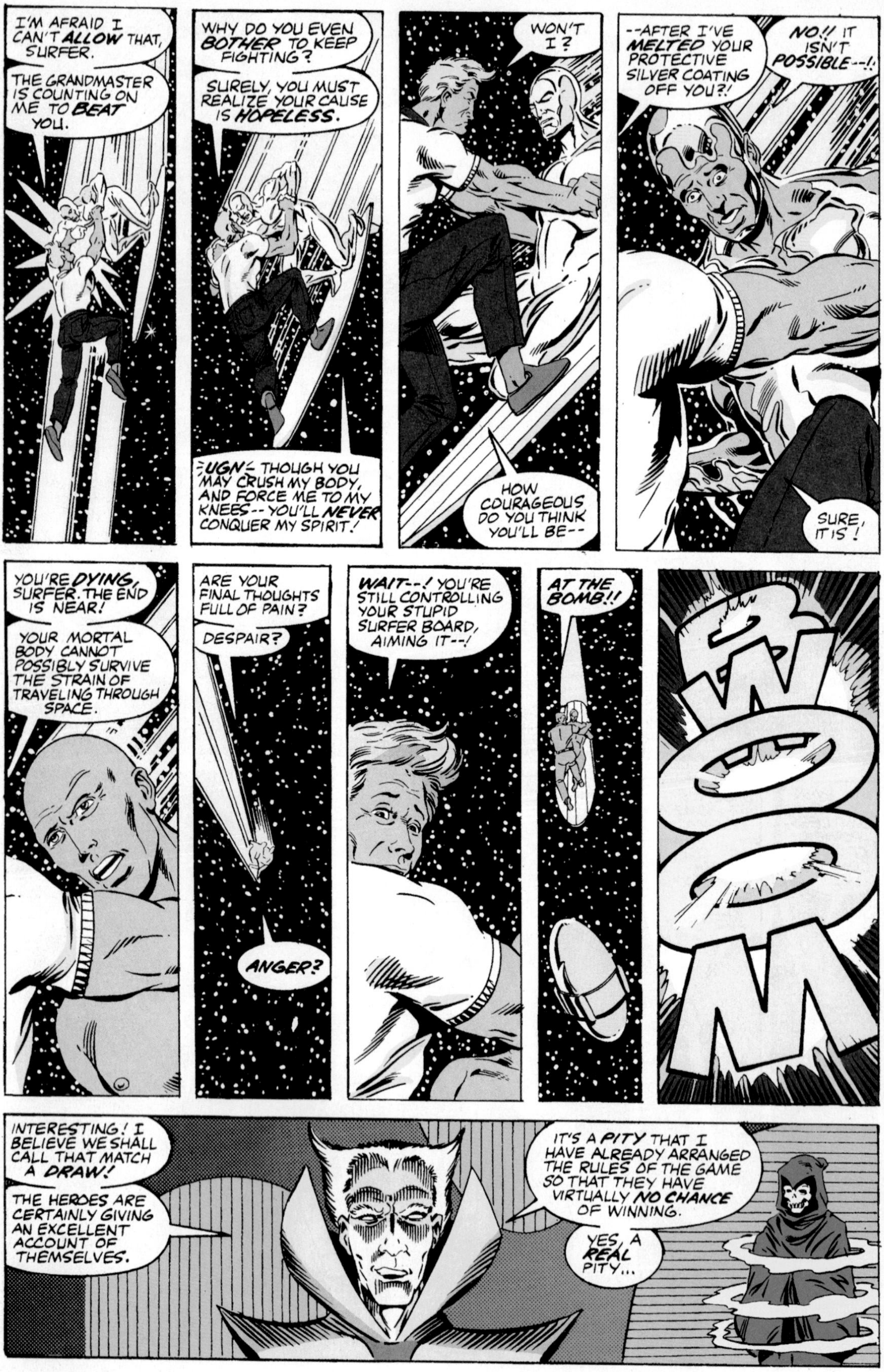
I'M AFRAID I CAN'T ALLOW THAT, SURFER.
THE GRANDMASTER IS COUNTING ON ME TO BEAT YOU.
WHY DO YOU EVEN BOTHER TO KEEP FIGHTING?
SURELY, YOU MUST REALIZE YOUR CAUSE IS HOPELESS.
=UGN= THOUGH YOU MAY CRUSH MY BODY, AND FORCE ME TO MY KNEES-- YOU'LL NEVER CONQUER MY SPIRIT!
WON'T I?
HOW COURAGEOUS DO YOU THINK YOU'LL BE--
--AFTER I'VE MELTED YOUR PROTECTIVE SILVER COATING OFF YOU?!
NO!! IT ISN'T POSSIBLE--!
SURE, IT IS!
YOU'RE DYING, SURFER. THE END IS NEAR!
YOUR MORTAL BODY CANNOT POSSIBLY SURVIVE THE STRAIN OF TRAVELING THROUGH SPACE.
ARE YOUR FINAL THOUGHTS FULL OF PAIN?
DESPAIR?
ANGER?
WAIT--! YOU'RE STILL CONTROLLING YOUR STUPID SURFER BOARD, AIMING IT--!
AT THE BOMB!!
BOOM
INTERESTING! I BELIEVE WE SHALL CALL THAT MATCH A DRAW!
THE HEROES ARE CERTAINLY GIVING AN EXCELLENT ACCOUNT OF THEMSELVES.
IT'S A PITY THAT I HAVE ALREADY ARRANGED THE RULES OF THE GAME SO THAT THEY HAVE VIRTUALLY NO CHANCE OF WINNING.
YES, A REAL PITY...

# CHAPTER FIVE:
IRON MAN!
MOCKINGBIRD!
THE BLACK KNIGHT!
DOCTOR DRUID!

**INTERESTING!** WE SEEM TO HAVE BEEN TRANSPORTED TO THE RUINS OF SOME ANCIENT *ALIEN CIVILIZATION!*

CALM DOWN, *DR. DRUID!* MUSTN'T OVER-EXCITE YOURSELF!

ANYBODY HAVE ANY IDEAS ON HOW WE FIND THE *LIFE-BOMB?*

WHAT A COLD FISH! SO ALOOF AND DETACHED! HE GIVES ME THE CREEPS!

I GATHER WE DON'T HAVE MUCH TIME BEFORE IT GOES BOOM!

I'M AFRAID WE'LL HAVE TO SPLIT UP, *KNIGHT!*

WE CAN COVER MUCH MORE GROUND THAT WAY--EVEN THOUGH WE'LL ALSO BE MORE VULNERABLE TO ATTACK!

HEY, *IRON MAN*, IF WE WANTED TO PLAY SAFE, WE WOULD HAVE JOINED PEE WEE'S PLAYHOUSE--NOT THE *AVENGERS!*

I AGREE WITH *MOCKINGBIRD!*

ALL RIGHT, WE'LL GO FOR IT!

SING OUT IF YOU FIND THE BOMB--OR RUN INTO TROUBLE YOU CAN'T HANDLE!

IT'S HARD FOR ME TO IMAGINE A MAN IN AN ARMORED SUIT LIKE THAT BEING VULNERABLE IN *ANY* FIGHT!

MOMENTS LATER...

THESE RUINS ARE FASCINATING! I WISH I HAD THE TIME TO STUDY THEM MORE CLOSELY!

*WAIT!* WHAT'S HAPPENING UP AHEAD? A PATCH OF MIST HAS SUDDENLY BEGUN TO SWIRL--

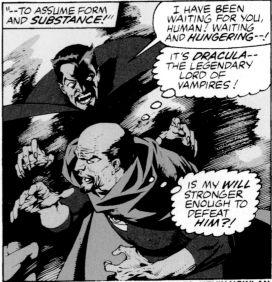

"--TO ASSUME FORM AND *SUBSTANCE!*"

I HAVE BEEN WAITING FOR YOU, HUMAN! WAITING AND *HUNGERING*--!

IT'S *DRACULA*-- THE LEGENDARY LORD OF VAMPIRES!

IS MY *WILL* STRONGER ENOUGH TO DEFEAT *HIM?!*

BREAKDOWNS: JACKSON GUICE

FINISHES: KEVIN NOWLAN

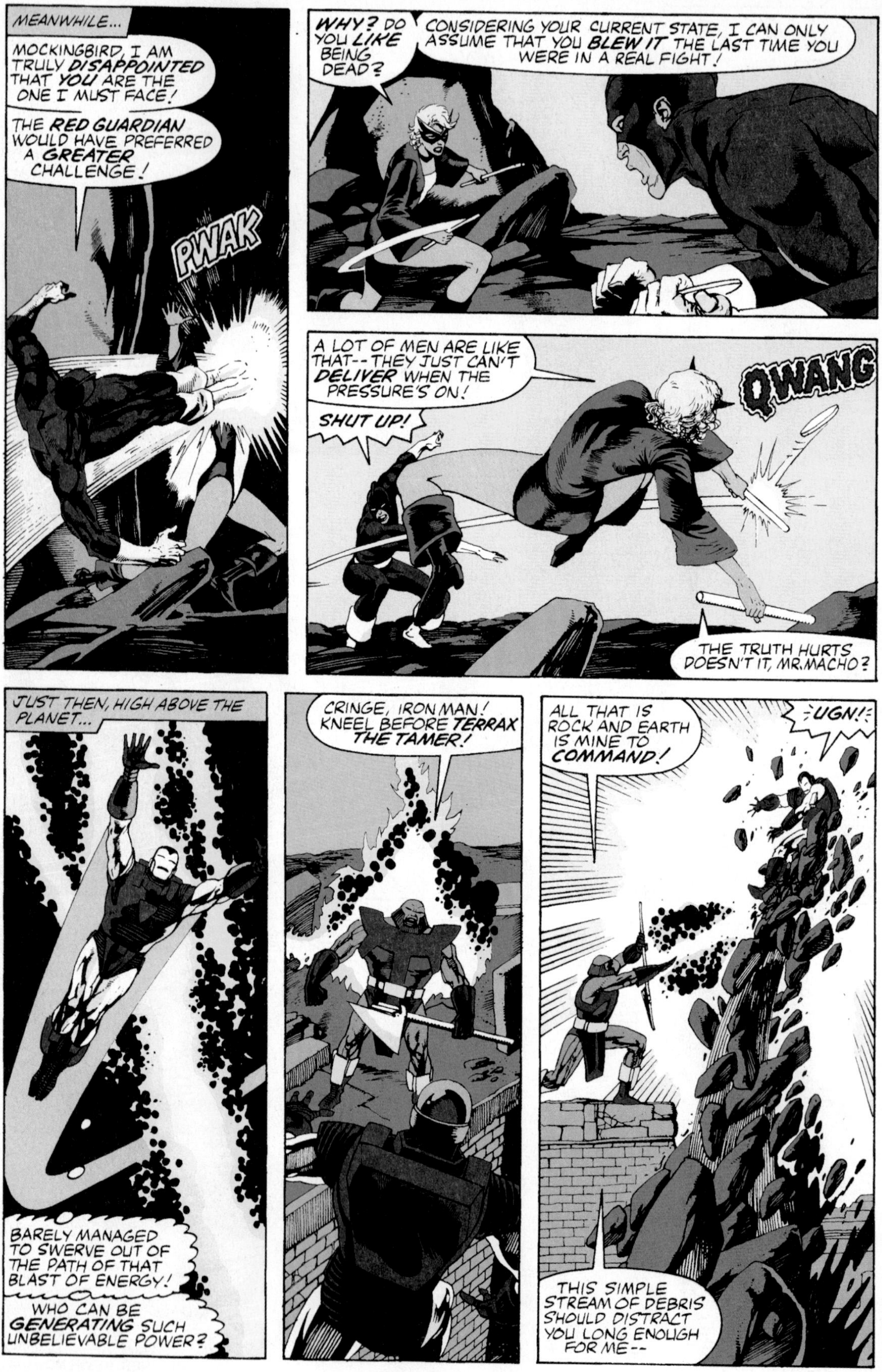
MEANWHILE...
MOCKINGBIRD, I AM TRULY DISAPPOINTED THAT YOU ARE THE ONE I MUST FACE!
THE RED GUARDIAN WOULD HAVE PREFERRED A GREATER CHALLENGE!
PWAK
WHY? DO YOU LIKE BEING DEAD?
CONSIDERING YOUR CURRENT STATE, I CAN ONLY ASSUME THAT YOU BLEW IT THE LAST TIME YOU WERE IN A REAL FIGHT!
A LOT OF MEN ARE LIKE THAT-- THEY JUST CAN'T DELIVER WHEN THE PRESSURE'S ON!
SHUT UP!
QWANG
THE TRUTH HURTS DOESN'T IT, MR. MACHO?
JUST THEN, HIGH ABOVE THE PLANET...
BARELY MANAGED TO SWERVE OUT OF THE PATH OF THAT BLAST OF ENERGY!
WHO CAN BE GENERATING SUCH UNBELIEVABLE POWER?
CRINGE, IRON MAN! KNEEL BEFORE TERRAX THE TAMER!
ALL THAT IS ROCK AND EARTH IS MINE TO COMMAND!
UGN!
THIS SIMPLE STREAM OF DEBRIS SHOULD DISTRACT YOU LONG ENOUGH FOR ME--

"--TO PREPARE A DEATH WHICH IS **WORTHY** FOR THE LIKES OF YOU!'"

**WHAT THE--?!**

HE JUST WAVED HIS **BATTLE-AX**--AND A CHUNK OF REAL ESTATE THE SIZE OF MANHATTAN SUDDENLY COMES FLYING AT ME!

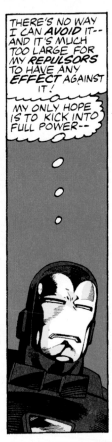

THERE'S NO WAY I CAN **AVOID** IT--AND IT'S MUCH TOO LARGE FOR MY **REPULSORS** TO HAVE ANY **EFFECT** AGAINST IT!

MY ONLY HOPE IS TO KICK INTO FULL POWER--

**KAR-PWOOM**

--AND HIT IT **STRAIGHT ON** WITH THE FORCE OF A ROCKET-POWERED MISSILE!

WHAT WAS **THAT**--?!

IT SOUNDED LIKE THE END OF A **WORLD!**

YOU NEED NOT CONCERN YOURSELF, SIR KNIGHT!

WHO--?

I AM **SIR PERCY OF SCANDIA**--THE RIGHTFUL WIELDER OF THE EBONY BLADE, AND A KNIGHT OF THE **ROUND TABLE** OF KING ARTHUR PENDRAGON!

YOU'RE ALSO THE ORIGINAL **BLACK KNIGHT,** AND MY FORMER TEACHER!

BUT, WHAT ARE **YOU** DOING HERE?

THOUGH MY **SPIRIT** ONCE SERVED AS YOUR MENTOR, AND INSTRUCTED YOU IN THE ARTS OF COMBAT, THE GRAND-MASTER HAS SENT ME HERE TO CHALLENGE YOU...**TO THE DEATH!**

**NO!** I WON'T FIGHT YOU! I **CAN'T**--!

THEN, YOU SHALL **DIE!**

143

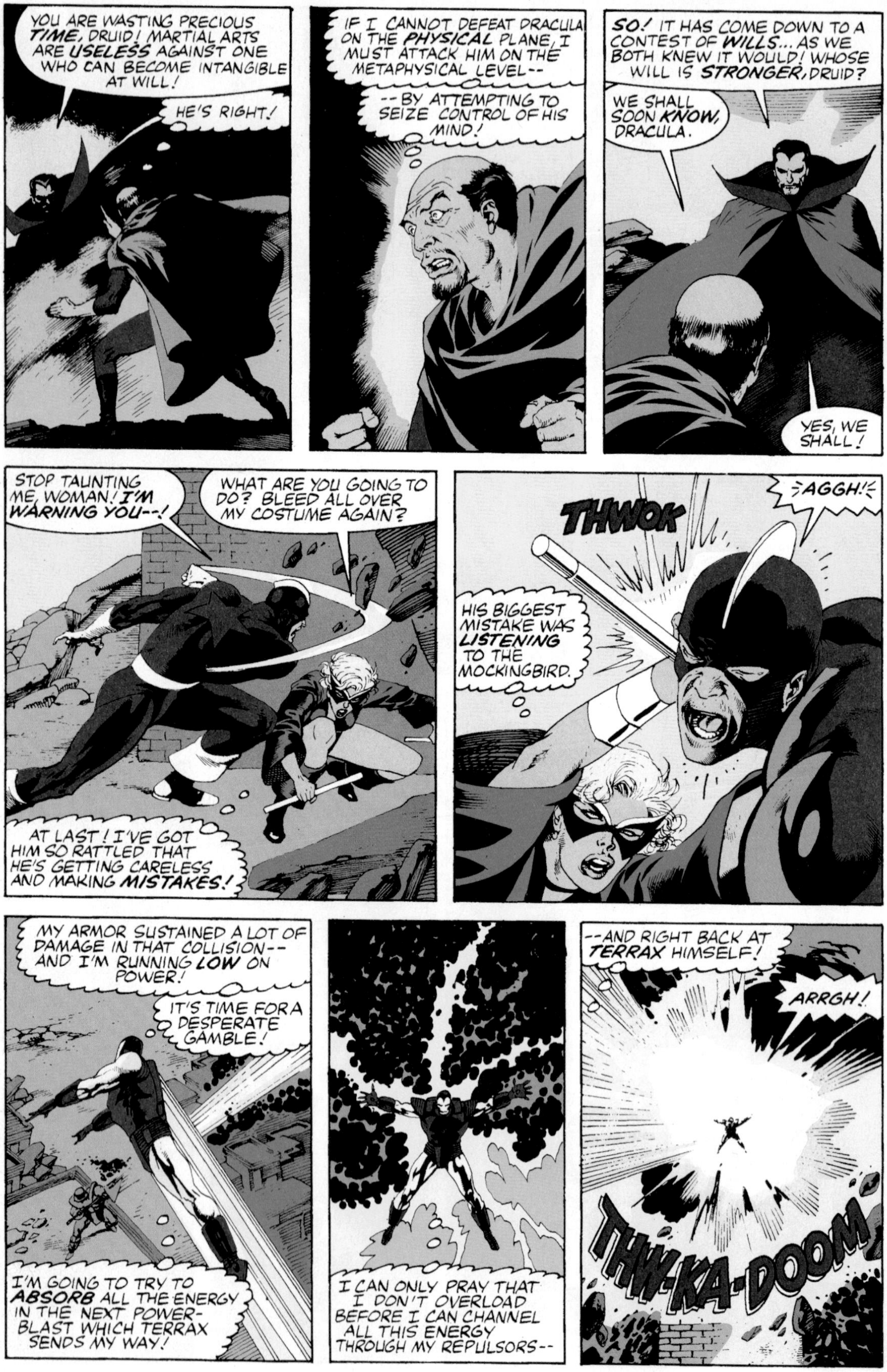
YOU ARE WASTING PRECIOUS TIME, DRUID! MARTIAL ARTS ARE USELESS AGAINST ONE WHO CAN BECOME INTANGIBLE AT WILL!
HE'S RIGHT!
IF I CANNOT DEFEAT DRACULA ON THE PHYSICAL PLANE, I MUST ATTACK HIM ON THE METAPHYSICAL LEVEL--
--BY ATTEMPTING TO SEIZE CONTROL OF HIS MIND!
SO! IT HAS COME DOWN TO A CONTEST OF WILLS... AS WE BOTH KNEW IT WOULD! WHOSE WILL IS STRONGER, DRUID?
WE SHALL SOON KNOW, DRACULA.
YES, WE SHALL!
STOP TAUNTING ME, WOMAN! I'M WARNING YOU--!
WHAT ARE YOU GOING TO DO? BLEED ALL OVER MY COSTUME AGAIN?
AT LAST! I'VE GOT HIM SO RATTLED THAT HE'S GETTING CARELESS AND MAKING MISTAKES!
THWOK
AGGH!
HIS BIGGEST MISTAKE WAS LISTENING TO THE MOCKINGBIRD.
MY ARMOR SUSTAINED A LOT OF DAMAGE IN THAT COLLISION-- AND I'M RUNNING LOW ON POWER!
IT'S TIME FOR A DESPERATE GAMBLE!
I'M GOING TO TRY TO ABSORB ALL THE ENERGY IN THE NEXT POWER-BLAST WHICH TERRAX SENDS MY WAY!
I CAN ONLY PRAY THAT I DON'T OVERLOAD BEFORE I CAN CHANNEL ALL THIS ENERGY THROUGH MY REPULSORS--
--AND RIGHT BACK AT TERRAX HIMSELF!
ARRGH!
THW-KA-DOOM

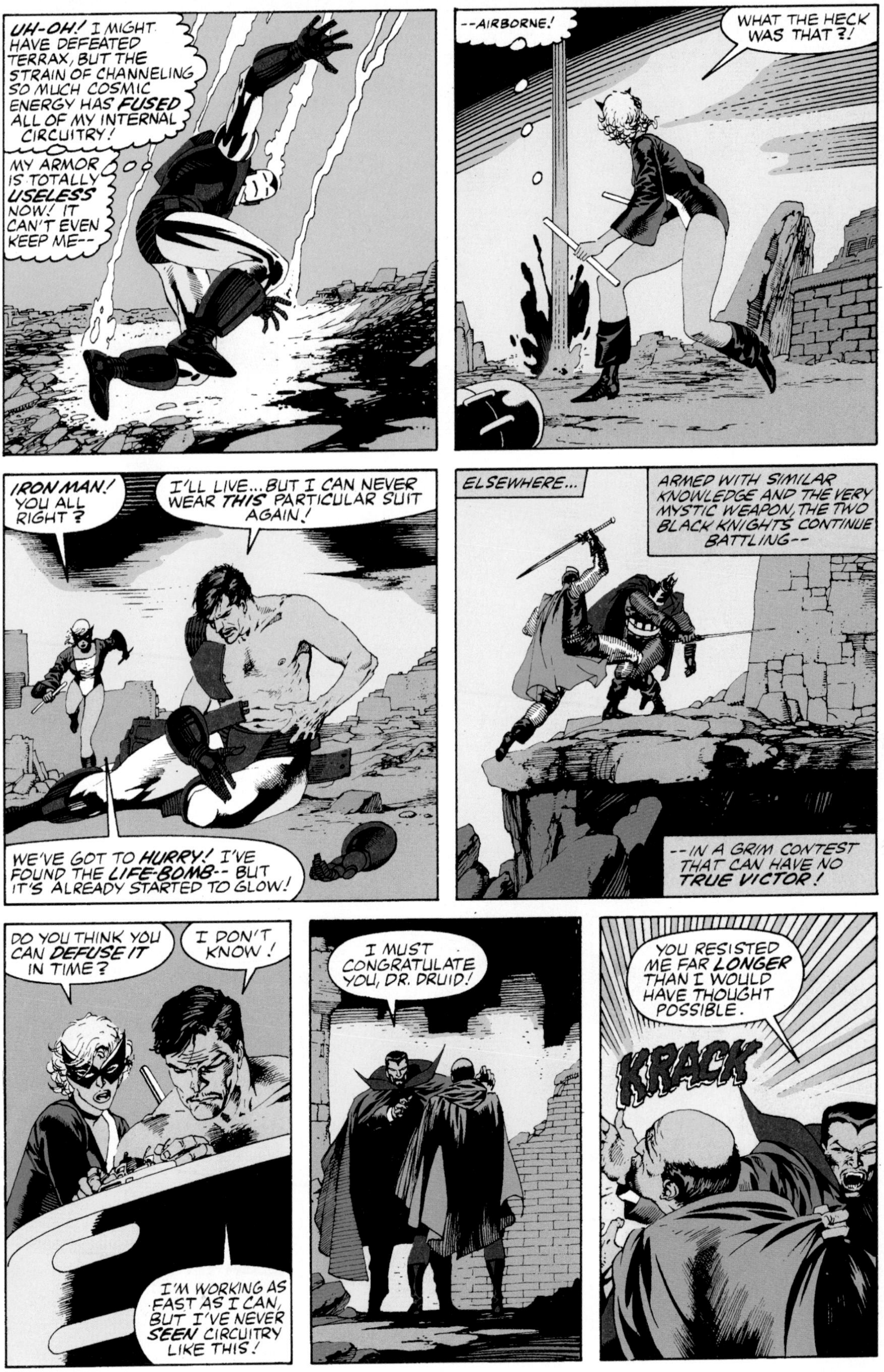
UH-OH! I MIGHT HAVE DEFEATED TERRAX, BUT THE STRAIN OF CHANNELING SO MUCH COSMIC ENERGY HAS FUSED ALL OF MY INTERNAL CIRCUITRY!
MY ARMOR IS TOTALLY USELESS NOW! IT CAN'T EVEN KEEP ME--
--AIRBORNE!
WHAT THE HECK WAS THAT?!
IRON MAN! YOU ALL RIGHT?
I'LL LIVE...BUT I CAN NEVER WEAR THIS PARTICULAR SUIT AGAIN!
WE'VE GOT TO HURRY! I'VE FOUND THE LIFE-BOMB-- BUT IT'S ALREADY STARTED TO GLOW!
ELSEWHERE...
ARMED WITH SIMILAR KNOWLEDGE AND THE VERY MYSTIC WEAPON, THE TWO BLACK KNIGHTS CONTINUE BATTLING--
--IN A GRIM CONTEST THAT CAN HAVE NO TRUE VICTOR!
DO YOU THINK YOU CAN DEFUSE IT IN TIME?
I DON'T KNOW!
I'M WORKING AS FAST AS I CAN, BUT I'VE NEVER SEEN CIRCUITRY LIKE THIS!
I MUST CONGRATULATE YOU, DR. DRUID!
YOU RESISTED ME FAR LONGER THAN I WOULD HAVE THOUGHT POSSIBLE.
KRACK

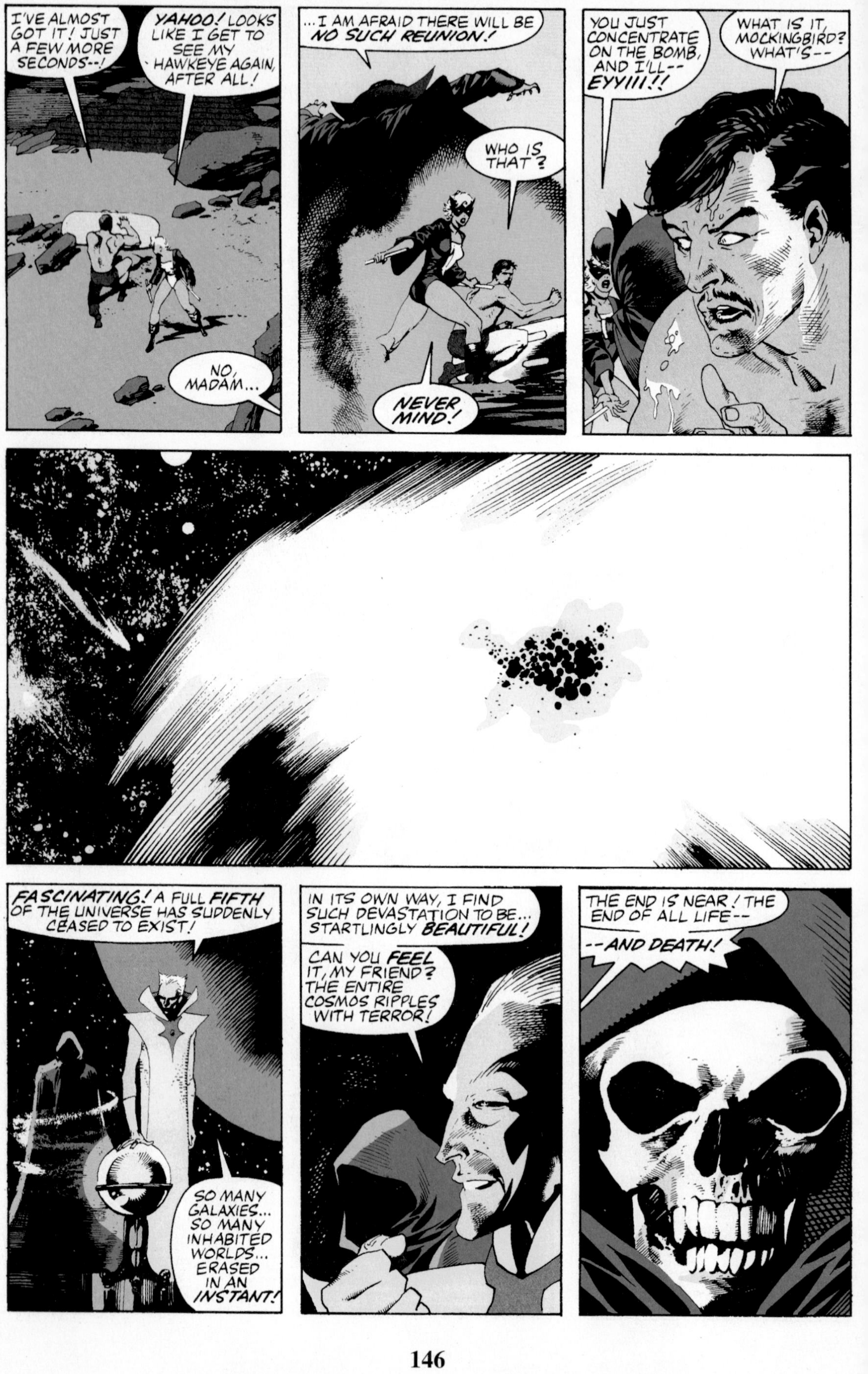
I'VE ALMOST GOT IT! JUST A FEW MORE SECONDS--!
YAHOO! LOOKS LIKE I GET TO SEE MY HAWKEYE AGAIN, AFTER ALL!
NO, MADAM...
...I AM AFRAID THERE WILL BE NO SUCH REUNION!
WHO IS THAT?
NEVER MIND!
YOU JUST CONCENTRATE ON THE BOMB, AND I'LL-- EYYIII!!
WHAT IS IT, MOCKINGBIRD? WHAT'S--
FASCINATING! A FULL FIFTH OF THE UNIVERSE HAS SUDDENLY CEASED TO EXIST!
SO MANY GALAXIES... SO MANY INHABITED WORLDS... ERASED IN AN INSTANT!
IN ITS OWN WAY, I FIND SUCH DEVASTATION TO BE... STARTLINGLY BEAUTIFUL!
CAN YOU FEEL IT, MY FRIEND? THE ENTIRE COSMOS RIPPLES WITH TERROR!
THE END IS NEAR! THE END OF ALL LIFE--
--AND DEATH!

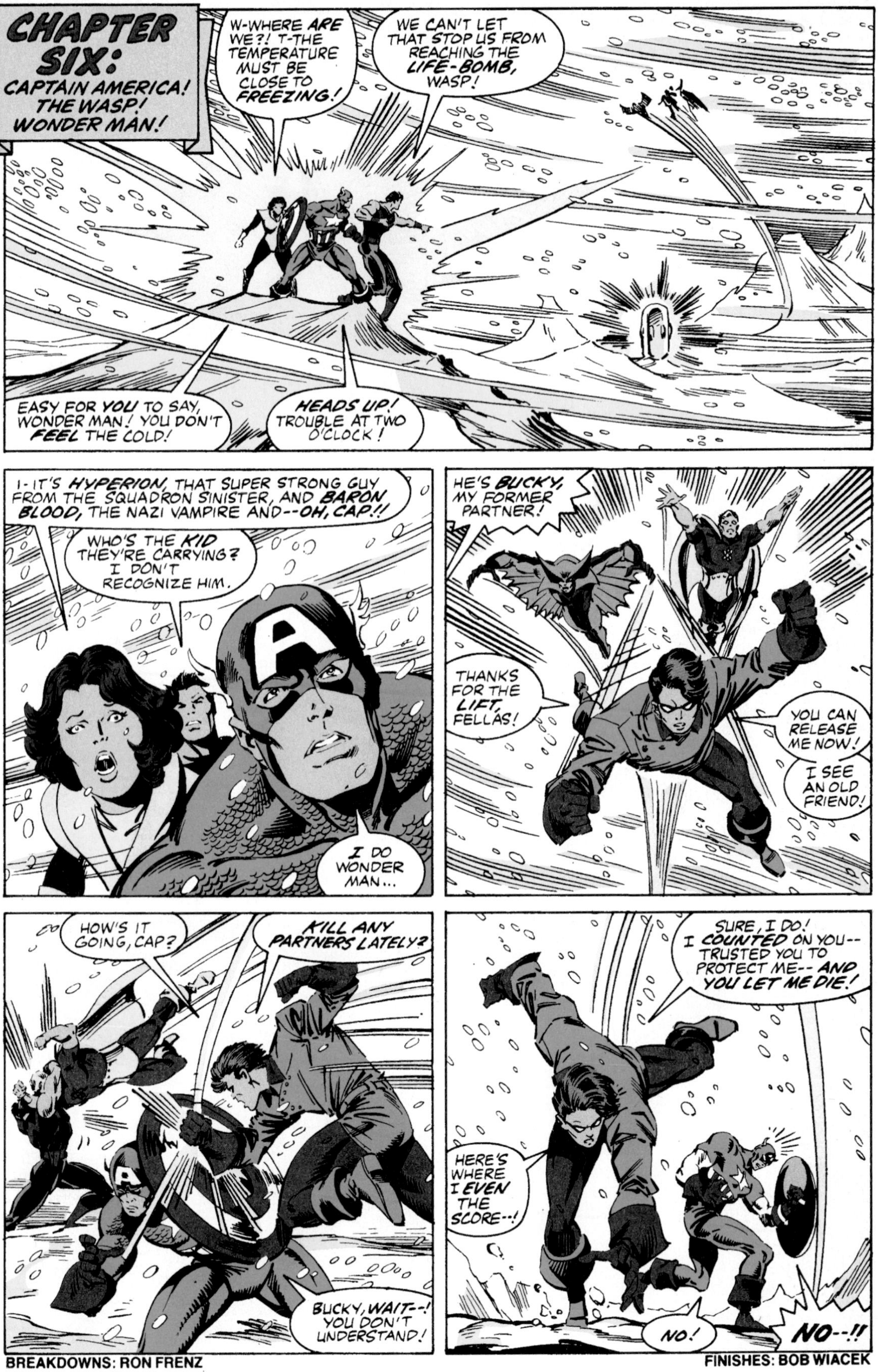

CHAPTER SIX: CAPTAIN AMERICA! THE WASP! WONDER MAN!
W-WHERE ARE WE?! T-THE TEMPERATURE MUST BE CLOSE TO FREEZING!
WE CAN'T LET THAT STOP US FROM REACHING THE LIFE-BOMB, WASP!
EASY FOR YOU TO SAY, WONDER MAN! YOU DON'T FEEL THE COLD!
HEADS UP! TROUBLE AT TWO O'CLOCK!
I-IT'S HYPERION, THAT SUPER STRONG GUY FROM THE SQUADRON SINISTER, AND BARON BLOOD, THE NAZI VAMPIRE AND--OH, CAP!!
WHO'S THE KID THEY'RE CARRYING? I DON'T RECOGNIZE HIM.
I DO WONDER MAN...
HE'S BUCKY, MY FORMER PARTNER!
THANKS FOR THE LIFT, FELLAS!
YOU CAN RELEASE ME NOW!
I SEE AN OLD FRIEND!
HOW'S IT GOING, CAP?
KILL ANY PARTNERS LATELY?
BUCKY, WAIT--! YOU DON'T UNDERSTAND!
SURE, I DO! I COUNTED ON YOU-- TRUSTED YOU TO PROTECT ME-- AND YOU LET ME DIE!
HERE'S WHERE I EVEN THE SCORE--!
NO!
NO--!!


BREAKDOWNS: RON FRENZ FINISHES: BOB WIACEK

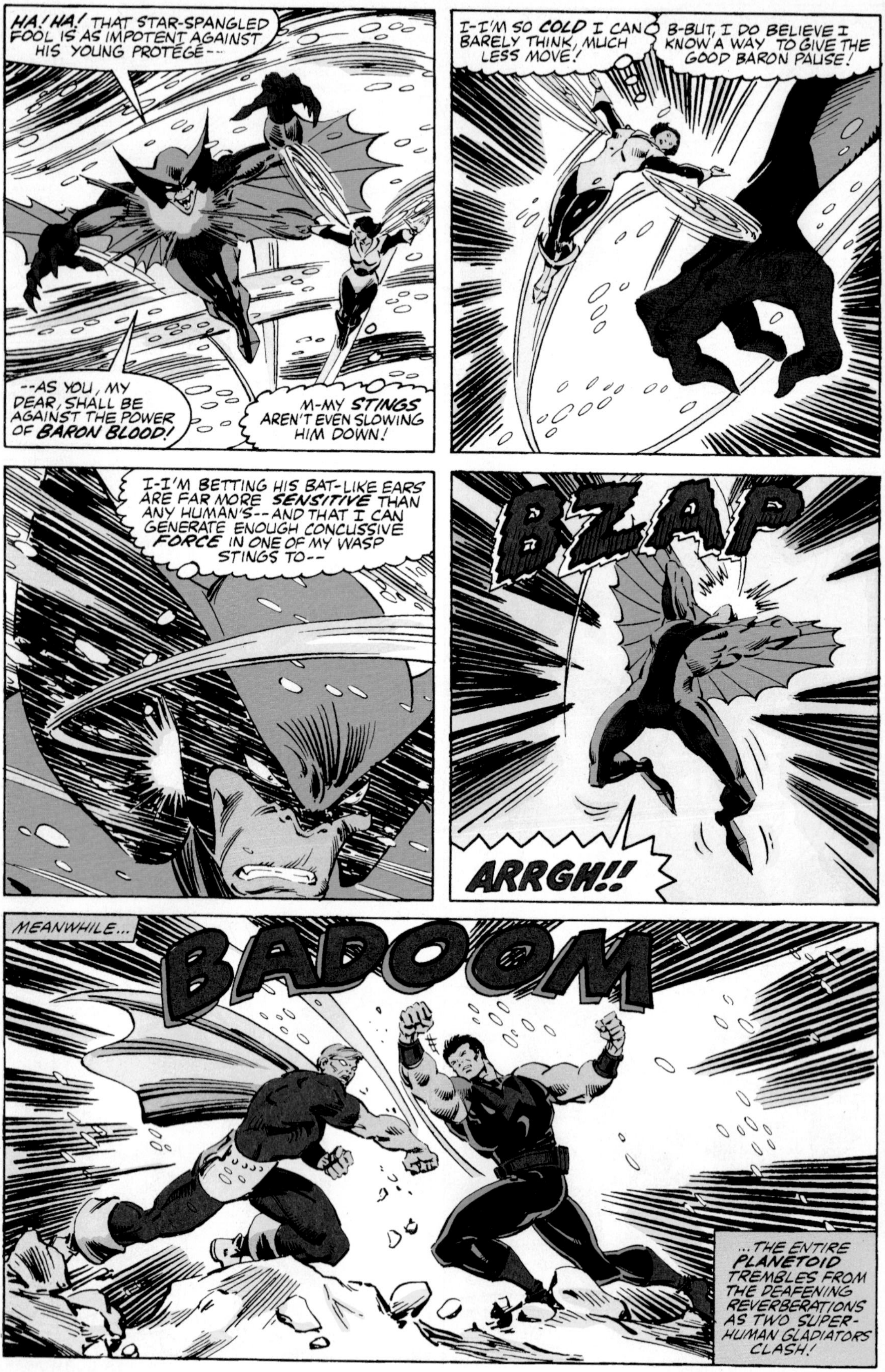

HA! HA! THAT STAR-SPANGLED FOOL IS AS IMPOTENT AGAINST HIS YOUNG PROTÉGÉ--
--AS YOU, MY DEAR, SHALL BE AGAINST THE POWER OF BARON BLOOD!
M-MY STINGS AREN'T EVEN SLOWING HIM DOWN!
I-I'M SO COLD I CAN BARELY THINK, MUCH LESS MOVE!
B-BUT, I DO BELIEVE I KNOW A WAY TO GIVE THE GOOD BARON PAUSE!
I-I'M BETTING HIS BAT-LIKE EARS ARE FAR MORE SENSITIVE THAN ANY HUMAN'S--AND THAT I CAN GENERATE ENOUGH CONCUSSIVE FORCE IN ONE OF MY WASP STINGS TO--
BZAP
ARRGH!!
MEANWHILE...
BADOOM
...THE ENTIRE PLANETOID TREMBLES FROM THE DEAFENING REVERBERATIONS AS TWO SUPER-HUMAN GLADIATORS CLASH!

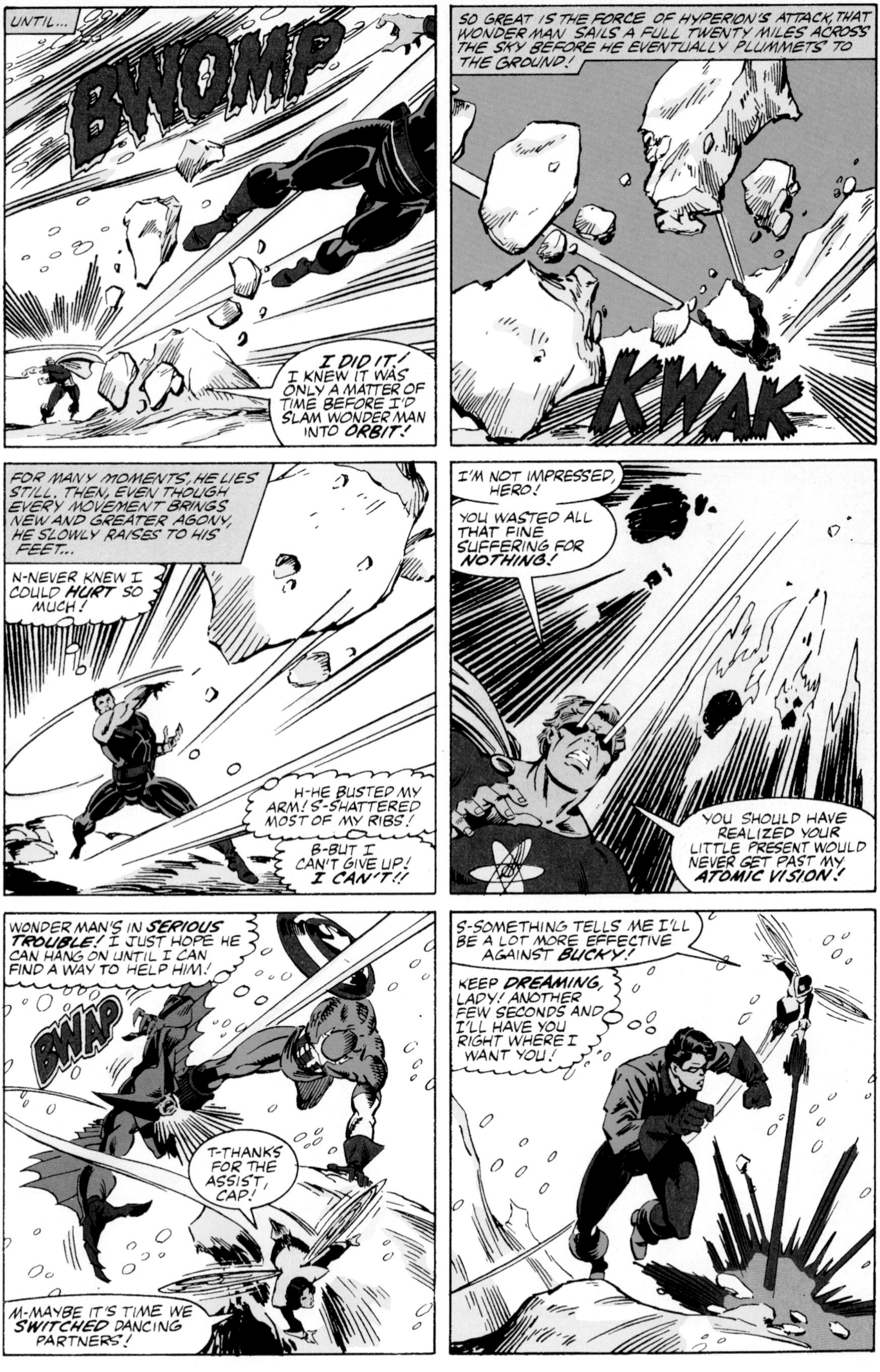
UNTIL...
BWOMP
I DID IT! I KNEW IT WAS ONLY A MATTER OF TIME BEFORE I'D SLAM WONDER MAN INTO ORBIT!
SO GREAT IS THE FORCE OF HYPERION'S ATTACK, THAT WONDER MAN SAILS A FULL TWENTY MILES ACROSS THE SKY BEFORE HE EVENTUALLY PLUMMETS TO THE GROUND!
KWAK
FOR MANY MOMENTS, HE LIES STILL. THEN, EVEN THOUGH EVERY MOVEMENT BRINGS NEW AND GREATER AGONY, HE SLOWLY RAISES TO HIS FEET...
N-NEVER KNEW I COULD HURT SO MUCH!
H-HE BUSTED MY ARM! S-SHATTERED MOST OF MY RIBS!
B-BUT I CAN'T GIVE UP! I CAN'T!!
I'M NOT IMPRESSED, HERO!
YOU WASTED ALL THAT FINE SUFFERING FOR NOTHING!
YOU SHOULD HAVE REALIZED YOUR LITTLE PRESENT WOULD NEVER GET PAST MY ATOMIC VISION!
WONDER MAN'S IN SERIOUS TROUBLE! I JUST HOPE HE CAN HANG ON UNTIL I CAN FIND A WAY TO HELP HIM!
BWAP
T-THANKS FOR THE ASSIST, CAP!
M-MAYBE IT'S TIME WE SWITCHED DANCING PARTNERS!
S-SOMETHING TELLS ME I'LL BE A LOT MORE EFFECTIVE AGAINST BUCKY!
KEEP DREAMING, LADY! ANOTHER FEW SECONDS AND I'LL HAVE YOU RIGHT WHERE I WANT YOU!

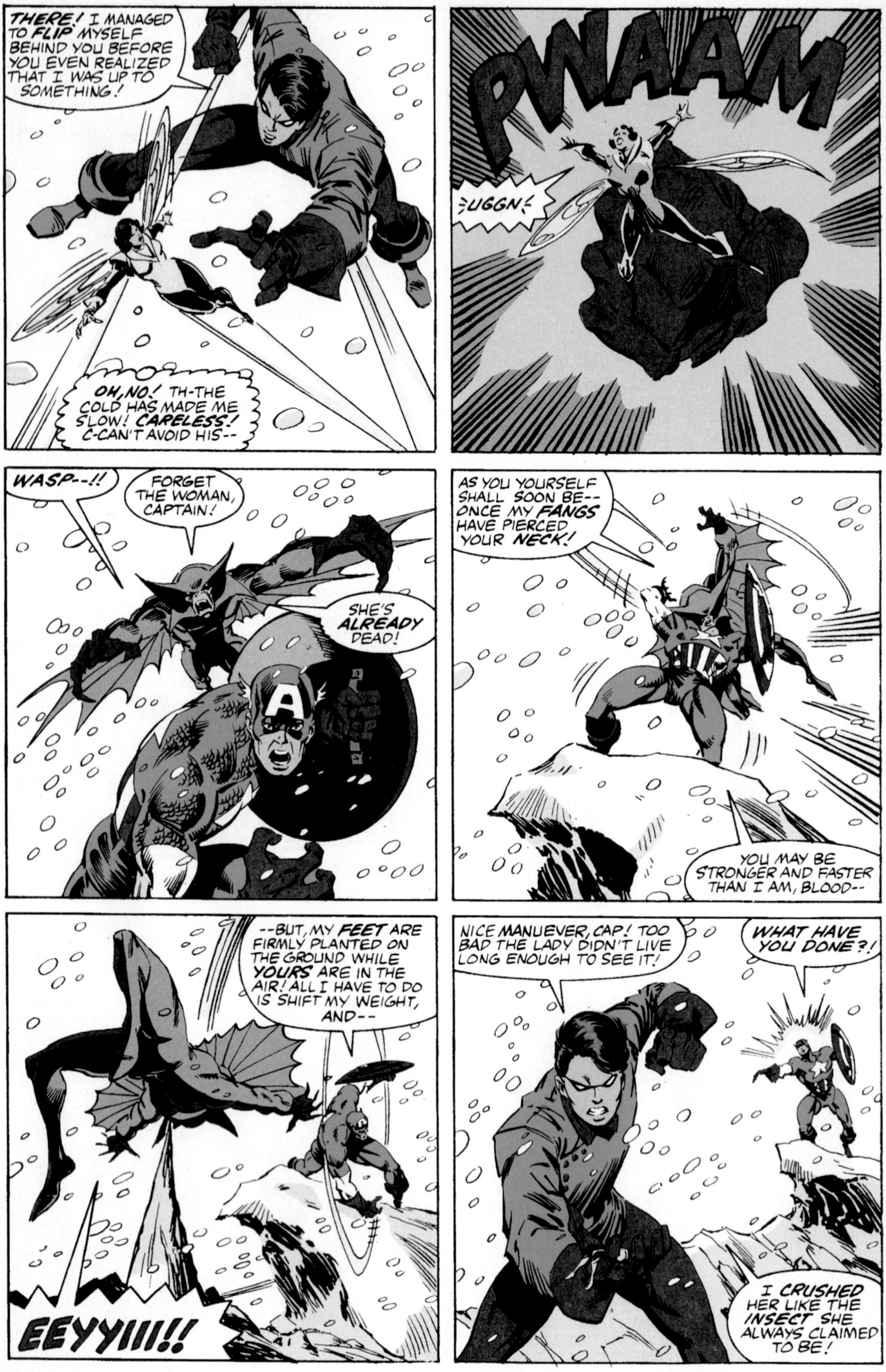
THERE! I MANAGED TO FLIP MYSELF BEHIND YOU BEFORE YOU EVEN REALIZED THAT I WAS UP TO SOMETHING!
OH, NO! TH-THE COLD HAS MADE ME SLOW! CARELESS! C-CAN'T AVOID HIS--
PWAAM
UGGN
WASP--!!
FORGET THE WOMAN, CAPTAIN!
SHE'S ALREADY DEAD!
AS YOU YOURSELF SHALL SOON BE-- ONCE MY FANGS HAVE PIERCED YOUR NECK!
YOU MAY BE STRONGER AND FASTER THAN I AM, BLOOD--
--BUT, MY FEET ARE FIRMLY PLANTED ON THE GROUND WHILE YOURS ARE IN THE AIR! ALL I HAVE TO DO IS SHIFT MY WEIGHT, AND--
EEYYIII!!
NICE MANUEVER, CAP! TOO BAD THE LADY DIDN'T LIVE LONG ENOUGH TO SEE IT!
WHAT HAVE YOU DONE?!
I CRUSHED HER LIKE THE INSECT SHE ALWAYS CLAIMED TO BE!

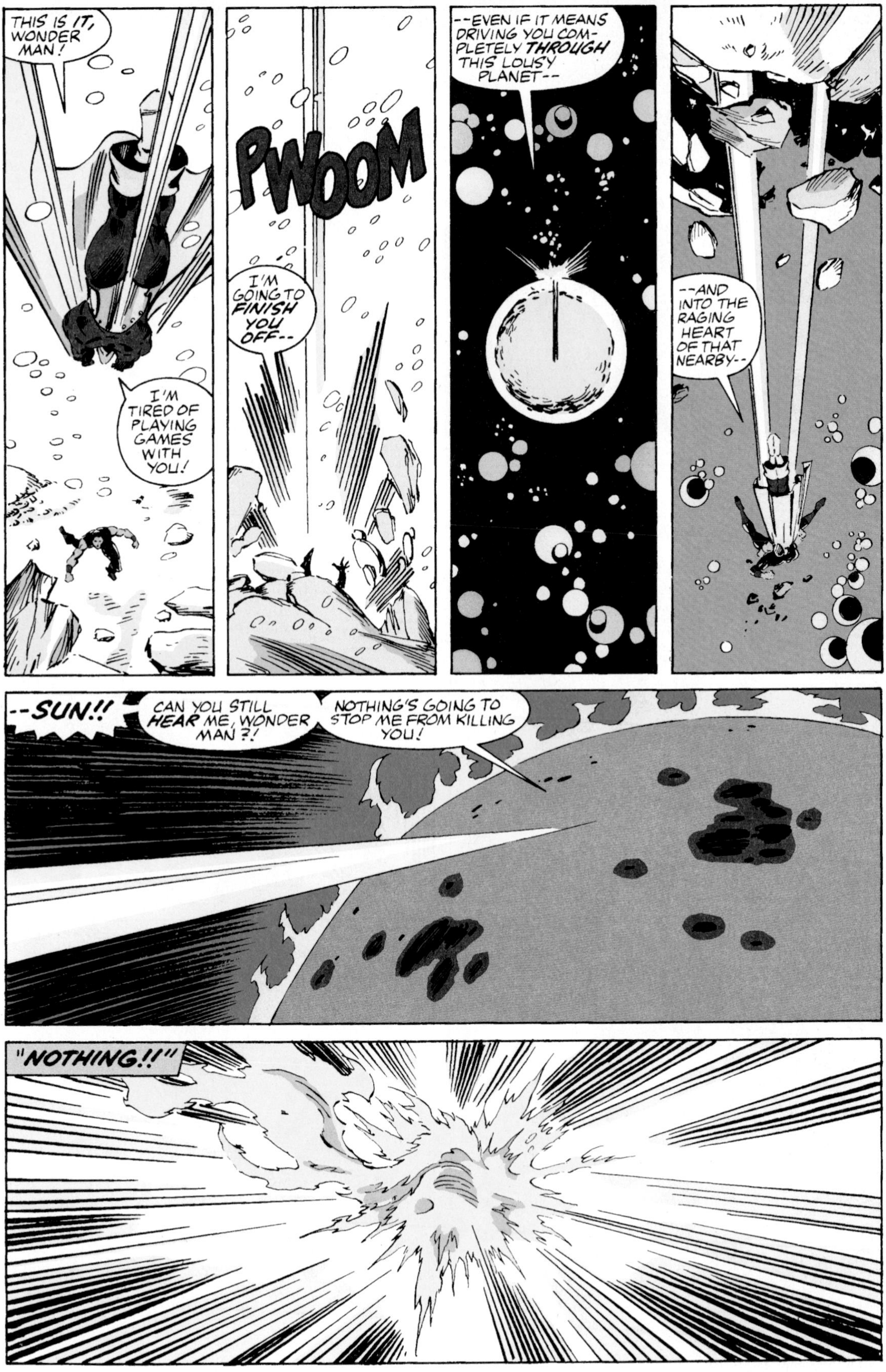
THIS IS IT, WONDER MAN!
I'M TIRED OF PLAYING GAMES WITH YOU!
PWOOM
I'M GOING TO FINISH YOU OFF--
--EVEN IF IT MEANS DRIVING YOU COMPLETELY THROUGH THIS LOUSY PLANET--
--AND INTO THE RAGING HEART OF THAT NEARBY--
--SUN!!
CAN YOU STILL HEAR ME, WONDER MAN?!
NOTHING'S GOING TO STOP ME FROM KILLING YOU!
"NOTHING!!"

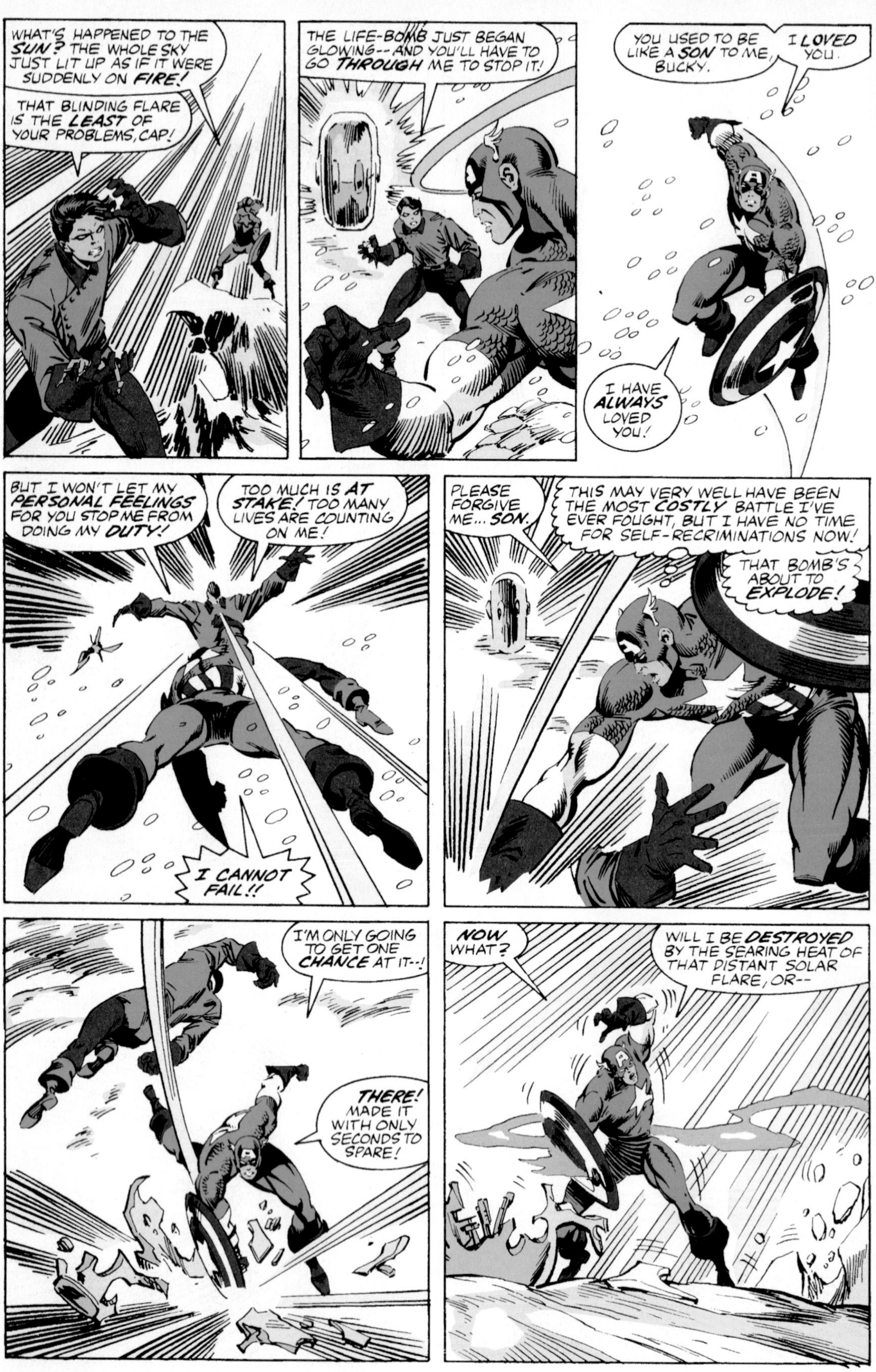
WHAT'S HAPPENED TO THE SUN? THE WHOLE SKY JUST LIT UP AS IF IT WERE SUDDENLY ON FIRE!
THAT BLINDING FLARE IS THE LEAST OF YOUR PROBLEMS, CAP!
THE LIFE-BOMB JUST BEGAN GLOWING-- AND YOU'LL HAVE TO GO THROUGH ME TO STOP IT!
YOU USED TO BE LIKE A SON TO ME, BUCKY.
I LOVED YOU.
I HAVE ALWAYS LOVED YOU!
BUT I WON'T LET MY PERSONAL FEELINGS FOR YOU STOP ME FROM DOING MY DUTY!
TOO MUCH IS AT STAKE! TOO MANY LIVES ARE COUNTING ON ME!
I CANNOT FAIL!!
PLEASE FORGIVE ME... SON.
THIS MAY VERY WELL HAVE BEEN THE MOST COSTLY BATTLE I'VE EVER FOUGHT, BUT I HAVE NO TIME FOR SELF-RECRIMINATIONS NOW!
THAT BOMB'S ABOUT TO EXPLODE!
I'M ONLY GOING TO GET ONE CHANCE AT IT--!
THERE! MADE IT WITH ONLY SECONDS TO SPARE!
NOW WHAT?
WILL I BE DESTROYED BY THE SEARING HEAT OF THAT DISTANT SOLAR FLARE, OR--

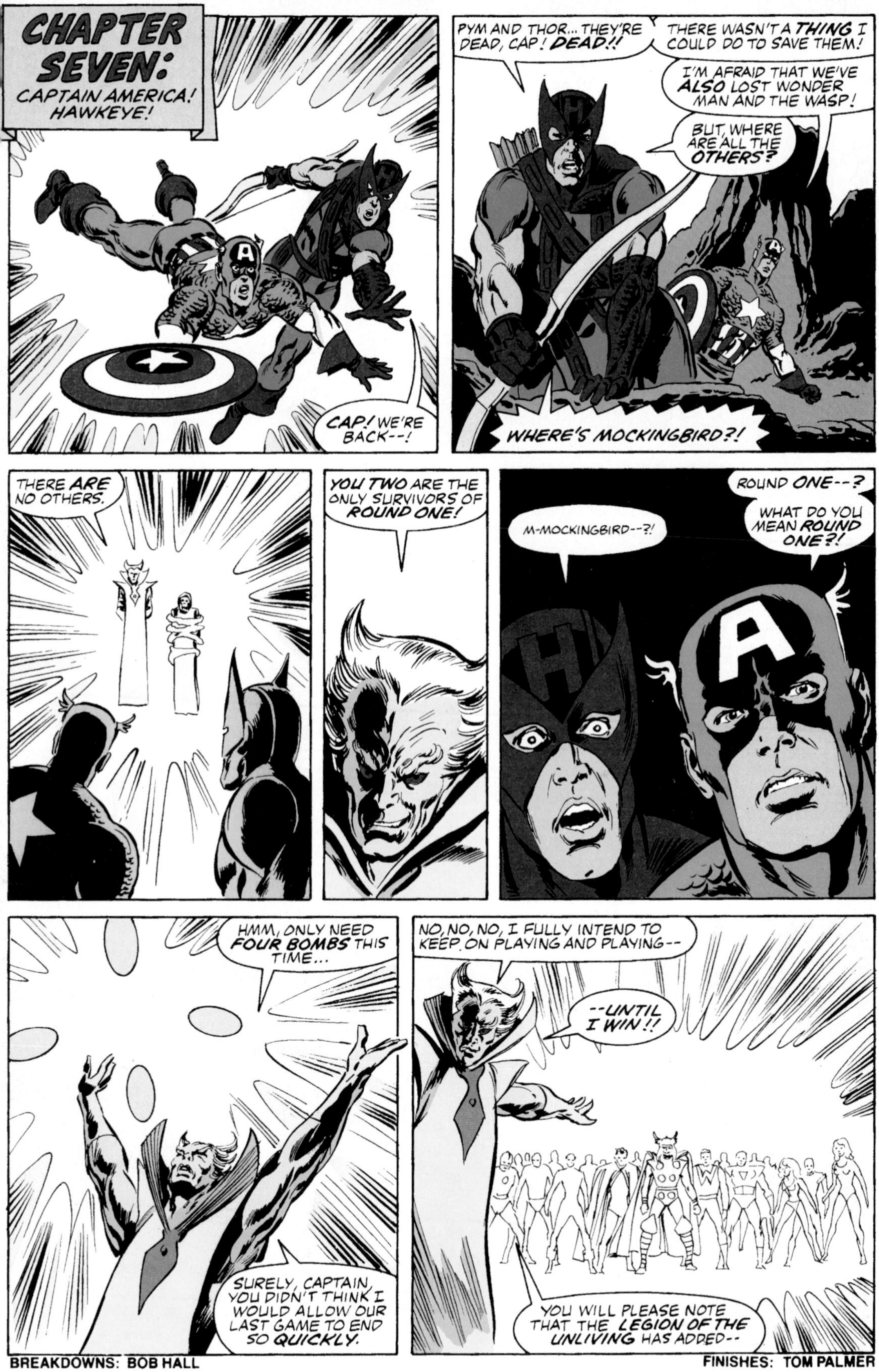
CHAPTER SEVEN:
CAPTAIN AMERICA! HAWKEYE!
CAP! WE'RE BACK--!
PYM AND THOR... THEY'RE DEAD, CAP! DEAD!!
THERE WASN'T A THING I COULD DO TO SAVE THEM!
I'M AFRAID THAT WE'VE ALSO LOST WONDER MAN AND THE WASP!
BUT, WHERE ARE ALL THE OTHERS?
WHERE'S MOCKINGBIRD?!
THERE ARE NO OTHERS.
YOU TWO ARE THE ONLY SURVIVORS OF ROUND ONE!
M-MOCKINGBIRD--?!
ROUND ONE--?
WHAT DO YOU MEAN ROUND ONE?!
HMM, ONLY NEED FOUR BOMBS THIS TIME...
SURELY, CAPTAIN, YOU DIDN'T THINK I WOULD ALLOW OUR LAST GAME TO END SO QUICKLY.
NO, NO, NO, I FULLY INTEND TO KEEP ON PLAYING AND PLAYING--
--UNTIL I WIN!!
YOU WILL PLEASE NOTE THAT THE LEGION OF THE UNLIVING HAS ADDED--

BREAKDOWNS: BOB HALL FINISHES: TOM PALMER

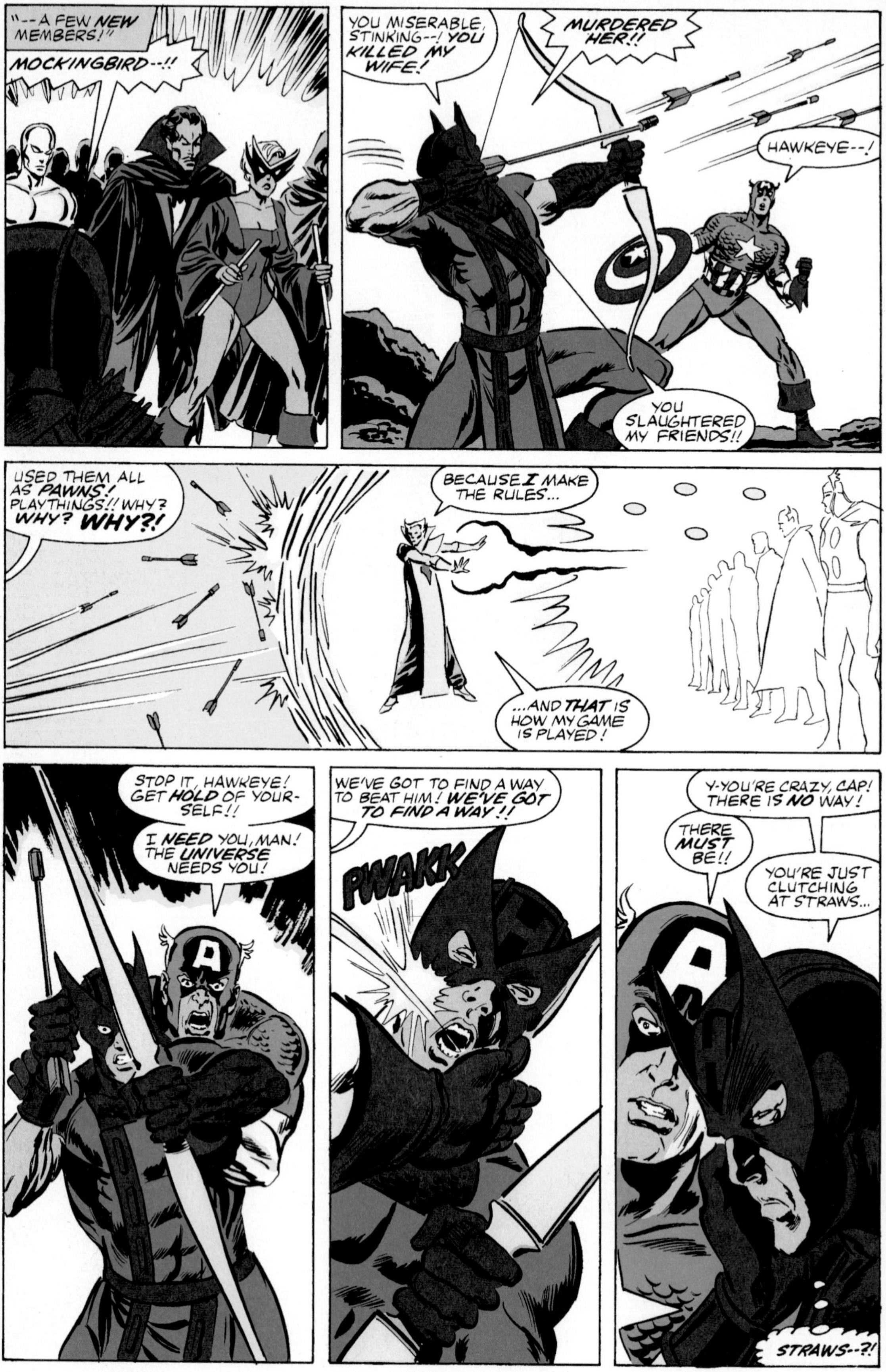
"--A FEW NEW MEMBERS!"
MOCKINGBIRD--!!
YOU MISERABLE, STINKING--! YOU KILLED MY WIFE!
MURDERED HER!!
HAWKEYE--!
YOU SLAUGHTERED MY FRIENDS!!
USED THEM ALL AS PAWNS! PLAYTHINGS!! WHY? WHY? WHY?!
BECAUSE I MAKE THE RULES...
...AND THAT IS HOW MY GAME IS PLAYED!
STOP IT, HAWKEYE! GET HOLD OF YOURSELF!!
I NEED YOU, MAN! THE UNIVERSE NEEDS YOU!
WE'VE GOT TO FIND A WAY TO BEAT HIM! WE'VE GOT TO FIND A WAY!!
PWAKK
Y-YOU'RE CRAZY, CAP! THERE IS NO WAY!
THERE MUST BE!!
YOU'RE JUST CLUTCHING AT STRAWS...
STRAWS--?!

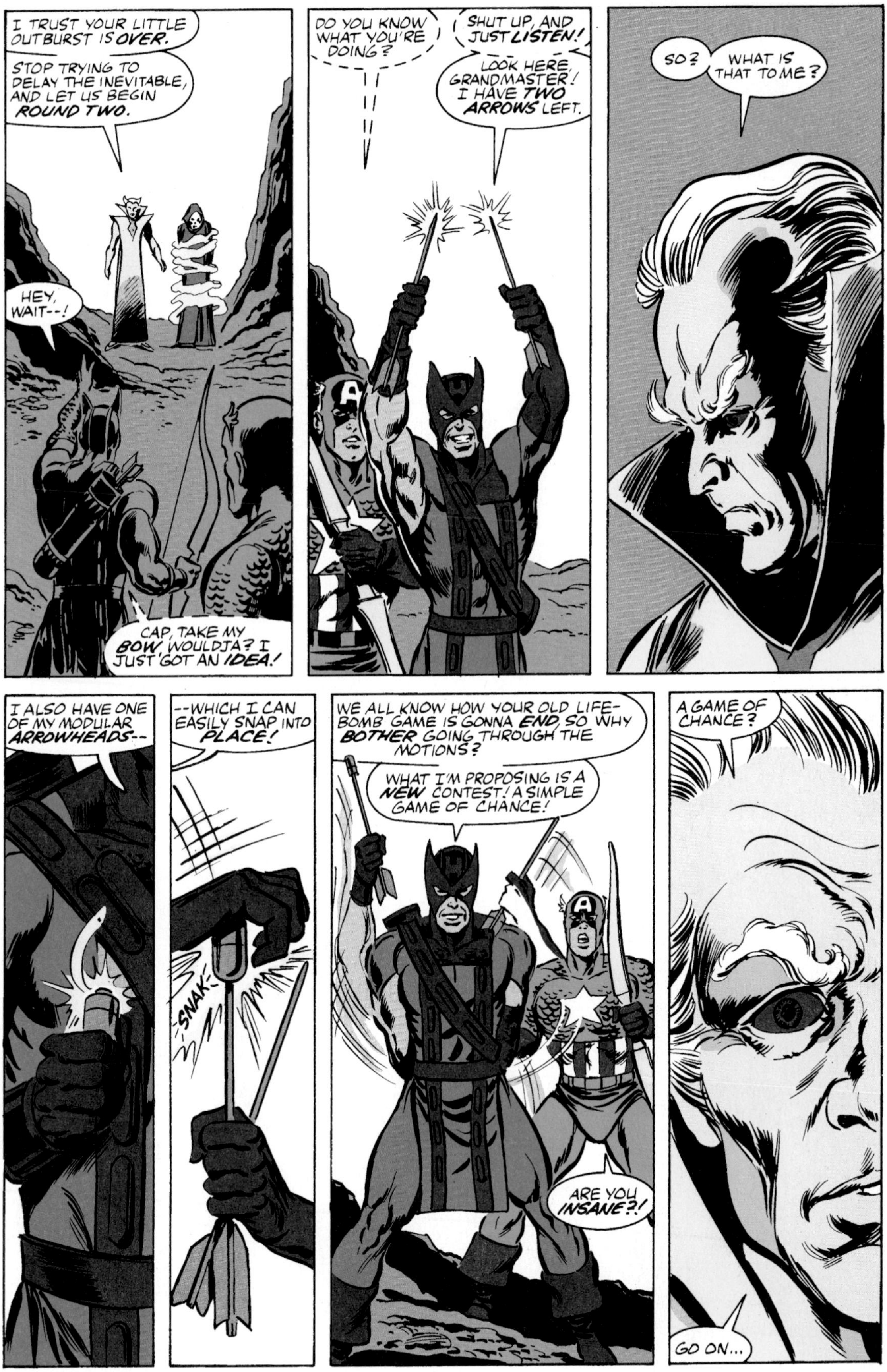

I TRUST YOUR LITTLE OUTBURST IS OVER.
STOP TRYING TO DELAY THE INEVITABLE, AND LET US BEGIN ROUND TWO.
HEY, WAIT--!
CAP, TAKE MY BOW, WOULDJA? I JUST GOT AN IDEA!
DO YOU KNOW WHAT YOU'RE DOING?
SHUT UP, AND JUST LISTEN!
LOOK HERE, GRANDMASTER! I HAVE TWO ARROWS LEFT.
SO?
WHAT IS THAT TO ME?
I ALSO HAVE ONE OF MY MODULAR ARROWHEADS--
--WHICH I CAN EASILY SNAP INTO PLACE!
SNAK
WE ALL KNOW HOW YOUR OLD LIFE-BOMB GAME IS GONNA END, SO WHY BOTHER GOING THROUGH THE MOTIONS?
WHAT I'M PROPOSING IS A NEW CONTEST! A SIMPLE GAME OF CHANCE!
ARE YOU INSANE?!
A GAME OF CHANCE?
GO ON...

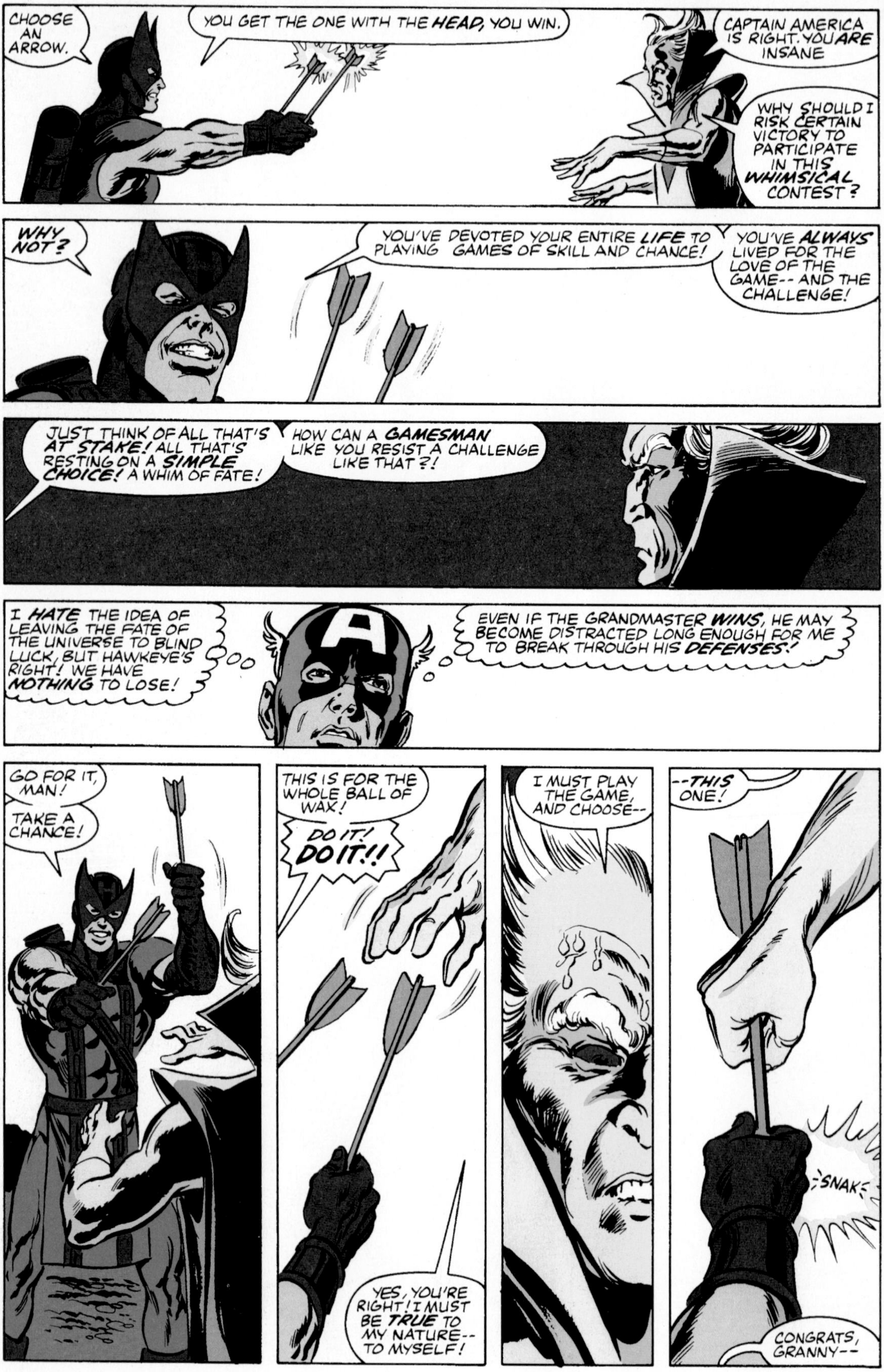
CHOOSE AN ARROW.
YOU GET THE ONE WITH THE HEAD, YOU WIN.
CAPTAIN AMERICA IS RIGHT. YOU ARE INSANE
WHY SHOULD I RISK CERTAIN VICTORY TO PARTICIPATE IN THIS WHIMSICAL CONTEST?
WHY NOT?
YOU'VE DEVOTED YOUR ENTIRE LIFE TO PLAYING GAMES OF SKILL AND CHANCE!
YOU'VE ALWAYS LIVED FOR THE LOVE OF THE GAME-- AND THE CHALLENGE!
JUST THINK OF ALL THAT'S AT STAKE! ALL THAT'S RESTING ON A SIMPLE CHOICE! A WHIM OF FATE!
HOW CAN A GAMESMAN LIKE YOU RESIST A CHALLENGE LIKE THAT?!
I HATE THE IDEA OF LEAVING THE FATE OF THE UNIVERSE TO BLIND LUCK, BUT HAWKEYE'S RIGHT! WE HAVE NOTHING TO LOSE!
EVEN IF THE GRANDMASTER WINS, HE MAY BECOME DISTRACTED LONG ENOUGH FOR ME TO BREAK THROUGH HIS DEFENSES!
GO FOR IT, MAN!
TAKE A CHANCE!
THIS IS FOR THE WHOLE BALL OF WAX!
DO IT! DO IT!!
YES, YOU'RE RIGHT! I MUST BE TRUE TO MY NATURE-- TO MYSELF!
I MUST PLAY THE GAME, AND CHOOSE--
--THIS ONE!
SNAK
CONGRATS, GRANNY--

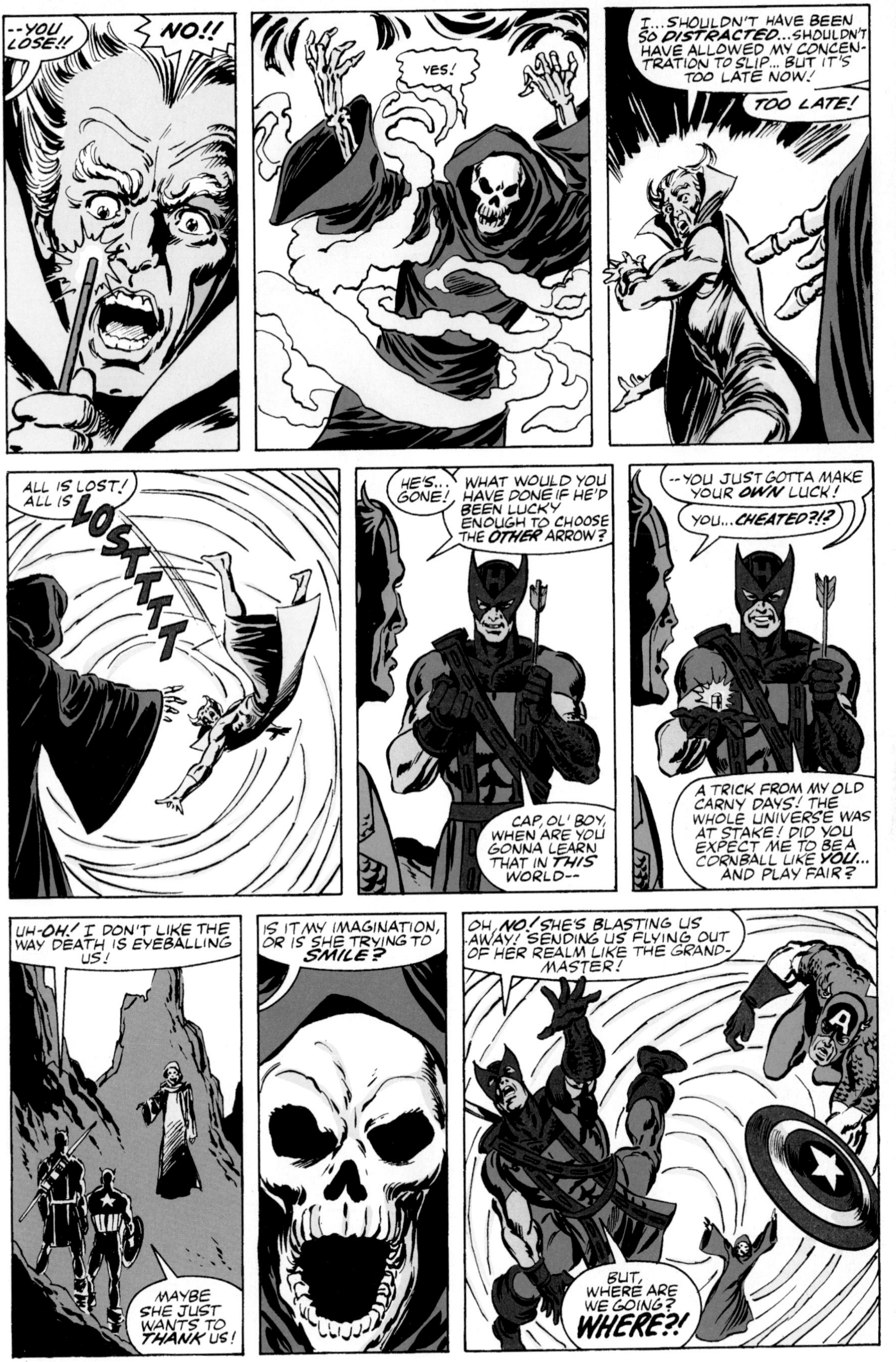

--YOU LOSE!!
NO!!
YES!
I... SHOULDN'T HAVE BEEN SO DISTRACTED... SHOULDN'T HAVE ALLOWED MY CONCENTRATION TO SLIP... BUT IT'S TOO LATE NOW!
TOO LATE!
ALL IS LOST! ALL IS LOSTTTTT
HE'S... GONE!
WHAT WOULD YOU HAVE DONE IF HE'D BEEN LUCKY ENOUGH TO CHOOSE THE OTHER ARROW?
CAP, OL' BOY, WHEN ARE YOU GONNA LEARN THAT IN THIS WORLD--
--YOU JUST GOTTA MAKE YOUR OWN LUCK!
YOU... CHEATED?!?
A TRICK FROM MY OLD CARNY DAYS! THE WHOLE UNIVERSE WAS AT STAKE! DID YOU EXPECT ME TO BE A CORNBALL LIKE YOU... AND PLAY FAIR?
UH-OH! I DON'T LIKE THE WAY DEATH IS EYEBALLING US!
MAYBE SHE JUST WANTS TO THANK US!
IS IT MY IMAGINATION, OR IS SHE TRYING TO SMILE?
OH, NO! SHE'S BLASTING US AWAY! SENDING US FLYING OUT OF HER REALM LIKE THE GRAND-MASTER!
BUT, WHERE ARE WE GOING? WHERE?!

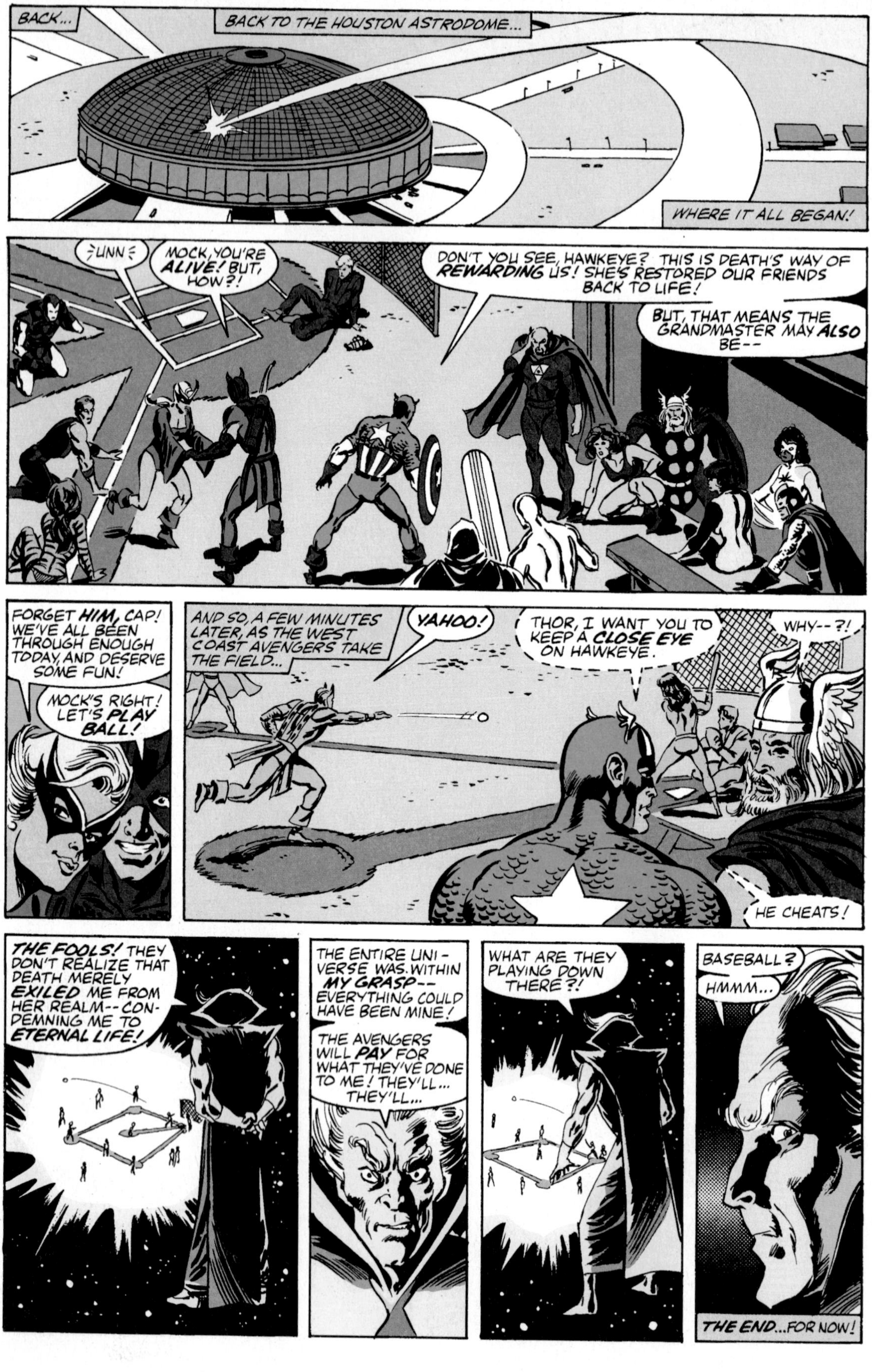
BACK...
BACK TO THE HOUSTON ASTRODOME...
WHERE IT ALL BEGAN!
UNN
MOCK, YOU'RE ALIVE! BUT, HOW?!
DON'T YOU SEE, HAWKEYE? THIS IS DEATH'S WAY OF REWARDING US! SHE'S RESTORED OUR FRIENDS BACK TO LIFE!
BUT, THAT MEANS THE GRANDMASTER MAY ALSO BE--
FORGET HIM, CAP! WE'VE ALL BEEN THROUGH ENOUGH TODAY, AND DESERVE SOME FUN!
MOCK'S RIGHT! LET'S PLAY BALL!
AND SO, A FEW MINUTES LATER, AS THE WEST COAST AVENGERS TAKE THE FIELD...
YAHOO!
THOR, I WANT YOU TO KEEP A CLOSE EYE ON HAWKEYE.
WHY--?!
HE CHEATS!
THE FOOLS! THEY DON'T REALIZE THAT DEATH MERELY EXILED ME FROM HER REALM--CONDEMNING ME TO ETERNAL LIFE!
THE ENTIRE UNIVERSE WAS WITHIN MY GRASP--EVERYTHING COULD HAVE BEEN MINE!
THE AVENGERS WILL PAY FOR WHAT THEY'VE DONE TO ME! THEY'LL... THEY'LL...
WHAT ARE THEY PLAYING DOWN THERE?!
BASEBALL?
HMMM...
THE END...FOR NOW!

# MARVEL SUPER HEROES–1982

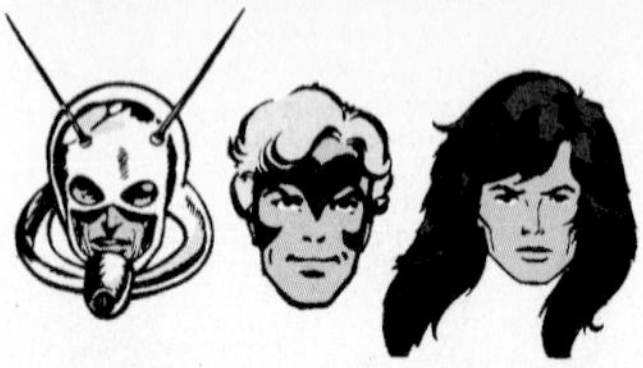

**Welcome, one and all, to mighty Marvel's very first *Limited Series*—a special, all-new kind of comic book series designed to run a finite number of issues. *Marvel Limited Series* based on such longtime favorites as HERCULES, WOLVERINE, THE VISION, and HAWKEYE will be rocketing their way to you in the months to come. But, as a very special treat to kick off this new format, we have chosen a project that encompasses *all* of Marvel's stalwart super-stars in a single senses-staggering epic ... the MARVEL SUPER HERO CONTEST OF CHAMPIONS!**

**The CONTEST OF CHAMPIONS has been a full two years in the making. Originally conceived in the winter of 1979 as a Treasury Edition based on the Summer Olympics, the book was stalled in mid-stream by the United States' withdrawal from the international games in early 1980. Since the basic story did not directly hinge upon the real Olympic games, we could easily eliminate the tie-in. But, between its inception and now, a lot of history has gone down in the mighty Marvel Universe, and the book required quite a bit of revamping so that it accurately reflected the current state of our super heroes.**

**We hope you enjoy this great mass assembly of super-humanity. It will be a long time before you see its like again ...**

**As a special bonus feature to commemorate this awesome gathering of super-stars, we've compiled—for the first time anywhere—a complete list of every single super hero alive today. We'll be serializing this riotous reference chart over the entire three-issue run of MARVEL SUPER HERO CONTEST OF CHAMPIONS! Buy all three issues for a ringside seat at the super hero event of the decade—and an up-to-the-minute list of the entire Marvel galaxy of super-stars!**

**ACROYEAR**
(Ex-King Acroyear of Spartak) Alien born in the Microversian world of Spartak, possessing super-strength, and wielding an energy sword. Current member of the Micronauts. Current whereabouts: Earth. First appearance: MICRONAUTS #1.

**EL ÁGUILA**
(Alejandro Montoya) Spanish mutant with the ability to shoot bio-electric energy when in contact with metal. Carries a sword. Current whereabouts: New York City. First appearance: POWER MAN/IRON FIST #58.

**AJAK**
(Name in own language unknown) Super-human belonging to the sub-species of humanity called the Eternals. Like his fellows, he can levitate. Current whereabouts: Earth. First appearance: ETERNALS #2.

**AMERICAN EAGLE**
(Jason Strongbow, tribal leader) American Indian possessing super-strength, endurance, and heightened senses. He carries a crossbow. Current whereabouts: American southwest. First appearance: MARVEL TWO-IN-ONE ANNUAL #6.

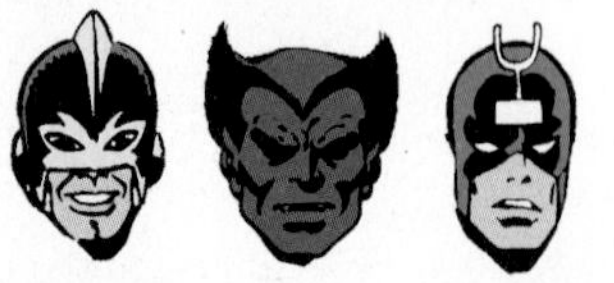

**ANGEL**
(Warren Worthington III, wealthy businessman) American mutant with large bird-like wings enabling him to fly. Former member of the X-Men and Champions. Current whereabouts: Los Angeles, California. First appearance: X-MEN #1.

**ANT-MAN**
(Scott Lang, technician) With the aid of a chemical invented by Henry Pym, he is able to shrink to the size of an insect and communicate cybernetically with ants. Current whereabouts: Long Island, New York. First appearance: MARVEL PREMIERE #47.

**AQUARIAN**
(Real name unknown, nicknamed "Wundarr") Alien who possesses a null-field about him capable of neutralizing all forms of energy. (For that reason, he could not be teleported to Grandmaster's game this issue!) Current whereabouts: Earth. First appearance: FEAR #17. First appearance (as Aquarian): MARVEL TWO-IN-ONE #58.

**ARABIAN KNIGHT**
(Abdul -- ,shiek) Arab possessing an enchanted energy scimitar, animated sash, and flying carpet. Current whereabouts: Saudi Arabia. First appearance: HULK #257.

**AURORA**
(Jeanne-Marie Beaubier) Canadian mutant with the ability of running and flying at super-speed. Member of Alpha Flight. Sister of Northstar. Current whereabouts: Canada. First appearance: X-MEN #121.

**BEAST**
(Henry McCoy, biochemist) American mutant with furry-skin and incredible agility and strength. Current whereabouts: New York vicinity. Former member of the X-Men and Avengers. First appearance: X-MEN #1. First appearance mutated to current state: AMAZING ADVENTURES #11.

**BLACK BOLT**
(Name in own language unknown) Ruler of the highly-evolved offshoot of humanity called the Inhumans. Possesses the ability to manipulate electrons and harness them to fly. Also has a voice so powerful it can shatter mountains. Current whereabouts: the Moon. First appearance: FANTASTIC FOUR #45.

**BLACK KNIGHT**
(Dane Whitman, physicist) American descendant of Arthurian-age champion who wields the ebony blade of his ancestor, and rides a winged horse. Last seen in Twelfth Century Britain, but is known to be back in the present. Current whereabouts: Britain. Former member of the Avengers. First appearance: AVENGERS #48.

**BLACK PANTHER**
(T'Challa, tribal leader of Wakanda) Jungle-born African possessing great natural strength, agility, and heightened senses. Former member of the Avengers. Current whereabouts: Africa. First appearance: FANTASTIC FOUR #52.

**BLACK WIDOW**
(Natasha Romanoff, heiress) Russian defector and secret agent possessing great agility and martial skills. Also uses suction-cups to stick to walls and an electric "widow's sting." current whereabouts: America. First appearance: TALES OF SUSPENSE #52.

**BLITZKRIEG**
(Real name unrevealed) West German with the ability to generate electricity and ride lightning-bolts. Current whereabouts: West Germany. First appearance: CONTEST OF CHAMPIONS #1.

**BLUE SHIELD**
(Joe Cartinelli, mob leader) American with super-human strength and a force field that protects him from harm. Current whereabouts: New York City. First appearance: DAZZLER #5.

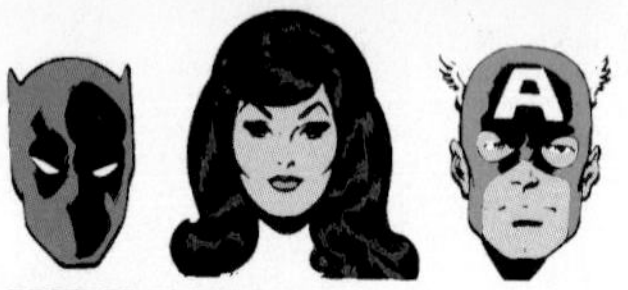

**BROTHER VOODOO**
(Jericho Drumm, physician) Haitian with minor mystical powers including immunity to fire, limited teleportation, and the ability to "possess" other people temporarily using his brother's shade as conduit. Current whereabouts: Haiti. First appearance: STRANGE TALES #169.

**BUG**
(Name in own language unknown) Denizen of the Microversian world of Kalikak with great acrobatic ability and fighting prowess. Current whereabouts: Earth. First appearance: MICRONAUTS #1.

**CAPTAIN AMERICA**
(Steve Rogers, artist) Recipient of the Super-Soldier formula endowing him with great strength, agility, and stamina. Carries a shield. Member of the Avengers. Current whereabouts: New York City. First appearance: AVENGERS #4.

**CAPTAIN BRITAIN**
(Brian Braddock, physics student) Englishman who inherited an amulet of power, granting him great agility, strength, and stamina. Uses a battle-sceptre. Current whereabouts: London, England. First appearance: MARVEL TEAM-UP #65.

**CAPTAIN ULTRA**
(Real name unrevealed) Would-be hero possessing flight, strength, and other powers but has a vulnerability to fire. Nationality unknown. Current whereabouts: unknown. First appearance: FANTASTIC FOUR #177.

**CAPTAIN UNIVERSE**
(Random recipient of Uni-Power) Uni-Power endows recipient with great strength, flight, and energy-powers. Current possessor: unknown. First appearance: MICRONAUTS #8.

**CLEA**
(No other name known) Sorceress from an alien dimension with minor mystic abilities. Current whereabouts: her home dimension. First appearance; STRANGE TALES #126.

**COLLECTIVE MAN**
(Tao-Yu, government workers) Red Chinese mutant brothers with the ability to merge into one super-being, can also summon the collective might of their race. Current whereabouts; China. First appearance: CONTEST OF CHAMPIONS #1.

**COLOSSUS**
(Peter Rasputin, student) Russian mutant with the ability to transmute his flesh to organic steel. Current whereabouts: Salem Center, New York. Current member of the X-Men. First appearance: GIANT-SIZE X-MEN #1.

**COMET**
(Real name unknown) American who possesses the ability to turn the lower half of his body on fire, enabling him to fly. Also shoots energy-blasts from his hands. First active in the 1950's. Current whereabouts; planet Xandar. First appearance: NOVA #22.

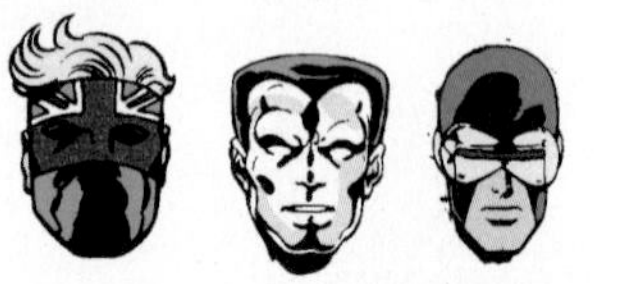

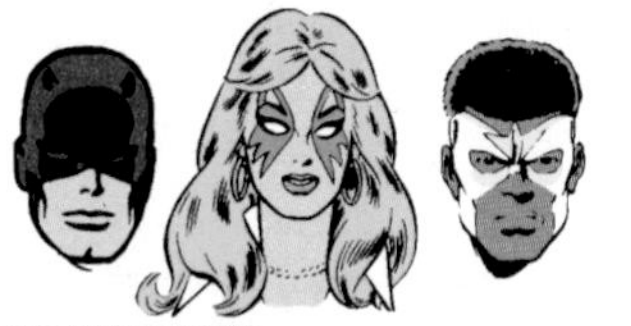

**CRIMSON DYNAMO**
(Dimitri Bukharin, government agent) Russian wearing mechanized armor granting strength, near-invulnerability, flight, energy-blasts. Current whereabouts: Moscow, Russia. First appearance: IRON MAN #109.

**CRYSTAL**
(Name in own language unknown) Inhuman with the ability to control the four ancient elements: fire, water, earth and air. Now married to Quicksilver. Current whereabouts: the Moon. First appearance: FANTASTIC FOUR #45.

**CYCLOPS**
(Scott Summers) American mutant whose eyes shoot energy-blasts. Brother to Havok. Current whereabouts: Salem Center, New York. Current member of the X-Men. First appearance: X-MEN #1.

**DAREDEVIL**
(Matt Murdock, lawyer) Blind American with heightened senses and incredible agility and fighting prowess. Uses billy club as a weapon. Current whereabouts: New York City. First appearance: DAREDEVIL #1

**DARKSTAR**
(Laynia Petrovna, government agent) Russian mutant with the ability to tap alien form of energy called the darkforce, enabling her to fly and project energy. Sister of Vanguard. Former member of the Champions. Current member of the Soviet Super-Soldiers. Current whereabouts: Moscow, Russia. First appearance: CHAMPIONS #7.

**DAZZLER**
(Alison Blaire, singer) American mutant with the ability to tranform sound into light. Current whereabouts: New York City. First appearance: X-MEN #130

**DEFENSOR**
(Real name unknown) Argentinian hero wielding armor, a sword, and shield, its properties still undetermined. Current whereabouts: Argentina. First appearance: CONTEST OF CHAMPIONS #1.

**DEVIL**
(No other name known) Furry animal-like alien from Tropica, a planet of the Microverse. Current member of the Micronauts. Current whereabouts: Earth. First appearance: MICRONAUTS #33.

**DEVIL-SLAYER**
(Eric Simon Payne, ex-marine, ex-hitman) Telepath who uses a transdimensional shadow cloak to teleport and to procure weapons from its pocket-dimensions. Current member of the Defenders. Current whereabouts: New York vicinity. First appearance: MARVEL SPOTLIGHT #33.

**DOC SAMSON**
(Leonard Samson, psychiatrist) Gamma-radiated American with super-strength. Current whereabouts: New Mexico. First appearance: HULK #141.

**DOCTOR DRUID**
(Anthony Druid, mysticist) British-born occult master with limited magical powers. Current whereabouts: unknown. First appearance: WEIRD WONDER TALES #19.

**DOCTOR STRANGE**
(Stephen Strange, ex-surgeon) The sorcerer supreme of Earth, commanding the greatest share of Earth's magical energies. Also uses a cloak of levitation and the amulet of Agomotto permitting him to see into persons souls. Current member of the Defenders. Current whereabouts: New York City. First appearance: STRANGE TALES #110.

**DRAX THE DESTROYER**
(formerly Art Douglas, real estate agent) Man reborn with powers of flight, strength, and energy-blasts. Father of Moondragon. Current whereabouts: space. First appearance: IRON MAN #55.

**EROS**
(No other name known) Super-human with the power of flight, born of the race of Titans. Son of Mentor. Current whereabouts: Titan, moon of Saturn. First appearance: CAPTAIN MARVEL #27.

**FALCON**
(Sam Wilson, social worker) American who uses an anti-gravitic suit with wings to fly, and has a nigh-telepathic link with his falcon Redwing. Former member of the Avengers. Current whereabouts: New York City. First appearance: CAPTAIN AMERICA #117.

**FIREBIRD**
(Bonita Juarez, social worker) American endowed with strange firebird-like energy phenomenon enabling her to fly and generate great amounts of energy. Current member of the Rangers. First appearance: HULK #255.

**FIRELORD**
(Commander Pyreus) Alien born on Xandar who became a herald of Galactus and was given the power of cosmic fire. Current whereabouts: space. First appearance: THOR #225.

**GARGOYLE**
(Isaac Christians, ex-mayor) American turned into a monster by a demon. Flies by means of wings and is able to sap or restore persons' life forces. Current member of the Defenders. Current whereabouts: New York vicinity. First appearance: DEFENDERS #94.

**GORGON**
(Name in own language unknown) Inhuman mutated to have hooves instead of feet capable of triggering seismic shock-waves. Brother to Karnak, member of the Royal Family of Inhumans. Current whereabouts: the Moon. First appearance: FANTASTIC FOUR #44.

**GUARDSMAN II**
(Michael O'Brien) American possessing armor enabling him to fly and shoot repulsor rays. Current whereabouts: unknown. First appearance: IRON MAN #96.

**HAVOK**
(Alex Summers, archaelogy student) American mutant whose body generates cosmic energy that can be siphoned off into explosions. Brother of Cyclops. Occasional member of the X-Men. Current whereabouts: Rio Diablo, New Mexico. First appearance: X-MEN #58.

**HAWKEYE**
(Clint Barton, security chief) American who has mastered the art of archery and uses various trick arrows. Occasional member of the Avengers. Current whereabouts: New York vicinity. First appearance: TALES OF SUSPENSE #57.

**HELLCAT**
(Patsy Walker) American with fantastic acrobatic abilities, agility, and battle prowess. Former member of the Avengers, current member of the Defenders. Current whereabouts: New York vicinity. First appearance: AVENGERS #144.

**HER**
(Formerly called "Paragon") Artificial human being created to be "perfect," capable of flying and generating cosmic energy to rearrange molecules. Current whereabouts: off Earth. First appearance (as Paragon): HULK ANNUAL #6. First appearance (as Her): MARVEL TWO-IN-ONE #61.

**HERCULES**
(Uses no regular alias) Olympian born man-god possessing super-strength. Son of Zeus. Former member of the Avengers. Current whereabouts: Hollywood, California. First appearance: THOR ANNUAL #1.

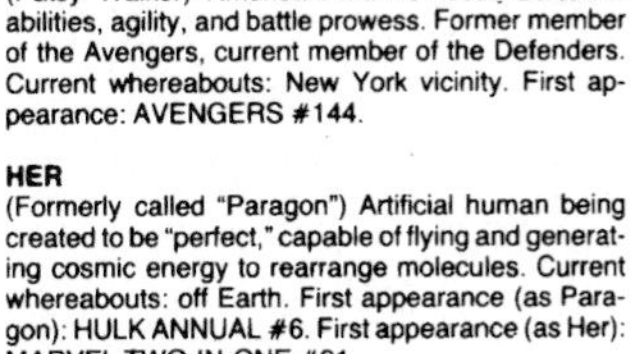

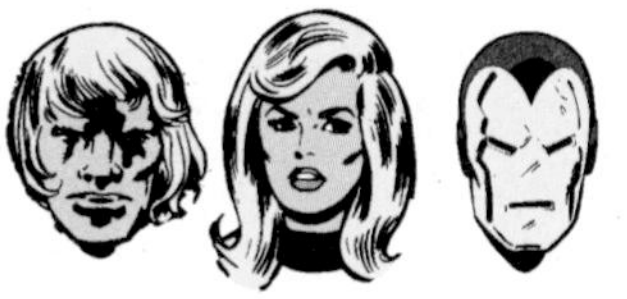

**HERO**
(Real name unknown) Earth-born Eternal with super-strength. Current whereabouts: unknown. First appearance: ETERNALS #13.

**HULK**
(Robert Bruce Banner, physicist) Gamma-radiated American possessing super-strength which increases in geometric proportion to anger. Former member of the Avengers, occasional member of the Defenders. Current whereabouts: New Mexico. First appearance: HULK #1.

**HUMAN TORCH**
(Johnny Storm, adventurer) American affected by cosmic rays, now able to turn his body into living flame. He can fly and create objects out of his own excess fire. Member of the Fantastic Four. Current whereabouts: New York City. First appearance: FANTASTIC FOUR #1.

**HUMAN TORCH II**
(Frankie Raye) American who is able to simulate many of John Storm's powers. Current whereabouts: New York City. First appearance: FANTASTIC FOUR #238.

**ICEMAN**
(Bob Drake, student) American mutant able to convert his skin to ice. He is able to control coldness and create frozen objects out of any moisture. Former member of the X-Men and Champions. Current whereabouts: upstate New York. First appearance: X-MEN #1.

**IKARIS**
(Ike Harris, archaeologist) Earth-born Eternal possessing the abilities of levitation, super-strength, and optic energy-beams. Current whereabouts: Earth. First appearance: ETERNALS #1.

**INVISIBLE GIRL**
(Susan Storm Richards, adventurer) American affected by cosmic rays, possessing the ability to turn invisible and create invisible force fields. Current member of the Fantastic Four. Wife of Mister Fantastic. Current whereabouts: New York City. First appearance: FANTASTIC FOUR #1.

**IRON FIST**
(Daniel Rand, investigator/bodyguard) American-born trained in the martial arts in the dimensional city of K'un-Lun, master of the "iron fist" technique. Current whereabouts: New York City. First appearance: MARVE PREMIERE #15.

**IRON MAN**
(Anthony Stark, industrialist) American clad in highly-technological, solar-powered armor, enabling him to fly, shoot repulsor rays, and other feats. Current member of the Avengers. Current whereabouts: New York vicinity. First appearance: TALES OF SUSPENSE #40.

**JACK OF HEARTS**
(Jack Hart, student) American endowed with strange energy, enabling him to fly and shoot energy rays, and computer-analyze machinery at a glance. Current whereabouts: Earth. First appearance: DEADLY HANDS OF KUNG FU #22.

**JOCASTA**
(No regular alias) A robot built by Ultron, possessing various cybernetic and super-humanoid abilities. Former member of the Avengers. Current whereabouts: Earth. First appearance: AVENGERS #162.

**KARNAK**
(Name in own language unknown) Inhuman possessing the zen-like ability to perceive stress points in all objects, has trained himself to be a master of karate. Brother to Gorgon, member of the Royal Family. First appearance: FANTASTIC FOUR #45.

***TO BE CONTINUED NEXT ISSUE!***

# MARVEL SUPER HEROES-1982

CONTINUED FROM LAST ISSUE

**KARKAS**
(No other name known) Huge red-skinned monster of the sub-species of humanity called the Deviants. Possesses great strength and intelligence. Current whereabouts: Earth. First appearance: ETERNALS #8.

**KA-ZAR**
(Lord Kevin Plunder) British nobleman raised in the jungle who has honed all of his natural abilities to their utmost level. Current whereabouts: Savage Land, Antarctica. First appearance: X-MEN #10.

**LIVING MUMMY**
(N'Kantu) African chieftain embalmed by Egyptian masters some 4000 years ago who has since awakened in recent years to possess super-strength and limited invulnerability. Current whereabouts: Egypt. First appearance: SUPERNATURAL THRILLERS #5.

**MACHINE MAN**
(Aaron Stack, insurance investigator) Robot possessing human-level intelligence and special mechanical abilities such as extendable limbs, electromagnetic circuitry, and superhuman strength. Current whereabouts: New York City. First appearance (as Mister Machine): 2001: A SPACE ODYSSEY #8. First appearance (as Machine Man): MACHINE MAN #1.

**MADROX**
(James Madrox) American mutant with the ability to create identical living duplicates of himself at will. Current whereabouts: Muir Island, Scotland. First appearance: GIANT- SIZE FANTASTIC FOUR #4.

**MAKKARI**
(Name in own language unknown) Eternal possessing super-speed and levitation powers. Current whereabouts: Earth. First appearance: ETERNALS #5.

**MARIONETTE**
(Princess Mari) Humanoid alien from the Microversian planet called Homeworld, possessing acrobatic skills and fighting prowess. Current whereabouts: Earth. Member of the Micronauts. First appearance: MICRONAUTS #1.

**MEDUSA**
(Name in own language unknown) Inhuman with the power to animate her long hair. Member of the Royal Family of Inhumans, Sister of Crystal. Current whereabouts: the Moon. First appearance: FANTASTIC FOUR #36.

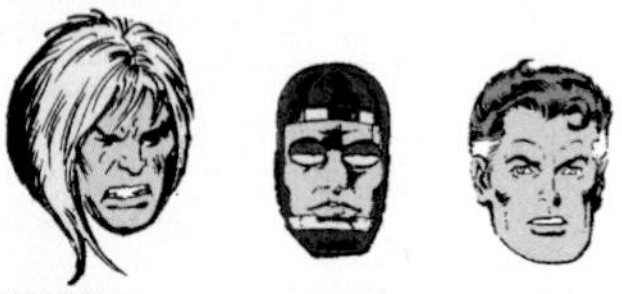

**MENTOR**
(A'Lars) Super-human possessing the power of flight, with Eternal ancestry. Father of Eros and Thanos, ruler of Titan. Current whereabouts: Titan. First appearance: CAPTAIN MARVEL #27.

**MICROTRON**
Non-humanoid robot constructed in the Microverse. Member of the Micronauts. Current whereabouts: Earth. First appearance: MICRONAUTS #1.

**MISTER FANTASTIC**
(Reed Richards, scientist/adventurer) American possessing cosmic ray-derived power of super-malleability. Able to stretch any part of his body to great lengths and mold his pliant flesh into numerous shapes. One of the great intellects of the world, he is the leader of the Fantastic Four. Husband of the Invisible Girl. Current whereabouts: New York City. First appearance: FANTASTIC FOUR #1.

**MOCKINGBIRD**
(Roberta Morse, physicist, ex-SHIELD agent) American possessing great natural agility and martial prowess. Uses battle-staves as a weapon. Current whereabouts: New York vicinity. First appearance (as Bobbi Morse): ASTONISHING TALES #6. First appearance (as Huntress): MARVEL SUPER-ACTION #1. First appearance (as Mockingbird): MARVEL TEAM-UP #95.

**MOONDRAGON**
(Heather Douglas) American-born priestess of Titan, trained in the martial arts, telepathy, and psychokinesis. Daughter of Drax the Destroyer. Occasional member of the Avengers. Current whereabouts: vicinity of the Earth. First appearance (as Madame MacEvil): IRON MAN #54. First appearance (as Moondragon): DAREDEVIL #105.

**MOON KNIGHT**
(Marc Spector, mercenary; alias Jake Lockley, cab driver; Steven Grant, millionaire) American possessing great natural strength and agility and mastery of martial arts. Uses crescent-darts, a truncheon, and glider-cape. Current whereabouts: New York vicinity. First appearance: WEREWOLF BY NIGHT #32.

**NAMORITA**
(alias Nita Prentiss, student) Atlantean amphibian able to breathe underwater and swim with incredible speed. Cousin to Namor. Current whereabouts: New York City. First appearance: SUB-MARINER #51.

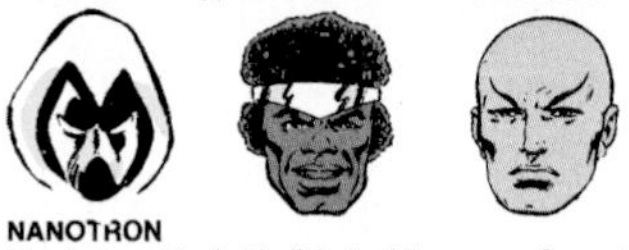

**NANOTRON**
Non-humanoid robot built in the Microverse. Current member of the Micronauts. Current whereabouts: Earth. First appearance: MICRONAUTS #30.

**NIGHTCRAWLER**
(Kurt Wagner, student) German mutant with dark blue skin, a prehensile tail, three-toed feet, pointed ears. Possesses the ability to teleport short distances and has natural acrobatic ability. Member of the X-Men. Current whereabouts: Salem Center, New York. First appearance: GIANT-SIZE X-MEN #1.

**NIGHTHAWK**
(Kyle Richmond, industrialist) American who took a serum to give him double human strength at night. Uses a jet-pack and wings. Occasional member of the Defenders. Current whereabouts: New York vicinity. First appearance: AVENGERS #70.

**NIGHT RIDER**
(Hamilton Slade, archeologist) American who becomes possessed by the spirit of his ancestor, granting him the ghostly powers of invisibility and intangibility. Carries a gun that shoots "phantom bullets" and a lariat. Rides Banshee, a ghostly horse that can fly. Member of the Rangers. Current whereabouts: American Southwest. First appearance: GHOST RIDER #56.

**PALADIN**
(Real name unknown) American mercenary possessing great agility and fighting prowess. Wears a bullet-proof vest and carries a gun. Current whereabouts: New York environs. First appearance: DAREDEVIL #150.

**LE PEREGRINE**
(Real name unknown) Frenchman who flies by means of artificial anti-gravitic wings. His name means "Falcon" in English. Current whereabouts: Paris, France. First appearance: CONTEST OF CHAMPIONS #1.

**POLARIS**
(Lorna Dane) American mutant with the ability to control magnetism. Current whereabouts: Rio Diablo, New Mexico. First appearance: X-MEN #49.

**POWERHOUSE**
(Name in own language unknown) Humanoid alien from planet Xandar who possesses ability to absorb power from whatever he touches. Member of the Syfon Warriors. Current whereabouts: planet Xandar. First appearance: NOVA #2.

**POWER MAN**
(Luke Cage) American possessing great strength and nearly-invulnerable skin. Partner of Iron Fist in Heroes for Hire. Former member of the Fantastic Four and Defenders. First appearance: HERO FOR HIRE #1.

**PROFESSOR X**
(Charles Xavier, headmaster) American mutant with the psionic powers of telepathy and astral projection. Founder of the X-Men. Confined to a wheelchair. Current whereabouts: Salem Center, New York. First appearance: X-MEN #1.

**QUASAR**
(Wendell Vaughn, security chief) American wielding a pair of power-bands from Uranus, capable of tapping any power-source and transforming that energy into solid objects or force-beams. Also enables him to fly. First appearance (as Marvel Man): CAPTAIN AMERICA #217. First appearance (as Quasar): HULK #234.

**QUICKSILVER**
(Pietro Frank – last name adopted) Romanian mutant possessing super-speed. Son of Magneto, brother of Scarlet Witch, husband of Crystal. Former member of the Avengers. Current whereabouts: the Moon. First appearance: X-MEN #4.

**RAZORBACK**
(Buford Hollis, truck driver) American with great natural strength and endurance, who uses various electronic gimmicks, such as an electrified costume. Drives a semi truck. Current whereabouts: Texarkana, Arkansas. First appearance: SPECTACULAR SPIDER-MAN #13.

**RED WOLF**
(Will Talltrees, construction worker, alias Tommy Thundercloud) American Indian with great fighting prowess, stamina, and agility. Carries a Coup Stick as a weapon. Accompanied by a pet wolf, Lobo. Member of the Rangers. Current whereabouts: American southwest. First appearance: AVENGERS#80.

**REJECT**
(No other name known) Human-looking offspring of the sub-species of humanity called the Deviants. Has great fighting strength and ferocity. Current whereabouts: Earth. First appearance: ETERNALS #8.

**ROM**
(No other name known) Humanoid alien in cybernetic armor from planet Galador. Is able to fly and has great strength and near-invulnerability. Carries a ray-gun capable of disintegrating aliens known as Dire Wraiths. Current whereabouts: Clairton, Virginia. First appearance: ROM #1.

**SABRA**
(Ruth Ben-Sera, policewoman) Israeli who was appointed by the government to be a costumed agent. Wears an anti-gravitic cape that shoots energy-quills, and possesses super-strength. "Sabra" means native-born Israeli. Current whereabouts: Israel. First appearance: HULK #256.

**SASQUATCH**
(Dr. Walter Langkowski, biophysicist) Canadian who drinks a serum to become a giant furry super-strong beast who retains his human intelligence. Member of Alpha Flight. Current whereabouts: Canada. First appearance: X-MEN #120.

**SCARLET WITCH**
(Wanda Frank – last name adopted) Romanian mutant who possesses a probability-altering "hex" that causes poltergeist-like phenomena. She has also trained in the actual art of magick. Daughter of Magneto, sister of Quicksilver, wife of the Vision. Former member of the Avengers. Current whereabouts: New York environs. First appearance: X-MEN #4.

**SERSI**
(No other name known) Eternal possessing the ability to transmute elements from one form to another. Can also levitate like all Eternals. Current whereabouts: Earth. First appearance: ETERNALS #3.

**SHAMAN**
(Dr. Michael Twoyoungmen, physician) Canadian Indian possessing various mystical abilities, such as animating totems, controlling the weather, etc. Member of Alpha Flight. Current whereabouts: Canada. First appearance: X-MEN #120.

**SHAMROCK**
(Real name unknown) Irish woman possessing great acrobatic prowess and a probability-field altering aura psychokinetically causing "good luck" to occur to her. Current whereabouts: Dublin, Ireland. First appearance: CONTEST OF CHAMPIONS #1.

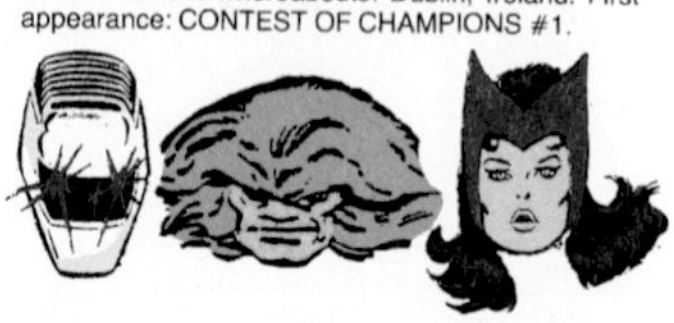

**SHANNA THE SHE-DEVIL**
(Shanna O'Hara, ex-veterinarian) Irish-American possessing great natural agility, fighting prowess, and stamina. Current whereabouts: the Savage Land, Antartica. First appearance: SHANNA THE SHE-DEVIL #1.

**SHE-HULK**
(Jennifer Walters, lawyer) American who can transform at will into a super-strong, green-skinned superhuman, due to gamma-irradiated blood in her system. Current whereabouts: Los Angeles. First appearance: SHE-HULK #1.

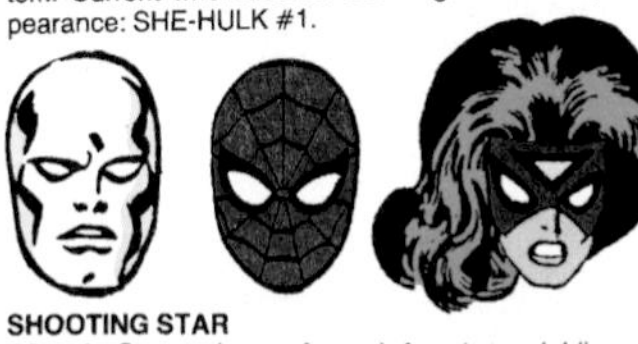

**SHOOTING STAR**
(Victoria Star, rodeo performer) American wielding two six-shooters which shoot paralysis-stars. Incredibly acrobatic and appears able to fly for short distances (whether this is natural power of by means of a device is not yet known). Member of the Rangers. Current whereabouts: American Southwest. First appearance: HULK #265.

**SHROUD**
(Real name unknown; uses no alias) American who was trained by the Cult of Kali in Tibet to be able to summon impenetrable darkness at will. He was also trained in the martial arts. Current whereabouts: Los Angeles. First appearance: SUPER-VILLAIN TEAM-UP #5.

**SILVER SURFER**
(Norrin Radd) Humanoid alien from Zenn-La with cosmic powers to rearrange molecules and shoot energy-blasts. Rides an indestructable flying surf board. Former herald of Galactus. Current whereabouts: space. First appearance: FANASTIC FOUR #48.

**SNOWBIRD**
(Corporal Anne McKenzie, Royal Canadian Mounted Police) Canadian able to fly and also bodily transform herself into various wild animals. Member of Alpha Flight. Current whereabouts: Canada. First appearance: X-MEN #120.

**SON OF SATAN**
(Daimon Hellstrom, occult expert) American whose father is an arch-demon. Possesses supernatural strength and wields a trident and rides a chariot driven by fiery horses. Occasional member of the Defenders. Current whereabouts: New York City. First appearance: MARVEL SPOTLIGHT #12.

**SPACE GLIDER**
(Commander Arcturus Rann) Humanoid alien born on the Microversian planet called Homeworld, possessing fighting prowess. Wields ray-guns and glider-wings. Counterpart of the Time Traveller. Leader of the Micronauts. Current whereabouts: Earth. First appearance: MICRONAUTS #1.

**SPIDER-MAN**
(Peter Parker, college student/freelance photographer) American possessing super-strength, super-reflexes, incredible agility, the ability to stick to virtually any surface, and a danger-detecting "spider-sense." Uses a chemical web-shooting device enabling him to swing from the rooftops, entangle persons or things, and create simple objects such as shields and spheres. Current whereabouts: New York City. First appearance: AMAZING ADULT FANTASY #15.

**SPIDER-WOMAN**
(Jessica Drew, private investigator) American possessing super-strength, super-reflexes, great agility, and a bio-electric discharge called a "venom blast." Uses "glider wings" to fly. Current whereabouts: San Francisco, California. First appearance: MARVEL SPOTLIGHT #32.

**SPRITE**
(Name in own language unknown) Eternal possessing the ability to transmute matter including own body. Is able to levitate like all members of his race. Current whereabouts: unknown. First appearance: ETERNALS #9.

**SPRITE II**
(Kathryn Pryde, student) American mutant possessing the ability to "phase" through solid objects at will. Current member of the X-Men. Current whereabouts: Salem Center, New York. First appearance: X-MEN #129.

**STAR-DANCER**
(Shanga) Humanoid alien from unidentified world who possesses cosmic power to rearrange molecules and fly, plus a special "matrix sense" by which to astrogate through space. Current whereabouts: space. First appearance: MARVEL TWO-IN-ONE #79.

**STINGRAY**
(Dr. Walter Newell, oceanographer) American who uses special deep-sea suit, enabling him to breathe underwater, withstand the ocean's pressure, swim with great speed, and glide through the air for short distances. Also uses an electrical sting-blast. Current whereabouts: Hydrobase, Atlantic Ocean. First appearance: SUB-MARINER #19.

**STORM**
(Ororo Munroe) African-American mutant possessing the ability to control the weather. Able to fly by riding the wind currents. Current leader of the X-Men. Current whereabouts: Salem Center, New York. First appearance: GIANT-SIZE X-MEN #1.

**SUB-MARINER**
(Prince Namor, ruler of Atlantis) Hybrid Atlantean-human possessing super-strength, the ability to breathe underwater, super-speed, and the ability to fly through the air for short distances by means of his ankle-wings. Occasional member of the Defenders. Current whereabouts: Atlantis. First appearance: FANTASTIC FOUR #4.

**SUNFIRE**
(Shiro Yoshida, student) Japanese mutant possessing the ability to discharge solar heat through his hands, and fly. Current whereabouts: Japan. First appearance: X-MEN #64.

**TAGAK THE LEOPARD LORD**
(No other name known) Extra-dimensional humanoid with great athletic ability and fighting prowess. Though blind, he is able to see by telepathic link with his pet leopard, Opar. Current whereabouts: his home dimension. First appearance: DAREDEVIL #72.

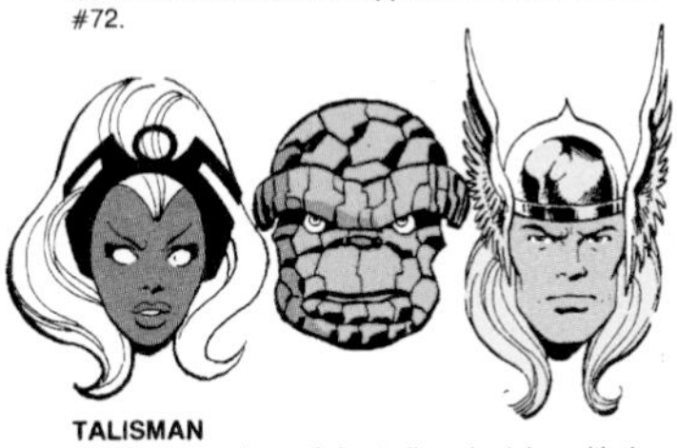

**TALISMAN**
(Real name unknown) Australian aborigine with the mystic power of entering "dream-time," the mythic realm beyond physical existence, enabling him to pass through objects and teleport short distances. Is also able to separate his astral form from his physical body. Uses the bull-roarer to open up a portal into "dream-time" large enough to engulf others inside First appearance: CONTEST OF CHAMPIONS #1.

**TAMARA**
(No other name known) Water-breathing humanoid extra-terrestrial able to withstand the ocean depths and swim with incredible speed. Current whereabouts: Atlantic Ocean. First appearance: SUB-MARINER #58.

**TEXAS TWISTER**
(Drew Daniels, rodeo performer, ex-SHIELD agent) American mutant possessing the power to create a vortex of air around his body, enabling him to fly and strike with hurricane force. Member of the Rangers. Current whereabouts: American Southwest. First appearance: FANTASTIC FOUR #177.

**THENA**
(Name in own language unknown) Eternal possessing her species' standard powers. Daughter of Zuras. Current whereabouts: unknown. First appearance: ETERNALS #5.

**THING**
(Benjamin Grimm, adventurer) American possessing super-strength and a rock-like epidermis making him impervious to virtually all harm. Member of the Fantasitc Four. Current whereabouts: New York City. First appearance: FANTASTIC FOUR #1.

**THOR**
(Donald Blake, physician) Asgardian man-god possessing great strength and stamina. Wields a mystic throwing hammer enabling him to fly and summon thunder, lightning, and rain. The hammer is enchanted so that it always returns to him and can be lifted by no other living being but Thor. Son of Odin, king of the Asgardians. Member of the Avengers. Current whereabouts: Chicago, Illinois. First appearance: JOURNEY INTO MYSTERY #83.

**3-D MAN**
(Hal Chandler, occupation unknown) American who can transform into a super-strong acrobat by donning the glasses in which his brother was transformed into a two-dimensional image. Active during the 1950's, now in semi-retirement. First appearance: MARVEL PREMIERE #35.

**THUNDRA**
(No other name known) Warrior from an alternate future of Earth genetically bred to be super-strong. Current whereabouts: her home reality. First appearance: FANTASTIC FOUR #129.

**TIGRA**
(Greer Nelson, ex-secretary) American able to change into a humanoid cat with various attributes: agility, strength, and reflexes. Former member of the Avengers. Current whereabouts: North America. First appearance (as The Cat): CLAWS OF THE CAT #1. First appearance (as Tigra): GIANT-SIZE CREATURES #1.

**TORPEDO**
(Brock Jones, ex-football player, ex-insurance agent, high school coach) American who wears strength-enhancing suit enabling him to fly at great speeds. Current whereabouts: Clairton, Virginia. First appearance: DAREDEVIL #126.

**TRITON**
(Name in own language unknown) Inhuman with aquatic abilities: able to breathe underwater, swim with great speed, and withstand undersea pressures. Member of the Royal Family of Inhumans. Current whereabouts: the Moon. First appearance: FANTASTIC FOUR #45.

**UNION JACK III**
(Joey Chapman) Britisher with natural acrobatic prowess. Carries daggers. Inherited the suit from the original Union Jack, Lord Falsworth. Current whereabouts: London, England. First appearance: CAPTAIN AMERICA #254.

**URSA MAJOR**
(Major Mikhail Ursus) Russian mutant with the ability to transform himself into a huge brown bear with superhuman strength. Member of the Soviet Super-Soldiers. Current whereabouts: Moscow, Russia. First appearance: HULK #258.

**VALKYRIE**
(No alias currently used) Asgardian goddess possessing great strength. Wields a sword and rides a winged horse, Aragon. Formerly a member of the Valkyrior, the Choosers of the Slain. Current member of the Defenders. Current whereabouts: New York City. First appearance (Enchantress possessing her form): AVENGERS #83. First appearance (in Barbara Norriss's mortal body): DEFENDERS #4. First appearance (in own body): DEFENDERS #109.

**VANGUARD**
(Nicolai Krylenko) Russian mutant with the ability to reflect an opponent's might against him/her. Uses a hammer and sickle to focus this power in the form of a power-bolt. Brother of Darkstar. Member of the Soviet Super-Soldiers. Current whereabouts: Moscow, Russia. First appearance: IRON MAN #109.

**VENUS**
(alias Victoria Starr, professor) Olympean goddess of love who sometimes takes leave of Olympus to live among mortals. Her main power seems to be making people love one another. Called Aphrodite among fellow gods. Current whereabouts: Olympus. First appearance: SUB-MARINER #57.

**VINDICATOR**
(James MacDonald Hudson, reasearch physicist) Canadian who uses a special uniform to fly, shoot energy bolts and create a force field around himself. Leader of Alpha Flight. Current whereabouts: Canada. First appearance (as Weapon Alpha): X-MEN #109. First appearance (as Vindicator): X-MEN #120.

**VISION**
(No regular alias used) Android possessing the ability to change his density at will, thus becoming intangible and lighter than air or as hard and heavy as diamond. Can also project solar-beams through his eyes. Believed to possess the body of the original Human Torch and the brain patterns of Simon Williams (Wonder Man). Former members of the Avengers. Husband of the Scarlet Witch. Current whereabouts: New York environs. First appearance: AVENGERS #57

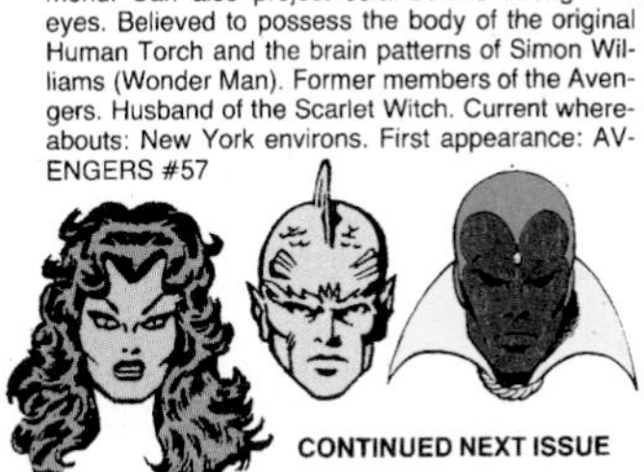

**CONTINUED NEXT ISSUE**

# MARVEL SUPER HEROES-1982

**CONTINUED FROM LAST ISSUE**

**WASP**
(Janet Van Dyne, heiress) American with the ability to shrink to insect-size and fly by means of surgically-implanted membrane-wings. Shoots a bio-electric "wasp's sting." Member of the Avengers. Ex-wife of Henry Pym (Yellowjacket), who concocted her powers. Current whereabouts: New York City. First appearance: TALES TO ASTONISH #44.

**WEREWOLF**
(Jack Russell, occupation unknown) American who inherited family curse to turn him into a werewolf. In such a state he has supernatural strength, agility, stamina, and ferocity. He is in command of his transformations and retains his human intelligence except during the three nights per month of the full moon. Current whereabouts: Los Angeles, California. First appearance: MARVEL SPOTLIGHT #2.

**WOLVERINE**
(Logan — , ex-soldier) Canadian mutant with great strength and agility, and the ability to heal very quickly. His bones were surgically reinforced with the steel-alloy Adamantium, and he was given retractable claws implanted in each hand. Member of the X-Men. Current whereabouts: Salem Center, New York. First appearance: HULK #181.

**WONDER MAN**
(Simon Williams, ex-industrialist, aspiring actor) American possessing enormous strength and near-invulnerability. The chemical processes of his metabolism have been replaced by some strange form of energy. Former member of the Avengers. Current whereabouts: Hollywood, California. First appearance: AVENGERS #8.

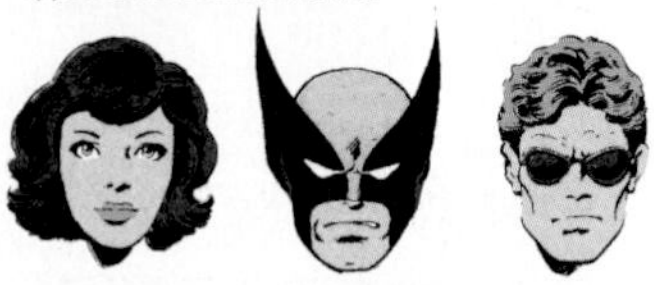

## INACTIVE SUPER HEROES

**BANSHEE**
(Sean Cassidy) Possessed sonic scream, ability to fly. Former member of X-Men. First appearance: X-MEN #28. Reason for retirement: loss of power.

**BIOTRON**
Humanoid robot from the Microversian planet of Homeworld. Former member of the Micronauts. First appearance: MICRONAUTS #1. Reason for retirement: was destroyed in MICRONAUTS #27.

**BLUE DIAMOND**
(Elton Morrow, anthropologist) American whose body could change to the density and strength of a diamond while still allowing mobility. Member of the Liberty Legion. First appearance: MARVEL PREMIERE #29. Reason for retirement: changed to living diamond and went off into space with the Star-dancer.

**CRIMSON CAVALIER**
(Real name unknown) Frenchman who used a fencing foil against the Germans during World War I. Member of the Freedom's Five. First appearance: INVADERS #7. Reason for retirement: (presumably) old age.

**DESTROYER II**
(Roger Aubrey) Britisher who had developed great strength, agility, stamina and fighting skills. Active during World War II. Second person to use costume and name, first being Brian Falsworth (Union Jack II). First appearance (as Dyna-Mite): INVADERS #14. First appearance (as Destroyer): INVADERS #26. Reason for retirement: (presumably) old age.

**DOMINIC FORTUNE**
(David Fortunoff, adventurer) American with acrobatic abilities, fighting prowess. Carried a gun. Active in the 1930's. First appearance: MARVEL PREVIEW #2. Reason for retirement: old age.

**FIN**
(Real name unknown) American who used aquatic powers during World War II. First appearance: INVADERS #5. Reason for retirement: (presumably) old age.

**GHOST RIDER**
(Johnny Blaze, motorcycle stunt rider) American who through sorcery became the host-body for a blazing skeletal demon who is able to create objects out of mystic flame, project soul-scalding Hellfire, and is super-strong and nearly impervious to to harm. First appearance MARVEL SPOTLIGHT #5. Reason for retirement: Blaze is no longer able to control the demon and force him to use his powers for good.

**GIANT-MAN II**
(Bill Foster, physicist) Black American who could mentally stimulate growth in height and mass up to about twenty-five feet. First appearance (as Bill Foster): AVENGERS #32. First appearance (as Black Goliath): POWER MAN #24. First appearance (as Giant-Man): MARVEL TWO-IN-ONE #55. Reason for retirement: radiation poisoning weakened body.

**GOLDEN GIRL**
(Gwenny Lou Sabuki) Japanese-American who possessed the ability to shoot solar beams from her hands, and fly. Member of the Kid Commandos. First appearance: INVADERS #28. Reason for retirement: (presumably) old age.

**GORILLA MAN**
(Ken Hale, occupation unknown) American who through African sorcery became a gorilla-creature with human intelligence. First appearance: WHAT IF #9. Reason for retirement: unknown.

**HUMAN ROBOT**
A humanoid robot created by an unnamed scientist in the 1950's who was reprogrammed by Marvel Boy's Uranian science to aid the cause of good. First appearance: WHAT IF #9. Reason for retirement: unknown.

**HUMAN TOP**
(David Mitchell) Black American who had the ability to spin about in circles at incredible speeds. Member of the Kid Commandos. First appearance: INVADERS #28. Reason for retirement: (presumably) old age.

**JACK FROST**
(No alias known) Humanoid of unknown origin who could command cold and ice. Member of the Liberty Legion. First appearance: MARVEL PREMIERE #29. Reason for retirement: unknown (whereabouts also unknown).

**MADAME MASQUE**
(Whitney Frost, ex-crime boss, alias Big M) American with no real super-powers who was briefly on the side of the law. First appearance: TALES OF SUSPENSE #97. Reason for retirement: resumed criminal career.

**MAN-WOLF**
(John Jameson, astronaut) American who was transformed into a powerful humanoid wolf by means of an alien gem called the moonstone, which attached itself parasitically to his body. First appearance: AMAZING SPIDER-MAN #124. Reason for retirement: the moonstone was surgically removed from Jameson's body in SPECTACULAR SPIDER-MAN ANNUAL #3.

**MANTIS**
(Real name unknown) Vietnamese empath who had a great mastery of the martial arts. First appearance: AVENGERS #114. Reason for retirement: abandoned corporeal life to become Celestial Madonna.

**MODRED THE MYSTIC**
(No other name known) Twelfth Century Britisher who gained great sorcerous powers from the elder demon Chthon and went into suspended animation till the 20th Century. Though he tried to wield his powers in the cause of good, the power itself was derived from evil, and so Modred became a pawn of the demon. First appearance: MARVEL FEATURE #1. Reason for retirement: succumbed to evil and had his intellect reduced to child's level.

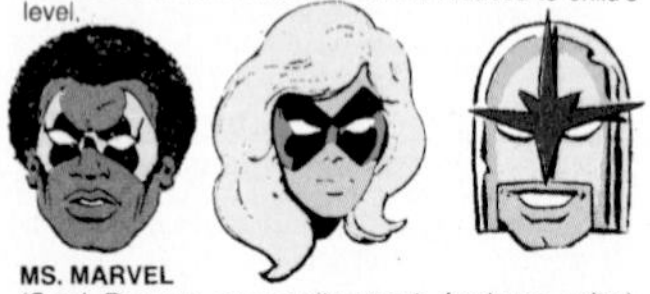

**MS. MARVEL**
(Carol Danvers, ex-security agent, freelance writer) American who possessed ability to fly, super-strength, heightened reflexes, and a precognitive Seventh Sense. Former member of the Avengers. First appearance: MS. MARVEL #1. Reason for retirement: loss of powers.

**NOVA**
(Richard Ryder, student) American who possessed super-strength and ability to fly. First appearance: NOVA #1. Reason for retirement: loss of powers.

**PATRIOT**
(Jeff Mace, reporter) American who used his natural athletic and fighting skills to battle crime. Member of the Liberty Legion. Became Captain America III following the original's presumed death in the late 1940's and was a member of the All-Winners Squad. First appearance (as the Patriot): MARVEL PREMIERE #29. First appearance (as Captain America III):WHAT IF #4. Reason for retirement: unknown

**PRESENSE**
(Sergei — , scientist) Russian mutant who gained vast cosmic powers through exposure to radiation. First appearance: DEFENDERS #52. Reason for retirement: left Earth to seek destiny.

**PROWLER**
(Hobie Brown, window washer) Black American who used various gimmicks to fight crime. First appearance: AMAZING SPIDER-MAN #78. Reason for retirement: voluntarily gave up costumed identity to devote time to civilian life.

**RED GUARDIAN**
(Dr. Tania Belinski, neurosurgeon) Russian possessing great agility and martial skills. Used discuses as weapons. First appearance: DEFENDERS #35. Reason for retirement: left Earth to seek destiny with the Presense.

**SCARECROW**
A mysterious unearthly figure of vengeance who guarded the portal to a demonic dimension on the surface of an oil painting, and could come to life to battle demons. First appearance: DEAD OF NIGHT #11. Reason for retirement: the oil painting was destroyed, sealing the portal between dimensions in MARVEL TWO-IN-ONE #18.

**SCARLET SCARAB**
(Abdul Faoul, archeologist) Egyptian who possessed an ancient power-object granting him abilities of flight, strength, and energy-blasts. First appearance: INVADERS #23. Reason for retirement: loss of scarab that granted powers

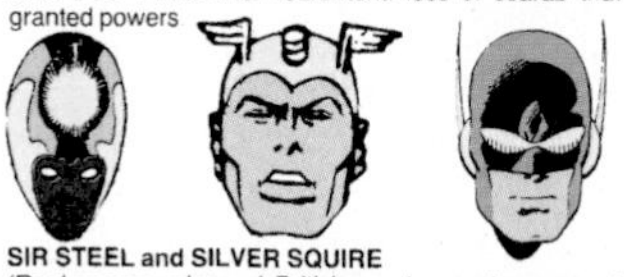

**SIR STEEL and SILVER SQUIRE**
(Real names unknown) Britishers who used armor and swords to fight the Germans during World War I. Members of the Freedom's Five. First appearance: INVADERS #7. Reason for retirement: (presumably) old age.

**SPITFIRE**
(Jacqueline Falsworth-Chrichton) Britisher who possessed the power of flight and heat rays. Member of the Invaders. First appearance: INVADERS #12. Reason for retirement: fading powers with old age.

**THIN MAN**
(Bruce Dickson, scientist) American who gained the ability to flatten his body to the width of paper. Member of the Liberty Legion. First appearance: MARVEL PREMIERE #29. Reason for retirement: (presumably) old age.

**TWO-GUN KID**
(Matt Hawk, gunslinger) Nineteenth Century American who donned mask and six-shooters to battle the lawless. Briefly came to the Twentieth Century via time machine. First appearance: TWO-GUN KID #1. Reason for retirement: returned to his own time.

**WHITE TIGER**
(Hector Ayala, student) Puerto Rican who used mystic amulets to grant him heightened strength, speed, agility, and fighting ability. First appearance: DEADLY HANDS OF KUNG FU #22. Reason for retirement: loss of amulets granting power.

**WHIZZER**
(Robert Frank, nuclear plant worker) American who gained the power of super-speed. Member of the Liberty Legion and Invaders. First appearance: GIANT-SIZE AVENGERS #1. Reason for retirement: old age (heart condition).

**WRAITH**
(Brian DeWolff, ex-policeman) American with telepathic and psychokinetic powers. Carries guns. Status as hero questionable. First appearance: MARVEL TEAM-UP #48. Reason for retirement: unknown.

**YELLOWJACKET**
(Henry Pym, biochemist, cyberneticist) American who invented serum enabling him to reduce to insect-size. Used bioelectric "stings." Former husband to Janet Van Dyne (Wasp). First appearance (as Dr. Pym): TALES TO ASTONISH #27. First appearance (as Ant-Man): TALES TO ASTONISH #35. First appearance (as Giant-Man): TALES TO ASTONISH #49. First appearance (as Goliath): AVENGERS #28. First appearance (as Yellowjacket): AVENGERS #59. Reason for retirement: began criminal career.

## HONOR ROLL OF THE
# DECEASED

**ADAM WARLOCK**
(Formerly called "Him") An artificial human being created to be "perfect," capable of harnessing cosmic energy to fly and shoot power-blasts. Later gained a symbiotic soul-gem which stole the souls of living beings, thus killing their bodies. First appearance (as Him): FANTASTIC FOUR #66. First appearance (as Adam Warlock): POWER OF WARLOCK #1. Died by cosmic suicide in AVENGERS ANNUAL #7.

**BLOODSTONE**
(Ulysses Bloodstone, adventurer) Primitve human who got strange energy blood-gem lodged in his chest, conferring upon him immortality. Had no real super-powers, carried guns and other weapons. First appearance: MARVEL PRESENTS #1. Died in battle in RAMPAGING HULK #8.

**BUCKY**
(Bucky Barnes, army mascot) American who trained himself athletically and in fighting skills. Partner to Captain America, member of the Invaders and Kid Commandos. Died trying to dismantle a bomb, as told in AVENGERS #4. First appearance: AVENGERS #4.

**CAPTAIN MARVEL**
(Mar-Vell, captain in Kree militia) Alien humanoid of the Kree Empire who had superhuman strength and fighting skills, photonic powers enabling him to fly, and a zen-like "cosmic awareness" which enabled him to perceive things extrasensorily. First appearance: MARVEL SUPER-HEROES #12. Died from cancer in THE DEATH OF CAPTAIN MARVEL graphic novel.

**CRIMEBUSTER**
(Frank — ) American who used various weapons and devices to battle crime. Son of the Comet. First appearance: NOVA #13. Died battling the alien Skrulls, as told in ROM #24.

**IT, THE LIVING COLOSSUS**
A thirty-foot stone statue animated telepathically by wheelchair-bound Bob O'Bryan. First appearance: TALES OF SUSPENSE #14. The statue was demolished by the Hulk in HULK #224.

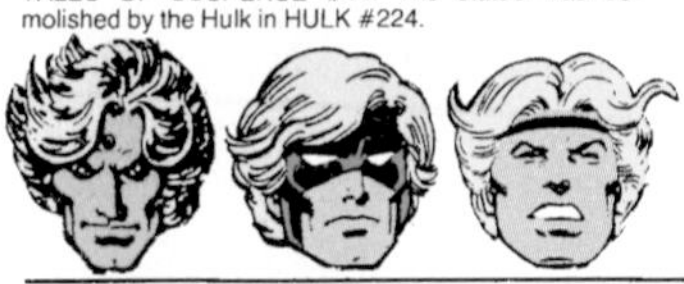

**MARVEL BOY**
(Robert Grayson) American who used power-bands from the planet Uranus to fly and dazzle his opponents. These power-bands were later used to better effect by Quasar. First appearance (as Crusader): FANTASTIC FOUR #164. Died by an energy overload in FANTASTIC FOUR #165.

**MIMIC**
(Calvin Rankin) American who gained the ability to duplicate the powers of any super-being nearby. Former member of the X-Men. First appearance: X-MEN #19. Died from an overdose of gamma radiation in HULK #161.

**MISS AMERICA**
(Madeline Joyce Frank) American who possessed the powers of flight and super-strength. Wife of the Whizzer. First appearance: MARVEL PREMIERE #29. Died from complications during childbirth, as told in GIANT-SIZE AVENGERS #1.

**OMEGA THE UNKNOWN**
(Real name unknown) A humanoid "organic robot" from an unspecified planet trained to be a perfect warrior. Possessed super-strength, enabling him to leap long distances, etc. Had empathic link with another organic robot, James-Michael Starling. First appearance: OMEGA #1. Died from a gunshot wound in OMEGA #10.

**PHANTOM EAGLE**
(Real name unknown) American air pilot who fought during World War I. Member of the Freedom's Five. First appearance: MARVEL SUPER-HEROES #16. Died in battle and lived on as a ghost, as told in GHOST RIDER #12.

**PHOENIX**
(Jean Grey, student) American mutant with psionic powers of telepathy and psychokinesis, who tapped into an incredible cosmic energy manifestation shaped like a fiery bird. Member of the X-Men. First appearance (as Marvel Girl): X-MEN #1. First appearance (as Phoenix): X-MEN #101. Died by cosmic suicide in X-MEN #137.

**RED RAVEN**
(Real name unknown) American given pair of anti-gravity wings by humanoid Bird-men. Member of the Liberty Legion. First appearance: X-MEN #44. Died in an explosion in SUB-MARINER #26.

**SPIRIT OF '76**
(Real name unknown) American who used his fighting prowess and bulletproof cloak during World War II. Became the second Captain America briefly after 1945 when the original was presumed dead. First appearance: INVADERS #14. Died in battle, as told in WHAT IF #4.

**SWORDSMAN**
(Real name unknown) American with great natural agility and fighting skill who became a master of the broadsword. Used an energy-shooting sword from time to time. Former member of the Avengers. First appearance: AVENGERS #19. Died in battle in GIANT-SIZE AVENGERS #4 but lived briefly as a ghost. Joined Mantis, the Celestial Madonna, in cosmic union after death.

**THUNDERBIRD**
(John Proudstar) American Indian mutant with great agility, strength and speed. Member of the X-Men. First appearance: GIANT-SIZE X-MEN #1. Died in plane crash in X-MEN #95.

**THUNDERBOLT**
(Bill Carver, assistant district attorney) Black American who possessed the power of super-speed. First appearance: POWER MAN #41. Died of accelerated old age in POWER MAN/IRON FIST #62

**TORO**
(Toro Raymond) American with the ability to burst on fire, fly, throw fireballs. Member of the Invaders and the Kid Commandos. First appearance: SUB-MARINER #14. Died in battle in SUB-MARINER #14.

**UNION JACK I**
(Lord Falsworth) Britisher who used his athletic and fighting skills to battle the Germans in World War I. Member of the Freedom's Five and the Invaders. First appearance: INVADERS #7. Died of old age in CAPTAIN AMERICA #254.

**UNION JACK II**
(Brian Falsworth) Britisher who used his athletic and fighting skills in World War II, first as the original Destroyer, then carrying on in his father's tradition as Union Jack. Member of the Invaders. Died in an automobile accident, as told in CAPTAIN AMERICA #253.

**ZURAS**
(Name in own language unknown) Eternal possessing the powers of levitation, molecular manipulation and energy beams. He was also the conduit by which the Eternals formed the ritual collective organism, the Uni-Mind. Father to Thena. First appearance: ETERNALS #5. Died in battle with the Celestials in THOR #300.

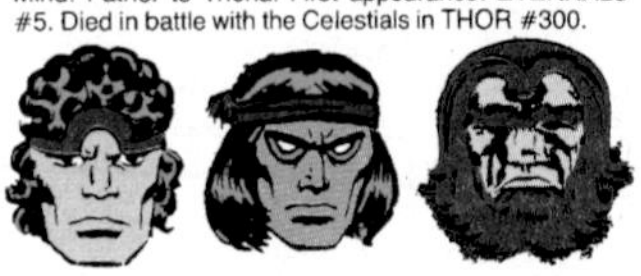

## SUPER HEROES OF
# OTHER WORLDS, OTHER TIMES

**AMERICAN EAGLE** (Squadron Supreme)
**ARKON** the Imperial
**ASTRA** (Imperial Guard of Shi'Ar)
**BALDER** (god of Asgard)
**CAP'N HAWK** (Squadron Supreme)
**CENTURION** (Rhomann Dey of Xandar)
**CHARLIE 27** (Guardians of the Galaxy)
**CHO'D** (Starjammers)
**CORSAIR** (Starjammers)
**DEATHLOK** (1990's)
**DOCTOR SPECTRUM** (Squadron Supreme)
**EARTHQUAKE** (Imperial Guard of Shi'Ar)
**FANDRAL** (Warriors Three of Asgard)
**FANG** (Imperial Guard of Shi'Ar)
**FIREFALL** of Galador
**GLADIATOR** (Imperial Guard of Shi'Ar)
**GOLDEN ARCHER** (Squadron Supreme)
**HEPZIBAH** (Starjammers)
**HOBGOBLIN** (Imperial Guard of Shi'Ar)
**HOGUN** (Warriors Three of Asgard)
**HORUS** (Falcon-god of Heliopolis)
**HUSSAR** (Imperial Guard of Shi'Ar)
**HYDRO-MAN** (Squadron Supreme)
**HYPERION** (Squadron Supreme)
**IMMORTUS**, Lord of Limbo
**IMPOSSIBLE MAN** of Poppup
**IMPET** (wife of Impossible Man)
**JAVELIN** of Galador
**KILLRAVEN** (2010's)
**LADY LARK** (Squadron Supreme)
**MANTA** (Imperial Guard of Shi'Ar)
**MARTINEX** (Guardians of the Galaxy)
**MENTOR** (Imperial Guard of Shi'Ar)
**MERCURIO** the 4-D Man
**NIKKI** (Guardians of the Galaxy)
**ORACLE** (Imperial Guard of Shi'Ar)
**PRESTER JOHN**
**PROTECTOR** (Prime Thoran of Xandar)
**RAZA** (Starjammers)
**RECORDER** (Rigellian robot)
**ROCKET RACOON**
**SIF** (goddess of Asgard)
**SMASHER** (Imperial Guard of Shi'Ar)
**STARBOLT** (Imperial Guard of Shi'Ar)
**STARHAWK** (Guardians of the Galaxy)
**STARSHINE** of Galador (deceased)
**TEMPEST** (Imperial Guard of Shi'Ar)
**TOM THUMB** (Squadron Supreme)
**VANCE ASTRO** (Guardians of the Galaxy)
**VOLSTAGG** (Warriors Three of Asgard)
**WARSTAR** (Imperial Guard of Shi'Ar)
**WHIZZER** (Squadron Supreme)
**YONDU** (Guardians of the Galaxy)

# QUASI-HEROES

**AGATHA HARKNESS** of New Salem
**ALPHA** the Ultimate Mutant
**BLADE** (Vampire Killer)
**CLOAK**
**COMBATRA** (Shogun Warriors)
**DAGGER**
**DANGARD ACE** (Shogun Warriors)
**DAUGHTERS OF THE DRAGON**
**DOC SAVAGE**
**DOMO** (Eternals)
**FUTURIST** (Dr. Randolph James)
**GABRIEL** the Exorcist
**GLORIAN**, Herald of the Shaper
**GOLEM**
**HIGH EVOLUTIONARY** (deceased)
**HOWARD THE DUCK**
**HUMAN FLY**
**IRIDIA** (Inhumans)
**JANN OF THE JUNGLE**
**JANUS**, Son of Dracula
**KARTHON THE QUESTOR** of Lemuria
**MAN-THING**, Guardian of the Nexus
**MURDOCH ADAMS** (Monster Hunter)
**NAMORA** of Atlantis (deceased)
**NICK FURY** Director of SHIELD
**PIP THE TROLL** (deceased)
**PUNISHER**
**RAYDEEN** (Shogun Warriors)
**RICK JONES**
**SKULL THE SLAYER**
**SONS OF THE TIGER**
**STUNTMASTER**
**VALKIN** (Eternal)
**WOODGOD**

MARVEL'S FINEST™

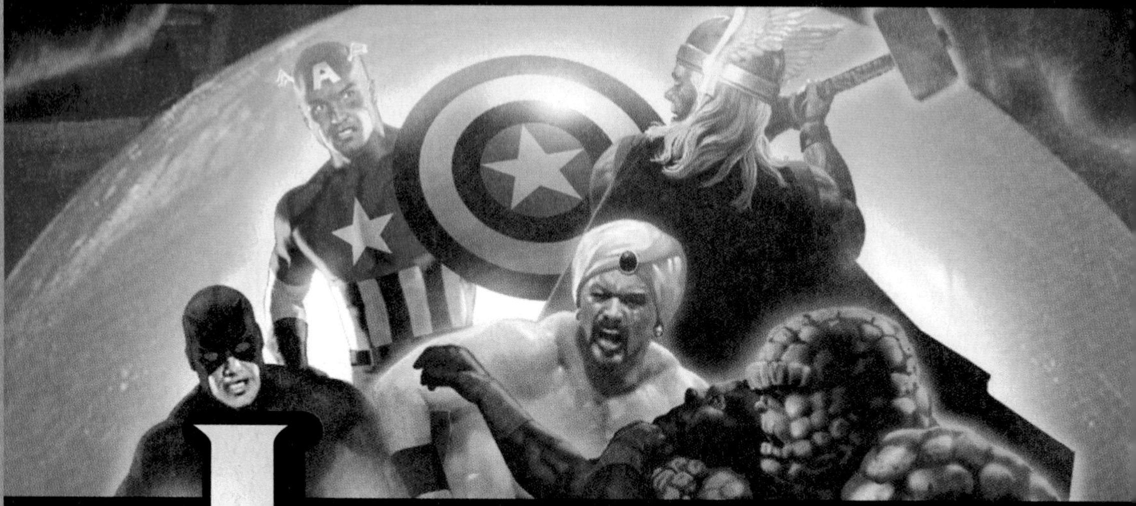

It begins with the disappearance of every living super hero on Earth.

Their abductors are the galactic gamesman known only as the Grandmaster and a mysterious entity called the Unknown.

Twenty-four of the mightiest heroes will be chosen to compete in a desperate contest of strength and skill – one which shall determine the fate of Earth itself!

With all life on the planet held hostage, the chosen come forth from the ranks of the X-Men, the Avengers, the Fantastic Four and more.

And thus the greatest competition of all begins – the CONTEST OF CHAMPIONS!

ISBN
0-7851-0726-6

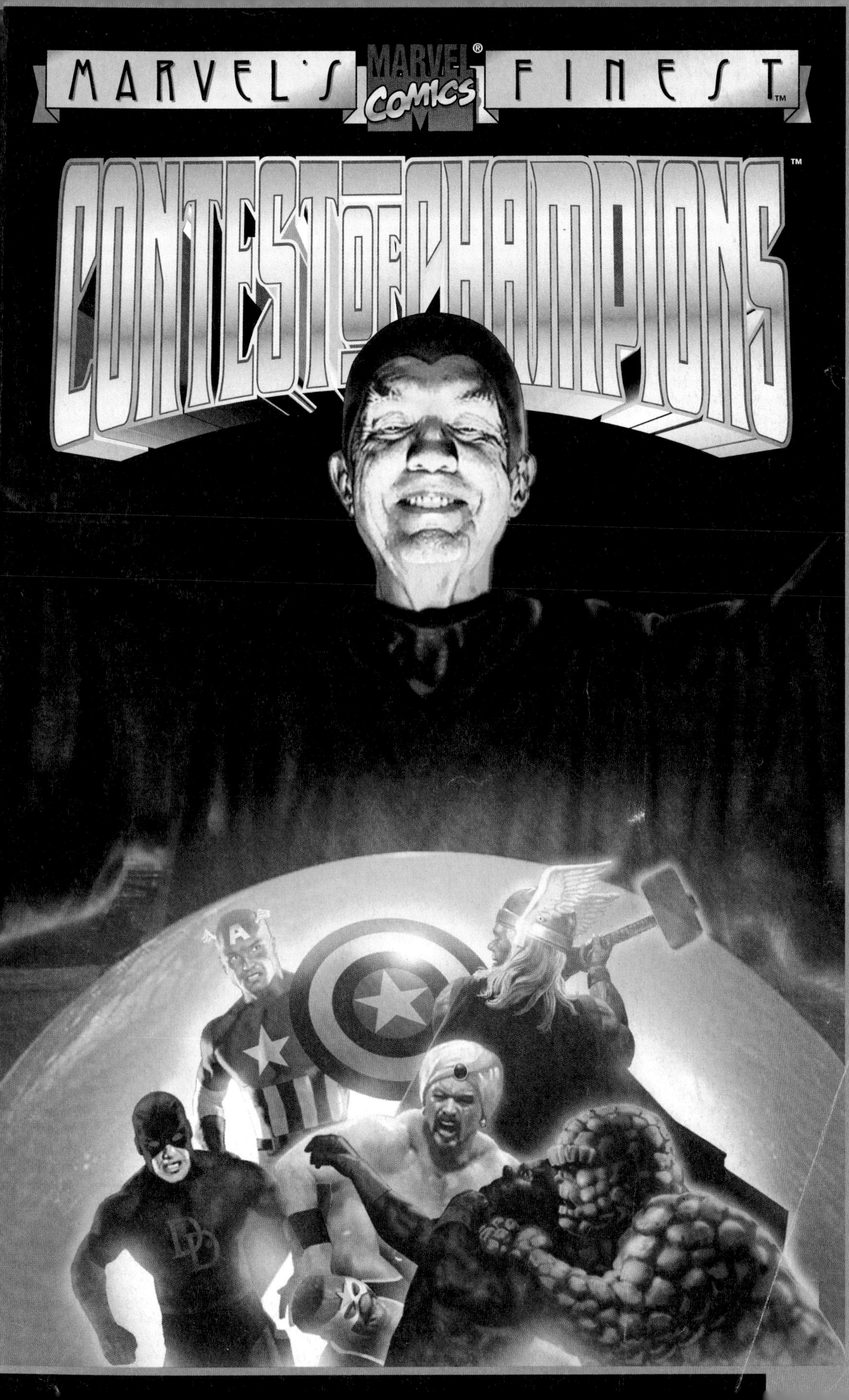
MARVEL'S FINEST
MARVEL COMICS
CONTEST OF CHAMPIONS

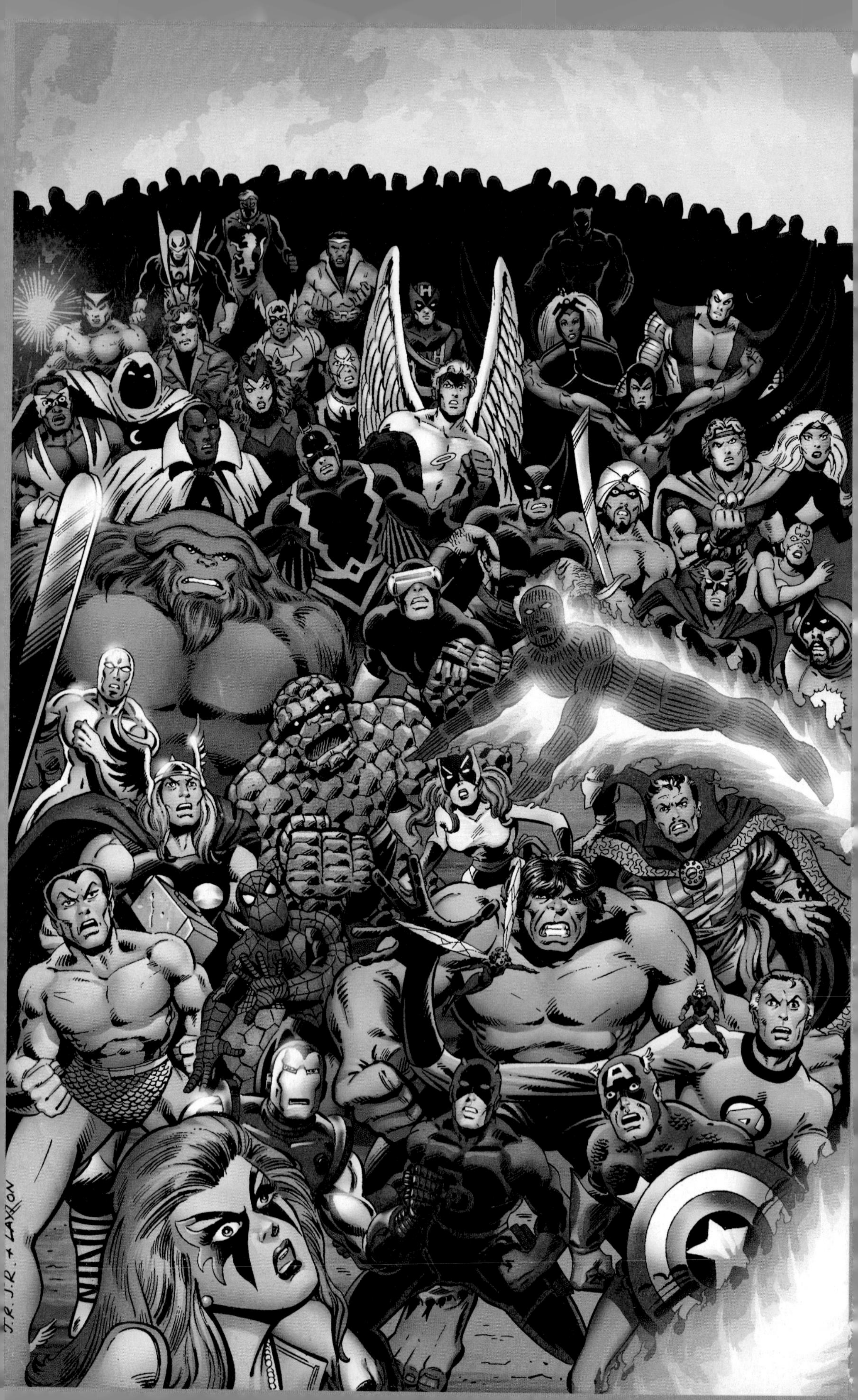
J.R. J.R. + LAYTON